Developme
in Globalising Africa
Beyond the Dichotomy

Edited by

Motoki Takahashi, Shuichi Oyama &
Herinjatovo Aimé Ramiarison

In collaboration

Langaa RPCIG
Mankon Bamenda

CAAS
Kyoto University

Publisher:
Langaa RPCIG
Langaa Research & Publishing Common Initiative Group
P.O. Box 902 Mankon
Bamenda
North West Region
Cameroon
Langaagrp@gmail.com
www.langaa-rpcig.net

In Collaboration with
The Center for African Area Studies, Kyoto University, Japan

Distributed in and outside N. America by African Books Collective
orders@africanbookscollective.com
www.africanbookscollective.com

ISBN-10: 9956-551-57-0

ISBN-13: 978-9956-551-57-6

Notes on Contributors

Simbarashe GUKURUME is Lecturer in the Department of Sociology and Social Anthropology at Great Zimbabwe University. He holds a PhD in Sociology from the University of Cape Town. His research interests fall more broadly on youth, informality and social movements, livelihoods and displacement in spaces of socio-economic and political fragility and crisis.

Godfrey HAMPWAYE is Senior Lecturer in the Department of Geography and Environmental Studies at the University of Zambia where he has been teaching for over 29 years. He is also a Senior Research Affiliate to the School of Tourism and Hospitality at the University of Johannesburg. He holds a PhD. His area of specialisation is economic geography with research interests in local economic development, urban agriculture and firm strategies and Asian investment in Africa. Over the past years, he has published scholarly papers and book chapters centred on his research interests.

Masaya HARA is Assistant Professor of Geography and Area Studies in the Graduate School of Human Development and Environment at Kobe University, Japan. His main research field is Zambia. His research topics are migration and people's livelihood changes since the colonial period. His major works include: 'Coexistence of multiple ethnic groups practicing different slash-and-burn cultivation systems adapted to field conditions in miombo woodlands in northwestern Zambia', *TROPICS*, 28 (4), pp. 75–89 (2020).

Mayu HAYAKAWA is Visiting Researcher at the National Museum of Ethnology, Japan. Her research fields are Zimbabwe and Lesotho. Her research topics are popular economy and money usage. Her major works include: *An Anthropology of Hyperinflation* (Jimbunshoin 2015, in Japanese) and 'Guided by weak conviction', in S. Moyo & Y. Mine (eds), *What Colonialism Ignored* (Langaa RPCIG 2016).

Kazuyo IDEUE is Lecturer of African Studies and Development Studies at Ritsumeikan University, Japan. Her research interests include economic development and history in sub-Saharan Africa and the relationship between the two. Her most recent publication is 'The relationship between sugar capital and industrialization in Mauritius: Focusing on the ownership and dominant structure of sugar-based capitalists and their investment to the industrial sectors', *Social System Study*, 41, pp. 43–70 (2020, in Japanese).

Hitomi KIRIKOSHI is Lecturer in the Department of Geography and Environmental Studies at Kokushikan University, Japan. She has conducted research in Sahel zones of Niger and savanna/forest zones in Ghana. She developed an academic interest in environmental issues, resident livelihoods, and inter-regional and inter-ethnic links through the historical kola nut trade in West Africa. She is also interested in the globalisation of West African merchants.

Motoji MATSUDA is Professor of Sociology and Anthropology, Kyoto University, Japan. His research fields are Nairobi and Western Kenya. His research topics are urbanisation, migration and conflict. His major works include: *Urbanisation from Below* (Kyoto University Press 1998); *The Manifesto of Anthropology of the Everyday Life World* (Sekai Shisosha 2008, in Japanese); *African Virtues in the Pursuit of Conviviality: Exploring Local Solutions in Light of Global Prescriptions* (co-edited with Itaru Ohta and Yntiso Gebre, Langaa RPCIG 2017) and *The Challenge of African Potentials: Conviviality, Informality and Futurity* (co-edited with Yaw Ofosu-Kusi, Langaa RPCIG 2020).

Garikai MEMBELE is Lecturer in the Department of Geography and Environmental Studies at the University of Zambia. He holds an MSc in Geo-information Science and Earth Observation from the University of Twente in the Netherlands. He is currently pursuing his PhD studies at the University of KwaZulu-Natal in South Africa. His area of specialisation is GIS, remote sensing and urban planning and management. Research interests include land governance, land use/cover analysis, vulnerability mapping and volunteered geographical information (VGI).

Atsuko MUNEMURA is Senior Assistant Professor in the Department of Economics at Chiba Keizai University, Japan. Her current research focuses on the fruits processing industry of South Africa from the historical perspective. Her major works include: 'The emergence of canning industry in Western Cape, 1930-1940s: South African second industrialization in rural economy', *Bulletin of Asia Pacific Studies*, 20, pp. 123–149 (2014, in Japanese). She also affiliates with the Japan Society for Afrasian Studies as a member of boards of directors.

Linda NAMAKANDO is a student in the Department of Geography and Environmental Studies at the University of Zambia. She is currently pursuing a Master of Science Degree in Spatial Planning. Her research interest is in urban agriculture, particularly how it is affected by urban developments.

Itaru OHTA is Emeritus Professor of the Centre for African Area Studies at Kyoto University, Japan. He has carried out anthropological research among the Turkana in Kenya and the Himba in Namibia. His major publications include: *Devoting Themselves to Convivial Negotiation: Property Relations among the East African Pastoral Societies* (Kyoto University Press 2021, in Japanese); *African Virtues in the Pursuit of Conviviality: Exploring Local Solutions in Light of Global Prescriptions* (co-edited, Langaa RPCIG 2017); *African Potentials* (editor-in-chief, a set of five volumes, Kyoto University Press 2016, in Japanese) and *Conflict Resolution and Coexistence: Realizing 'African Potentials'* (co-edited, Kyoto University 2014).

Masumi OWA is Associate Professor of Global Studies at Chukyo University in Japan. Her research topics are global governance in the field of international development, international cooperation and African development. Her publications include contributing chapters to *Japanese Development Cooperation: The Making of an Aid Architecture Pivoting to Asia* (Routledge 2016) and *New Asian Approaches to Africa: Rivalries and Collaborations* (Vernon Press 2020).

Shuichi OYAMA is Professor at the Center for African Area Studies, Kyoto University, Japan. He conducted multi-disciplinary research based on geography, anthropology, ecology and agronomy in Zambia, Uganda, Niger and Djibouti. His main publications include: 'Action research and reverse thinking for anti-desertification methods', in T. Haller & C. Zingerli (eds), *Towards Shared Research: Participatory and Integrative Approaches in Researching African Environments* (Transcript Publishers 2020).

Herinjatovo Aimé RAMIARISON is Professor of Economics and acting as General Coordinator of the University of Antananarivo Madagascar. He holds a PhD in Commerce from Meiji University, Tokyo, Japan. His research interests are in development economics, and he primarily focused his research on the development experiences of East Asian countries. Since 2002, his fields of study have covered development issues in sub-Saharan Africa and in Madagascar, more particularly in industrialisation, employment, labour markets and globalisation. His recent work is 'Les facteurs d'informalité et les opportunités de transition vers l'économie informelle à travers l'étude diagnostic de la filière de commercialisation du vivrier marchand à Madagascar', in F. Lapeyre & S. Barussaud (eds), *La Formalisation Vue d'En Bas: Enjeux pour La Transition vers l'Economie Informelle*, pp. 207–248 (Academia-l'Harmattan 2019).

Toru SAGAWA is Associate Professor in the Faculty of Letters at Keio University, Japan. He has conducted field research in East Africa. His recent works include: 'Naturalography of co-existence among East African pastoral societies: An introductory overview of Japanese scholarship', *African Study Monographs*, 40 (2/3) (2019 with I. Hazama) and 'Waiting on a friend: Hospitality and gift to the "enemy" in the Daasanach', *Nilo-Ethiopian Studies*, 23 (2019).

Makiko SAKAI is Associate Professor of Sociology at Tokyo University of Foreign Studies (TUFS), Japan. Her main research fields are western Cameroon, central Tanzania and southern Chad. Her field topics are rural development viewed from local communities, subsistence agriculture and small-scale economic activities. Her major works include: 'Famines and moral economy in agro-pastoralist society: Analysis of Gogo strategies from a historical perspective', in S. Maghimbi, K. Sugimura & D. Mwamfupe (eds), *Endogenous Development, Moral Economy and Globalization in Agro-pastoral Communities in Central Tanzania* (Dar es Salaam University Press 2016), and *Characteristics of Bike Taxis in African Rural Society: A Case Study of Dschang, West Cameroon* (Fondation France-Japon de l'EHESS 2020).

Manasa SIBANDA is an anthropologist and currently Chairperson of Sociology and Social Anthropology Department at the Great Zimbabwe University. He holds a PhD in Social Anthropology from the University of Fort Hare, RSA. His research interests are rural livelihoods, conflicts, migration and conservation. He has also consulted on a wide range of development programmes and planning as well as social dimension in Environmental Impact Assessments (EIAs) issues for municipalities and non-profit organisations.

Yuko SUGIYAMA is Professor of Anthropology in the Faculty of Humanities and Social Sciences at Hirosaki University, Japan. Her research focuses on the folk innovation process and its history among the rural farmers of Zambia, Tanzania and Japan. Her recent works include: 'Cooperative behavior of food processing, food sharing and survival of children', in K. Kawai (ed.), *Extremity: The Evolution of Human Sociality* (Kyoto University Press 2020, in Japanese), and 'Moral economy and social stratification in rural Africa: Are we moving towards a new platform?', in T. Tsuruta (ed.), *Proceedings of 7th International Workshop on African Moral Economy* (Kindai University 2018).

Motoki TAKAHASHI is Professor of Graduate School of Asian and African Area Studies and Center for African Area Studies at Kyoto University, Japan. He is also a Professor Emeritus at Kobe University, Japan. His main research fields are socio-economic development in sub-Saharan Africa and foreign aid to low-income countries. His academic works include: *African Potentials: Their Diversity and Dynamism and Challenges* (edited, Kyoto University 2018); *Contemporary African Economies: A Changing Continent under Globalization* (co-edited with K. Kitagawa, African Development Bank 2016); 'TICADs under the changing global landscape: Japan's role in African development reconsidered', in T. Iwata (ed.), *New Asian Approaches to Africa: Rivalries and Collaborations*, pp. 83–107 (Vernon Press 2020), and 'Development, and social cohesion in Africa: Overview', in H. Hino, A. Langer, J. Lonsdale & F. Stewart (eds), *From Divided Pasts to Cohesive Futures: Reflection on Africa,* pp.161–189 (co-authored with Bruce J. Berman, Cambridge University Press 2019).

Tadasu TSURUTA is Professor in the Faculty of Agriculture at Kindai University, Japan. He has focused much of his research on the comparative study of peasant societies in Africa and Southeast Asia. He is a co-editor with G. Hyden & K. Sugimura of *Rethinking African Agriculture: How Non-Agrarian Factors Shape Peasant Livelihoods* (Routledge 2020). He also contributed a chapter on agro-pastoralism in Tanzania to J. Abbink (ed.), *The Ecological Crunch in Africa: Growth Narratives vs. Local Environmental Realities* (Palgrave-Macmillan 2018).

Yuki YOSHIMURA graduated from Graduate School of Asian and African Area Studies, Kyoto University, Japan. She studied in northern Zambia and currently works for SAKA NO TOCHU Co., Ltd., aiming to achieve sustainable farming.

Table of Contents

African Potentials for Convivial World-Making

Motoji Matsuda

1. The Idea of 'African Potentials'

The *African Potentials* series is based on the findings since 2011 of the African Potentials research project, an international collaboration involving researchers based in Japan and Africa. This project examines how to tackle the challenges of today's world using the experiences and wisdom (ingenuity and responsiveness) of African society. It has identified field sites across a variety of social domains, including areas of conflict, conciliation, environmental degradation, conservation, social development and equality, and attempts to shed light on the potential of African society to address the problems therein. Naturally, such an inquiry is deeply intertwined with the political and economic systems that control the contemporary world, and with knowledge frameworks that have long dominated the perceptions and understanding of our world. Building on unique, long-standing collaborative relationships developed between researchers in Japan and Africa, the project suggests new ways to challenge the prevailing worldview on humans, society and history, enabling those worldviews to be relativised, decentred and pluralised.

After the rose-coloured dreams of the 1960s, African society entered an era of darkness in the 1980s and 1990s. It was beleaguered by problems that included civil conflict, military dictatorship, national economic collapse, commodity shortages, environmental degradation and destruction, over-urbanisation and rampant contagious disease. In the early 21st century, the fortunes of Africa were reversed as it underwent economic growth by leveraging its abundant natural resources. However, an unequal redistribution of wealth increased social disparities and led to the emergence of new forms of conflict and discrimination. The challenges facing African society appear to be more profound than ever.

The governments of African states and the international community have attempted to resolve the many problems Africa has experienced. For example, the perpetrators of crimes during times of civil conflict have been punished by international tribunals, support for democratisation has been offered to states ruled by dictators and despots and environmental degradation has been tackled by scientific awareness campaigns conducted at huge expense.

Nonetheless, to us – the Japanese and African researchers engaging with African society in this era – the huge monetary and organisational resources expended, and scientifically grounded measures pursued, seem to have had little effect on the lives of ordinary people. The punishment of perpetrators did not consider the coexistence of perpetrators and victims, while the propagation of democratic ideals and training to raise scientific awareness was far removed from people's lived experiences. Nevertheless, while many of these 'top-down' measures prescribed to solve Africa's challenges proved ineffective, African society has found ways to heal post-conflict communities and to develop practices of political participation and environmental conservation.

Why did this happen? This question led us to examine ideas and practices African society has formulated for tackling the contemporary difficulties it has experienced. These were developed at sites where ordinary Africans live. 'African Potentials' is the name we gave to these home-grown ideas and the potential to engender them.

2. African Forum: A Unique Intellectual Collaboration between Japan and Africa

As the concept of African Potentials emerged, it required further reflection to develop ideas that could be applied in the humanities and social sciences. The context for these processes was the African Forum: a meeting held in a different part of Africa each year where African researchers from different regions and Japanese researchers studying in each of those regions came together to engage in frank discussion. The attendance of all core members of the project sympathetic to the idea of African Potentials ensured the continuity of the discussions at these African Forums. The core members who drove the project forward from the African side included Edward Kirumira (Uganda and South Africa), Kennedy Mkutu (Kenya), Yntiso Gebre (Ethiopia), the late Samson Wassara (South Sudan), the late Sam Moyo (Zimbabwe), Michael Neocosmos (South Africa), Francis B. Nyamnjoh (Cameroon and South Africa) and Yaw Ofosu-Kusi (Ghana). The researchers from Japan specialised in extremely diverse fields, including political science, sociology, anthropology, development economics, education, ecology and geography. As they built creative interdisciplinary spaces for interaction across fields over the course of a decade, project members have produced many major outcomes that serve as research models for intellectual and academic exchange between Japan and Africa, and experimental cases of educational practice in the mutual cultivation and guidance of young researchers.

African Forums have been held in Nairobi (2011), Harare (2012), Juba (2013), Yaoundé (2014), Addis Ababa (2015), Kampala (2016), Grahamstown (now Makhanda, 2017), Accra (2018) and Lusaka (2019). These meetings fostered deeper discussion of the conceptual isation and generalisation of African Potentials. This led to the development of a framework for approaching African Potentials and its distinguishing features.

3. What are African Potentials?

The first aim of African Potentials is to 'de-romanticise' the traditional values and institutions of Africa. For example, when studying conflict resolution, members of African Potentials are not interested in excessive idealisation of traditional means of conflict resolution and unconditional endorsement of a return to African traditions as an 'alternative' to modern Western conflict-resolution methods, because such ideas fix African Potentials in a static mode as they speak to a fantasy that ignores the complexities of the contemporary world; they are cognate with the mentality that depreciates African culture.

Rendering African culture static displaces it from its original context and uses it to fabricate 'African-flavoured' theatrical events, as we have seen in different conflict situations. Typical of this tendency is the 'theatre' of traditional dance by performers dressed in ethnic costume and the ceremonial slaughter of cows in an imitation of the rituals of mediation and reconciliation once observed in inter-ethnic conflicts. In our African Forums, we have criticised this tendency as the 'technologisation' and 'compartmentalisation' of traditional rituals.

Naturally, a stance that arbitrarily deems certain conflict-resolution cultures to be 'subaltern', 'backward' or 'uncivilised' needs to be critiqued and it is important to re-evaluate approaches that have been written off in this way. This does not mean that we should level unconditional praise on a fixed subject. With globalisation, African society is experiencing great changes brought about by the circulation of diverse ideas, institutions, information and physical goods. African Potentials can be found in the power to generate cultures of conflict-resolution autonomously under these fluid conditions, while re-aligning elements that were previously labelled 'traditional' and 'indigenous'. In the African Potentials project, we call this the power of 'interface function': the capacity to forge combinations and connections within assemblages of diverse values, ideas and practices that belong to disparate dimensions and different historical phases. In one sense, this is a kind of 'bricolage' created by dismantling pre-existing values and institutions and recombining them freely. It is also a convivial process in the sense that it involves enabling the coexistence of diverse, multi-dimensional elements to create new strengths that are used in contemporary society. The terms 'bricolage' and 'conviviality' are apt expressions characterising the 'interface functions' of African Potentials.

Following this outline, we can identify two features distinguishing African Potentials. First, African Potentials comprise not fixed, unchanging entities but, rather, an open process that is always dynamic and in flux. To treat African traditions and history as static is to fall into the trap of modernist thinking, in which Africa is scorned as barbaric and uncivilised, and the knowledge and practices generated there treated as subaltern and irrational – or a diametrically opposed revivalist mindset that romanticises traditions unconditionally and imbues them with exaggerated significance.

The second feature of African Potentials is its aspiration to pluralism rather than unity. For example, a basic principle of modern civil society is that conflict resolution should occur in accordance with law and judicial process. This principle is deemed to be based on common sense in our society, which means that any resolution method that runs counter to the principle is regarded as 'mistaken' from the outset. This constitutes an aspiration toward unity. It supposes that there is a single way of thinking in relation to the achievement of justice and deems all other approaches peripheral, informal and inferior. The standpoint of Africa's cultural potential, however, renders untenable the idea of a single absolute approach that represents all others as mistaken or deserving of rejection. Here, we can identify a pluralist aspiration that embraces both legal/judicial approaches and extrajudicial solutions.

An aspiration to unity, reduced to the level of dogma, can find eventual culmination in beliefs about 'purity'. In other words, thoughts, values and methods can be regarded as an absolute good, while any attempt to incorporate other (impure) elements is stridently denounced as improper behaviour that compromises purity and perfection. In direct contrast, African Potentials affirm the complexity and multiplicity of a range of elements, and attach value to that which is incomplete. This signifies a more tolerant, open attitude to ideas and values, one that differs from those of the more developed world. African Potentials are grounded in this kind of openness and tolerance.

As we have seen, African cultural potentials are distinguished by their dynamism, flexibility, pluralism, complexity, tolerance and openness. These features are completely at odds with the notion that there is a perfect, pure, uniquely correct mode of existence that competes with others in a confrontational, non-conciliatory manner – one that repels, subordinates and controls them, and occupies the position of an absolute victor. African Potentials can lead us to worldviews on humans, society and history that differ from the hegemonic worldviews that dominate contemporary realms of knowledge.

4. The African Potentials Series

In this way, the concept of African Potentials has enabled researchers from Japan and Africa to organise themselves and pursue activities in multidisciplinary research teams. The products of these activities have been classified into seven different fields for publication in this series. The authors and editors were selected by and from both Japanese and African researchers, and the resulting publications advance the research that has grown out of discussion in the African Forums. The overall structure of the series is as follows:

Volume 1

Title: *African Politics of Survival: Extraversion and Informality in the Contemporary World*

Editors: Mitsugi Endo (The University of Tokyo), Ato Kwamena Onoma (CODESRIA) and Michael Neocosmos (Rhodes University)

Volume 2

Title: *Knowledge, Education and Social Structure in Africa*

Editors: Shoko Yamada (Nagoya University), Akira Takada (Kyoto University) and Shose Kessi (University of Cape Town)

Volume 3

Title: *People, Predicaments and Potentials in Africa*

Editors: Takehiko Ochiai (Ryukoku University), Misa Hirano-Nomoto (Kyoto University) and Daniel E. Agbiboa (Harvard University)

Volume 4

Title: *Development and Subsistence in Globalising Africa: Beyond the*

Dichotomy

Editors: Motoki Takahashi (Kyoto University), Shuichi Oyama (Kyoto University) and Herinjatovo Aimé Ramiarison (University of Antananarivo)

Volume 5

Title: *Dynamism in African Languages and Literature: Towards Conceptualisation of African Potentials*

Editors: Keiko Takemura (Osaka University) and Francis B. Nyamnjoh (University of Cape Town)

Volume 6

Title: *'African Potentials' for Wildlife Conservation and Natural Resource Management: Against the Images of 'Deficiency' and Tyranny of 'Fortress'*

Editors: Toshio Meguro (Hiroshima City University), Chihiro Ito (Fukuoka University) and Kariuki Kirigia (McGill University)

Volume 7

Title: *Contemporary Gender and Sexuality in Africa: African-Japanese Anthropological Approach*

Editors: Wakana Shiino (Tokyo University of Foreign Studies) and Christine Mbabazi Mpyangu (Makerere University)

Acknowledgements

This publication is based on the research project supported by the JSPS KAKENHI Grant Number JP16H06318: 'African Potential' and Overcoming the Difficulties of Modern World: Comprehensive Area Studies that will Provide a New Perspective for the Future of Humanity.

Introduction

Development and Subsistence in Globalising Africa: Beyond the Dichotomy

Motoki Takahashi, Shuichi Oyama and Herinjatovo Aimé Ramiarison

1. Development and Subsistence

In a part of the literature on developing countries, development has been viewed as inimical to people's subsistence and livelihoods. This view has been stronger in the literature on sub-Saharan Africa. It has been all the stronger in cases where development interventions have been brought in from abroad through aid or foreign direct investment, or from above by governments.

Today, this view is still shared by some academics and activists (e.g., Carmody 2011), who observe that after the turn of the century, not only governments of, and multi-national corporations (MNCs) from, developed countries but also emerging economies, represented by China, have been rushing into Africa. Official Development Assistance (ODA) from developed countries, aid from emerging ones and foreign direct investment (FDI) rapidly increased. It was often understood that those massive inflows of money were motivated by abundant mineral resources and potentially promising markets in Africa. Also, negative phenomena such as environmental destruction, land grabbing (see Chapter 1) and deindustrialisation (decrease in the relative importance of manufacturing in national economies) have been seen as ensuing from the greed of the external actors mentioned above. It is said that deindustrialisation in Africa has been due to the erosion of domestic markets by rapidly expanding imports of manufactured goods from emerging economies, especially China (Edwards and Jenkins 2015).

Despite these negative views, at the time of the third wave of democratisation in developing countries and Africa, especially following the end of the Cold War, development study scholars and practitioners together started to speak about 'participatory development', 'growth with equity', 'inclusive development with no one left behind', 'human-centred development' and 'sustainable livelihoods' (Huntington 1991; Lynch and Crawford 2011). Though facing negative responses, such as criticism that such discourse was hypocritical, many pro-development people have now turned to discussing these concepts enthusiastically.

Apart from pro-development views, several African area studies scholars have been paying increasing attention to other aspects of the relationship between development and subsistence and now articulate a more complex understanding of interaction between them.

We find the word 'development' almost every day in newspapers in African countries. Throughout the territories of each nation of Africa, including relatively densely populated rural areas, it would be hard to drive a car along trunk roads for one hour without seeing construction sites for roads or buildings, or signboards advertising development projects. Above all, a large majority of African people are inevitably involved in the process of development that has originated either from home or abroad.

It is certain that there are still a number of classical cases where large infrastructure construction projects have negatively impacted people's livelihoods. We must be aware of the details not only of positive outcomes, as pro-development people desire, but also of the negative impacts of development interventions initiated from abroad and above. At the same time, we should turn our eyes on people's resilience, which enables them to survive such negative impacts through geographical shifts and reconstruction of their livelihoods (See Chapter 1). They are struggling to reconcile development with their subsistence or to make use of development interventions for their subsistence. The first theme of this volume involves an exploration of complex relations between development and subsistence, citing empirical evidence.

2. Globalisation and African People

African people striving to live and survive under complex interactions between development and subsistence have been directly or indirectly feeling the influence of globalisation. Typical of Chinese cases, aid and investment are intricately linked with the promotion of exports and imports to/from developing countries including Africa (Brautigam 2011). Globalisation, as well as development mentioned above, is not necessarily simply positive or negative for people.

We have referred to deindustrialisation as a result of increasingly large amounts of imports from China. Yet, Chinese products have been welcomed by African consumers, import traders and some manufacturing sectors as they are cheaper and of better quality than some domestic products. The products include consumer goods (Chapter 11), machines and materials for production by manufacturers (Chapter 10) and motorbikes driven by transporters (Chapter 12), as they are cheaper and of better quality than some domestic products. Notably, imports from China have been associated with a consumption boom in Africa and have facilitated growth in import-dependent manufacturing and service provision among a wide range of African nations.

While the definition of globalisation varies from author to author, there seems to be a broad consensus among economic historians and development studies scholars to regard it as a series of processes strengthening (though often intermittently) the interlinkages of economy, politics and culture among different societies across the world. Sub-Saharan Africa is now deeply involved and participating in globalisation with the spread of phenomena related to development.

As Hutchinson (2011) argues, globalisation has been a series of historically sustained changes over a long duration. In this series, strengthening and weakening processes in terms of cross-border linkages have alternated over and over again. Since the post-Cold War, when change was rather drastic and widely spread geographically, the focus has been on contemporary change. This change is said to be led by neoliberalism or at least promoted by neoliberalists, so we can call it neoliberal globalisation (Fuchs 2015; Crotty 2003; Shizha 2010). Globalisation, however, is not limited to neoliberal globalisation.

With regard to Africa, globalisation started when Africa encountered the modern West's advance into the region, either at the beginning of the slave trade in the 16th century as Wallerstein (1975) suggests, if we correctly understood him, or at the time of the 'Scramble for Africa' in the latter half of the 19th century. When colonial rulers or entrepreneurial farmers started trading with nations outside the region, it may be said that globalisation came to Africa (Chapters 5 and 6). Since then, Africa has been an integral part of the world economy through trade. Africa has been taking part in a globalising process over a long time. In this book, we are going to present Africa and African peoples' experiences and their potential to respond proactively to, and interact with, societies outside Africa. This is the second theme of the book.

Immigrants and their offspring have played special roles in building connections with overseas markets (Chapter 5), mobilising domestic capital and negotiating with governments in importing countries (Chapter 6), thus laying bases for the expansion of external trade and economic development. Indigenised immigrants and their offspring can be called *Africans* as well. While their dominance involved an unbalanced power distribution, which resulted in an unwelcome and often oppressive rule over the population of 'African (or black) races' along with economic disparity between the two, immigrants and offspring, if they are indigenised and have no place to 'go back to', are integral members of African societies. In this book, European and Indian immigrants and their offspring appear as leading *African* actors. Their roles are the third theme of this book.

3. Synchronisation and Similarisation but not Homogenisation under Globalisation

As Africa globalises further, social phenomena are apparently synchronising or similarising with those in the rest of the world, especially developed countries at present or in the past.

Widening economic disparity is in the process of both synchronising and similarising in Africa with the outside world. With regard to synchronising, African countries are undergoing widening income gaps, in step with other countries. Yet in other countries, developed and East Asian, widening disparity in the past was associated with industrialisation, not with deindustrilisation. Developed countries afterwards experienced narrowing disparity due to redistribution policies by national governments and the diffusion of education. Historical backgrounds and contexts differ in Africa and, therefore, we can call these trends not as homogenisation but as similarisation. Also, African people are resisting this synchronising and similarising trend in widening gaps, as elaborated in Chapters 3, 10 and 12.

Almost every country has experienced urbanisation since the beginning of modern times, which is another phenomenon of similarisation with outside the African region. One of the causes of urbanisation is globalisation as large cities are pivots for linkages with the outside world, being capitals foreigners often visit, seaports, other transportation hubs and/or production bases for leading export commodities. Chapters 6, 7, 8, 10, 11, 12 and 13 describe activities vibrantly unfolding in African cities. Recent urbanisation, however, in Africa has been more rapid than in the past developed countries if measured by the increase in the proportions of urban inhabitants in total populations.

Urbanisation involves people and their resources migrating from villages to cities, permanently or temporarily, leading to population concentration and growth in cities. Migration is often key to African peoples' livelihoods as it broadens life opportunities and increases the remittances earned by migrant labourers. Migration occurs not only between villages and cities but also from development back to subsistence. People recirculate back from cities to villages to retire or to settle back into subsistence, which is another remarkable phenomenon in contemporary Africa (Chapter 7). To finance industrialisation by domestic resources, capital should be transferred from rural to urban areas. If this capital transfer can take place smoothly, industrialisation has more chance of being successful (cf. Chapter 6). The geographical expansion of cities means that cultivated fields are converted into residential and industrial sites (Chapter 8), i.e., that land is transformed from rural to urban uses.

Finally, the rapid advancement and spread of Information and Communication Technology (ICT) has been a major factor in promoting neoliberal globalisation. One of origins of the present ICT revolution in Africa was the development of an inter-continental infrastructure as discussed in Chapter 5. The ICT spread has also facilitated learning of knowledge in manufacturing, derived from overseas, as mentioned in Chapter 10.

Africa has never been homogenised with developed nations or other areas. African people have been attempting to preserve their communal rules (Chapter 2), and to maintain equality (Chapter 3), or to create their own ways of production for subsistence (Chapters 4 and 10).

4. Africans' Initiatives for Development and Subsistence

As previously discussed, the chapter authors explore, through field work or surveying primary source documents, African peoples' own initiatives for development and subsistence.

In Chapter 1, Sagawa discusses the negative impacts of large development projects, such as opening commercial farms, dam construction and food aid policy on the Daasanach people, agro-pastoralists in south-western Ethiopia. The dam construction created risks for their self-sufficiency, which had been based on crops and livestock. Food and cash aid has had the unexpected result of categorising people and aggravating local dependence on the state, but people continue to survive or live together and reconstruct their livelihoods through mutual assistance, making use of their ability to shift location to find other places for subsistence.

Chapter 2 is concerned with the Turkana people, one of the major pastoralist groups in arid parts of Kenya and neighbouring countries. Ohta, based on his more than 40 years of fieldwork, describes vividly the ways the Turkana people determine entitlement with regard to disposing of livestock, their most important property, through communal relations. Facing increasing opportunities, such as border trade, to sell livestock to earn cash, the Turkana people still try to preserve a communal order. In their ideology, livestock belong to the head of family but with multi-layered rights held by various other people. This 'bundle' of rights can be understood as resistance to the strong penetration of private ownership into localities under globalisation and an attempt to reconcile development with subsistence.

Oyama and Yoshimura present an empirical study in Chapter 3, on the positive and negative impacts of piecework as a levelling mechanism in northern Zambia's Bemba society. This study provided an interesting case for considering the symbiosis of development and subsistence in a farming village. The main purpose of offering piecework has been to expand private farmland and crop production but, in addition, employers use it as means of sharing wealth with others so as to limit envy and the practice of witchcraft. In the broader economy, piecework exacerbates economic disparities but, within villages, it also can serve as a mechanism to promote the distribution of wealth. This piecework provided the interesting case to consider the symbiotic relations of development and subsistence at a farming village.

The development or renewal of production processes occurred not only through interventions from outside or above, but was also achieved by the initiatives of individual people. In Chapter 4,

Sugiyama and Tsuruta continue their collaborative work on the cumulative process of numerous trials and errors by individual Bemba farmers in northern Zambia. This process is regarded as folk innovation history. The external technologies and newly introduced crops were integrated into the existing paradigm and strategies, based on woodland ecology and an economy of sharing. Influenced by the monetisation of the national economy, the farmers tackle the challenge of reducing economic disparities within the village. This intrinsic levelling mechanism played a central role in Bemba communities, allowing the resource-poor villagers access to essential resources.

Munemura discusses, in Chapter 5, the historical significance of the laying of inter-continental submarine cables between Europe and locations in the southern hemisphere such as South Africa. It is not very well known that submarine cable constituted indispensable infrastructure for the development of international communication and information exchange. The author sheds light on the importance of the submarine cable for African exports of agricultural commodities in general, and especially fruits. Without it, timely and efficient export of perishable primary commodities such as fruits would have been impossible. African people engaged with those exports relied on intercontinental information networks, which, in turn, relying on submarine cables. Globalisation, therefore, would not have reached the present stage without them.

Chapter 6 by Ideue elucidates internal factors leading to the export-oriented industrialisation of Mauritius, a small island African country. At the time of independence in 1968, Franco-Mauritian sugar estate owners, descendants of French colonial settlers and a small ethnic minority, had accumulated abundant capital, while Indian immigrants and their descendants, the majority group, held political power. The success of Mauritian post-independence industrialisation, the leading sector of which is garment production for export to the West, has been attributed to FDI inflows from East Asia. However, Ideue also shows that the role of Franco-Mauritian capitalists who invested in the garment sector was significant and that the government, led by Indian Mauritians, negotiated to secure preferential access to European markets. The Mauritian experience could be a useful precedent for other African countries currently depending on agricultural exports that are seeking possibilities to accumulate foreign exchange revenue. Additionally, in Africa there are numerous cases in which an ethnic majority has dominated government and antagonised wealthy ethnic minorities, resulting in negative economic outcomes.

Hara describes, in Chapter 7, a Lunda family's migration trajectory in Zambia. A late family member migrated from a village in the north-western area of the country to a large mining city in colonial times and then came back to the village after losing his job. Due to an unfortunate event, he then left the home village and moved around in search of a stable place to live. After becoming acquainted with a Luvale man, he found a place to live and, with permission of a local chief, created a new village together with his family. The introduction by the Luvale man was highly significant in this outcome. The mobility of the Lunda man and his newly obtained reliable relation with the Luvale man offered the potential for a new livelihood. This case is an example of inter-ethnic collaboration, like that in Mauritius but in a different dimension.

Hampwaye, Membele and Namakando discuss, in Chapter 8, the fast-paced spatial expansion of Lusaka, the capital of and largest city in Zambia. Agricultural land has been converted to other uses impacting people's livelihoods, especially those of the poor. The authors, focusing on an area in the city of Lusaka, analysed impacts through applying geographic information techniques and interviewing residents. They argue that the capital's expansion and consequent agricultural land conversion have contributed to loss of food production by urban agriculture, a rise in food prices and increased food insecurity among low-income residents, all of which have negatively influenced the livelihood of urban poor people.

Ramiarison explores, in Chapter 9, the difficulty and potential of the informal economic sector in Madagascar. While informal economic activities span society in each African country, academic attention has focused on urban informal enterprises. Ramiarison expands this perspective to incorporate rural and non-agricultural informal enterprises, which is valuable for obtaining a more holistic understanding of the informal sector. He argues that informal enterprises are based on the logic of subsistence or survival and experience harsh competition. There is a vicious circle constraining their development between the following factors: cycle of low income, low savings, low investment and low capital constraining their development. According to his detailed statistical analyses, however, there is a large disparity among informal enterprises with the same production activity in terms of size, production and willingness to innovate. The author finally finds that there is a strong potential for informal enterprises to innovate and adopt a logic of development through technical transfer of knowledge, the introduction of new machines and equipment and skill-learning through on-the-job training, thereby allowing them to break the abovementioned vicious circle and to effectively exploit their rich potential.

In Chapter 10, Takahashi, Owa and Ideue discuss horizontal development whereby informal vendors of low-price products in a sofa-making cluster in Nairobi, Kenya, are increasing not in terms of the size of individual enterprises but in terms of the number of enterprises. As many as 55 vendors concentrate in a small area and production activities unfold in an open-air situation. Stakeholders in the cluster share knowledge of basic sizes and standards of sofa sets. Workers learn through apprenticeship under more experienced workers and develop their skills on the job. The vendors and workers imitate others' ideas and skills through observing, which senior people tolerate. Workers can work for different vendors and learn more. Consequently, knowledge-sharing by a wide range of stakeholders has led to horizontal development. There are, however, innovations, differentiation of knowledge and some segregation along the line of ethnicity and gender.

Kirikoshi, in Chapter 11, explores Ghanaian traders' trust acquisition and connection building with Chinese businesspeople. As already mentioned, Chinese products have become popular among African people but Chinese nationals, with their visible activities, have faced anti-alien actions on the part of Ghanaian and local governments, which are influenced by the Africanisation tendency in the country. Exclusion of Chinese is particularly strong in Kumasi, one of the largest cities in Ghana. There, contacts with Chinese have become so difficult that it is a privilege oligopolised by those who have acquired *gaskiya* (trustworthiness) in trading. Their *gaskiya* has been acquired by demonstrating truth, honesty and fairness mainly through intraregional kola trading. *Gaskiya*, intraregional trustworthiness, has become a platform for interregional connection, which is a characteristic factor in Africa's participation in globalisation.

Most African nations are ethnically heterogenous and regionally disparate. Sakai, in Chapter 12, clarifies the difficult situation in western Cameroon, borders on the Anglophone Regions where the conflict with the government is intensifying. Despite the well-known entrepreneurship of the local people, the Bamiléké, the Western area has been largely alienated from national economic and political development. The situation is aggravated by western Cameroon's political and economic disadvantages. While many young people in western Cameroon are highly educated, they have difficulty finding formal or qualified employment opportunities. These under-employed people go out into the streets to find a means of subsistence in motorbike driving. A strike of bike taxi drivers in August 2019 cannot be understood only from the economic viewpoint, and its politics are important to national history. To achieve inclusive development, such circumstances should be reconsidered with attention to civic rights.

In Chapter 13, Sibanda, Gukurume and Hayakawa discuss the means Zimbabweans used to survive inflation caused by international isolation and government macroeconomic mismanagement. The authors conducted field research in two major cities in the country, Harare and Masvingo, on responses to quickly changing policies and the economic situation. Though the Zimbabwean government formally tried to regulate and restrain parallel money markets, various actors engaged in money trading joined in the proliferation of parallel markets to mitigate painful shocks by inflation, i.e., the daily decrease in value of the official currency people held. The government and the banking sector lost public trust due to their incapacity to respond to people's ongoing need for cash. Money traders invented various alternative measures including the introduction of foreign exchanges for circulating money. Alternative measures were officially illegal but politicians and elite bankers backed money traders' operations informally, which meant, in all likelihood, that the operations were linked with high-level corruption. The measures were also telling representations of Zimbabwean city dwellers' resilience in defending their livelihoods.

5. From Victimisation to Engagement

Africa and its peoples have long been portrayed as victims, subject to the actions of external forces such as foreign aid donors or MNCs, or their own national and local governments. According to our field research, such portrayals are not totally appropriate as Africans are not always passive in the face of impacts from external policies, large-scale aid projects or the operations of MNCs. African people initiate their own development efforts and make use of resources introduced through external or internal development interventions. As well, they mitigate the negative impacts of development on their lives by shifting geographically, devising their own subsistence measures or reconstructing their livelihoods, sometimes forging bonds with political and economic elites to survive in business and sustain their livelihoods and, if they are fortunate, to thrive.

The dichotomic distinction between development and subsistence is outdated. Every day, African people reconcile or bridge the two as capable actors. Though it is not easy to achieve, they are striving for survival, protection or betterment of their livelihoods. African area studies scholars should reconstruct their understanding of African people's engagement with changing realities. We should not be satisfied with lamenting Africans' predicaments, specifying some of the perpetrators, and criticising them. Needless to say, we should beware of expected negative impacts of development interventions and try best to prevent and rectify them. Nevertheless, while doing so, we should pay attention to patience, flexibility, robustness, ingenuity and creativity in development, sometimes skilful responses to development interventions from outside and above, and subsistence of African people. Thereby we can grasp Africans' potentials in opening up their own future.

Challenges to African people such as negative impacts caused by development interventions, government failures, growing intra-regional and inter-regional trade, widening income disparity, urbanisation, ICT spread, migration, needs for improving production ways, informality, unemployment and macroeconomic instability as discussed in this volume, are also common throughout the world. Such commonalities, however, do not mean that Africa has been homogenised with the rest of the world; for example, a factor that makes Africa unique is Africans' aptitude for living with complex relations between development and subsistence.

If we can discern ways to solve problems emanating from our common challenges among Africans' activities and experiences, we should be able to learn more from Africa. Africans have potentials to contribute to the world by sharing knowledge acquired through their everyday struggle with development and subsistence, and their bridging of the two.

Acknowledgements

This work was supported by JSPS KAKENHI Grant Number JP16H06318.

References

Brautigam, D. (2011) *Dragon's Gift: The Real Story of China in Africa*, Oxford: Oxford University Press.

Carmody, P. R. (2011) *The New Scramble for Africa*, Cambridge: Polity.

Crotty, J. (2003) 'The neoliberal paradox: The impact of destructive product market competition and impatient finance on nonfinancial corporations in the neoliberal era', *Review of Radical Political Economics*, Vol. 35, Issue 3, pp. 271–279.

Edwards, L. and Jenkins, R. (2015) 'The impact of Chinese import penetration on the South African manufacturing sector', *The Journal of Development Studies.* Vol. 51, Issue 4, pp. 447–463.

Fuchs, C. (2015) 'Neoliberal globalization', Encyclopædia Britannica (https://www.britannica.com/event/antiglobalization#ref1180923) (accessed: 15 November 2020).

Huntington, S. P. (1991) *The Third Wave: Democratization in the Late Twentieth Century*, Norman: University of Oklahoma Press.

Hutchinson, J. (2011) 'Globalisation and nation formation in the longue durée', in D. Halikiopoulou and S. Vasilopoulou (eds) *Nationalism and Globalisation: Conflicting or Complementary?*, London: Routledge, pp. 84–99.

Lynch, G. and Crawford, G. (2011) 'Democratization in Africa 1990–2010: An assessment', *Democratization*, Vol. 18, Issue 2, pp. 275–310.

Shizha, E. (2010) 'The Interface of neoliberal globalization, science education and indigenous African knowledges in Africa', *Journal of Alternative Perspectives in the Social Sciences*, Vol. 2, No. 1, pp. 27–58.

Wallerstein, I. M. (1975) *The Modern World-System I: Capitalist Agriculture and the Origins of the European World-Economy in the Sixteenth Century*, New York: Academic Press.

Part I

Customs and Renewals in Rural Societies in Africa

Chapter 1

Large-Scale Development Projects, Food Security Policy and Livelihoods of Agro-Pastoralists in Southwestern Ethiopia

Toru Sagawa

1. Introduction

Ethiopia has been one of the leading countries in 'developing Africa' in the 21st century. In 2004, it achieved a 13.5 per cent gross domestic product growth rate and continued double digit growth until 2008. Although the growth rate of many other African countries slowed in the 2010s, Ethiopia has maintained its high rate of growth. Rapid growth is reflected in major cities such as Addis Ababa, which are booming and rife with high-rise buildings. Concurrently, there has been a distortion in economic growth.

In rural areas, ambitious policy attempts to improve food security for local people; however, various development projects that can deprive local people of their livelihoods have been ongoing. In 2005, the Ethiopian government implemented the Productive Safety Net Programme (PSNP), which is 'the largest social protection programme operating in sub-Saharan Africa' outside of South Africa (Gilligan et al. 2009: 1685). Because the Ethiopian people have experienced serious drought and starvation many times, this large-scale social protection programme has been well received. It represents the 'the new politics of distribution', which Ferguson (2015) discussed mainly in the context of southern African countries.

On the other hand, large-scale development projects have been underway since the mid-2000s, especially in historically marginalised areas, under the guise of 'democratic developmentalism'. In western and southern Ethiopia, the construction and operation of large-scale commercial farms has resulted in loss of access to the land and water that was the primary means of food production for local people. There have been reports of conflicts, sometimes violent, among local people, companies, migrant labourers and police over commercial farms; these conflicts have occurred in the Gambella (HRW 2012a), Benishangula-Gumuz (Tsegaye 2015) and Southern Nations, Nationalities, and Peoples' (SNNP) regions (HRW 2012b; Oakland Institute 2013).

In previous studies, the two policies have tended to be analysed separately. While the 'achievements' of PSNP were examined quantitatively (e.g., Gilligan et al. 2009; Bethelhem et al. 2015), negative impacts on local societies have been reported as a result of large-scale development projects (e.g., Dessalegn 2011; Tsegaye 2015). Lavers criticised the majority of research regarding the PSNP, stating that it did not consider the PSNP's political intentions or the relationships of the PSNP with other policies (Lavers 2013; cf. Bishop and Hilhorst 2010). Stevenson and Buffavand (2018: 125) researched food security among the Bodi – who have faced systematic forced displacement and villagisation – and warned that, '[i]n focusing only on the villagization piece of what is in fact a much wider set of interventions, our food access survey risks presenting a misleading picture'.

In contemporary Ethiopian society, plural policies which could drastically change local livelihoods are operated simultaneously and influenced mutually. By only examining the 'achievements' of single policies – ignoring their relationships with other policies – the research thus far fails to analyse how government policies, including the PSNP, have influenced local food security and changed the relationship between the government and the local people.

In this chapter, I analyse how large-scale development projects and food security policies overall have influenced local livelihoods, as well as how the people have attempted to adapt to a new social environment. The examination led to the theme of this book: the relationship between development and subsistence economies.

The African Potential Projects have emphasised the problem-solving capacity of 'ordinal people' in Africa (e.g., Ofosu-Kusi and Matsuda (eds) 2020). Many papers in the Projects have noted that 'ordinal people' are neither solely conservative nor entrepreneurs; they are flexible and resilient, capable of communicating traditional (internal) and modern (external) elements and creating hybridised methods of thinking and practising. I describe the devastating effects of development policies on local livelihoods; I also emphasise the creative management of 'ordinal people' in responding to those effects.

2. Large-Scale Development Projects and Their Influences on Local Food Security

2-1. Object Area

The subject of this chapter is the Daasanach *woreda* (district), located in southwestern Ethiopia in the South Omo zone of the SNNP region on the border area of Ethiopia, Kenya and South Sudan. This remote area has changed from a peripheral area far from the centre of the state to the frontline of development on which Ethiopian state's prestige has been staked. Large-scale commercial farms, exploratory oil drilling, and mega-scale dam construction began in the mid-2000s and early 2010s. The field research for this chapter was conducted during periods of one or two weeks in 2013, 2014, 2016 and 2017.

The estimated population of the Daasanach *woreda* in 2016 was 65,353; the majority are Daasanach. These residents depend on pastoralism and flood-retreat cultivation for their subsistence (Carr 1977; Almagor 1978). The Omo River, which flows from the Ethiopian highlands into Lake Turkana, floods the downstream areas annually in July. Flooding in the Daasanach land, which is located at the lower end of the river, is substantial. As the flooded water withdraws in August and September, the residents plant sorghum and other crops in the fertile floodplain and riverbank soils, which are also used for herding livestock. Although the average annual precipitation of the Daasanach land is approximately 350 to 400 millimetres, a relatively abundant amount of food can be produced. Neighbouring peoples, such as the Turkana and Gabra, come to the Daasanach land during periods of drought and starvation to ask for food. The Daasanach often entertain these visitors and give ample quantities of sorghum and other crops without requesting anything in immediate return (Sagawa 2010, 2019a). Whereas it was previously the centre of food security in the area, food production in the Daasanach land has drastically changed since large-scale development projects began.

2-2. Commercial Farms Projects

Since the latter half of the 2000s, external investors have made large-scale land acquisitions, sometimes described as 'land grabs', in various areas of the world, especially in sub-Saharan Africa. The direct impetus for these acquisitions was a sudden rise in food prices traded internationally in 2007–2008; other factors also contributed, such as the growing concern for food security in many countries, the increased demand for biofuels in the global market and the focus on land as a safe haven for capital after the Lehman Shock. Though Sassen (2013) examined how land grabs escalate the process of 'de-nationalisation' and transform national territories into commodities for the global market, this analysis does not apply well to Ethiopia (Lavers 2016).

Ethiopia is one of the main target countries for land grabs. The government of the Ethiopian People's Revolutionary Democratic Front (EPRDF) adopted an Agricultural Development Led Industrialisation (ADLI) policy which made much account of small-scale peasants from around 1993. However, mainly because of the stagnation in agricultural productivity, the EPRDF changed its policy direction and began to accept the development of large-scale commercial farms in the early 2000s (Dessalegn 2014; Shete and Rutten 2015).

Land grabs in Ethiopia can be characterised in six ways (Dessalegn 2011; Lavers 2012; Nalepa 2013; Keeley et al. 2014; Tsegaye 2015): (1) a vast expanse of land is available for transaction in a short period of time;[1] (2) agreements are made regarding conditions that are advantageous for investors (e.g. the lease period is several decades and the lease rate is extremely low); (3) primarily foreign investors acquire tens of thousands of hectares of land, although dozens to thousands of hectares are also acquired by domestic investors; (4) most of the land available for transaction is in the southern and western parts of the country, which have been marginalised by past administrations; (5) acquired land is referred to as 'unused' or 'marginal' land in government documents, although the majority of it has been used by pastoralists, agro-pastoralists and shifting cultivators; and (6) in areas where acquired land is developed for agricultural use, residents are given neither sufficient prior explanation nor compensation for eviction.

The majority of acquisitions involve unregistered land in arid and semi-arid areas. In rural Ethiopia, land registration has been facilitated by the Tigray, Amhara, Oromia and SNNP regions. According to a report released in 2013 by the government, land registration has been completed for more than 90 per cent of households in those areas. However, there have been delays in other regions. Even in remote areas of the above four regions that are inhabited by pastoralists, registration has been behind schedule (Imeru 2010; Bezu and Holden 2014: 195; Lavers 2012: 804; Abebe and Solomon 2013: 188).[2] These lands, which had generally been marginalised by successive central governments, began to be registered as investor land and controlled under the state's land law right as the land deals were completed.

Domestic investors, especially those from Tigray occupying the core of the EPRDF regime from 1991 to 2018, were leased hundreds to thousands of hectares of land. The Oakland Institute (2011) noted that the central government intended to spread the state's authority to the corners of the country through developing its peripheral areas by loyal regime supporters. In addition, one-third of land deals involving more than one thousand hectares from 2005 to 2012 were with state-owned enterprises (Keeley et al. 2014). The main crop cultivated in plantations owned by these state enterprises is sugarcane, which was identified in the 2010 'Growth and Transformation Plan' as the core product with which to achieve economic growth as a means to reach Ethiopia's development goal of becoming a middle-income country by 2025. In sum, the central government, which identified its political intention to strengthen its authority in peripheral areas and expand the production of exportable agricultural products, actively promoted land deals and development that would support this objective.

In the Daasanach *woreda*, at least eight farm agreements were made with investors from Italy, India and Tigray as of 2015. Of these farms, five were already in operation, cultivating mainly maize and cotton. The size of the farms varied from 1,000 to 30,000 hectares; all were located in the centre of the inhabited area of Daasanach on the flatlands along the Omo River suitable for irrigation. Consistent with the reports from other areas, residents were not given proper prior explanation regarding the land transactions; because land registration had not begun in these villages, no compensations were given. Sugarcane plantations owned by state-owned enterprises, totalling 100,000 hectares, have been operating in the Salamago *woreda* of the northern South Omo zone (100 km north of the Daasanach land); these areas are inhabited by agro-pastoralists such as the Mursi and Bodi (Kamski 2016, 2018).

2-3. Dam Construction and Its Downstream Impacts

The Gibe III Dam, located in the middle valley of the Omo River approximately 200 kilometres northwest of the Daasanach land, began construction in 2006 and has operated since 2015. At the time of its construction, the dam was intended to be the highest in sub-Saharan Africa and cost more than any other infrastructure project in Ethiopia (1.55 billion Euro). Many dams have been built in

Ethiopia since 2001, resulting in a production capacity of electric power tenfold greater than the capacity in 2000 (Mains 2019: 29). Mega-scale hydroelectric projects to meet domestic and neighbouring electricity demand are expected to take a leading role in promoting the economic growth of Ethiopia. These dams also enable investors and the government to operate downstream commercial irrigated farms by controlling the flow of the river upstream.

The construction of Gibe III Dam has been criticised, mainly by Western civil-based organisations. For example, International Rivers (2009) estimated that dam construction would have negative impacts on the livelihoods of approximately 300,000 people who live in the lower Omo valley and around Lake Turkana. Many actors have warned that the dam would reduce the flow of the river, stop flooding in downstream areas and increase the salinity of Lake Turkana.

The environmental and social assessment report of the Gibe III Dam, which was only publicised after construction began, reported that the dam would enable the control of river flow and 'protect' people who had 'suffered' from flooding. The report also described the negative influence of flood stoppage on local livelihoods; accordingly, it proposed the alternative measure of a ten-day 'simulated flood' (Agriconsulting SpA. and Mid-Day International Consulting Engineers 2008). The report insisted that the simulated flood would maintain the positive effects of natural flooding. Independent expert groups that assessed the impacts of the dam criticised this report (ARWG 2009). These groups stated that there have been no successful examples of simulated floods and that this measure would be inadequate.

2-4. Opposition against Development Projects

In view of the problems caused by these development projects, it is supposed that agro-pastoralists in the lower Omo Valley presumably attempted to protect their rights with support from various international indigenous peoples' movements. Since the

1990s, the cooperation of international and local NGOs focused on indigenous rights has flourished in sub-Saharan Africa. International NGOs in the West launched an opposition campaign to the Gibe III Dam on the global stage, but no local Ethiopian NGOs responded or become involved. The Ethiopian government implemented 'Proclamation No. 621/2009', which prohibited all foreign NGOs and domestic NGOs with at least 10 per cent foreign funding from engaging in activities or issues concerning human rights and conflict. As a result, international NGOs could not cooperate with domestic NGOs, and they failed to mobilise local people in the opposition movement.

The political party in power at the time, which was facing the upcoming 2010 national election, was motivated to enforce the Proclamation. The party analysed that one of the causes on a hard fight in previous election in 2005 was the advocacy activities by NGOs which acquired the activity fund from Western organisations (Dereje 2011). The late Meles Zenawi, Prime Minister of Ethiopia from 1995 to 2012, held a strong negative attitude towards the 'trickle up democracy' promoted by NGOs (Meles 2006).

A policy that strongly restricts civil society activities might be a target of criticism from Western countries and negatively influence relations with international NGOs engaged in development and support activities in Ethiopia. There are two factors that enable the Ethiopian government to enforce the proclamation, with varying risks (Miyawaki and Tonegawa 2018). The first factor is the global situation after 11 September 2001. The Ethiopian state, which neighbours Sudan and Somalia, has become an important strategic ally of the USA. The second factor is Ethiopia's close relationship with China, whereby China's large investments since the turn of the century have reduced Ethiopia's dependence on support from international NGOs. Based on its relationships with these two powerful nations, the Ethiopian state has been advancing towards an 'authoritarian' developmental state, rather than a 'democratic' state.

2-5. Influences of Development Projects on Local Livelihoods

Large-scale development projects have already influenced livelihoods in the Daasanach. Table 1 shows the meal composition of a household in a semi-sedentary settlement located at the centre of Daasanach land along the Omo River. The household exhibits a mid-range economic status in terms of the number of livestock and area of cultivated land. Table 1A describes the meals in March and August of 2006; Table 1B describes the meals in March of 2017 and August through September of 2016.

The majority of meals in 2006 were composed mainly of sorghum, common beans (*Phaseolus vulgaris*), milk from small livestock (sheep and goat) and butter. The second harvest of sorghum had been completed in March. August was between seasons when the stored amount of sorghum was becoming low, although a moderate amount had been stored due to a large flood in 2005. The household herded its cattle in a livestock camp and obtained its supply of milk from small livestock. There was substantial milking in March because the livestock had been herded in a green floodplain. In August, butter made from cow's milk was brought from the livestock camp when the amount of milking decreased. Although the numbers of meals in 2006 were fewer than in the numbers in 2016 and 2017, the amount of food in each meal in 2006 was much larger and members of the household ate less frequently.

Meal composition in 2016 and 2017 drastically changed, compared with 2006. Sorghum only appeared once day,[3] and wheat was eaten as a substitute for sorghum. While there was often milk from small livestock (see Table 1B), the quantity of milk was low; a small child could consume it in a single swallow. There was no butter from the livestock camp because insufficient pastureland was available. Because the amount of wheat in each meal could not sustain a family, the family often slaughtered small livestock for meat. Local beer and *injela*, a staple food in the Ethiopian highlands, were brought in from the town of Omorate by a member of the household or other residents in the village who sold mainly small livestock – including females – to afford them. While selling livestock to buy everyday goods has not been uncommon since approximately 2000, the sale of female livestock, which are indispensable for reproduction and increasing herd sizes, is very rare. One of my Daasanach colleagues said after seeing a woman go to town with a female goat: 'our stomachs make us mad'.

Table 1. Comparison of meal composition between 2006 and 2016–17

Table 1A: 2006

Date	Morning	Daytime	Evening
12 March		sorghum, common bean, sour milk	sorghum, common bean
13 March		sorghum	sorghum, sour milk
14 March		sorghum, sour milk	sorghum, milk of small livestock
15 March		sorghum, common bean	sorghum, common bean
12 August	sorghum, meat	sorghum	sorghum, milk of small livestock
13 August	sorghum, milk of small livestock	sorghum	sorghum, meat
14 August	milk of small livestock		sorghum, milk of small livestock
15 August	milk of small livestock	sorghum	sorghum
16 August	milk of small livestock	sorghum, butter	sorghum, butter

Table 1B: 2016 (August and September) and 2017 (March)

Date	Morning	Daytime	Evening
18 March	sorghum	meat	sorghum, meat
19 March			wheat, meat
20 March	injera, meat	wheat	wheat, meat
21 March	wheat	local beer	maize
28 August	wheat	wheat	wheat, milk of small livestock, meat
29 August	wheat, milk of small livestock	local beer, meat	wheat, milk of small livestock, meat
30 August	wheat, milk of small livestock	wheat, meat	wheat, milk of small livestock, meat
31 August	wheat, milk of small livestock	wheat	wheat, milk of small livestock
1 September	wheat, milk of small livestock	wheat	wheat, milk of small livestock, cat fish

Source: Author's data.

Although Table 1 shows data from only one household, the change from self-sufficiency to dependence on external supplies reflects the general change in meal composition for households that mainly depend on flood-retreat cultivation and pastoralism for their livelihood. Similar tendencies have been reported among the Bodi (Stevenson and Buffavand 2018; Fana 2019) and Nyangatom (Hodbod, Sharma, et al. 2019; Tebbs et al. 2019) in the South Omo zone.

The primary reason for the drastic change in meal composition within such a short period of time was that the Omo River did not flood in 2015 (which influenced the meal composition in August and September of 2016) and 2016 (which influenced the meal composition in March of 2017). As a result, the area suitable for herding decreased and the residents could not cultivate crops in previous floodplains and riverbanks. Daasanach elders explained that, while they remembered many years with no floods, there were never two consecutive years without flooding. This lack of flooding was related to the construction of the Gibe III Dam; as International Rivers and other organisations warned, the dam led to a cessation of flooding after its completion in 2015.[4] Local government officials revealed that the planned simulated floods in August of 2016 were cancelled because they might devastate the plantations along the Omo River. Residents of the Daasanach are now compelled to make a living without the aid of the flood. The number of PSNP beneficiaries has increased, such that this programme replaces the supportive role of the floods.

3. Allocation of PSNP and Emergency Aid Beneficiaries

3-1. PSNP and Emergency Aid

Residents of the Daasanach did not cultivate and eat wheat prior to receiving it from the PSNP or other emergency aid (see Table 1B). They cooked wheat the same way they did sorghum – only boiling or grinding and making a thick gruel – and described it as 'very bad' with 'no taste', compared to the 'very good' and 'very tasty' sorghum and 'second best' maize.

The Ethiopian government began the PSNP in 2005. The government previously regarded the food shortage as the result of natural disasters and as the focus of emergency aid. After the serious food crises in 2002 and 2003, the government shifted its attitude towards regarding food shortages as a development problem (Kodama 2014) and enacted a new food security policy in 2003 with the PSNP as its core project.

The PSNP attempts to prevent the exhaustion of household assets by supplying food and cash regularly for half the year. Through this programme, beneficiaries must engage in specified work and are supplied with food or cash corresponding to 2,100 kilocalories per day for six months of each year for five years. Elderly individuals and persons with disabilities are unconditionally provisioned with food or cash, which is referred to as 'direct support' (comprising approximately ten per cent of beneficiaries), whereas the main portion of the programme comprises 'public work'. Beneficiaries also participate in the Complementary Community Investment Program and Household Asset Building Program to improve the food security of households and communities. Households that become food secure graduate from the programme.

The PSNP has had multiple phases: the first and second phases were from 2005 to 2009, the third phase was from 2010 to 2014 and the fourth phase began in 2015. There were approximately five million beneficiaries during the first and second phases, living in the Amhara, Oromia, SNNP and Tigray regions. As of 2009, the programme extended into four other regions and *woredas* (districts) mainly inhabited by pastoral people. Approximately ten million people have been registered during the fourth phase so far.

3-2. Uneven Allocation of Beneficiaries in the District

The PSNP began in the Daasanach *woreda* during the third phase of the programme. There were 9,514 beneficiaries in 2013, which increased drastically to 24,969 in 2016 during the fourth phase (2.6 times greater than the number of beneficiaries during the third phase). The population of the Daasanach *woreda* in 2016 was estimated at 65,353; thus, PSNP beneficiaries comprised 38.2 per cent of the total population. In addition to the PSNP, the Daasanach *woreda* has been the recipient of emergency food aid. The 'Humanitarian Requirements Documents', which predict the probability of starvation based on data such as the previous year's precipitation, designated the Daasanach *woreda* as a 'hot spot' in 2016 (Joint Government and Humanitarian Partners 2016). As a result, 23,267 people (35.6 per cent of the population) received emergency aid in the same amount of food and cash as PSNP beneficiaries. Between the PSNP and emergency aid programmes, 48,236 people

(73.8 per cent of total population) were expected to be provisioned with food or cash for six months in 2016.

The Daasanach *woreda* consists of 41 *kebeles* (villages); the population of each *kebele* ranged from 993 to 3,358 in 2016. There were large differences in the percentage of PSNP and emergency aid beneficiaries in each *kebele*. While the total percentage of beneficiaries in the *woreda* was 73.8 per cent of the population, the percentage of beneficiaries in the total population was 100 per cent, or almost 100 per cent in each of 16 *kebeles* (hereafter, 'focused target *kebeles*'). The percentage of beneficiaries in the remaining 25 *kebeles* was less than 85.4 per cent of the total population.

The focused target *kebeles* can be classified into three categories in terms of their political-geographical conditions. The first category includes five *kebeles*, located in northwestern Daasanach along the Omo River, that were identified as plantation development sites. People in these *kebeles* lost access to the land for housing, cultivation and herding. The second category includes six *kebeles*, in northeastern Daasanach along the Omo River, identified as resettlement sites for people displaced by the plantation developments (people from the first category of *kebeles*). The local government planned to use the PSNP 'public work' to build irrigated lands for resettled people who did not have a means of subsistence. The third category consists of four *kebeles* in southwestern Daasanach land in the border zone with Kenya where the Daasanach and Kenyan Turkana have fought for many years. The local government reportedly intends to make a buffer zone between the Daasanach and Turkana to mitigate conflict by transforming livestock pasture into irrigated land for cultivation. Ironically, food security in the focused target *kebeles* was originally stable, compared to *kebeles* located far from the Omo River, because they were able to engage in riverbank cultivation in most years (Sagawa 2019b).

Local government officials unanimously stated that large-scale development projects were forced by the federal and/or regional governments and that they were required to accept these projects.

Markakis (2011: 8) has noted that only elites in the centre of the modern and contemporary Ethiopian government take part in political decision making; auxiliary elites on the periphery simply enforce the decisions of the centre. Officials within the local government identified themselves as auxiliary elites. While auxiliary elites are subordinate to the decisions of the central elites, they need to comply to a certain degree with local resident requests to maintain their status. Local government officials have recognised the PSNP and emergency aid as political resources, strategically allocated in phases, to soften the disappointment of residents about development projects decided upon by the central elites.

3-3. Allocation within Villages

In the *kebeles* in which the percentage of beneficiaries was lower than 85.4 per cent, some people were registered and some were not. According to the Programme Implementation Manual for the fourth phase (MOA 2014), the criteria for choosing beneficiaries are the level of household food security in the previous three years, such as level of support from other households, and availability of labour in each household. '*Kebele* Food Security Task Forces', which comprise the administrative head and agricultural extension workers in each *kebele*, make the final decision.

As an example, in Y *kebele* in the middle of Daasanach land along the Omo River, where beneficiaries of the PSNP and emergency aid comprise 50.75 per cent of the total population (2,807), a commercial farm operated by a domestic investor began operations in 2009 but closed in 2012 due to funding problems. Because of this withdrawal, the percentage of beneficiaries has remained lower than other *kebeles* where commercial farms have been in operation or are preparing to open.

According to the author's research, the residents of Y *kebele* gathered at a meeting to decide who would receive PSNP and emergency food aid in 2015 and 2016. The administrative head walked through the group, pointed at people saying, 'this one';

agricultural extension workers who were appointed by the Ministry of Agriculture recorded the names of these identified individuals as beneficiaries. Some villagers reported that only fortunate people were registered by chance. Other villagers told me that people with personal or close relationships with administrators were registered preferentially. Some villagers recognised that persons who opposed plantation development were not registered. Because the author does not have systematic data regarding relationships between administrators and registrants or the economic statuses of registered and unregistered, he cannot analyse whether the selection had been done 'fairly' or not. The problem is that some villagers reckoned that the selection was done arbitrarily and unregistered persons experienced unfairness.

Under the situation in which mutual distrust among villagers might arise and strengthen, many beneficiaries in Y *kebele* attempt to avoid distrust and divides within the community by sharing their food and money from the PSNP and emergency aid. For example, a middle-aged woman gave her food and cash to her co-wife, mother's family, neighbours and friends in the same and different villages who were not registered as PSNP beneficiaries. As a result, her stock of food and money ran short early. Because the provision time of PSNP and emergency aid were different, she was given food and/or money from beneficiaries of emergency aid and got through to next provision of PSNP. It is pointed out that the sharing and distribution of supplied food and money are not regarded positively from the point of view of the PSNP which is for food secure households to 'graduate' from the programme. The government considers sharing to 'dilute' the effect of the PSNP (Sabates-Wheeler et al. 2013); from the perspective of the residents in the community, voluntary sharing and distribution prevents differentiation between 'haves' and 'have nots'.

Sun reported that villagers in Rendille in northern Kenya took food aid from the Food and Agriculture Organisation to one location and redistributed it to all the villagers during a period of serious hardship (Sun 2017). My observations did not reveal similar instances of this in the Daasanach, where sharing was performed on an interpersonal basis only. While the Rendille society is strongly organised under the clan system, the Daasanach is organised under a network of invididual relations. The sharing and distribution of goods from the outside world reflects social structures within each community.

4. Conclusion

Most previous studies (e.g., Gilligan et al. 2009; Bethelhem et al. 2015), examining the impact of the PSNP on its beneficiaries, did not fully consider the programme's political motivations or the relationship between the PSNP and other development projects. In this chapter, I analysed the impact of dam construction and the operation of commercial farms on the subsistence economy and food security of agro-pastoral people in southwestern Ethiopia. I noted that food and money provided through the PSNP and emergency aid were appropriated to make up for the negative impacts of the dam and plantations on subsistence livelihoods. The PSNP and other development projects have increased people's dependence on the state. While current government policies can divide the community between those who benefit from the PSNP and those who do not, people have managed to survive through helping each other. On the one hand, this action which was taken to deal with development policy can be positioned as a potential of local communities. On the other hand, as the government does not have a political motivation to consider and improve the livelihoods of people who can survive through their mutual assistance, this 'spontaneous' action may contribute to the continuation of an unreasonable development policy.

Lastly, I note that, because many households that registered for the PSNP or emergency aid did not receive the prescribed amount of food and cash, people were compelled to slaughter and/or sell livestock, which depleted their assets. This means that the basic purpose of the PSNP, which was to prevent the exhaustion of household property, has not been achieved. In addition, the government has not provided proper alternatives for people whose livelihoods were lost to large-scale development projects. While the government has a plan to distribute irrigated land to each household (0.5 ha per household) through mobilising PSNP public works, there has been a long delay. As of August 2017, only 73 people in Y *kebele* (total population is 2,807) had access to 0.22 ha of land on average. The food security situation in the area should be carefully monitored.

Endnotes

[1] The total amount of transacted land is uncertain. The following estimates have been proposed: 3,619,590 ha from 2008 to January 2011 (Oakland Institute 2011); approximately 1,500,000 ha from 2003 to 2010 (Dessalegn 2011); 1,060,000 ha from 2005 to 2012 (Keeley et al. 2014); and more than 2,100,100 ha from 1992 to 2013 (Shete and Rutten 2015).

[2] Article 3(1) of the Expropriation of Landholdings for Public Purposes and Payment of Compensation Proclamation stipulates, 'A woreda [district] … have the power to expropriate rural or urban landholdings for public purpose where it believes that it should be used for a better development project to be carried out by public entities, private investors …'. Part 3 of the same proclamation stipulates the procedures related to the compensation paid upon expropriation of land, but no compensations shall be paid upon expropriation of unregistered land (Daniel 2013).

[3] This sorghum was gifted from a member of a household which was located at the northern shore of Lake Turkana. While there was no flooding of the Omo River in 2015, the water level of the Lake Turkana rose slightly, such that households along Lake Turkana could cultivate and harvest a small amount of sorghum after the water had receded.

[4] See Hodbod, Stevenson, et al. (2019) regarding the overall impact of the Gibe III Dam on the area.

Acknowledgements

This work was supported by JSPS KAKENHI Grant Number JP16H06318.

References

Abebe, M. and Solomon, B. (2013) 'The need to strengthen land laws in Ethiopia to protect pastoral rights', in A. Catley, J. Lind and I. Scoones (eds) *Pastoralism and Development in Africa*, London: Routledge, pp. 186–194.

Agriconsulting SpA. and Mid-Day International Consulting Engineers (2008) *Gibe III Hydroelectric Project: Environmental Impact Assessment Additional Study of Downstream Impact.*

Almagor, U. (1978) *Pastoral Partners: Affinity and Bond Partnership among the Dassanetch of South-West Ethiopia*, Manchester: Manchester University Press.

ARWG (Africa Resources Working Group) (2009) *A Commentary on the Environmental, Socioeconomic and Human Rights Impacts of the Proposed Gibe III Dam in the Lower Omo River Basin of Ethiopia.*

Bethelhem, L. D., Shively, G. and Holden, S. T. (2015) 'Does Ethiopia's Productive Safety Net Program improve child nutrition', *Food Security*, Vol. 7, pp. 1273–1289.

Bezu, S. and Holden, S. (2014) 'Demand for second-stage land certification in Ethiopia: Evidence from household panel date', *Land Use Policy*, Vol. 41, pp. 193–205.

Bishop, C. and Hilhorst, D. (2010) 'From food aid to food security: The case of the safety net policy in Ethiopia', *Journal of Modern African Studies*, Vol. 48, No. 2, pp. 181–202.

Carr, C. (1977) *Pastoralism in Crisis: The Dasanetch and their Ethiopian Lands*, Chicago: The University of Chicago.

Daniel, W. A. (2013) 'Land rights and expropriation in Ethiopia', Doctoral thesis, Royal Institute of Technology.

Dereje, F. (2011) 'Aid negotiation: The uneasy "partnership" between EPRDF and the donors', *Journal of Eastern African Studies*, Vol. 5 No. 4, pp. 788–817.

Dessalegn, R. (2011) *Land to Investors: Large-scale Land Transfers in Ethiopia*, Addis Ababa: Forum for Social Studies.

______ (2014) 'The perils of development from above: Land deals in Ethiopia', *African Identities*, Vol. 12, No. 1, pp. 26–44.

Fana, G. (2019) 'Transforming the Bodi from pastoralists to outgrowers: Land and state capitalism in South Omo, southwest Ethiopia', in A. O. Akinola and H. Wissink (eds) *Trajectory of Land Reform in Post-Colonial African States: The Quest for Sustainable Development and Utilization*, Cham: Springer, pp. 43–55.

Ferguson, J. (2015) *Give a Man a Fish: Reflections on the New Politics of Distribution*, Durham: Duke University Press.

Gilligan, D. O., Hoddinott, J. and Alemayehu, S. T. (2009) 'The impact of Ethiopia's Productive Safety Net Programme and its linkages', *The Journal of Development Studies,* Vol. 45, No. 10, pp. 1684–1706.

Hodbod, J., Stevenson, E. G. J., Akall, G., Akuja, T., Angelei, I., Bedasso, E. A., Buffavand, L., Derbyshire, S., Eulenberger, I., Gownaris, N., Kamski, B., Kurewa, A., Lokuruka, M., Mulugeta, M. F., Okenwa, D., Rodgers, C. and Tebbs, E. J. (2019) 'Social-ecological change in the Omo-Turkana basin: A synthesis of current developments', *Ambio*, Vol. 48, No. 10, pp. 1099–1115.

Hodbod, J., Sharma, S., Pertaub, D.-V., Tebbes, E. J. and Chan, K. (2019) *Coping Strategies in Nyangatom, Ethiopia, SIDERA Briefing Note #3*, Michigan: Omo-Turkana Research Network.

HRW (Human Rights Watch) (2012a) *Waiting Here for Death: Forced Displacement and 'Villagization' in Ethiopia's Gambella*, New York: Human Rights Watch.

______ (2012b) *'What will Happen if Hunger Comes?' Abuses against the Indigenous Peoples of Ethiopia's Lower Omo Valley*, New York: Human Rights Watch.

Imeru, T. (2010) 'Governance of large scale agricultural investments in Africa: The case of Ethiopia', *World Bank Annual Conference on Land Policy and Administration*, Washington DC, 26–27 April 2010.

International Rivers (2009) *Fact Sheet: Gibe III Dam, Ethiopia*, Oakland: International Rivers.

Joint Government and Humanitarian Partners (2016) *2016 Ethiopia Humanitarian Requirement Document*, Joint Government and Humanitarian Partners.

Kamski, B. (2016) 'The Kuraz Sugar Development Project (KSDP) in Ethiopia: Between "sweet visions" and mounting challenges', *Journal of Eastern African Studies*, Vol. 10, No. 3, pp. 568–580.

______ (2018) 'Water, sugar, and growth: The practical effects of a "failed" development intervention in the southwestern lowlands of Ethiopia', *Journal of Eastern African Studies*, Vol. 13, No. 4, pp. 621–641.

Keeley, J., Michago, W., Eid, S. A. and Kidewa, A. L. (2014) *Large-scale Land Deals in Ethiopia: Scale, Trends, Features and Outcomes to Date*, London: IIED (International Institute for Environment and Development).

Kodama, Y. (2014) 'The changes in food and cash benefit policies and international food aid policies in Ethiopia', in K. Usami and K. Makino (eds) *Cash Transfer Policies in Emerging Countries*, Chiba: Institute of Developing Economies, pp. 131–165 (in Japanese).

Lavers, T. (2012) 'Patterns of agrarian transformation in Ethiopia: State-mediated commercialization and the "land grab"', *The Journal of Peasant Studies*, Vol. 39, No. 3-4, pp. 795–822.

______ (2013) 'Food security and social protection in highland Ethiopia: Linking the Productive Safety Net to the land question', *Journal of Modern African Studies*, Vol. 51, No. 3, pp. 459–485.

______ (2016) 'Agricultural investment in Ethiopia: Undermining national sovereignty or tool for state building', *Development and Change*, Vol. 47, No. 5, pp. 1078–1101.

Mains, D. (2019) *Under Construction: Technologies of Development in Urban Ethiopia*, Durham: Duke University Press.

Markakis, J. (2011) *Ethiopia: The Last Two Frontiers*, Melton: James

Currey.
Miyawaki, Y. and Tonegawa, Y. (2018) 'State, civil society and NGO: Perspective from Ethiopia', in Y. Miyawaki (ed.) *State Domination and Peoples' Power*, Sakai: Osaka Municipal Universities Press, pp. 10–36 (in Japanese).
Meles, Z. (2006) *African Development: Dead Ends and New Beginnings*, unpublished paper.
MOA (Ministry of Agriculture) (2014) *Productive Safety Net Programme Phase IV Programme Implementation Manual, Version 1.0*, Addis Ababa: Ministry of Agriculture.
Nalepa, R. A. (2013) *Land for Agricultural Development in the Era of 'Land Grabbing', LDPI Working Paper 40*, Land Deal Politics Initiative.
Oakland Institute (2011) *Understanding Land Investment Deals in Africa, Country Report: Ethiopia*, Oakland: The Oakland Institute.
______ (2013) *Understanding Land Investment Deals in Africa: Ignoring Abuse in Ethiopia: DFID and USAID in the Lower Omo Valley*, Oakland: The Oakland Institute.
Ofosu-Kusi, Y. and Matsuda, M. (eds) (2020) *The Challenge of African Potentials: Conviviality, Informality and Futurity*, Bamenda: Langaa RPCIG.
Sabates-Wheeler, R., Lind, J. and Hoddinott, J. (2013) 'Implementing social protection in agro-pastoralist and pastoralist areas: How local distribution structures moderate PSNP outcomes in Ethiopia', *World Development*, Vol. 50, No. 1, pp. 1–12.
Sagawa, T. (2010) 'Local potential for peace: Trans-ethnic cross-cutting ties among the Daasanech and their neighbors', in C. Echi-Gabbert and S. Thubauville (eds) *To Live with Others: Essays on Cultural Neighborhood in Southern Ethiopia*, Köln: Rüdiger Köppe Verlag, pp.99–127.
______ (2019a) 'Waiting on a friend: Hospitality and gift to the "enemy" in the Daasanach', *Nilo-Ethiopian Studies*, Vol. 23, pp. 1–16.
______ (2019b) 'Food security policy and the suddenly changing

livelihood of agro-pastoralists in southwestern Ethiopia', *Journal of African Studies (Africa-Kenkyu)*, Vol. 95, pp. 13–25 (in Japanese with English abstract).

Sassen, S. (2013) 'Land grabs today: Feeding the disassembling of national territory', *Globalizations*, Vol. 10, No. 1, pp. 25–46.

Shete, M. and Rutten, M. (2015) 'Large-scale land acquisitions in Ethiopia: Implications for agricultural transformation and livelihood security', in R. Hall, I. Scoones and D. Tsikata (eds) *Africa's Land Rush*, Melton: James Currey, pp. 65–82.

Stevenson, E. G. J. and Buffavand, L. (2018) '"Do our bodies know their ways?" Villagization, food insecurity, and ill-being in Ethiopia's lower Omo valley', *African Studies Review*, Vol. 61, No. 1, pp. 109–133.

Sun, X. (2017) 'Strengthening local safety nets as a key to enhancing the food security of pastoralists in East Africa: A case study of the Rendille of northern Kenya', *African Study Monographs, Supplementary Issue*, Vol. 53, pp. 19–33.

Tebbs, E. J., Hodbod, J., Pertaub, D.-P., Gebresenbet, F., Stevenson, E. G. J., Chan, K. and Mulugeta, M. F. (2019) *Multiple Environmental Shocks Impacting Livelihoods and Food Security in Nyangatom, the Lower Omo, Ethiopia, SIDERA Briefing Note #1*, Michigan: Omo-Turkana Research Network.

Tsegaye, M. (2015) 'Listening to their silence? The political reaction of affected communities to large-scale land acquisitions', *Journal of Peasant Studies*, Vol. 42, No. 3-4, pp. 517–539.

Chapter 2

Creating Mutual Recognition and Respect in Property Relations: Negotiation Regarding Livestock Ownership and Usufruct in East African Pastoral Societies

Itaru Ohta

1. Introduction

This chapter examines the complex property relations involving livestock held by East African pastoralists and discusses how they constantly reconstruct social relations through conversation and negotiation with others regarding what rights one may have over livestock. When their livestock rights are called into question, these peoples strive to defend their rights through ardent negotiation and to persuade other people of the legitimacy of those rights. They are persistent negotiators. I have argued that African people are preeminent in talking to, listening to and negotiating with others (Ohta 2017). This chapter expands that discussion by exploring how East African pastoralists negotiate and settle conflicts over their livestock rights by persevering in negotiations. In some sense, their property rights are not firmly established by laws such as those in developed countries. However, I point out that such uncertainty over one's rights is not a problem but, rather, a strength in that mutual recognition and respect are continuously recreated between one person and the other through negotiations over livestock ownership and usufruct, a process, I would argue, that serves as a manifestation of African Potentials.

In East African pastoral societies, livestock not only provide food such as milk and meat for the pastoralists but are also sold to purchase daily necessities or pay medical bills and school fees.

Livestock are also a crucial medium for creating and maintaining social relationships through gifting and exchange. In a marriage, livestock are given to the bride's family by the bridegroom's family as bridewealth, a process involving many actors (Ohta 2007). Important rituals call for livestock as an offering. This is to say that livestock are not only an economic resource but also of crucial social and religious significance as well.

In this chapter, I will analyse how the Turkana pastoralists in northern Kenya, whom I studied first-hand, deal with property issues involving livestock and discuss these issues in Rendille and Gabra societies based on rich existing ethnographic literature.

The Turkana have a word meaning livestock, *e-bar-asit* (sing.; pl. *ngi-bar-en*), that is also used to mean 'property'. Strictly speaking, this word does not apply to cats and dogs; *e-bar-asit* includes five kinds of livestock: cattle, camels, donkeys, goats and sheep. A verb that shares the same root, *aki-bar*, means 'to multiply livestock', which is 'to become rich'. Similarly, *eka-bar-an* (pl. *ngika-bar-ak*) denotes 'a rich man', the owner of many head of livestock. Thus, for the Turkana, livestock means property. The importance of livestock is thus succinctly expressed through their vocabulary.

2. How Can We Deal with Property Relations?

2-1. Four Layers of Property Relations

Property issues have been investigated in various social science disciplines including law, economics, sociology, anthropology and others. One of the most widely respected frameworks, that of Benda-Beckmann et al. (2006: 15), posits that property should be analysed in four layers:

(1) cultural ideals and ideologies;
(2) legal institutions;
(3) actual social relationships; and
(4) social practices.

According to Benda-Beckmann et al. (2006: 15), although each layer is closely related to the others, they each cover different kinds of social phenomena, 'just as marriage ideologies and legal rules about marriage are different from the actual relations between two married people and their daily interactions'.

The first layer is ideological, and it supplies property with its cultural status. The second layer (legal institutions) provides a legitimate scheme for property relationships. Benda-Beckmann et al. (2006: 16) called property relationships at this layer 'categorical' because property holders, property objects and the rights and obligations attached to these are specified as legal-institutional categories.

At the third layer, property relationships are more 'concretised' (Benda-Beckmann et al. 2006: 19). At this layer, we can explore actual social relationships between property-right holders with respect to certain concrete valuables. At the fourth layer, that of social practices, people use, transfer and inherit concrete property in the form of objects or enter into disputes over their property rights. People might also discuss the appropriateness of property rules and these social practices, in turn, cause changes at the first, second and third layers of property relationships, again showing that these four layers are closely interrelated (Benda-Beckmann et al. 2006).

In the areas of legal anthropology and the anthropology of law, considerable research has accumulated dealing with the rules and authority that bind people's actions based on case studies in various societies. Discussions about ownership and usufruct rights over property comprise a part of this literature. Researchers have pointed out the pitfalls of unwittingly applying to different societies the modern, West European paradigm of the law as a set of coercive rules. Turner (2017: 31) states that the 'most convincing framework' for analysing property relations is to differentiate the four analytical layers of property relations advanced by Benda-Beckmann et al. (2006).

Comaroff and Roberts (1981) analysed the ways in which the

Tswana people are bound by normative rules and do follow them, yet at the same time, use the rules to assert their own rights in negotiation with another. In disputes and negotiations among the Tswana, specific rules are invoked and become tools for political manoeuvring. The rules take on meaning and value in each individual setting during the negotiations and the dispute (Hayden 1984). In line with the four layers of property relations, Comaroff and Roberts (1981) identified and emphasised the importance of exploring daily practices, giving close attention to the interactions among the four layers.

2-2. Multiple Property Rights in Livestock in Africa

In the introduction to the book titled *Who Owns the Stock? Collective and Multiple Property Rights in Animals*, Khazanov and Schlee (2012: 7) stated, 'most complicated, multiple and overlapping rights in stock are characteristic of African pastoralists'. They classified property rights in livestock into the following five basic types:

(1) Full rights of ownership, which implies the ultimate rights of allocation, disposal and sale of animals.
(2) Nominal rights of ownership, where rights of control or even disposal belong to another person.
(3) Shared ownership (co-ownership, joint ownership), which implies different degrees of rights and even different percentages of ownership in individual animals.
(4) Usufruct rights, such as the right to milking or transportation, which are often temporary.
(5) The right to the offspring or a defined portion of the offspring of an animal. Often calves are promised to hired cowherds for their services.

In the above-mentioned book, five chapters focused on African societies, and all of them described and analysed complicated livestock rights. For example, according to Pelican (2012: 219), among the Fulbe (Mbororo) of northwestern Cameroon, sons are given livestock by their fathers, but the son has only 'nominal ownership' and 'cannot legitimately make use of his ownership rights' until his father agrees that the son may build his own family based on his independent herd. Before this, the father has 'the ultimate rights of allocation and alienation' of livestock. He may even sell his son's animals. Furthermore, although the father is 'morally required to at least inform the [son] and replace the animal as soon as possible, this obligation is often overlooked'. Women have 'usufruct rights' to their own animals, but 'the final right' lies with the household head. Schlee (2012: 260) also stated that pastoral people may have 'shared rights' in an animal. For example, when an animal is given as a loan, both the holder and the owner have their own rights in the 'shared' animal.

In terms of the four-layer framework of property relations presented by Benda-Beckmann et al. (2006), to which layers do these statements refer? It is evident that the above-mentioned proposal by Khazanov and Schlee (2012), classifying various livestock rights into five basic types ('categories'), belongs to the first and second layers. Although this approach, i.e., classifying the multiple rights to animals into several categories, seems to make complicated ownership of livestock clearly understandable, it has a significant drawback in that these rights are wrongly construed as definite legal ones which have strong binding force.

Among African pastoral societies, it is not significant to distinguish between the above-mentioned first and second layers, namely, ideologies and legal institutions. People mutually concede that there are proper ways of obtaining, utilising, and disposing of livestock. Such forms of consent can be termed cultural ideologies, beliefs, norms or rules. However, because local rules and norms are not put into statutory form, it is difficult to clearly differentiate among ideologies, laws and legal institutions.

For example, pastoral people may declare their rights in livestock, stating, 'I am the owner of this animal' or 'my wife utilises milk of this cow'. However, it is sometimes not clear whether these statements imply rigid rules, refer to moral requirements or are mere descriptions of actual practices. There are also ethical norms, such as 'those who live together must all share ample milk to drink, especially with the children when there is a shortage'. Furthermore, there are value-neutral rules, such as 'the offspring of my livestock are also mine'. Some norms may have an accompanying and direct sanction in case of violation, but many others do not.

Among pastoral societies, wider social networks should be considered when trying to understand concretised property relationships, as people have many other social ties, such as kinship relations. In such cases, these rights are often subject to dispute and negotiation (in the fourth layer) when people demand their own rights in reference to diverse forms of normative legitimation. Thus, people make various claims and counterclaims on the contested livestock.

Previous studies of property relationships with regard to livestock in African pastoral societies have mainly focused on the first and second layers, that is, cultural ideas and legal-institutional structures. However, in the descriptions of these studies, we find many ethnographic descriptions dealing with the third and fourth layers. For example, Schlee (2012: 263) stated, referring to Spencer's (1973) research, that livestock ownership is always contested and negotiated among the Samburu. A Samburu bridegroom should transfer eight cattle as a bridewealth payment but, after the marriage, the family members of the bride continue to demand gifts from the bridegroom and his patrilineal family members on various occasions. When they feel that their claims are refused unreasonably, they may place a curse on the other party. Also, a Samburu man cannot sell his own livestock freely because members of a clan are morally obliged to assist one another (Spencer 1973 in Schlee 2012: 263).

Dahl (1987) explored women's status and roles in pastoral societies. She emphasised that, although ideologies or cultural models in pastoral societies grant broad authority to males, and females tend to be located by their behavioural norms as inferior to males, these norms belong only to the sphere of ideas and ideologies. She states that wives sometimes resist the suggestions of their husbands, abiding instead by their own convictions, and that their informal influence plays an important role in managing livestock herds and building/maintaining social relations. That is, she maintained that we should pay attention to the third and fourth layers of property relationships.

2-3. 'Bundle of Rights'

When several persons have overlapping rights in an animal, as pointed out by Khazanov and Schlee (2012), their property relationships may be analysed using the metaphor of a 'bundle of rights'. Baxter (1975: 212) coined the term 'mobile' bundle of rights in a study of African pastoral societies. Pelican (2012: 213) also indicated that property rights could be understood as a bundle of rights.

Benda-Beckmann et al. (2006: 16–21) argued the 'bundle of rights metaphor' is effective when we examine property relationships in the second (legal institutions) and third (actual social relationships) layers mentioned above. For example, a man may be the owner of a specific farm, but he may have conferred the right of its management to another person. The latter may have leased the farm to a tenant, who may have contracted a share cropping arrangement with several persons. In this case, the 'sticks' (or 'sub-bundles') of property rights that constitute the 'bundle of rights' to the farm are widely shared among different actors.

In this example, each actor's property right seems to be clearly defined, because each right is exclusively specified by relevant laws in the society. However, this state of affairs cannot be applied unconditionally to other societies, as people in those societies engage in various negotiations corresponding to their specific social context. Max Gluckman (1965a, 1965b) used the 'bundle (cluster) of rights' metaphor in the field of social anthropology. He argued that all property relations are ultimately social and political relations. He rejected the commonplace view in which property is conceived in terms of the relationship of persons to things. A person's right over a specific thing is better understood by examining his/her relationships with other persons. As Gluckman (1965a: 36) stated, 'What is owned in fact is a *claim* to have power to do certain things with the land or property, to possess immunities against the encroachment of others on one's rights in them, and to exercise certain privileges in respect of them'. Thus, '*ownership cannot be absolute*, for the critical thing about property is the role that it plays in a nexus of specific relationships' (1965b: 45, emphasis mine).

The 'bundle of rights' does not exist as a solid and unchanging entity. It always emerges 'performatively' in the process of a negotiation at a specific time and place, and it undergoes metamorphosis as members and their social relationships change among the parties concerned. I use this term 'performatively' to emphasise that a specific 'bundle of rights' emerges in a process of specific interactions at a specific time and place and that this 'bundle of rights' is a temporal one. East African pastoralists do not place absolute trust in it.[1]

3. Owning Livestock in Turkana Society

The Turkana, whom I have studied over the years since 1978, live in arid north-western Kenya. Their population is roughly 1,016,000 (KNBS 2019: 424), and most of them live in Turkana County. The annual average rainfall in Lodwar, the administrative centre of Turkana County, is no more than 200 millimetres. The people raise five types of livestock: cattle, camels, goats, sheep, and donkeys. They speak an Eastern Nilotic language (Gregersen 1977) and reckon descent patrilineally.

3-1. Possession and Use of Livestock by the 'Basic Family'

I have studied and discussed in detail how the Turkana own and utilise livestock (Ohta 2019). Below is a discussion based on this study of the property rights the Turkana hold over each head of their livestock.

First, we will look at a family group consisting of an adult man, considered the head of the family, his wife and children. The family head may have multiple wives, the grown son(s) may have wives and children and these, along with unwed daughters with children, may all cohabit as a family group. I will call this group 'the basic family' for convenience.[2] We should note here that, because the Turkana generally keep their livestock in multiple camps according to the ecological and physiological needs of each animal type, members of a basic family reside separately in different camps, and they often live with members of other basic families, managing their livestock together (Ohta 1980). The wives and unwed daughters with children may have their own huts at their residence and conduct separate lives.

If the Turkana are asked, 'Who owns the livestock you are raising?' they will say that all the livestock belong to the family head.[3] However, it is too simplistic to think that the family head alone has ownership rights to the livestock. One reason is that all of the livestock are, in fact, allotted among the women, i.e., the wives and the unwed daughters with children.

It is not difficult to understand the practicality of the above arrangement if one stops to think that female livestock will eventually reproduce and give milk, and milking is labour assigned to women and children. Each mother will thus have milk from her allotted livestock as food for herself and her children. Secondly, when an individual animal is consumed for meat, it is slaughtered by the woman to whom the livestock had been allotted, and she distributes its meat to family members.[4] In other words, the protocol for consuming what was produced by livestock, including milk, is determined for each head of livestock according to which woman has the central stake. I will call this woman 'the main charge' below.

Each new livestock offspring is allotted to the woman who is the main charge of the mother animal. Sometimes the Turkana exchange a male head of livestock for a female animal with a kin or friend (Ohta 2001). The new female animal is allotted to the woman who was the main charge of the original male animal. The allotment of livestock is thus automatically determined and agreed upon.

The Turkana use the cash gained through the sale of livestock to buy foodstuffs such as grain, clothes or cooking utensils, or to pay medical bills or school fees. They also slaughter the livestock for various rituals. When these necessities arise, a woman and her children use the livestock allotted to her. If a head of livestock is injured or falls ill, people try to cure it, with the main charge playing the central role. Upon the death of the family head, the main charge and her children inherit the livestock allotted to her.

Within the basic family, each head of livestock has a main charge. This raises the question of how we should understand livestock 'ownership' in Turkana society. For example, can the head of the family, who is said to be the 'owner of all livestock within a family', sell any head of livestock as he pleases to gain cash to buy his clothes? If a Turkana is asked such a question, the answer will be that the family head must first consult with the main charge. However, I have heard from some Turkana that if the family head is not a good person, he may sell an animal without consultation.

Nevertheless, the family head is expected to negotiate with the main charge of an animal that he wants to sell. If he ignores this process, the main charge and other family members are likely to protest his actions. Some family members may physically try to block the family head's attempt to take the animal to sell, although how vigorous the protest becomes will depend on the composition of the family, that is, whether the main charge has a grown-up son, etc. Thus, the family head's discretion is strictly regulated by other members of his family.

In Turkana society, gender differences are emphasised in many situations. For example, only men can negotiate bridewealth in public (Ohta 2007). The division of labour in terms of the family's livelihood is also markedly gender-based. However, my impression from living among the Turkana is that women have considerable power to dictate day-to-day activities. I witnessed first-hand the slaughter or sale of livestock for which the family head always consulted with the main charge; moreover, sometimes an animal other than the one selected by the family head was chosen for the occasion. At other times, the consultation turned into a long discussion that was not settled overnight. There were also times when I felt that the family head truly had power, but even so, his final decision was never despotic.

The children of the main charge sometimes partake in such consultations. The children's say over livestock increases as they mature (Ohta 2019). The sons will eventually inherit the livestock allotted to their mother, and the daughters will have milked and taken care of the animals over time. For these reasons, sons and daughters may well feel strongly about the disposal of specific animals, whether by selling, slaughtering or gifting them. Moreover, if the sons already have wives, those wives would have assumed the main charge of the animals, and the family head must think twice about disposing of such animals himself.

The reality that the livestock held by a basic family are in fact allotted to the women in the family and that the children's say in their disposal will increase as they grow older complicates any decision about livestock. Some livestock were gained by the family head as bridewealth and gifting, and he would have allotted these to his wives, and others were gained by the wives and the children themselves in similar processes. The history of how each head of livestock was gained determines how much power a given individual has over the animal. It would be quite misleading to think that, in this situation, the family head has 'ownership' of all livestock and that the other members of the family only have usufruct rights over them. Rather, one must realise that the situation is affected by various factors, and the members of the family must repeatedly negotiate any decision.

Gulliver (1955), who studied the Turkana before I did, has described the rights held over livestock. He wrote that the family head 'legally owns the stock' (1955: 125). The sons growing up increasingly demand ownership over livestock allotted to their mothers, but '(t)his factor lies rather at the level of moral attitudes and sentiments than at the level of legal rights and relations' (Gulliver 1955: 135). In other words, Gulliver observed that the family head had 'legal' ownership over the livestock, yet this was, in effect, in the realm of a cultural idea and the legal institutions of the Turkana.

3-2. Daily Practice of Livestock Management and the Rights over Livestock

I wrote above that the women of the basic family are the main charges of each head of livestock and that they, together with their children, take care of the animals in health, sickness and injury, playing an important role in livestock management. When the need arises for them to assert their rights over a specific head of livestock, they recount how they toiled over the animal.

The livestock of the basic family's main charges are taken to day-trip herding every day. The herder must control the livestock, ensuring that they graze well, planning a good watering spot on the way to and from the grazing grounds. This continues from early morning to late evening. I acquired, by purchase and gifting, a few head of livestock that were being cared for by the family with whom I was staying. The young man of the family who acted as the herder would often come to me and say, 'I graze your livestock for you. Do you have something to give me?' This is one expression of how, at times, the herder would assert his rights over the livestock, sometimes very petulantly.

The Turkana sometimes dig very deep wells to provide water for their livestock. They must repeatedly lower a container to the bottom of the well to fetch water, which must be gathered into a larger container from which the livestock can drink. This is very hard labour, especially in the dry season. One basic family may jointly create a grazing camp along with one or more other families, and all livestock from the multiple families sometimes graze together. In such cases, members from the families work together to secure water for the animals. When an animal goes astray during grazing or is stolen, the families managing the livestock cooperate to rectify the matter. The youths and grown men organise a search party, and they may return home with the stray or stolen animal after covering several tens of kilometres. The village neighbours will also join and cooperate in such an expedition.

The members of a Turkana basic family not only co-manage their livestock but they also cooperate with other families to maintain the grazing camps and are helped by their neighbours when some problem arises. These cooperative activities do not at all blur the livestock ownership rights of the basic family. The rights held over the livestock owned by each basic family are quite clear. However, since cooperation is a matter of daily life, it is not hard to imagine that the ownership rights pertaining to livestock held by the basic family are neither completely exclusive nor monopolistic.

This delicate mutuality is quite visible when a head of cattle or a camel is slaughtered for meat. Feasting on goat or sheep occurs within the family or with cohabiting individuals, but this is not the case for cattle or camel meat. People from outside the village gather for the occasion; they join in the feast, and the women receive a share to take back to their village from the women of the hosting family. The right to participation in such events is a given to neighbouring villagers. When the neighbours feel that they are not being treated well, they are likely to assert their rights, focusing on their roles in livestock management.

4. Trust and Ownership of Camels in the Rendille and Gabra Societies

Here, we will see how livestock are owned and used among the pastoralist Rendille and Gabra in northern Kenya. The Rendille, a comparatively minor group, have a population of roughly 96,000 (KNBS 2019: 423). The annual rainfall on the Kaist Desert, the Rendille central residential area, is only about 200 millimetres. The Gabra, who live in northern Kenya and southern Ethiopia, include about 141,000 people in Kenya (KNBS 2019: 423) and several tens of thousands in Ethiopia.

The Rendille and the Gabra are neighbours and speak related Eastern Cushitic languages (Greenberg 1966). They intermarry, form friendships and share considerable culture. Both groups reckon descent on the father's side. They raise and live on camels, cattle, goats and sheep, of which the most important is camels. As they live in a rather arid semi-desert, camels are physiologically and ecologically well adapted to the environment. The camel is the most important provider of food for both societies. Bridewealth must be in camels, and camel sacrifice is also necessary for any ritual of importance. The value of the camel is supreme, both socially and religiously.

4-1. Camel Trust

Both the Rendille and the Gabra have a unique strategy for lending out a camel to others indefinitely. In the discussion below, I will call this system 'camel trust', and at times refer to detailed studies by Sato (1991, 1992a, 1992b), Soga (1997a, 1997b, 1998) and Schlee (2012). I will add here that when a family does not have enough camels giving milk to provide for family members, they can rent a lactating camel from another family for a defined period.[5] This type of limited lending of a camel is differentiated from the camel trust, and there are separate vocabularies for each. I will refer to the lender in the camel trust as the 'depositor' and to the renter in this system as the 'trustee'.

The camel trust is practised with a unique set of rules. The first pertains to the social relationship between the depositor and trustee. If someone wishes to rent a camel, he goes to and pleads with a person who has camels. For the Gabra, such target persons would include the 'in-laws (for example, the mother's brothers, brothers-in-law through the wife or sisters), same-clan members, an acquaintance formerly living in the same village whose camel one had cared for, or a fellow herder and friend who once worked together at the grazing camp, or the biological father' (Soga 1998: 38). For the Rendille, such persons are the father, brothers, in-laws (the father and brothers of the wife, the husbands of the sisters), mother's brothers and their clan members, or members of the same clan (Figure 4 in Sato 1992b: 116). In either case, the trust relation is limited to people who already have close social ties. It is possible for two men to mutually lend and rent camels.

The camel used in tying the trust must be a heifer but, in a rare instance, it may be a parous female (Sato 1992b: 144). When a trust relation is successfully tied, all subsequent female offspring of this camel belong to the original depositor, along with the original heifer. In other words, any female camel produced in the trust becomes a trust camel. The male offspring belong to the trustee, who is free to dispose of these animals in any way, whether by sale, slaughter or gift. The trustee can also use the milk from the female camels. The relation tied in a camel trust continues as long as female offspring from the original heifer continue to exist, and the depositor's and trustee's sons inherit and assume their roles in the dyadic relation if the first generation dies. Thus, the camel trust can cover a long span of time.

The interesting point of this trust mechanism is that the trustee can become the depositor of a female offspring from the original camel, lending it to someone else. Such double and triple trust relations can be repeated to form a long chain of trust dyads: W with X, X with Y, Y with Z, etc. Here, the depositor of the original heifer will be termed the 'owner'. All female camels belong to the original owner, W, at the top of the chain of trust, and all male camels belong to the trustees.

If a need arises, W may ask X to return to him one or several trust camels. If X does not have a suitable animal on hand, he can go to Y and ask that a camel be returned to W. However, W cannot go directly to Y for an animal. In this chain of trust, only the members in the depositor–trustee dyadic relationship are beholden to each other to arrange the return of an animal.

4-2. Negotiations for the Return of a Trust Camel

As noted above, W, the original depositor, has ownership of all female camels (trust camels) in the trust chain, whereas X, Y, Z and others in the trust chain can be described as having only the usufruct, or the usage right of female camels (Sato 1991: 277, 1992b: 144). However, contrary to general thinking, ownership does not entail free use and disposal of what is owned, as explained below.

First, the return of a trust camel cannot be demanded at just any time. Sato (1991: 287) wrote that if brothers became tied in a camel trust, they themselves would refrain from demanding the return of the trusted camels until their sons inherited the trust. If someone other than close patrilineal kin should demand the return of a camel in a trust, the first return may wait until the renter has three to four female offspring from the heifer, and then another may be returned after his son has inherited the trust. In other words, in the absence of a very pressing circumstance, the other female camels need not be returned.

The depositor must also have his demand for the return of the trust camel recognised as legitimate by the society. Such legitimate occasions are limited to the imminent need for payment of bridewealth, a funeral requiring that an animal be slaughtered or when most of the livestock are lost due to a drought or raid, resulting in a catastrophic food shortage. Another occasion may be when the depositor deems that the trustee's care of the animal is poor (Sato 1991: 277–278; Soga 1998: 38). The above occasions illustrate how it is not possible for a depositor to demand a return of the trust camel at just any time. Furthermore, among the Rendille, no more than one heifer needs to be returned by the trustee (Sato 1991: 286). The depositor who repeatedly and without legitimate reason demands the return of a trust camel will become a nuisance and may even have the camel trust terminated by the trustee (Sato 1991: 288).

On the other hand, even if a depositor in legitimate need asks for the return of a trust camel, his wish may not be fulfilled at an opportune time. The trustee may try to postpone the demand, arguing that there are not enough female camels in his herd or that he is in a dire circumstance at the moment. He might also ask the depositor to check back with him after several years. Schlee (2012: 252–253) wrote that, although the camel trust was a loan, the trusted camel 'would normally never be recovered' by the depositor. In this sense, the ownership held by the depositor is 'nominal'. For the depositor to have a trust camel returned to him, he must endure a long period of negotiation, argue for the legitimacy of the demand, and finally persuade the trustee. In the camel trust, the scope of the depositor's ownership is thus quite limited.

However, if the depositor comes to believe that the trustee is not properly managing the camel or if the social relations between the dyad deteriorate for some reason, he may forcefully take back the trust camel. The fact that such incidents do occur seems to indicate that the Rendille and Gabra societies recognise a kind of 'absolute ownership', i.e., the right of the owner to freely claim and dispose of what belongs to him. However, a close look into people's actions in reality indicates that the right of the owner is usually more mired in the complex social relations among the people than such a conclusion suggests. Consider the three interesting cases below.

[Case 1] (Soga 1998: 43)

X, a Gabra, trusted a heifer to Y in 1962.[6] In 1973, having lost his livestock to the drought, X went to Y and demanded a lactating camel, a cargo male camel and some goats and sheep. To this, Y said, 'Everybody is suffering from this drought, and it is not possible to meet your demand.' But X was not persuaded and demanded his share of the camel trust by force. To this, Y said, 'If you insist on your demand, first have the elders agree with you.' The matter was brought to the meeting of elders, and they all tried to dissuade X from his excessive demand. However, X gave no heed, and took away his share of camels.

This case raises three points of interest. First, X's demand to Y included a cargo camel as well as goats and sheep, which exceeded X's rightful share of the camel trust, but Y was not totally unwilling to comply with such a demand. This indicates that the Gabra mutually recognise each other's livestock rights, which are not rigidly limited to the ownership and usufruct right to specific animals. The ownership of the depositor and the usufruct of the trustee are seemingly well defined in the rules of camel trust but, in fact, more complex factors must be considered beyond ownership and usufruct that defy simplistic understanding. The second point is that the legitimacy of recovering one's share from the trust was viewed as an issue worthy of convening an elders' meeting. In other words, ownership is far from an absolute right to be exercised at any time. The third point is that some people act as if ownership were always at their command, enabling them to recover their share of camels.

The forceful taking back of trust camels is referred to in Gabra society as 'dirty evil of digging muck' (Soga 1998: 43). This act is viewed with the utmost disgust. To engage in such an act is to unilaterally cut off social relations, sending enormous shock waves throughout the society. It is believed that the person who commits such an act will die by the roadside, or the retrieved camels will all die off from a disease or cease to produce milk. A tragic fate will certainly befall the person who exerts his ownership at any cost.

In at least one reported case, the person who forcefully retrieved camels had to 'compensate' for his action later when his deed was judged inappropriate.

[Case 2] (Schlee 2012: 253)

X, an elder among the Rendille, retrieved his camels in a camel trust with Y, and Y was indignant. Sometime afterwards, X proposed to a family to marry their daughter as his second wife. The girl's family belonged to the same clan as Y, and X ended up having to appease Y and his clan members by paying a 'penalty' so that he could marry the girl.

The camel that X forcefully retrieved was indeed his, but the way he exerted his right was illegitimate, and this had to be rectified when he was in a weakened position of seeking a wife.

The next case demonstrates how each trust relation is intertwined with other trust relations, which are themselves social relations that, at times, must be reconciled.

[Case 3] (Sato 1991: 284, 1992a: 77)

Two Rendille men, X and Y, had a fight and charged at each other with big clubs. The next morning, X went to Y's livestock enclosure and forcibly retrieved two female camels that Y got in trust from Z, a parallel cousin of X. The elders convened a meeting to discuss the matter. It took them two days to refer the matter to Z, who decided not to side with his cousin X, but with Y, and had the retrieved camels brought back to Y. He feared that, had he done otherwise, the camels trusted to him by a close relative of Y would be taken away from him.

The above three cases demonstrate the ideas and beliefs pertaining to the camel trust in two societies and the associated day-to-day social interactions and negotiations. There is no doubt that the Rendille and the Gabra think of the original depositor as having ownership of the camels. But it is also their thinking that the ownership rights may not be freely exerted at any time. Realising the return of the camels requires legitimate reasons, and grave misfortune may befall if one retrieves camels without consent from the trustee. In this sense, the right of ownership in the camel trust is far from absolute but is, rather, 'nominal', as Schlee (2012: 253) has pointed out, and crucially open to negotiation at all times.

Categorising the rights involved in the camel trust into ownership and usufruct is seemingly clear cut, yet this is only because we think of private ownership as an absolute right. For us to understand Rendille and Gabra rights pertaining to livestock, we must consider not only who can demand what of whom but also under which circumstance and with which conditions. This is why people spend days in lengthy discussions and negotiations seeking a mutually satisfactory solution.

4-3. Various Negotiations over Livestock Ownership

The Rendille and the Gabra conduct various negotiations over livestock besides the camel trust. Here, I will describe an impressive case where a demand to have a livestock exchange from the past annulled was granted after much negotiation.

[Case 4] (Sato 1991: 278, 1992a: 77)

X exchanged a young heifer camel for a castrated camel with Y of the same clan. The original heifer and its offspring reproduced well and, 16 years later, Y had nine female camels. X saw this and demanded that the previous exchange be cancelled. X argued that because the original heifer reproduced so well, the exchange in the past was no longer fair and that Y should return the nine female camels to X because they were 'his'. The matter called for many meetings held among many men, and Y eventually returned eight of the nine female camels to X.[7]

The Rendille think of a mature castrated camel as equal in value to a young heifer, and the two are often exchanged (Sato 1991: 280). As this was an exchange, the heifer that Y obtained was not a trust camel. It is easier for us to think that, because the animal was obtained in a balanced exchange, Y would have the ownership once the exchange was complete, and with it, the total of nine female camels. But X made a stunning demand for the animals, saying the exchange made in the past was imbalanced, so Y should return to him not only the original heifer but all of its descendants. It might be true that the original heifer reproduced extremely well. But reproduction itself was expected at the time of the exchange, and X's demand seems improbable to us. Furthermore, X referred to all descendants of the original heifer as belonging to him, and the immediate society's acceptance of this demand as legitimate indicates how X continued to hold a certain property right over the original heifer after the exchange. The original exchange of the heifer with a castrated camel was not what we would think of as 'balanced exchange'. We are familiar with exchanging goods where good balance and equal value are taken for granted. But it is indeed wrong for us to naively apply the concept of 'equal value' (Ohta 2001) to the Rendille and the Gabra.

Below, we examine how the Rendille and the Gabra handle the rights pertaining to livestock within a family.[8] The ultimate right over livestock, or the right to their disposal, is deemed to rest with the father, the head of the family (Sato 1992a; Soga 1997b). Both the Rendille and the Gabra practice primogeniture, where the eldest son of the first wife (the 'eldest son' in the following paragraphs for simplicity) inherits most of the livestock held by the father. These people emphasise the ideal oneness of the father and eldest son in narratives, and they value this in daily life as well. The father's livestock is never gifted to his eldest son before he dies. On the other hand, the father may gift female camels to his second and younger sons for occasions such as a circumcision or wedding that would mark a passage in an individual's life stages.

Soga (1996) has described in detail the rights of the Gabra father and sons over livestock and how they assert these rights. The Gabra sons must live with the father after they marry, and all livestock raised by the family group, which consists of the father, his wives and married sons, belong to the father. However, in the case of the second or younger sons, Soga (1996) reports a conflicting narrative. That is, when female livestock are given to the second or younger sons, these animals and their female offspring belong to the sons. Their male offspring belong to the father before the sons get married but, after they marry, the sons acquire ownership of these animals. However, the right to dispose of any individual animal is said to be held by the father. The second or younger sons may be given a heifer by someone from outside the family group, and such an animal is likewise said to fall under the disposal right of the father. In other words, livestock ownership on the part of the sons is strongly restricted, whereas the father is free to dispose of the livestock held by the sons.

However, in real life, the father does not take livestock away from his second and younger sons except under extreme circumstances (Soga 1996). When the father must take away the animal, he does his best to find a suitable replacement. If he does not, it is said that the livestock held by the father may die off, stop giving milk or cease to reproduce. As I mentioned, similar misfortune is said to befall the Gabra man who forcibly retrieves his camels in a trust relation. Yet, such retrieval does happen. Thus, we can assume that the father who disposes of his son's livestock may not always compensate his son, presenting the sons with the need to sternly assert their rights. But Soga (1996) wrote that these conflicts between a father and his second or younger sons almost never occur.

In contrast, the father and his eldest son are often in conflict (Soga 1996). As Gabra society is based upon primogeniture, oneness of the father and the eldest son is desirable, and the son does not have any livestock of his own. Although they believe that all livestock belong to the father and that children must obey the father, there coexists a conflicting idea that the father must have the eldest son's consent to dispose of any head of livestock. The father has his own economic or social necessities and may try to give away or sell the livestock, but the eldest son's wish may not coincide with the father's. If the two happen to disagree, and the quarrel is not resolved, the matter must be brought before a meeting of the elders, where the two argue their stance and seek a compromise.

Not all fathers and eldest sons reach the point of conflict, and Soga (1996) reported that their relationship is more likely to be very close. He analysed the reasons for this and found that the first was the social maturation of the eldest son. Before marrying, Gabra men lead a highly mobile lifestyle as they move away from the father's village to graze the livestock in outlying camps. After they marry, they return to the father's village with a wife, and rather than grazing the livestock themselves, they direct their children and younger men in the task. As eldest sons mature in their social status, they may or may not have reason to oppose the father's wishes pertaining to livestock.

The second reason given by Soga (1996) is closely related to the first: the father in fact transfers more and more patriarchal rights to the eldest son as the son matures. The father may let the eldest son distribute foodstuffs, including meat, to family members or let him allot the lactating camels to the women of the family so that there is a balance in the amount of milk available to feed the children. The Gabra do not have a prescribed protocol on these matters. Rather, these changes are realised through daily discussion and negotiation between the father and the eldest son. This is to say that, even though the Gabra hold that all livestock belong to the father, as realistic adjustments are made in tandem with the emerging social maturity of the eldest son, the father's rights over his livestock are affected and change over time. This is also true in the Turkana society in that members of the 'basic family' must repeatedly negotiate any decision, as I explained in Section 3 of this chapter.

5. Conclusion: The Self That Is Open to the Other

In the ideology of East African pastoralist societies, livestock most often belong to the head of the family. These groups have ideas and rules relating to livestock ownership and usufruct. Multi-layered rights of multiple people exist, all intertwined, for each head of livestock, which can be described as a 'bundle of rights'. However, in this chapter, I did not try to comprehensively describe and list these rules because, even if they were neatly categorised into ownership and usufruct, or practical ownership rights and nominal ownership rights, we would still be far from understanding people's practices related to their ownership of livestock. It is misleading to regard the 'bundle of rights' as something tangible that dictates the actions of the stakeholders for each individual animal. The rights held by the people exist in a flux, perpetually renewed and recreated through people's negotiations with 'the other'.[9]

Here lies the thematic conundrum, 'What is ownership?' as well as the question of, 'Who is "the other"?' with whom the negotiation must be conducted. What kind of an existence is 'the other' for the Turkana? Kitamura (2019: 29) pointed out that, for the Turkana faced with a negotiation, '[t]here always will be room for mutual interaction that ensures the facility and desirability of the continued negotiation'. He also wrote that the 'positivist rule that people will cooperate … is unerringly applied in all social interactions' (Kitamura 2002: 104).[10] This is to say that, for the Turkana, 'the other' is a counterpart whose action directed to oneself must be taken seriously and acted upon, never neglected.

For us in Japan, 'the other's' existence is often conveniently presumed absent, and interactions with such others are more likely to be discontinued. Thus, the way the Turkana deal with the other is quite striking. What follows is an episode from the period during which I was conducting fieldwork among the Turkana. In an outing to buy necessities in town with some friends, I was approached by an old woman who said, 'Give me some money.' She may have thought that I was some kind of rich white man, willing to part with cash for her. My friends at first told her, 'Leave our friend alone.' However, the old woman replied, 'What's wrong with my begging him for money?' My friends grimaced and laughed, saying, 'All right, all right.' I had secretly hoped that my friends would shoo the burdensome old woman away, but for the Turkana, she, whoever she was, had a legitimate right to approach anybody in the way she did.

Now, this does not mean that my friends were sympathetic to the old woman, nor did they feel kind-hearted toward her. For them, 'the other' is never a being who gently understands 'the self' without engaging in verbal communication, nor a being who will imagine a convenient circumstance of the self. The other is an existence and a counterpart whose relationship with the self must be constantly renewed through direct mutual interaction.

Another impressive incident occurred after the livestock being raised by the family with whom I was staying were looted by a neighbouring people. The head of the family subsequently visited relatives and friends to solicit livestock. One day, he declared he was visiting a friend living very far away. I happened to know this friend and was secretly convinced that he would offer help, but asked aloud, 'Would he offer you some livestock?' To this, the family head replied, 'He was a good friend of mine in the past, but I cannot say this is still the case with us now' (Ohta 1986: 209). For the Turkana, 'the other' is an unknowable, inviolable entity that exists beyond one's manoeuvring or management. They take this as a given and delve into negotiations on the principle that people must cooperate, which at the same time means that room for communication must always be secure. 'The other' and 'the self' are just such open entities for the Turkana (Ohta 2017).

Let us compare our property relations and our image of 'the other' with those of East African pastoralists. The pastoralists, who continuously engage in negotiations with the other over livestock ownership, strike us as mercenary, each simply interested in maximising their own advantage. For us in Japan, they are very calculating, and all parties seem to end up either a winner or a loser after negotiations. However, we are completely mistaken to think that the pastoralists are self-centred and constantly asserting their desires just because they repeatedly engage in negotiations over livestock. This is because we have projected our view of private ownership and the profit motive onto their society.

Because private ownership is taken for granted in the capitalist market economy, to own something is a state that exists regardless of whether there is an 'other' or not. Yet for the pastoralists, their rights over their livestock cannot be separated from perpetual acknowledgement from 'the other'. Without 'the other', there is no property or ownership. Their rights over livestock can only mean something when there is an 'other' with whom one must negotiate.

The title of the volume by Benda-Beckmann et al. (eds) (2006) introduced in the beginning of this chapter is *Changing Properties of*

Property. There are two meanings of property/properties here. One is ownership and the objects owned. The second involves the characteristics, qualities, specificities and uniqueness that are attributed to what is owned. Washida (2000) argued that the two meanings of the word 'property' are in opposition to each other. The reason for this, he wrote, is that to own something signifies the possibility of giving or trading that something away, whereas the attribute of specificity signifies that it is not exchangeable with anything else. When used to refer to people, the term denotes the uniqueness (i.e. singularity) of a person.

Washida (2000) used the two Japanese words *sho-yuu* (to own) and *ko-yuu* (specific to), used in translating the duality of the French word *propriété*, to discuss the characteristics of modern society. The institutionalisation of private ownership was the necessary condition to guarantee the civic freedom of individuals in modern times. We usually take this for granted and never doubt whether we are free to dispose of what we own as we please. At the same time, we extrapolate our understanding of ownership to all aspects of life and believe that our specificity (individuality) and identity are based on a similar, inherent rule. It is as if we are obsessed with seeking the *raison d'être* of our individual, singular existence in the attributes of ourselves, independent of 'the other'. Washida (2000) pointed out that we continue to discuss property using the vocabulary of control over and disposal of things, where the other is absent. He proposed that it might be necessary for us to employ the vocabulary of communication in reconsidering the problematic idea of ownership because communication and interaction presume the existence of 'the other'.

As Gluckman (1965a) illustrated, in thinking about property rights, we should focus on relationships between people rather than the relationship between people and things. Generally, ownership exists only in relation to 'the other'. However, because it is assumed that private ownership exists unconditionally in the capitalist market economy and because we have yielded to law any decision as to where specific ownership rests in our society, we have negated the existence of 'the other'. In contrast, the East African pastoralists perpetually hold their property rights in negotiation with the other. The self and the other are always in a direct face-off with each other because the other is an uncertainty, an inviolable being, and an existence beyond one's manipulation or management. Such a relationship between the self and the other may seem extremely harsh and stringent to us yet, for the pastoralists, this is their domain, one that constantly regenerates mutual recognition and respect.

I was always impressed with their way of conducting face-to-face interaction, through which they establish and vitalise their social relationships, and I am confident that it is a superb manifestation of African Potentials. Their property relationships seem not to be legally formalised to a high degree, which, one might think, causes uncertainties with regard to property rights. However, as Nyamnjoh (2017) argues, incompleteness is the normal order of things. African people do not place their trust in hard logic and/or rigid rules. 'It is one's interest and the interest of others to acknowledge that being and becoming is an eternal process of incompleteness' (Nyamnjoh 2017: 259). Recognition of being incomplete leads us to convivial conversations and interactions with others.

Endnotes

[1] See, Bourdieu's (1990) argument for a theory of practice and Butler's (1990) theory of performativity.

[2] Gulliver (1955: 124) called this unit 'a nuclear family'.

[3] Only outsiders, including anthropologists, ask these questions. The Turkana can identify not only the individual animals that they own but also each head of livestock owned by their neighbours. A visitor from a village far away may ask, 'Who owns the livestock?' when he sees some livestock grazing in front of him. If the person asked happens to be the herder, he will reply, 'They are mine.' This is to say that the Turkana would never ask

the question independently of a context. This is comparable to the situation where we may ask someone, 'Who owns the house we are standing near?' and someone else replies with the name of the head of the family living there. It is not necessarily the case that the head of the family residing there actually owns the house.

[4] Livestock meat consumed within a family would be slaughtered and skinned at this woman's hut, and she would distribute the meat symbolically, as each family has a predetermined way of sharing meat among its members.

[5] These short-term loans of lactating camels are called *kharasime* in Rendille (Sato 1992a) or *karashime* in Gabra (Soga 1997).

[6] Both the Rendille and the Gabra use an intricate lunar calendar system to mark the day, week, month and year. This is observed in conducting rituals and daily activities. The calendar year is denoted by the names of the days of the week, with the name repeated every seven years (Sato 1992b).

[7] Sato (1991, 1992a) did not report whether X returned the original castrated camel to Y, but my guess is that he did not. It is my guess that the very fact that X could demand that Y annul the camel loan was probably influenced by the two men's belonging to the same clan, but Sato (1991, 1992a) did not speak to this either.

[8] The definition of 'family' among the Rendille and Gabra will not be discussed in detail here.

[9] I stress the importance of negotiation here but do not negate the importance of ideology nor the importance of the different rights and obligations allotted to various subsets of people, for example, men and women, husband and wife or father and son.

[10] For Kitamura's papers written in English, see, Kitamura (1990, 1997).

Acknowledgements

This work was supported by JSPS KAKENHI Grant Numbers JP16H06318, JP19K12502 and JP16K01978.

References

Baxter, P. T. (1975) 'Some consequences of sedentarisation for social relationships', in T. Monod (ed.) *Pastoralism in Tropical Africa*, London: Oxford University Press, pp. 206–229.

Benda-Beckmann, F. von, Benda-Beckmann, K. von, and Wiber, M. G. (2006) 'The properties of property', in F. von Benda-Beckmann, K. von Benda-Beckmann and M. G. Wiber (eds) *Changing Properties of Property*, New York and Oxford: Berghahn Books, pp. 1–39.

Bourdieu, P. (1990) *The Logic of Practice*, Redwood: Stanford University Press.

Butler, J. P. (1990) *Gender Trouble: Feminism and the Subversion of Identity*, New York: Routledge.

Comaroff, J. L. and Roberts, S. (1981) *Rules and Processes*, Chicago: University of Chicago Press.

Dahl, G. (1987) 'Women in pastoral production: Some theoretical notes on roles and resources', *Ethnos*, Vol. 52, Issue 1-2, pp. 246–279.

Gluckman, M. (1965a) *The Ideas in Barotse Jurisprudence*, Manchester: Manchester University Press.

———— (1965b) *Politics, Law and Ritual in Tribal Society*, Oxford: Basil Blackwell.

Greenberg, J. H. (1966) *The Languages of Africa*, Bloomington: Indiana University.

Gregersen, E. H. (1977) *Language in Africa: An Introductory Survey*, New York: Gordon and Breach.

Gulliver, P. H. (1955) *Family Herds*, London: Routledge & Kegan Paul.

Hayden, R. M. (1984) 'Rules, processes, and interpretations: Geertz, Comaroff, and Roberts', *American Bar Foundation Research Journal*, Vol. 9, No. 2, pp. 469–478.

Khazanov, A. M. and Schlee, G. (2012) 'Introduction', in A. M. Khazanov and G. Schlee (eds) *Who Owns the Stock? Collective and Multiple Property Rights in Animals*, New York and Oxford:

Berghahn Books, pp. 1–23.

Kitamura, K. (1990) 'Deep involvement in social interactions among the Turkana', *African Study Monographs, Supplementary Issue*, No. 12, pp. 51–58.

——— (1997) 'Communication for "negotiation" among the Turkana', *African Study Monographs*, Vol. 18, No. 3-4, pp. 241–256.

——— (2002) 'Uniqueness of pastoral epistemology: "Art of living" of the Turkana in northern Kenya', in S. Sato (ed.) *The World of Pastoralists*, Kyoto: Kyoto University Press, pp. 87–135 (in Japanese).

——— (2019) 'What supports self-affirming way of life: "Begging" communication among the Turkana', in I. Ohta and T. Soga (eds) *Thoughts of Nomadic Pastoralism: Anthropological Perspectives on Drastically Changing Africa*, Kyoto: Showado, pp. 17–35 (in Japanese).

KNBS (Kenya National Bureau of Statistics) (2019) *2019 Kenya Population and Housing Census, Volume 4: Population by Socio-Economic Characteristics*, Nairobi: Kenya National Bureau of Statistics.

Nyamnjoh, F. B. (2017) 'Incompleteness: Frontier Africa and the currency of conviviality', *Journal of Asian and African Studies*, Vol. 52, Issue 3, pp. 253–270.

Ohta, I. (1980) 'Property unit and nomadic unit of the Turkana', in J. Tanaka (ed.) *A Study of Ecological Anthropology on Pastoral and Agrico-Pastoral Peoples in Northern Kenya*, Inuyama: Kyoto University Primate Research Institute, pp. 55–77.

——— (1986) 'Reciprocity and begging among the Turkana', in J. Itani and J. Tanaka (eds) *Anthropological Studies on Nature-dependent Societies in Africa*, Kyoto: Academia Shuppankai, pp. 181–215 (in Japanese).

——— (2001) 'Motivations, negotiations, and animal individuality: Livestock exchange of the Turkana in northwestern Kenya', *Nilo-Ethiopian Studies*, No. 7, pp. 45–61.

——— (2007) 'Marriage and bridewealth negotiations among the Turkana in northwestern Kenya', *African Study Monographs,*

Supplementary Issue, No. 37, pp. 3–26.
——— (2017) 'The power to speak, listen, and negotiate in the local meetings of Africa: The palaver of the Bakongo, clan gathering of the Borana, and bridewealth negotiation of the Turkana', in Y. Gebre, I. Ohta and M. Matsuda (eds) *African Virtues in the Pursuit of Conviviality: Exploring Local Solutions in Light of Global Prescriptions*, Bamanda: Langaa RPCIG, pp. 249–274.
——— (2019) 'Rules and negotiations: Livestock ownership among the Turkana in northwestern Kenya', *African Study Monographs*, Vol. 40, No. 2-3, pp. 109–131.
Pelican, M. (2012) 'From cultural property to market goods: Changes in the economic strategies and herd management rationales of agro-pastoral Fulbe in north west Cameroon', in A. M. Khazanov and G. Schlee (eds) *Who Owns the Stock? Collective and Multiple Property Rights in Animals*, New York and Oxford: Berghahn Books, pp. 213–230.
Sato, S. (1991) 'Camel transfer system of the Rendille in northern Kenya', in J. Tanaka and M. Kakeya (eds) *Natural History of Mankind,* Tokyo: Heibonsha, pp. 271–292 (in Japanese).
——— (1992a) 'The camel trust system in the Rendille society of northern Kenya', *African Study Monographs*, Vol. 13, No. 2, pp. 69–89.
——— (1992b) *The Rendille: A Society of Camel Herders in Northern Kenya*, Tokyo: Koubundo (in Japanese).
Schlee, G. (2012) 'Multiple rights in animals: An East African overview', in A. M. Khazanov and G. Schlee (eds) *Who Owns the Stock? Collective and Multiple Property Rights in Animals*, New York and Oxford: Berghahn Books, pp. 247–294.
Soga, T. (1996) 'Inequality in the livestock inheritance system: Conflict between father and his sons among the Gabra', in J. Tanaka, M. Kakeya, M. Ichikawa and I. Ohta (eds) *Anthropological Studies on the Nature-Dependent Societies in Africa, Part 2*, Kyoto: Academia Shuppankai, pp. 215–242 (in Japanese).
——— (1997a) 'System and reality: The camel trust system of the

Gabra', *African Study Monographs*, Vol. 18, No. 3-4, pp. 157–174.

——— (1997b) 'The camel exchange system among the Gabra: Patterns and consequences of inheritance', in K. Fukui, E. Kurimoto and M. Shigeta (eds) *Ethiopia in Broader Perspective Vol. 2*, Kyoto: Shokado Book Sellers, pp. 597–615.

——— (1998) 'The ties of camel exchange: The camel trust system of the Gabra, pastoralists of northern Kenya', *Journal of African Studies (Africa-Kenkyu)*, No. 52, pp. 29–49 (in Japanese with English abstract).

Spencer, P. (1973) *Nomads in Alliance: Symbiosis and Growth among the Rendille and Samburu of Kenya*, London: Oxford University Press.

Turner, B. (2017) 'The anthropology of property', in M. Graziadei and L. Smith (eds) *Comparative Property Law*, Cheltenham: Edward Elgar Publishing, pp. 26–46.

Washida, K. (2000) 'Ownership and specificity: On the concept of propriété', in T. Oba and K. Washida (eds) *Ethics of Ownership*, Kyoto: Nakanishiya Shuppan, pp. 4–41 (in Japanese).

Chapter 3

Levelling Mechanisms and Growing Economic Disparities Associated with Piecework Performed by the Bemba People of Zambia

Shuichi Oyama and Yuki Yoshimura

1. Piecework

From 2011 through 2019, the authors surveyed a farming village of the Bemba people who live in the northern part of Zambia. The first few days after our entry into the village entailed the greatest expense of the entire study period. Upon our arrival at the village, we were surrounded by a group of villagers who gave us warnings such as, 'The straw roof on your house is old, and it doesn't look good; you should really have it redone', and, 'The roof will leak when it rains, so you should add some straw to it'. They even offered to carry out the repair work themselves. The conversation then moved on to the house provided to us by Elias, the owner, with offers to repair the goat stall and to build a new chicken coop. We looked to Elias to help us with these negotiations, but he pretended not to hear us and waited it out. We were obliged to negotiate by ourselves, refusing offers to help and determining the wages for the work to be done.

Villagers not immediately offered a job sat beside the garden, where they would wait several hours for us to talk with them. It was not easy to refuse villagers who sought work, as they told us of the troubles they faced in their daily lives, their need for money to keep their children in school or the lack of food they faced during the rainy season.

Three days after we arrived in the village, with new straw on the roof and a very clean goat stall as well as a fresh chicken coop, our living environment was now significantly improved. In this village, work for wages is called 'piecework'. Piecework, of course, is work that is paid per job, and the Bemba villagers use this English term. In the Bemba language, the verb *bombela* is used to describe payment made for work. That is, since the term 'piecework' alone is not sufficient to indicate the precise type of payment to be made, the addition of another word to *bombela* can more specifically convey payment type: *bombela impiya* means work paid in cash, while *bombela amataba* is work paid in maize, the main staple food.

Just as the villagers requested that the authors give them work, they also asked the owners of large maize fields to provide them with jobs. Many villagers obtain piecework in these maize fields after negotiation with the field owners (i.e., the employers), who pay them in cash or maize.

Makoto Kakeya and Yuko Sugiyama, Japanese anthropologists have researched the Bemba society continuously since 1983. While earning their living performing shifting (slash-and-burn) agriculture, the Bemba have traditionally lived autonomously by being self-sufficient. Despite the Zambian government having adopted an agricultural modernisation policy centred on maize cultivation, the Bemba have relied on shifting cultivation as their main livelihood while flexibly responding to various changes in external society (Kakeya et al. 2006). Bemba village society upholds the following shared commitment: 'When there is someone who doesn't have enough food, then I will take some of mine and share it (even if it is not that much), because I want to help.' Research indicates that as a backdrop to levelling (equalisation) mechanisms with respect to wealth in agricultural villages – particularly equality in terms of food – people fear the envy and jealousy of others.

Our project is focused on the 'latent potential of Africa' and related international symposia and forums attended by scholars from Japan and several African nations, which have been held in Kyoto, Nairobi, Harare, Juba, Yaoundé, Addis Ababa, Accra and Lusaka, among other locations. At such exchanges, African scholars have pointed out that Japanese researchers, in their studies of African farming villages, often focus on the human relationships within a community. In these exchanges with international researchers, we were reminded again of our interest (as Japanese scholars) in eliciting 'Africa's potentials' in daily human relationships within a community, via the avoidance of conflict and the realisation of shared harmony. We decided that we should reconsider a key theme in Bemba-related research: that of levelling (equalising) mechanisms, viewed as a form of latent power for peaceful coexistence in small villages.

Significant economic disparities have recently been observed in African village society (e.g., Asiimwe 2017; Nakazawa 2017; Oyama 2017), which has traditionally endeavoured to equalise wealth. In Bemba villages, some households manage large-scale maize-growing land, while others acquire considerable incomes by running shops or stores. Several households earn hardly any cash income, and some even lack self sufficiency in terms of food. In Bemba society, where food has traditionally been shared, such economic disparities are growing. This chapter analyses economic differences among households in present-day Bemba farming villages. It focuses on the hired labour that links the poor and the wealthy and considers the merits and demerits of levelling mechanisms in contemporary African farming villages.

2. Zambian Agricultural Policies and Bemba Farming

We surveyed the village of ML, located in the Mpika District of Muchinga Province in northern Zambia (Figure 1). Mpika District is 640 kilometres from the capital, Lusaka, and the surveyed area can be reached by a 40 kilometres unpaved road from the city of Mpika. The villages in this region are situated along this road, like points along a string, while many residents have homes alongside it. In 2013, the population of this village was 272 persons, with 47 households. Miombo woodlands – which contain open and sparse

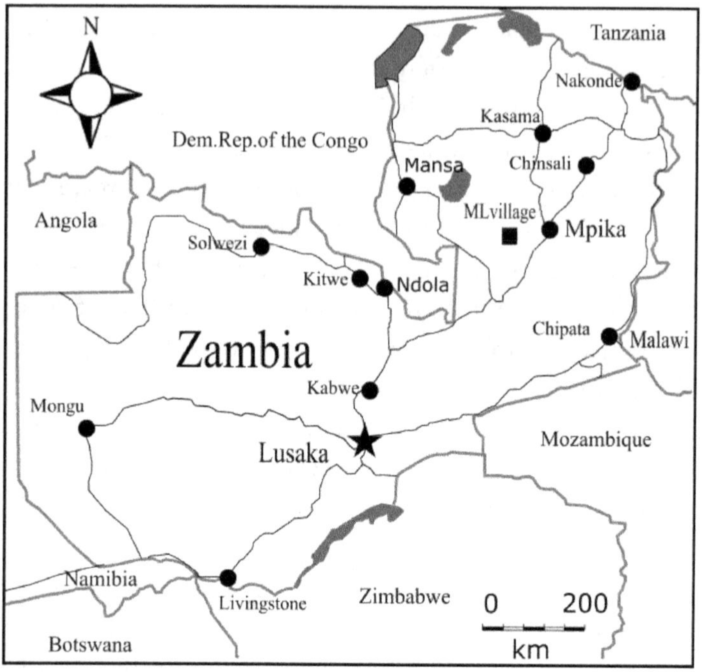

Figure 1. Research area of northern Zambia

forests – stretch across this part of northern Zambia. Villagers clear the miombo forests and cultivate fields.

Seventy-three ethnic groups live in Zambia; among them, the Bemba constitute a large group, and the Bemba language is widely used as the official language. Northern Zambia, where the surveyed village is located, is the centre of Bemba society. Before the country became a British colony at the beginning of the 20th century, the Bemba formed a powerful kingdom based on trade and military prowess. One of the characteristics of Bemba society is its matrilineal system.

The Bemba who live in our surveyed area implement a unique shifting cultivation system called *citemene*, which constitutes their main economic source (Richards 1939; Kakeya and Sugiyama 1985; Moore and Vaughan 1994). *Citemene* has three distinct aspects. The first is that a tree is not felled from the trunk; instead, a man climbs up the tree and cuts the branches only (*kusaila*). The second is that the women collect the cut branches and stack them in a circular form in the central part of the cutting district, where they are set on fire. The third is that *citemene* has a three- or four-year rotation system. Here, in the first year, *Eleusine coracana* (finger millet) is cultivated, while peanuts and *Vigna subterranean* (Bambara nut) are planted in the second year. From the third year onward, cassava planted in the first year is harvested. In the fourth year, the fields may be furrowed and common beans (*Phaseolus vulgaris*) grown. When all of these have been completely harvested, the field is abandoned or left to lie fallow.

In addition to finger millet and beans, *citemene* includes the mixed cultivation of various crops, including maize, pumpkin, edible gourds, tomatoes, cucumbers and watermelon. The Bemba divide the seasons into a wet season (mid-November through April), a cold dry season (May through August) and a hot dry season (September through early November). The end of February through March (the second half of the wet season) is an off-peak period when food is in short supply. During this phase, local people frequently eat boiled pumpkin and edible gourds.

Until the mid-1980s, the people in the surveyed area were self-sufficient, subsisting primarily on the agricultural products produced under *citemene* and the meat of wild animals caught in the miombo woodlands that spread outward from the vicinity of the village. Finger millet, produced with *citemene*, was a source of cash income to be sold to itinerant merchants or used as material for brewing millet beer (Kakeya and Sugiyama 1985; Kakeya et al. 2006).

After Zambia attained independence in 1964, the economy's monocultural structure continued as before, relying on copper and cobalt, among other materials. Copper prices plunged following the oil shock of the 1970s and the Zambian government sought to break away from the monocultural economy, with agricultural reform on its agenda. Since then, the development of agricultural villages has been a key issue for the country. Under agricultural modernisation policies, maize cultivation became widespread in Zambia. In 1987, maize cultivation began to spread throughout the surveyed area, bringing about major changes in people's lives (Kakeya and Sugiyama 1987; Kakeya et al. 2006).

The Zambian government provided large subsidies to help fund maize cultivation in districts that were far from the capital and from Copperbelt Province. The price of fertiliser was reduced, while the price of maize buy-in was raised (Wood 1990). To ensure a cheap supply of staple food (i.e., maize) to city residents, large subsidies were provided to keep consumer prices from rising. Since small-scale farmers struggled to purchase chemical fertilisers and maize seed at market prices, the government set official prices for the agricultural inputs required for maize cultivation and introduced a subsidy system to ensure that farmers could easily obtain what they needed. Boosted by these government policies, maize cultivation became a mainstay, even in remote districts like our surveyed area; nevertheless, the villagers did not abandon their *citemene* practices.

Zambia's finances became strained as a result of these policies, which required large subsidies. During the 1990s, the government accepted the Structural Adjustment Program (SAP) proposed by the International Monetary Fund (IMF). Economic liberalisation witnessed progress under this programme, and subsidies for agricultural inputs were discontinued (Krugmann 1995). Having lost this source of financial support, ordinary farmers struggled to purchase chemical fertilisers and first filial generation (F1) seed. Farm cultivation underwent a rapid decline in the surveyed village, and strategies developed for the combined practice of *citemene* and ordinary farming were abandoned in favour of a lifestyle centred on *citemene*.

Villagers unable to continue with farm cultivation sought cash income from sources other than maize cultivation, and economic activities diversified (Kakeya et al. 2006). For example, villages with extensive remnants of miombo woodlands, perfect for *citemene* cultivation, turned to *citemene* as their primary livelihood. Harvests were not simply consumed by each household; some were diverted to sales. Economic liberalisation resulted in large seasonal fluctuations in agricultural product prices. Aware of these price changes, during the off-peak season described above, villagers could frequently be seen riding their bicycles and laden with farm products destined for the marketplace.

Farming villages outside cities could not easily cultivate crops under *citemene*, as the surrounding miombo woodlands frequently had sandy and infertile soil (Stromgaard 1985; Chidumayo 1994; Oyama 1996). Thus, in lieu of slash-and-burn farming, many villages turned to charcoal production. Tree-cutting to produce charcoal again depleted forests, a vicious cycle that threatened the continuation of *citemene*. Charcoal prices were easily influenced by market fluctuations, meaning that life with autonomy based on *citemene* was under the sway of market forces.

Thus, as farm cultivation rose and fell in tandem with government policy changes, farming and lifestyles were deeply affected. Nevertheless, even in the often violent shifts during each period of modern history, the Bemba people never abandoned *citemene*; rather, *citemene* became entrenched as the basis of self-support, even as means of survival diversified (Kakeya et al. 2006). This is the foundation for the above assertion that the Bemba responded flexibly to modifications in agricultural policies. Meanwhile, the spread of farm cultivation caused the miombo woodlands to deteriorate. Where the forest was severely depleted, *citemene* cultivation could not continue; this eliminated people's self-sufficiency, which they had secured under *citemene*. Households that could not maintain *citemene* practices were thus more easily affected by shifts in external society.

3. The Current Status of Bemba Farming Villages

The year 1997 marked a turning point in the decline of subsidies for maize production that resulted from structural adjustment policies. With the re-election of President Chiluba, the subsidy system was revived, beginning with the Fertiliser Credit Programme (FCP). With these subsidies, farmers could buy chemical fertilisers in cash at 10 per cent off the market price, and pay back the difference (90 per cent) with cash or maize after the harvest. This made chemical fertiliser available through a loan, without the obligation to provide cash up front. The Fertiliser Support Programme (FSP) was introduced in 2002 and facilitated the further investment of subsidy monies in agriculture. The FSP differed from traditional loan schemes, with prices now restrained by these subsidies, enabling farmers to purchase chemical fertilisers and F1 seed maize at low prices. The ratio of subsidy money was 50 per cent at the launch of the FSP and was increased year-on-year until it had reached 75 per cent by 2008. While this subsidy system was maintained, in 2013 President Sata announced a cut in subsidies. Attempts are currently under way to reduce or abolish agricultural subsidies.

The Zambian government also intervened in maize distribution. The Food Reserve Agency (FRA) was created in 1996 as a public organ for the storage of maize to respond to domestic food shortages. Currently, this is not limited to maize purchased directly from farmers but has expanded to include sales of maize to domestic markets as well as the export of maize. Criticism has been levelled at the government's excessive intervention in markets via the FRA (Muyanwa 2015).

The revival of a subsidy system for maize production has renewed the expansion of farm cultivation in the surveyed area. The present state of production of *citemene* and farm cultivation can be ascertained from the findings of our intensive survey, which was undertaken in ML village in 2012 and 2013.

Regarding the cultivation of new fields (shifting agriculture) during the two-year survey period, approximately 70 per cent of households have maintained *citemene* (Table 1). Only two households

Table 1. Number of households (HH) cultivating *citemene* (C) and maize farm (MF) in research village (2012 and 2013 cropping seasons)

	C+MF	Only C	Only MF	No fields	Total HH
2012	24	11	5	6	46
	(52%)	(24%)	(11%)	(13%)	(100%)
2013	15	20	7	5	47
	(32%)	(43%)	(15%)	(11%)	(100%)

over the previous ten-year period relied solely on farm cultivation, with zero production of new fields under *citemene*. While the number of households working in farm cultivation was high, at 29 households (63 per cent) in 2012 and 22 households (47 per cent) in 2013, only 18 had pursued farm cultivation for two consecutive years. Farm cultivation depends on the supply of chemical fertiliser, meaning that the inconsistent supply of such fertiliser has had a major impact on the number of households working in farm cultivation.

When villagers have secured enough maize for their needs, the surplus may be sold to the FRA. However, only seven households (15 per cent) in 2012 and four households (9 per cent) in 2013 sold maize to the FRA. Maize filling 50 kilogram bags is the minimum unit for sale to the FRA. Households with less than 50 kg of maize in off-peak seasons can join with other households for bag shipments, or maize can be carried by bicycle to the market in Mpika Township.

While residents of the surveyed village used government-provided subsidies to invest in their farms, this caused various problems. For example, some farmers were unable to obtain the necessary amount of fertiliser they needed due to insufficient funds and/or supply insufficiencies. Additionally, due to late deliveries of seed and fertiliser, planting and fertilisation could not be performed at the appropriate times. The government's announcement in 2013 of its plans to cut subsidies led to an increase in fertiliser prices, and many farmers had to refrain from purchasing fertiliser as they were unable to raise sufficient cash. Such repeated changes in farming policies involving the supply of fertiliser have resulted in major fluctuations in maize production in Zambia; livelihoods in the surveyed village were also deeply impacted by these fluctuations. The inconsistent supply of fertilisers makes annual large-scale maize cultivation difficult, and the number of households growing maize on a small scale has increased.

Using the analytical methods of Oyama and Takamura (2001) and Kakeya and Sugiyama (1985) in their research on farming villages in the same region, we scrutinised food self-sufficiency based on the extent of *citemene* and maize production. To determine the status of self-sufficiency in our Bemba farming village, we used Kakeya's concept of actual household-constituent consumer numbers (Man-Value). Man-Value follows the classical nutritional surveys performed by Richards and Widdowson (1937), whereby values are assigned to surveyed persons as follows: males aged 14 and older are 1.0; females aged 14 and older are 0.8; males and females aged 6 to 13 are 0.7; and children younger than 6 are 0.4, with the exception of infants, who are not assigned a value. To determine whether a household is self-sufficient with respect to food, one must not only consider farm production due to *citemene* and farm cultivation but also the family composition (i.e., the number of people) of each household. Production amounts per adult male are then calculated to determine the probability of self-sufficiency. Here, with a *citemene* average area of 9 R (1 R = 100 square metres) per Man-Value being cultivated each year, it is possible for the household to secure enough food.

To investigate the possibility of food self-sufficiency grounded in farm cultivation, the required annual maize production was calculated. With the cooperation of adult males from the village, an approximation was made of the amount of maize consumed per meal, with the finding that per capita adult males eat an average of

330 gram of maize per meal. In Bemba villages, meals are commonly taken at noon and at night. Thus, considering that a person eats two meals per day, 240 kilograms was the estimate for the amount of maize consumed in a one-year period. A household was thus considered capable of farm food sufficiency if maize weighing 240 kilograms could be consumed per Man-Value per household. In a 1995 analysis, a portion of the maize harvested by a farmer was used for loan payments; disposable (consumable) maize amounts could then be established by subtracting this figure from the quantity of harvested maize. In 2013, villagers would sell their crops for cash to buy fertiliser for the following fiscal year. However, since the quantity of fertiliser to be supplied by the government could not be forecast, at times, no fertiliser could be purchased (even with advance payments), with only a portion of paid monies returned in some cases. In 2013, it was difficult to determine the amount of cash money needed for the following year's fertiliser purchase based solely on the production quantities of *citemene* and maize farming. For that analysis, food sufficiency probability per household had to be calculated from that year's production numbers.

Figure 2 shows the 2013 food sufficiency status of all households in ML village. Food sufficiency from farm cultivation (on the vertical axis) was computed as follows: 100 per cent indicates 240 kg of maize necessary for one year's consumption by an adult male (i.e., one person Man-Value), which is the volume of maize produced per household divided by the Man-Value of that household. The vertical axis thus depicts that percentage. Data collected from surveying the villagers were used to determine maize production amounts. Since villagers store their harvested maize in 50-kilogram bags, recording the number of bags and multiplying that sum by 50-kilogram facilitates the calculation of maize production amounts.

The x-axis in Figure 2 reveals self-sufficiency based on *citemene*. Here, *citemene* land area per household is divided by Man-Value; 100

per cent indicates a *citemene* area of 9 R per one male adult. The horizontal axis indicates that proportion. The line connecting 100 per cent self-sufficiency grounded in farm cultivation (240 kilogram maize) on the vertical axis with 100 per cent self-sufficiency (9 R) on the horizontal axis combines *citemene* with regular farm cultivation, thereby demonstrating whether a household was food-sufficient. A household with 100 per cent food self-sufficiency, through farm cultivation or *citemene* (or a combination of both), was deemed self-sufficient with respect to staple foods.

Our surveyed villagers showed differences according to household regarding their respective efforts in *citemene* and farm cultivation. Seven households specialised solely in farm cultivation; of these, only two had attained food self-sufficiency. Meanwhile, 20 households specialised in *citemene* alone; only six produced stable amounts of food to exceed self-sufficiency. Eight households

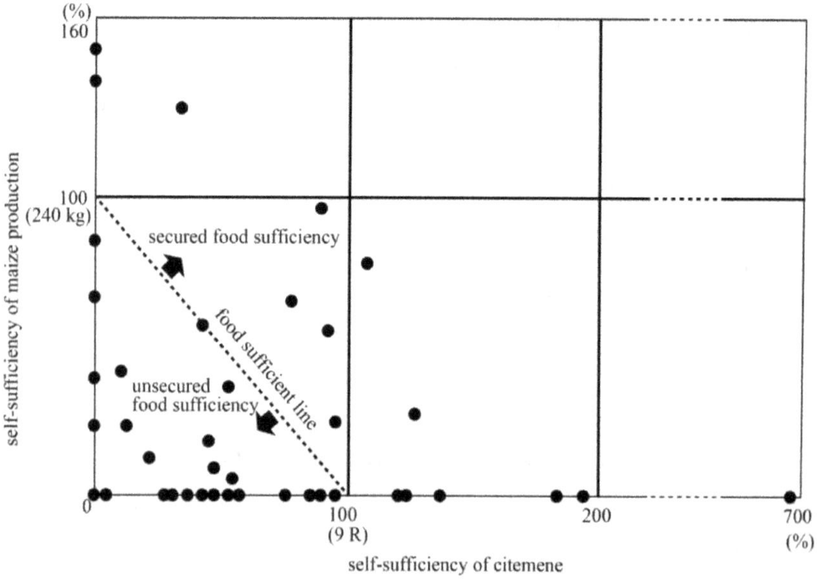

Figure 2. Staple food self-sufficiency of all households in ML village (2012 cropping season)

achieved food self-sufficiency by combining *citemene* with farm cultivation. Yet even combining *citemene* with farm cultivation, 31 households (66 per cent) experienced difficulty in relation to food self-sufficiency. For such households, it is a challenge to make the investments required for the following year's maize production, including sales of their products and purchases of chemical fertiliser.

Among the 31 households who experienced food self-sufficiency problems, some individuals were able to purchase agricultural products to meet their needs by peddling (itinerant sales), raising livestock (chickens, goats, pigs) and selling charcoal. Many also work for the people who live near them, labouring in their fields or helping to build houses – this is piecework, performed to support one's livelihood in terms of foodstuffs and money.

4. Piecework Performed in the Village

Piecework itself is nothing new in Bemba farming villages. For example, today, one still sees women who brew finger millet beer when requesting the clearing of new land for *citemene*; the man is given the cultivation work in exchange for the beer. This is included in the piecework concept. Examples of piecework in agriculture (i.e. farm cultivation) include tillage, fertilisation, sowing, weeding, maize harvest, threshing and transport (Figure 3). In *citemene*, the tasks of cutting trees, carrying branches, and building and repairing houses and food storage bins count as piecework.

Among these types of piecework, those involving farm cultivation have critical implications for the livelihoods of many villagers. The time at which farm cultivation-related work is in highest demand corresponds to the period of greatest food insufficiency for numerous households. In the surveyed village, piecework in maize fields begins around October, and is mainly performed during the period thereafter from December to February. Piecework during this time is an indispensable means of preserving livelihoods.

Piecework in recent years has been characterised by two major aspects. The first is the increased number of cases for which cash is paid in remuneration. This is due to the growing need for cash and the increase in the number of those who now have it. Nonetheless, during the off-peak period for foodstuffs, payment in maize is preferred over money. The other aspect is that of the increased opportunities for household owners of large maize fields to request that multiple villagers perform short-term piecework.

Piecework opportunities occur according to the two patterns described next. The first is when an employer requests piecework, and the villagers gather at that site. In the case of small-scale piecework where only one or two people are employed, specific individuals are asked directly. However, when many workers are needed on a large-scale maize farm, prior notification is given along the lines of, 'Furrowing piecework is needed on 15 December on

Figure 3. The villagers engaged at the fertilisation for piecework. Within a short period, the farmers must complete tillage, fertilisation, sowing, weeding, maize harvest, threshing and transport

such-and-such maize farm'. The information is disseminated throughout the village, and many people show up on the designated date. Whether from the same village or other ones, no one who comes is denied work; rather, all are accepted on a first-come, first-served basis until the desired quota has been filled. Some work is assigned by gender (i.e., some for men, some for women).

The other piecework pattern is the offering of piecework services to households who are likely to comprise villagers seeking employment. Villagers will approach the owner of a large maize field or a person known to have cash and ask him/her whether he/she has any work that needs to be done. They may even ask specifically (e.g., 'Please let me do some work in your maize field'). This can generate piecework opportunities.

Regarding the details of the work and its remuneration, the person who does the work (below, 'the worker') attends the worksite, where he/she is informed of such by the employer. After being told by the employer about the kind and amount of work to be performed and the remuneration to be paid, the worker begins the labour if he/she agrees with the stated conditions. Take, for example, the case of M, who was assigned the task of furrowing work in a maize field. A furrow length of 20 metres was set as the unit for one furrow, with one kwacha (0.2 United States Dollar) to be paid for each furrow. In addition to the cash, further details were established: one egg per one furrow, 2.5 litres of beer for six furrows and five litres of maize for seven furrows. This request for work details and pay was communicated to the workers at the time the labour was to be carried out.

Workers who have agreed to the stated work and pay may then work at their own pace; in most cases, they themselves determine when the work has been completed. When they finish their work, they go to the employer and report it. At this time, the employer may request modifications, among other adjustments.

Once the employer is satisfied with the work, the worker receives his/her pay, and the contract is concluded (Figure 4). Nonetheless, hard labour must be performed for long hours before any pay is received. In the case of M described above, since remuneration was determined based on furrow-length units of 20 metres, it was necessary to measure the length of each furrow. M prepared a scale that could measure 50 metres, after which he divided the total to determine how many furrow units he had finished. He would record the number of furrows on a sheet of paper; these served as receipts that were presented to each individual worker. The workers would stand by whenever a measurement was made and often say something like, 'That should be longer. Please measure it again.' In this way, the determination of precisely what work must be done is often a difficult process.

Employers other than M would repeatedly perform the same kind of give-and-take with their employees, such that in some cases, the negotiations regarding payment would take as long as the piecework itself. Even for work details that have been agreed on,

Figure 4. Women pieceworkers. They received the maize for the piecework pay and hurried home in the evening

some negotiation (conflict) will inevitably arise at the time of payment. Some slight change may occur in the relative positions of the employer and the employee before and after the work is performed. Workers who have finished a job appear to have a strong right to comment, and a relationship of equality exists between the employer and employee with respect to piecework.

5. The Ambiguities of Piecework

Many workers who toil in maize fields during the off-peak period are householders who struggle to achieve food self-sufficiency. Currently, in Bemba farming villages, piecework is key to sustaining food self-sufficiency, with its redistribution of money and foodstuffs. Until piecework became an active phenomenon in society, with the establishment of farm cultivation in the 1980s, both young and middle-aged (hereinafter, 'mature') householders cleared forests for *citemene*, and produced enough finger millet and cassava for their own consumption needs, selling the excess (if any). Meanwhile, older couples and women-headed households brewed finger millet beer and sold it to younger generations, allowing cash to spread to each part of the village.

Thereafter, with the diffusion of farm cultivation, one livelihood strategy involved balancing *citemene* and farm cultivation, while young and mature householders often dedicated themselves to farm cultivation, since it involved greater profits. However, the instability in fertiliser supply resulted in large fluctuations in annual maize production amounts, and households began to experience food insufficiency during the off-peak period. During this time, older females who continued to pursue *citemene* without rushing to perform maize cultivation contributed to their villages' food self-sufficiency. Households run by older women have no major year-on-year changes in the area they use for *citemene*. They either live alone or have been responsible for raising several grandchildren, meaning that, in many cases, they have enjoyed a surplus of food.

In the off-peak season, these individuals (i.e., older mothers) share their surplus with the households of their sons and daughters (Oyama and Takamura 2001).

Even today, gifts of food and money are given within a narrow scope of kinship between children and parents, as well as among siblings. To realise self-sufficiency, household owners of large maize fields play a major role, as they distribute food and money via cultivation-related piecework performed in these fields. Piecework is not only indispensable in maintaining households directly faced with food shortages but also plays an important role in the expansion of economic activities. Employer households with a surplus of food sell a portion of their maize on the market. Efforts are made to then set aside cash obtained from sales to the FRA, so that it can be used to pay wages for piecework conducted during farm cultivation the following year. In this way, efforts are made to secure an annual workforce.

Among households who own large maize fields and produce a surplus of maize are people who have returned to their villages with retirement money after having worked for wages for several years in the city or as elementary school teachers. Meanwhile, some owners and operators of large maize fields have made their money not by working and being paid wages in a city but by making and selling beer and agricultural products or from the proceeds of their hunting and gathering. Alternatively, they may have sold fish as itinerant merchants. Such villagers use the money gained from the sale of surplus maize as capital for the expansion their economic activities. For example, one household has begun to operate a bar that sells an alcoholic beverage called 'wine' made from sugar and yeast, while another runs a grocery store selling merchandise procured from wholesale facilities in the town (Figure 5). Yet another has bought a milling machine for maize and is now in the milling business. These villagers differ from wage earners in that their business is continuous, necessitating the continued production of surplus maize for capital to grow their enterprises further. The main objective of piecework for employers, then, is to allow themselves to maintain and expand their separate business activities.

Piecework requested by employers from employees not only serves to enlarge the employer's personal assets but also helps support the daily lives of surrounding villagers. Mr F, for instance, who often requests piecework, explained, 'My neighbours who worry about money or food will ask for piecework. They can't live without piecework.' Mr F further asserted, 'I won't ask villagers who have food and money to do piecework.' The authors themselves heard statements in the research area on piecework requests, including advice to 'first employ the woman who has lost her husband' and 'rather than asking people who performed work before to do a new job, you should first ask someone new to perform it.'

Mr K, a teacher at an elementary school, said that, 'Piecework empowers local people. Doing piecework gives villagers cash income. This helps them to buy chemical fertiliser, and also to buy

Figure 5. Grocery store selling merchandise in the farming village

food if necessary.' Mr K was asked whether he would consider buying a tractor rather than hiring many people to do piecework. He declined, asserting that, 'If I bought a machine, there would be no more work for villagers to do, so I won't buy one.' Mr K would frequently observe that, 'Life in the village is full of trouble because there is so much envy,' indicating his strong awareness of others' views and their envy. His desire to deflect such envy is evident in his remarks.

There exists a strong awareness among employers that piecework functions as a means of helping neighbours in need. They say, '*Uluse* exists in piecework.' *Uluse* is a Bemba term that broadly means generosity, consideration for others, kindness, charity, salvation and forgiveness. Thus, the provision of piecework expresses kindness, generosity and consideration for one's neighbours. It is said that everyone in Bemba society should practise *uluse*.

By offering piecework, employers try to prevent a limited number of people from benefiting from it. Therefore, villagers are assigned piecework in the order in which they arrive at the worksite, and no elements of intimacy or deepening of friendship are involved in piecework. Villagers who come in search of piecework are not refused or rejected out of hand, and repeated negotiations take place requiring careful attention to the opinions of people who have performed the work with respect to their pay prior to the final remuneration – these, too, are expressions of *uluse*. The request that one's neighbours perform piecework requires considerable work and may be a source of annoyance. Yet, from the employer's perspective, the interactions sustained in piecework help to preserve good neighbourly relations and allow one to live a peaceful, satisfying daily life.

6. Economic Disparities Resulting from Levelling Mechanisms

Kakeya et al. (2006) indicated that social mechanisms in Bemba society, which regulate a general equality of possessions (one cannot own much more than others do) and that render the uneven distribution of goods taboo, give one a glimpse of levelling mechanisms that help to control disparities. While differences in labour abilities (resulting from varied household composition) have fostered divergences in agricultural production, such differences are levelled (equalised) through the distribution and consumption of produced goods. In this way, a stable livelihood is maintained for the entire village.

In Bemba farming villages today, significant economic disparities exist between households who have trouble sustaining food self-sufficiency and households who produce a surplus of maize. Nevertheless, the surplus maize and money generated by households who own and operate large-scale maize fields are passed on to households who worry about obtaining food via piecework. The outcome is that the entire village achieves food self-sufficiency.

Employers who provide piecework require a large labour force year-on-year so that they can continue to produce surplus maize. Such labour is secured via piecework. The major aim of piecework for an employer, then, is to expand personal economic activities; at the same time, however, the employer is aware of the opportunity offered by piecework to become familiar with their neighbours' lives and to provide support therewith for households who are concerned about food sufficiency. Here, wealthier people do not intend to ignore their neighbours' food needs but, rather, endeavour to provide piecework upon request to those with insufficient food, thereby avoiding the envy of others. Piecework helps to rectify food and money disparities positively in the village. In other words, piecework, as observed in contemporary Bemba society, has a levelling function that helps to protect others' livelihoods.

One negative aspect of piecework in modern Bemba society should be noted, namely, that it exacerbates economic disparities. Not only do employers who provide piecework have their own farmlands cultivated; they also clear new farms every year. This expansion leads to increased employment opportunities in the village, thereby helping to raise livelihood levels. Nonetheless, employees who perform piecework are busy carrying out work for others and have no time to develop their own maize fields. This cycle of piecework leads to increased economic disparities between employers and employees. Growth via shifting cultivation not only causes environmental deterioration but also creates problems for future generations with regard to uneven ownership of land resources and the fixing of economic disparities (Oyama 2016).

As researchers, we have admired the consideration for others and generosity associated with piecework as sources of 'the latent potential of Africa', having observed that the provision of piecework by the wealthy to their neighbours aims to level consumption. Piecework, as practised today, enables numerous neighbours who worry about food insufficiency to seek work and obtain the money and food they need to survive. In this sense, piecework has served as a mechanism within villages to promote the equalisation of wealth. We have observed this levelling of wealth to have the potential to maintain peace in village society. However, piecework in the maize fields has also highlighted disparities between the wealthy and the non-wealthy. The resulting expansion of the maize fields of the wealthy has prompted the rapid clearing of the miombo woodlands and the decline of the forest. Will piecework be continued in the future as a means of helping sustain villagers' livelihoods? Or will it become the spark that ignites the divisions in society, whereby wealthy employers absorb workers' labour powers, leading to a society where few are rich while many are poor? The current symbiotic status of Bemba farming villages now stands at a crossroads.

Acknowledgements

This work was supported by JSPS KAKENHI Grant Number JP15H02591, JP16H06318, JP17H04506, and JP17H02235.

References

Asiimwe, F. A. (2017) 'Gender inequality of high income households in Uganda: Exploring women's rights to land and property at the household level', *Japanese Journal of Human Geography*, Vol. 69, No. 1, pp. 87–99.

Chidumayo, E. N. (1994) *Miombo Ecology and Management: An Introduction*, London: Intermediate Technology Publications.

Kakeya, M. and Sugiyama, Y. (1985) '*Citemene*, finger millet and Bemba culture: A socio-ecological study of slash-and-burn cultivation in northeastern Zambia', *African Study Monographs, Supplementary Issue*, No. 4, pp. 1–24.

—— (1987) 'Agricultural change and its mechanism in the Bemba villages of northeastern Zambia', *African Study Monographs, Supplementary Issue*, No. 6, pp. 1–13.

Kakeya, M., Sugiyama, Y. and Oyama, S. (2006) 'The *citemene* system, social leveling mechanism, and agrarian changes in the Bemba villages of northern Zambia: An overview of 23 years of "fixed-point" research', *African Study Monographs,* Vol. 27, No. 1, pp. 27–38.

Krugmann, H. (1995) 'Overcoming Africa's crisis: Adjusting structural adjustment towards sustainable development in Africa', in K. Mengisteab and B. I. Logan (eds) *Beyond Economic Liberalization in Africa: Structural Adjustment and the Alternatives*, London: Zed Books, pp. 129–162.

Moore, H. L. and Vaughan, M. (1994) *Cutting Down Trees: Gender, Nutrition, and Agricultural Change in the Northern Province of Zambia, 1890–1990*, London: Heinemann.

Muyanwa, J. (2015) 'Policy analysis: Examining FRA's role', *Times of Zambia*, 20 January 2015 (http://www.times.co.zm/?p=48374) (accessed: 29 November 2020).

Nakazawa, M. (2017) 'Unstable landownership and economic differentiation among female-headed households in rural area of southwestern Uganda', *Japanese Journal of Human Geography*, Vol. 69, No. 1, pp. 57–72.

Oyama, S. (1996) 'Regeneration process of the miombo woodland at abandoned citemene shifting cultivation field in northern Zambia', *African Study Monographs*, Vol. 17, No. 3, pp. 101–116.

—— (2016) 'Guardian or misfeasor? Chief's roles in land administration under the new 1995 Land Act in Zambia', in S. Moyo and Y. Mine (eds) *What Colonialism Ignored: 'African Potentials' for Resolving Conflicts in Southern Africa*, Bamenda: Langaa RPCIG, pp. 103–128.

—— (2017) 'Food and land in economic differentiation of sub-Saharan Africa', *Japanese Journal of Human Geography*, Vol. 69, No. 1, pp. 1–8.

Oyama, S. and Takamura, T. Y. (2001) 'Agrarian changes and coping strategies for subsistence of Bemba shifting cultivators in northern Zambia in the mid-1990's', *Journal of Tropical Agriculture*, Vol. 45 No. 2, pp. 84–97.

Richards, A. I. (1939) *Land, Labour and Diet in Northern Rhodesia: An Economic Study of the Bemba Tribe*, London: Oxford University Press.

Richards, A. and Widdowson, E. (1937) 'A dietary study in Northern Rhodesia', *Africa*, No. 9, pp. 166–196.

Stromgaard, P. (1985) 'A subsistence society under pressure: The Bemba of northern Zambia', *Africa*, No. 55, pp. 39–58.

Wood, A. P. (1990) 'Agricultural policy since independence', in A. P. Wood, S. A. Kean, J. T. Milimo and D. M. Warren (eds) *The Dynamics of Agricultural Policy and Reform in Zambia*, Ames: Iowa State University, pp. 21–58.

Chapter 4

Conflicting Paradigms and Strategies of Local Innovation: A Case Study among the Bemba, Northern Zambia

Yuko Sugiyama and Tadasu Tsuruta

1. Introduction

Interest in grassroots innovation in rural Africa has been growing over the last two decades. Recognising the failure of the previous top-down and unilateral approaches for facilitating rural innovation, Reij and Waters-Bayer (eds) (2001) focused on farmer-innovators in Africa who tried out novel methods of their own initiative, without direct support from formal research and extension agencies. At the onset of the International Year of Family Farming, declared by the United Nations in 2014, the Food and Agriculture Organization of the United Nations (FAO 2014: 5) stressed that farmers' knowledge and experience should inform the process of on-farm innovation to achieve food security, poverty reduction and sustainable development simultaneously. Agricultural innovation is a complex process involving multiple actors, including farmers, research institutions, extension workers and other stakeholders, all of who make up the entire system of innovation (World Bank 2007). Among these actors, the FAO (2014) asserts that farmers should be the protagonists, rather than mere recipients, in the innovation process. Although recent studies on the 'innovation system' approach in sub-Saharan Africa have demonstrated that there have been some successful cases of innovation, which have increased the capacity of villagers (Adekunle et al. 2012; Triomphe et al. 2013), little is known about how they displayed their initiatives, particularly in the process of incorporating new technologies into the local context that includes existing farming systems and communal relations.

Analyses on agricultural innovation have largely been made on the basis of either past Western experiences of agricultural modernisation or Asian experiences of the Green Revolution. A particularly influential work on this theme is that of Hayami and Ruttan (1985), who attempted to create a model of 'induced innovation' in the agricultural sector, in which farmers, along with public research institutions, have the incentive to innovate in response to changes in the relative prices of certain factors of production. Their basic assumption was that farmers are highly responsive to price signals and research institutions, for their part, are able to fulfil farmers' demands for alternative technologies to reduce production costs, thus creating an ideal interaction between the two. Examining the applicability of this innovation model to Africa, Goran Hyden (2007) points out that the basic attitude of African peasant farmers tends to be more risk-averse than their counterparts in Asia, from which Hayami and Ruttan derived their model on market (and government)-induced innovation.

Hyden's emphasis on African peasants' reluctance to take part in market-oriented production has often been misunderstood as asserting that they are not willing to change (Williams 1987). His larger point was, however, that African villagers also pursue change, but do so according to their own principles (Hyden 1983). Although recent studies have emphasised that African villagers are highly responsive to market-driven innovation (Haggblade and Hazell (eds) 2010; Adekunle et al. 2012), this perspective does not recognise the fact that most African peasants assign a high priority to securing subsistence,[1] and that, as they live in village communities, they cannot easily escape from existing communal ties. Through her longitudinal study among the Bemba in northern Zambia, the first author found that villagers have introduced several types of innovation into their farming systems to make subsistence more stable, and that these on-farm innovations have been closely associated with changes in socioeconomic relationships among villagers, particularly in the spheres of exchange and consumption. The economic gap stemming from the adoption of new technologies has tended to be reduced by the act of sharing scarce resources, which was also driven by local cash circulation.

Innovation is thus not only a matter of technical change per se; rather, it is a dynamic process involving villagers' reactions to ever-changing socioeconomic and environmental circumstances. In the case of the Bemba, foreign technologies (and crops) have often been adopted in accordance with existing dynamics of change in human-to-human relationships and human-to-nature relationships. To understand the process by which external technologies are modified, it may be helpful to use the concept of a *paradigm*, which here denotes a dominant pattern, or way in which villagers adapt themselves to the surrounding natural environment, along with their worldview. The term 'paradigm' was first applied to the history of science by Thomas Kuhn (1970), who regarded it as denoting a set of concepts and practices shared by members of an academic community. In the context of an African village, a paradigm can be regarded as a set of dominant values and practices in terms of the villagers' interaction with nature, in particular land utilisation. A particular innovation may be developed according to a certain paradigm, but it can be shifted to another paradigm once it has been adopted by a certain community. At the same time, to reveal the social mechanism behind this process, we also need to focus on villagers' livelihood strategies, particularly in terms of social exchange, as one of the driving forces of *paradigm shifts*.[2]

In the next section, we describe the background of the site where the first author carried out field research from 1983 until 2000.[3] This is followed by a description of the everyday on-farm trials and errors of Bemba villagers, after which a brief history of the Bemba's innovation over the past one hundred years is sketched out. This highlights three landmark innovations that have contributed greatly to sustaining villagers' livelihood to this day. Finally, the development of these major innovations will be examined through the framework of different paradigms and strategies of innovation.

2. Background of the Research Site

The Bemba people are shifting cultivators living in *miombo* woodland[4] in northern Zambia (Figure 1). Their kinship system is

Figure 1. Study area (before 2011)

Source: Author.

Note : This map shows city centres and provinces before 2011, when Muchinga Province was created by combining four districts from Northern Province and one district from Eastern Province.

matrilineal, with an uxorilocal pattern of residence. The core section of a village is made up of a male headman and his matrilineal kin. Due to a high rate of divorce, there are a considerable number of female-headed households in each village. Their farming system is characterised by a unique method of swidden agriculture known locally as *citemene*. In this system, unlike swidden farming in rainforests, where a whole tree is felled and burnt, only branches are lopped off by male villagers. The fallen branches are piled on the ground by women and then burnt to make a swidden field. The branches are collected from a much wider area than the field itself, and the trees whose branches were trimmed off regenerate over a period of around 15 years outside the field, and 30 years inside the field (or 'in-field') (Oyama 2013).

Another arresting feature of the present *citemene* method is its unique cropping pattern, characterised by a crop rotation system and mixed-cropping. The crop rotation proceeds according to the following five-year cycle. In the first year, villagers grow sweet potatoes and pumpkins (plus tomato, spinach, beans and gourds) on the mounds built on the fringes of the *citemene* field, at the centre of which cassava and finger millet are planted. In the second year, groundnuts and Bambara nuts are grown. Mature cassava is harvested in the third and fourth years. After harvesting cassava, oval shaped mounds are built at the centre, on which beans are grown in the fourth and fifth years, before leaving it fallow for more than ten years. The present system has been elaborated through a number of on-farm innovations over the past one hundred years, as we shall see in detail further below.

Citemene food production is supplemented by farming in *ibala*, which are small semi-permanent fields with mounds introduced during colonial times. *Ibala* are normally cleared near the home and vegetables are grown there for around seven years, during which time soil fertility is occasionally replenished using weeds as green manure. From the 1980s onward, villagers have grown hybrid maize in semi-permanent fields with subsidised chemical fertiliser. Locally called *faamu* (derived from the English word farm) cultivation, this method diffused widely from the late 1980s to the early 1990s as it yielded a considerable profit at the time.

Villagers' farming activities are based on a clear gender division of labour. Commercial maize production in *faamu* is chiefly practised by male villagers. On the other hand, women are primarily responsible for *citemene* crop production for domestic consumption, although they cannot clear *citemene* fields without a male workforce to climb up the trees and cut the branches off. The size of the *citemene* field of each household (and the amount of food secured), therefore, is heavily dependent on the number of male members. The economic gap between female-headed households and those with abundant male-labour, however, is mitigated by the sale of finger millet beer made by women. Male villagers rich in food and cash are required to buy more beer than they need, and to distribute it to others. The cash is then used by female household heads to buy daily necessities and secure a labour force to clear the *citemene* field. Behind this cash flow lies a persistent norm of sharing among villagers, which has survived despite the increasing penetration of the cash economy. The *haves* have a moral obligation to help the *have-nots* by sharing scarce resources, in particular food. This levelling mechanism guarantees villagers' subsistence in case of any eventuality.

Villagers also utilise the surrounding natural and semi-natural environments, including fallow fields in the process of regenerating the trees, in multiple ways: for hunting, gathering wild plants and edible worms, and fishing. The first author has discussed this multi-faceted utilisation of the natural environment elsewhere (Sugiyama 1998), which is based on the Bemba villagers' ample ecological knowledge, which in turn forms the basis for innovation in subsistence activities.

The *citemene* system is also related to the cycles of fission and fusion of Bemba villages. A reorganisation of settlements occurs, along with a change in village political authority, with each new generation. Villagers tend to leave an old village site to create a new village every 30 years, a cycle that corresponds with the regeneration cycle of *miombo* in the *citemene* in-field (Oyama 2013). Given the mobility of villages and the villagers, village sizes remain rather small, thereby limiting human impact on the environment. *Miombo* woodland is considered to belong primarily to the ancestral spirits, in particular the deceased Bemba chiefs who established and governed the Bemba chiefdom. Although the living chiefs are the legal representatives of the Bemba territories under Zambian law, they only represent communal ownership of the woodland, along with village headmen who act under commission of the chiefs. They only retain their authority for as long as they can attract support from villagers by fulfilling the task of praying to the ancestral spirits for good harvests and a stable life through various rituals.

3. Everyday Forms of On-Farm Innovation

3-1. The Beginning of On-farm Innovation through Small Scale Trial and Error

The introduction of new crops and new farming techniques is an everyday affair for the Bemba villagers. As shown in Table 1, Mr A, B, C and D introduce novel crops and techniques most frequently among the villagers. It is worth noting that all these individuals are outsiders, hailing from other villages. Mr A moved into his wife's village after his marriage. As he often makes peddling tours around different districts, he tends to have the latest information about government policies and the recent market trends for farm products. He was the first to start hybrid maize cultivation, based on a government loan system in the mid-1980s. As soon as he perceived a delay in the government's fertiliser supply in the early 1990s, he shifted his fields to remote areas where the soil was still intact, to reduce the use of chemical fertilisers for hybrid maize cultivation, and then tried to maintain the soil fertility by utilising a crop rotation system. Mr B had once worked for a European farm in the Copperbelt Province before settling in his wife's village. He actively pursued a better way of *ibala* cultivation, experimenting with new methods and crops which he observed in the Copperbelt Province and other areas. Mr C, who used to work as a company employee in the Copperbelt Province, came to live in his wife's home village after his retirement. He tried to find drought tolerant cash crops (including sorghum) suited to the *citemene* fields, in addition to cultivating hybrid maize. He utilised the social networks he established during his stay in the Copperbelt Province to acquire new crop seeds for his trials. It is also notable that both Mr A and Mr C tried to grow wheat as a new crop, although they obtained wheat seeds through different channels.

Social marginality is an important factor in facilitating innovation, even for village-born males, as shown in the cases of Mr E, F, and G (Table1). As their social status is somewhat marginal for one reason or another, they are at greater liberty to explore novel methods and crops than other male villagers. As such, social marginality gives them an excuse to be not as strict as other villagers in sharing goods, and they are able to monopolise the fruits of their trials to some extent. At the same time, even when their trials fail, a certain level of livelihood is secured because their wives are engaged in *citemene* farming for self-consumption and the mechanisms for sharing between villagers provide them with supplementary food for daily use.

Table 1. Villagers' on-farm trials

Birthplace and gender	Individual villager	Field	Year	Trials of new crops and new methods	Sources of information or seeds
Males hailing from other areas	A	*Ibala*	1978	Maize for sale	Agricultural college (Kasama)
			1985	Hybrid maize production with a loan from government	Other chief areas
			1988	Soybean	Observed in other areas
			1990	Improved variety of sorghum	Other chief areas and a brewery
			1992	Wheat	Experience in Copperbelt, seeds obtained from relatives in another chief area
	B	*Ibala*	1980	Maize for sale	A European farmer who formerly employed B, seeds obtained from a government depot
			1988	Cultivating a garden after a long fallow to avoid animal damage	His own experience
			1992	Testing groundnuts' fertilising effect	Following practices of agricultural extension workers in Chibwa
	C	*Citemene*	1991	Improved variety of sorghum	A brewery
			1992	Wheat	His own experience in Copperbelt, seeds obtained from relatives in Mpika
			1992	Soybean	His own experience in Copperbelt
	D	*Citemene*	1984	Maize for sale	Friends in other chief areas
Village-born males	E	*Dambo**	1993	Guava and other fruit trees	Observation in other areas
	F	*Ibala*	around 1990	Wheat	Bought at Chinsali market
	G	Homestead	1992	Fruit trees	Agricultural college
Village-born females	H	*Citemene*	1984-	Tomato	Seeds taken from tomatoes sold in town market
			1987	Sweet potato	Another chief area
			1992	An improved variety of finger millet	Kasama Rural Development Centre
	I	*Citemene*	1988	Beans and edible gourd	Daughter in another area
			around 1990	Cassava, sorghum	Friends in other areas
	J	*Citemene*	1991	Late sowing	Memory of J's parents' practice

Table 1. (*continued*)

Village-born females	K	*Citemene*	1989	Vegetables incl. onions	Daughter in another area
		Ibala	1992	Improved variety of sorghum	Seminar held by a beer brewery
	L	*Citemene*	1989?	Groundnuts, beans	Brother in another area
	M	*Ibala*	around 1990	Tobacco and Irish potato	Gift from relatives who visited other areas
	N	*Ibala*	1992	Tobacco	A relative in another village
	O	*Ibala*	1991	Improved variety of maize	Seminar of a seed company

Source: Field survey.

Note*: *Dambo* denotes a field made in lower wet areas.

On-farm trials are also common among non-marginal villagers. In particular, female villagers are always eager to find new varieties of crops and easier methods to secure harvests. Some examples follow. An elderly woman, Ms H, tried to plant seeds taken from tomatoes that she bought at the town market and found very tasty. In 1987, she started planting some new types of sweet potatoes brought from another chief area, where she had stayed for a few months. In 1992, she succeeded in obtaining seeds of an improved variety of finger millet developed by the Kasama Rural Development Centre, by asking one of her acquaintances in Kasama for them. A middle-aged woman, Ms J, found the rainfall pattern was changing and tried late sowing (of finger millet and beans) in 1991, recalling that her deceased parents practiced that to avoid the risks incurred by delays to the start of rain. Another middle-aged woman, Ms K, introduced an improved variety of sorghum after attending a seminar held by a brewery, which promised to buy the harvest at a higher price than common sorghum.

At the beginning, these trials were undertaken separately in a decentralised manner, according to each person's needs and perspectives. As can be seen in Table 1, the channels used to obtain new crop seeds vary in terms of the social ties involved. Later on, some of the new crop seeds or methods may become popular throughout the innovators' networks, via the sharing economy, by exchanging the seeds themselves, or by sharing information about them.

3-2. Principles Guiding Adoption of New Crops and Farming Methods

The crop repertoire of the Bemba villagers has changed significantly over time. First, their staple food shifted from sorghum to finger millet during the 18th and 19th centuries, and other options such as cassava and maize were added in the 20th century (Table 2). Several varieties of beans were introduced from neighbouring areas in the early 20th century.

In addition to the introduction of crops by individual villagers, chiefly through exchanges with other ethnic groups, there were several official projects to bring new crops into the area. Institutions initiating such projects included Christian missionaries, colonial and post-colonial governments and NGOs. Table 2 summarises crops of external origin introduced through these official projects. Some projects aimed to produce food for the miners in the Copperbelt, while others attempted to increase the variety of crops to improve the rural economy. Of the 15 new crops introduced, however, only four were successful; these are indicated by the shaded areas in Table 2. Only cassava, sweet potatoes (both introduced before World War II) and beans (introduced in the 1950s), along with the second wave of hybrid maize in the 1980s, were adopted by the villagers to create new combinations of crops.

It is noteworthy that new crops have been consistently introduced by the villagers themselves through various channels other than by official institutions or influential local leaders, as indicated in Table 1. In addition to the crops mentioned above, new crops such as Irish potatoes and varieties of sweet cassava were introduced, many of which gradually disappeared and some of which were adopted. Notably, cassava became an important staple food for surviving the hunger season.[5] According to Richards (1939), the colonial government carried out a campaign to introduce cassava, after a famine was triggered by serious damage to crops caused by locusts. A variety of cassava cultivars, however, were sporadically introduced through informal channels rather than through formal routes.

Table 2. Introduction of new crops by external institutions

Year	Missionaries	Colonial government	Zambian government and ODA from foreign countries*	Foreign NGOs	Staple food for villagers
18th century					Sorghum
19th century					Sorghum + finger millet
1910s	Sunhemp	Coffee **Sweet potato (during WWI)**			Finger millet
1920s	Wheat, chick peas	Maize			
1930s	Castor-oil plant	**Cassava**			
1940s	Sunhemp (as green manure)	**Sweet potato (a new variety)**			Finger millet + cassava (+ sweet potato)
1950s		**Common beans**			
1960s	Sunflower		Maize		
1970s					
1980s			**Hybrid maize**		
1990s			Finger millet (improved) Paprika	Castor-oil plant Soybean	Finger millet + cassava + maize
2000s			Soybean Sorghum (improved)	Orange	

Source: Field survey and Kakeya (2017: 386).

Note. *These include UK, Netherland, Norway and Sweden.

The Bemba evaluation standard in adopting crops primarily lies in whether they contribute to food security. As an elderly woman put it:

> The most important thing for us is that it [a new crop] can be our food for daily life. If you cannot eat it, it doesn't help us in the long run. You should not lose the ways of feeding your own children.

Labour distribution in a household is another important standard in deciding whether to adopt a certain crop, as an elderly woman told the first author:

> Maize may have a good harvest, but if you concentrate only on maize, you cannot finish planting cassava. Our labour force is limited.

The cases of maize introduction in the 1960s and 1980s were in conflict with the villagers' evaluation standards for the adoption of new crops, as it was introduced primarily as a cash crop, and not as food. In the 1960s, some villages abandoned *citemene* fields and shifted to mostly maize cultivation. But this did not last due to famine followed by drought, which caused the maize harvest to fail. As one of the elders explained:

> Most of us did not stop cultivating *citemene*, even though we tried maize cultivation in a small field. Thanks to that decision, we hardly suffered from hunger, while those who shifted to the maize cultivation did suffer; they even starved and asked us for help. That experience made us convinced that you must not stop making *citemene* fields if you wish to lead a life without worries.

Drawing a lesson from this experience, villagers only added maize cultivation to the *citemene* cultivation in the 1980s. Thus, an important principle for villagers in adopting new crops and technologies is that they do not replace old crops or strategies with new ones, but simply add new practices to their existing repertoire, without abandoning old strategies. Thus, however eager a person may be for cash crop production, it is necessary, as a safeguard, to continue to maintain existing subsistence activities, including *citemene* farming, along with gathering, hunting and fishing activities.

4. Three Landmark Innovations over 100 Years

4-1. The First Innovation: Establishment of the Citemene *System*

Over the past one hundred years, there have been three major innovations that have provided villagers with stable and reliable livelihood bases: (1) the establishment of the crop rotation system in *citemene* fields in the 1930s; (2) the creation of the cash circulation system in the 1940s; and (3) the establishment of the dual livelihood strategy, combining hybrid maize cultivation (*faamu*) with *citemene* farming in the 1980s and 1990s (Table 3). Note that the second off-farm innovation provided the basis for the third innovation, which diffused throughout the community regardless of the existing economic disparity between households.

In the original *citemene* system practised more than one hundred years ago, the Bemba villagers cultivated finger millet and sorghum (and groundnuts) only once, and then left the field fallow. When a famine broke out due to crop failure in the late 19th century, they temporarily moved to neighbouring areas occupied by the Lungu and Fipa peoples. After returning to the Bemba land, the villagers started to grow finger millet for two consecutive years in the same *citemene* field, following the method learned from their neighbours. This practice contributed to increasing the production of grain and alleviating hunger.[6]

The colonial government consistently banned *citemene*, as it was regarded by officials as a primitive and irrational farming method. Villagers, however, not only continued to practice *citemene* but also tried to elaborate it by introducing external technologies and crops. The *citemene* crop rotation system was further prolonged by mound cultivation, which was introduced on an extensive scale by the colonial government to secure food for soldiers during the World War I. Each adult villager was forced to grow sweet potatoes and beans on 200 mounds per person in semi-permanent fields. After the war, this practice was abandoned, but the mound cultivation technique continued to be used in case of necessity. At around the same time, common beans were brought into the village by the neighbouring Lala people. Even before compulsory cultivation, some villagers attempted mound cultivation after it was introduced through their contact with neighbouring ethnic groups. Added to this, in the 1930s, a village woman came back with cassava stems and a mound cultivation technique from neighbouring Bisa land, where she engaged in wage labour. Soon after, some villagers

Table 3. Chronology of local innovation among the Bemba

	Macroeconomic situation and policy intervention	Mainstream livelihood strategy	Major innovations in farming system and other economic activities
1800s	Famine, out-migration		Introduction of continuous cropping Introduction of mound cultivation
1900s	Colonization, a ban on *citemene* farming	Premordial *citemene* without crop rotation	
1910s	World War I, obligatory mound cultivation		Mound cultivation in semi-permanent fields spread widely, and then disappeared after World War I
1920s			Mound cultivation was adopted into *citemene* system
1930s	Labour migration to copper mines, introduction of poll tax	*Citemene* with crop rotation	**Creation of crop rotation system in *citemene*** Groundnuts cultivation increased both for sale and self-consumption
1940s			**Creation of cash circulation system within the village** Female villagers started to sell finger millet beer brewed using a new method
1950s			Trial of cattle keeping
1960s	A Christian mission tried to introduce green manure Maize as a cash crop	*Citemene* plus income -generating activities	Some villagers adopted maize cultivation but abandoned this as they suffered from hunger
1964	Independence		
1966	Chief Luchembe refused to accept government announcement that *citemene* should be abolished		
1970s	Chemical fertilizer supply depots were established		
1980s	Promotion of hybrid-maize cultivation with subsidized inputs		Some male villagers started hybrid maize cultivation by receiving a loan from the government **Creation of dual livelihood strategy**
1990s	Structural adjustment programme Subsidies for chemical fertilizer ended	Expansion of *faamu* (1986–1994)	A new method of brewing beer was introduced, which gave women the economic strength to hire male workers
2000s		Returning to *citemene* (1995–)	Introduction of pig-raising Goat-keeping in pens

Source: Field survey.

attempted to create mounds in *citemene* fields, and the mound cultivation of sweet potatoes and common beans became incorporated into the existing *citemene* cultivation practice, establishing the present crop rotation system. As noted previously, the period of *citemene* cultivation was further extended by the introduction of cassava, various cultivars of which were brought about through multiple informal routes.

The establishment of the present crop rotation system in *citemene* is the result of a series of innovations that occurred in the early 20th century. It is remarkable that almost all the techniques and seeds were adopted to refine existing woodland cultivation to stabilise food production for self-consumption. It must also be noted that the high mobility of the Bemba is an important factor in their history of innovation.

4-2. Second Major Innovation: The Creation of a Local Cash Circulation System

The second important innovation was made in off-farm activities: the introduction of local beer sales, and the ensuing creation of a cash circulation system within the village. In the 1930s, a poll tax system was introduced by the colonial government and labour migration to copper mines became increasingly popular. Those who migrated to the Copperbelt Province and neighbouring areas came back with cash and ideas for new cash-generating activities: wage labour in farming work and a new method of brewing local beer for sale.

By the 1920s, the sole alcoholic drink made by villagers was *cipumu*, which was used only for communal occasions such as rituals and cooperative labour events. It was never exchanged for cash. However, after some women returned from the Copperbelt Province with a new brewing technique, they began to sell a new type of finger millet beer (*katata*) to fellow male villagers. This innovation was welcomed by men who had already experienced urban life and were accustomed to purchasing beer, which facilitated the flow of cash from wealthier males to less-privileged females.

At almost the same time, it became common practice to hire

labour in exchange for cash or goods. Formerly, villagers with labour shortages had to depend on their kin networks along matrilineal lines. However, after the creation of the cash circulation system within the village, households short of labour, especially female-headed households, came to rely on labour hired in exchange for either cash or goods. The exchange between labour and goods (or cash) also created an avenue through which cash or valuable resources could be obtained by those without such.

In the mid-1980s, the first author closely observed how the Bemba villagers strived to obtain cash and how they used it (Sugiyama 2007). As the villagers did not keep livestock, hoarding cash was almost the only means to accumulate wealth, but few villagers succeeded in doing so. It is notable that, in the first place, cash was procured only when necessary and, once obtained, it was consumed immediately, for example, by purchasing daily necessities. By the mid-1980s, the main source of income was based on finger millet grown in *citemene* fields. Men would go to the villages of neighbouring Bisa people and exchange finger millet for dried fish, which were then sold in the market in town. Most of the cash obtained from selling dried fish was immediately used to purchase goods, such as school uniforms, stationery for children, clothes and daily utensils for the family use. The remaining cash was used to purchase second-hand clothes, soaps, salt and cooking oil which were then taken back to the village to sell in request of other villagers. At the same time, cash was also spent on local *katata* beer made of finger millet by female villagers, who sold it only when they needed cash to purchase the commodities listed above from outside.

Occasions for selling or providing local beer are at the core of the levelling mechanism, which evens out the economic gap stemming from different sizes of *citemene* and the different amounts of cash income in each household. As noted earlier, wealthier males tend to treat less-privileged villagers to local beer brewed by women, which can boost beer sales and help female household heads to buy daily necessities and secure male labour for *citemene* cultivation. Wives of these wealthier males also often brew finger millet beer, which is distributed freely among villagers. At the same time, half of the materials needed to brew *katata* beer for sale are left to brew *cipumu*, which is provided free of charge to villagers the next day. Thus, the introduction of *katata* has not wiped out the communal aspects of drinking traditional beer (*cipumu*). This practice also places some constraint on the brewers' accumulation of wealth.

4-3. The Third Major Innovation: Introduction of Hybrid Maize in the 1980s

The third major innovation was the introduction of hybrid maize cultivation in semi-permanent fields (*faamu*) grown with subsidised chemical fertiliser. Unlike the *citemene* system, *faamu* fields have to be cleared by uprooting trees before hoeing over the entire surface of the land. *Faamu*, therefore, requires enormous amounts of labour to initiate, in contrast to the innovations of the 1930s. After individual trials by some pioneering marginal persons, *faamu* was introduced by young and middle-aged males, as it brought about a considerable amount of profit. Their households established a dual livelihood strategy, being engaged in both subsistence production in *citemene*, and cash crop production in *faamu*. As they strived to expand *faamu* fields in suitable locations, other villagers experienced an acute shortage of labour for clearing *citemene*.

Initially, female-headed households were excluded from this innovation, as these women lacked the male labour required to clear *citemene* and *faamu* fields. They had to eke out a subsistence by being hired by male households in exchange for cash or other daily necessities (salt and soaps), and later for maize. Sales of finger millet beer, which were almost the sole source of income for females, stagnated due to steep inflation at the time. Thus, there was a growing economic gap between households with abundant male labour and those without it.

However, not long after, women gradually became involved in the innovation process, because the once declining levelling mechanism was revitalised. This process was associated with two important changes in villagers' daily lives: (1) the incorporation of maize into the everyday food repertoire; and (2) the cooperation and division of labour between older and younger female household heads, which was accompanied by the introduction of a new method for brewing beer. Originally, maize was introduced as a cash crop and not as food, with the villagers regarding maize as *cash equivalent.* According to the ethics of the Bemba villagers, there is no room for sharing cash, and the owner of cash (or cash equivalent) has an exclusive right to it. Asking for money is an unacceptable act, and is considered shameful. An elderly woman explained the distinction between food and money as follows:

> Claiming food is very good when you don't have enough, but you cannot ask someone to give you money. It's as though we were a bunch of beggars. No Bemba does such a shameful thing!

The adoption process of maize as one of the staples is related to the aforementioned fact that female household heads were often hired as farm hands by those families with a large acreage of *faamu* fields. The hired women were sometimes paid in maize (as a cash equivalent), which gave them opportunities to taste it. Eventually, they found that maize was useful as a substitute for cassava during the rainy season, when it takes longer to dry soaked cassava before milling it. It is also notable that wage labour was considered a way of 'sharing' cash or cash equivalents, which could not be shared through other transaction channels. The households with a male labour force, in a sense, helped female household heads by hiring them so that they could have a chance to earn their daily bread. At the same time, the hirers could not obtain private ownership of the land, no matter how extensively they cleared woodland to create *faamu* fields.

As maize was accepted as a daily food, the symbolic meaning of it changed from a cash equivalent to food, i.e., something to be shared. If one is short of it, one has the right to claim it, or to ask for help in acquiring it. Some young female household heads succeeded in creating a *faamu* with the help of their brothers, who agreed to be hired at exceptionally low wages. Thus, the male labour force and maize itself became available, even for those who were short of these resources.

Another important factor is the diffusion of a new economic

and time-saving method for brewing beer. This was introduced in 1991 by a young female household head, who learned the method when visiting a relative living in a nearby town. As the new beer (*vestini*) can be brewed with considerably less effort and material, and can be sold at a higher price than the old beer, female household heads could raise enough money to hire males to create their own *faamu* and *citemene*. Cash, labour and foods began to circulate again among villagers. Young females who sold *vestini* also induced male customers to help those women's mothers and maternal aunts to create *faamu*. Younger women may in turn have relied on subsistence foods harvested from the *citemene* of their mothers. As new forms of cooperation between mothers and daughters (or aunts and nieces) emerged, female-headed households found it much easier to survive. Finally, even female-headed households succeeded in adopting *faamu* cultivation, establishing a dual livelihood strategy by combining *citemene* and *faamu* production (Sugiyama 2020).

5. Conflicting Paradigms and Strategies of Innovation: Embedding Foreign Technologies in the Local Context

5-1. First and Second Innovations: Before the 1960s

The landmark innovations mentioned above took more than ten years to be assimilated into the villagers' livelihood activities, during which time numerous assays by each villager had taken place. Although these foreign techniques (or systems) were originally developed in different contexts, they were eventually accommodated into local systems. To understand this process, it may be useful to suppose a pair of paradigms (dominant modes of land use and concomitant settlement patterns and ideologies). At the same time, we assume that there is a pair of livelihood strategies (particularly in terms of social and economic exchange) for villagers, and that this is one of the driving forces causing a *paradigm shift* in relation to a particular innovation.

Figure 2 shows paradigms and strategies of (both on-farm and off-farm) innovations, divided into four quadrants partitioned by vertical and horizontal axes. The ends of the vertical line indicate

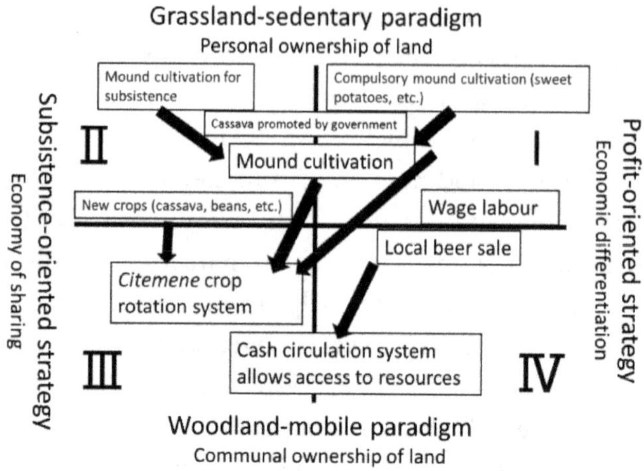

Figure 2. Paradigms and strategies of local innovation (before the 1960s)

Source: Authors.

two contrasting paradigms, each of which is based on different human–nature relationships and the ensuing settlement and land ownership patterns. Here, we contrast original woodland ecology with grassland ecology, in each of which villagers created soil-enriching methods characteristic of the respective vegetation.[7] The upper end represents grassland ecology and the sedentary mode of life, in which personal ownership of land predominates ('grassland-sedentary paradigm'). Meanwhile, the lower end constitutes the mobile pattern of livelihood in woodland, characterised by the communal ownership of land ('woodland-mobile paradigm'). In the woodland-mobile paradigm, replenishment of the soil relies on the regeneration of trees, and land without trees has no value. Its landscape is characterised by patches of different vegetation created by shifting cultivation. Meanwhile, in the grassland-sedentary paradigm, land itself has a value as a valuable resource, and its soil fertility is maintained only when villagers carry on the additional work of fertilising. The ends of the horizontal line indicate two contrasting livelihood strategies, which also show the socioeconomic orientation of a particular innovation. The right side indicates that a particular technique, or economic system, is based on a profit-oriented strategy and works to enhance economic differentiation, while the left side indicates a subsistence-oriented strategy that serves to achieve food security and maintain the original function of the levelling mechanism.

While a paradigm associated with land use is based on longstanding collective beliefs and values held by most community members, livelihood strategies may reflect the personal behaviours of each individual, based on short-term considerations. Note also that none of these four quadrants represents a monolithic unit of paradigm-strategy combination. There are gradations between the poles of grassland-sedentary and woodland-mobile paradigms, and also between profit-oriented and subsistence-oriented strategies. For instance, a farming system utilising grassland ecology is not necessarily based on a sedentary mode of livelihood. In fact, the Bemba villagers introduced grassland cultivation but still retain a certain degree of mobility. Likewise, an economic strategy may fall somewhere between two opposites. The placement of each technology (or system) in this coordinate system is determined by the balance between opposing tendencies.

The Bemba's original paradigm-strategy lies in the lower left quadrant (Quadrant III). The *citemene* system is based on shifting cultivation within a woodland environment, which is communally controlled. Bemba subsistence production is supported by the social ethic of sharing, which functions to even out economic differences through a levelling mechanism. The direction towards Quadrant III denotes maintaining the original Bemba pattern, while the opposite direction depicts the Bemba's changing paradigm and strategy.

Figure 2 also classifies items and methods (including economic systems) introduced by the 1940s into four quadrants, along with the direction of the modification of these techniques after their introduction (indicated by arrows). In their original contexts (or in the original intention), newly introduced techniques may have had different functions and orientations from those of the Bemba context. An example of this is the mound cultivation technique, which was originally developed as a farming method for the sustainable use of grassland rather than woodland. It requires constant labour input to maintain the grassland environment and its fertility. As the period of cultivation in the same field is prolonged compared to shifting cultivation, this technique develops some awareness of ownership of the plots under cultivation and, as such, is in conflict with the Bemba's shifting cultivation system, which is based on common ownership of woodlands.

Similarly, wage labour in the case of the Bemba may be placed in different social contexts from the original context of this practice. Normally, wage labour is enlisted individually between an employer and the employee. The money earned in this way belongs to the hired individual, who exerts his/her free will when deciding how to use it. Therefore, in theory, the penetration of wage labour can enhance individualism and magnify the economic differentiation between those who can be hired and those who cannot. Again, this is in conflict with the Bemba's interpersonal relationships, which are based on the ethic of sharing. Thus, these foreign techniques and economic systems were developed in such different original contexts and functions that they could have drastically changed the Bemba livelihood. However, these innovations were eventually modified upon incorporation into the Bemba's own context.

Figure 2 shows that most of the early on-farm innovations are situated in either Quadrants I or II. The technologies in Quadrant II, such as mound cultivation and cassava cultivation, were originally developed in grassland environments and oriented to enabling self-sufficiency and food security. In Quadrant I, one can find the most unfamiliar techniques to the villagers: the obligatory mound cultivation of sweet potatoes and beans in a permanent field, with a purpose other than self-consumption. At the same time, wage labour was introduced by those who had been salaried workers in the colonial economy. The techniques or systems placed in Quadrant I are potentially associated with surplus production, and are therefore oriented toward economic differentiation and the tendency to change from cultivation of woodlands to cultivation of grasslands for personal profit. Mound cultivation techniques and new crops, however, were eventually incorporated into the *citemene* crop rotation system, shifting into Quadrant III, which includes the original paradigm and livelihood strategy of the Bemba communities, where food security was based on the cyclical use of woodland and the function of the levelling mechanism was maintained.

Wage labour and the sales of local beer are to the right of the horizontal axis, and are notable landmark innovations in the economic system. Both innovations were introduced during the 1930s and 1940s, and seem to have promoted an orientation toward cash-centred personal-profit, creating economic disparity among the households. However, not long afterwards, a communal drinking party was required to be held on the day following the beer sale. This held back the potential for unlimited moneymaking by brewers. Thus, women acquired an income-generating measure of their own, and a local circulation system involving cash and labour was created within the village, allowing resource-poor villagers access to scarce resources.

5-2. Introduction of Hybrid Maize Cultivation in the 1980s and 1990s

A similar scheme can also be applied to the process of adopting hybrid maize cultivation in the 1980s and 1990s, the third landmark innovation (Figure 3). Hybrid maize cultivation was originally introduced to promote cash crop production in semi-permanent fields (*faamu*), but later came closer to subsistence production, as maize began to be consumed by villagers as a part of their staple food. It should also be noted that, even before the introduction of maize cultivation subsidised by the government, some villagers initiated their own trials to grow hybrid maize. Being aware of the precarious nature of government policy, the *citemene* continued to be cleared even after the diffusion of *faamu* cultivation, and most villagers eventually came to apply a dual livelihood strategy, combining subsistence farming and cash crop production.

As examined earlier, the levelling mechanism lies behind the widespread adoption of hybrid maize cultivation, which had declined but was revitalised due to innovation in brewing methods. The new method not only reduced labour requirements and the cost of brewing but also boosted the sales of beer,[8] thereby contributing to shifting cash from the wealthy to underprivileged female household heads. Coupled with the new division of labour between older and younger women along matrilineal lines, the new flow or circulation of cash updated the levelling mechanism to fit the new economic situation. The incorporation of hybrid maize

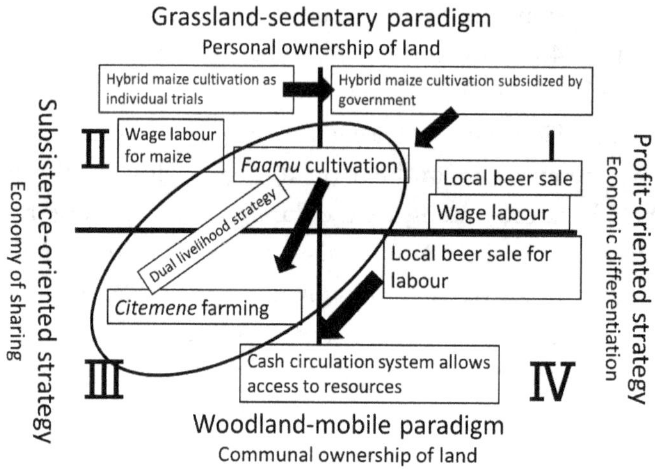

Figure 3. Paradigms and strategies of local innovation (early 1990s)

Source: Authors.

(originally a cash crop) to the local context of food sharing also served to activate the levelling mechanism. This transformed what had been genuine cash crop production into something closer to subsistence production, which can be helped by other households.

Our investigation of the innovation processes in Bemba villages over the past one hundred years, as detailed above, shows that it has always been influenced by the villagers' strategies to secure the long-term stability of their livelihoods, which should be supported by the *miombo* woodland ecology and good relationships with their relatives and neighbours. In the changes introduced in the 1930s and 1980s, foreign techniques and systems oriented toward personal profit tended to be combined with other techniques and methods upon their incorporation into the communal context of the Bemba sharing economy and local food security. The creation (and revitalisation) of a cash circulation system was key to allowing villagers access to scarce resources and labour, in particular. The villagers incorporated transactions mediated by cash into the context of communal life by converting cash into other sharable resources.

Researchers agree on the important role played by the cash economy to induce on-farm innovations in rural Africa, in the sense that villagers can be connected with the market economy through the medium of money (Tiffen et al. 1994). In the case of the Bemba, however, cash not only plays the role of linking villagers with the outside economy but also enables them to share scarce resources, the male labour force in particular, as an indispensable means of subsistence. In this sense, it is not helpful to consider the cash and subsistence economies as existing in a state of mutual conflict. In their argument on the role of money in communal systems of exchange, Bloch and Parry (1989: 24–30) divided economic transactions into two types based on different terms of transaction cycles: the individualistic and private profit-oriented 'short-term transaction', on one hand, and the 'long-term transaction' concerned with the continuous reproduction of social order, on the other. To understand the process of innovation among Bemba villagers as a way of accommodating new techniques or products into their livelihood, it is useful to consider short- and long-term transactions in their economic system. Villagers always seek new opportunities through short-term transactions, while trying to maintain social relations and secure subsistence through long-term transactions. Cash can serve to facilitate both types of transactions. The important point here is how the villagers articulated the communal village economy with the national economy by combining two types of transactions, thereby weakening the potentially subversive force of the market economy.

5-3. After the mid-1990s: Return to Citemene

Hybrid maize cultivation had spread widely in the village by 1992. Although most villagers did not pay back loans for the subsidised chemical fertiliser, efforts to recover the loans were not consistent at that time. The heyday of *faamu* cultivation, however, did not last long. In 1993, subsidies for maize cultivation were officially abolished and the collection of the loans became stricter. Most villagers then had to abandon *faamu* fields and return to the former strategy of only cultivating *citemene* fields.

Missing out on the lucrative business of hybrid maize production, villagers began to seek diversification of livelihood activities while depending on the *citemene* for their subsistence food production. However, the basic conditions that made *citemene* farming possible, the abundant *miombo* woodland, was gradually being undermined. Furthermore, the Land Act was amended to promote private ownership of land in 1995. By 1997, pressure on the land increased due to a new government settlement scheme, which invited outsiders to live in this area. It became increasingly difficult to secure enough *miombo* woodland to implement *citemene* farming. The small semi-permanent field, *ibala*, had once been abandoned, but was restored for both subsistence and cash crop production. Some villagers started to sell finger millet, which had seldom been sold for cash. Other new sources of income include pig-rearing and charcoal production. Pig-rearing was first introduced in 1994 and had spread among almost all the households by 1998. Behind this rapid diffusion lies a social mechanism similar to that of past innovations, in which villagers acquired pigs by offering either cash, maize or goats, and even resource-poor villagers gained access to pigs by exchanging their labour for animals. For several reasons, however, most villagers ceased raising pigs by 2000, which did not lead to any significant form of wealth accumulation, or social stratification after all. Since then, because of a serious land shortage, villagers could not secure enough land for *citemene* and became more dependent on farming in *ibala* or *faamu*.[9] Some wealthier villagers succeeded in consolidating large landholdings, leading to a widening gap between them and other villagers lacking sufficient landed property (see Oyama 2016 for further details).

6. Concluding Remarks

The Bemba's innovation history is a cumulative process of numerous trials and errors carried out by individual villagers. Newly introduced crops and techniques are evaluated through people's daily lives: some are accepted, and others are stored in memory and may be re-evaluated as useful later on. When a new method or crop has an element of appeal to other villagers, it may spread widely through a complex social process without any centre of diffusion. Existing levelling mechanisms, along with the local cash circulation system, contributed to allowing resource-poor villagers (especially female-headed households) access to necessary resources.

By using a framework representing different combinations of paradigms and strategies of innovation, we illustrated how external technologies (and crops) were integrated into (or came closer to) the existing Bemba paradigm and strategy based on woodland ecology and the economy of sharing. The levelling mechanism inherent in Bemba communities played a central role in the social process, eventually leading to a paradigm shift. Thus, the common, simple dichotomy of a levelling mechanism (or the economy of sharing) as traditional and static, versus the cash economy as modern and dynamic, is misleading and inaccurate. The levelling mechanism itself is a dynamic process and can be revitalised by the potentially threatening force of the cash economy, establishing a local transaction system that contributes significantly to extending the benefits of innovations throughout the village community. Even though the cash economy has penetrated deeply into local life, people are not fully involved in it; rather, they invent ways to articulate the local exchange system only partially to the national cash economy.

This dual economy is possible as long as the villagers can continue with their subsistence *citemene* production, which requires a sufficiently large area of *miombo* woodland. The woodland ecology, the very basis of their food security, however, is under considerable threat. Due to the government's seizure of woodland and its policy to promote land privatisation, *miombo* woodland around the study area has deteriorated, which made it impossible for villagers to adhere to the original woodland-mobile paradigm. Bemba villagers today have to tackle the challenge of narrowing the growing wealth gap, as well as establishing a sustainable farming system that is based on a balance between the grassland-sedentary and the woodland-mobile patterns of livelihood.

Endnotes

[1] Among 57 cases of agricultural innovation in Benin, Kenya and South Africa, degradation of natural resources (declining soil fertility, deforestation, etc.) was one of the most common triggers of innovation, suggesting that a considerable part of innovation in rural Africa was actually pursued to secure subsistence food production rather than driven by market opportunities (Triomphe et al. 2013: 317)

[2] A paradigm shift can also be triggered by changes in physical environment, for example, degradation of farmlands caused by overpopulation.

[3] Part of the first author's study on the innovation history of the Bemba has already been published (Sugiyama 2011, 2020).

[4] *Miombo* is a local term denoting tree species belonging to the genus *Brachystegia.* This vegetation is located between drier savanna and rainforest, occupying as much as one quarter of sub-Saharan Africa (Kakeya 2017: 359).

[5] In the 1930s, the period from January to March was a hunger season for Bemba villagers (Richards 1939), which has been mitigated by the introduction of cassava since the 1940s.

[6] A similar account can also be found in Richards (1939). According to her, the Bemba cultivated the same *citemene* field for only one year in the late 19th century, but later learned that finger millet can be grown twice in the same field, a practice that had spread widely among the Bemba by the 1930s.

[7] Woodland/grassland typology here owes much to Itani (2002), who classified a variety of indigenous farming systems practised in *miombo* woodlands (including areas whose primary vegetation was dominated by *miombo*) into two major types (woodland-fallow and grassland-fallow types) by focusing on the different nutrient cycles based on different vegetation.

[8] As the sale of new beer was not restricted by the existing rules for 'traditional' beer, those young men who had not been allowed to buy beer in the village became steady customers, thereby considerably increasing beer sales.

[9] Since the 2000s, *ibala* has gradually replaced *faamu* as the term referring to semi-permanent maize fields (see Oyama and Yoshimura,

chapter 3 in this volume).

Acknowledgements

This work was supported by JSPS KAKENHI Grant Number JP16H06318.

References

Adekunle, A. A., Ellis-Jones, J., Ajibefun, I., Nyikal, R. A., Bangali, S., Fatunbi, O. and Ange, A. (2012) *Agricultural Innovation in Sub-Saharan Africa: Experiences from Multiple-stakeholder Approaches*, Accra: Forum for Agricultural Research in Africa (FARA).

Bloch, M. and Parry, J. (1989) 'Introduction: Money and the morality of exchange', in J. Parry and M. Bloch (eds) *Money and the Morality of Exchange*, New York: Cambridge University Press.

FAO (Food and Agriculture Organization) (2014) *The State of Food and Agriculture 2014: Innovation in Family Farming*, Rome: FAO.

Haggblade, S. and Hazell, P. B. R. (eds) (2010) *Successes in African Agriculture: Lessons for the Future*, Baltimore: Johns Hopkins University Press.

Hayami, Y. and Ruttan, V. (1985) *Agricultural Development: An International Perspective* (revised and expanded edition), Baltimore and London: Johns Hopkins University Press.

Hyden, G. (1983) *No Shortcuts to Progress: African Development Management in Perspective*, London: Heinemann.

——— (2007) 'Governance and poverty reduction in Africa', *Proceedings of the National Academy of Sciences of the United States of America (PNAS)*, Vol. 104, No. 43, pp. 16751–16756.

Itani, J. (2002) 'Indigenous farming systems in miombo woodlands and surrounding areas in East Africa', *Asian and African Area Studies*, Vol. 2, pp. 88–104 (in Japanese with English abstract).

Kakeya, M. (2017) *Collected Works of Makoto Kakeya I*, Kyoto: Kyoto University Press (in Japanese).

Kuhn, T. S. (1970) *The Structure of Scientific Revolutions* (Second edition, enlarged), Chicago and London: The University of Chicago Press.

Oyama, S. (2013) 'Miombo woodland and citemene shifting cultivation of Bemba people in northern Zambia: Specifying and calculating a concept of optimum fallow period', *Ökumene Research*, Vol. 2, pp. 21–37 (in Japanese).

———— (2016) 'Guardian or misfeasor? Chief's roles in land administration under the new 1995 Land Act in Zambia', in S. Moyo and Y. Mine (eds) *What Colonialism Ignored: 'African Potentials' for Resolving Conflicts in Southern Africa*, Bamenda: Langaa RPCIG, pp. 103–128.

Reij, C. and Waters-Bayer, A. (eds) (2001) *Farmer Innovation in Africa: A Source of Inspiration for Agricultural Development*, London: Earthscan Publications.

Richards, A. I. (1939) *Land, Labour and Diet in the Northern Rhodesia*, New York and London: Oxford University Press.

Sugiyama, Y. (1998) 'Cutting trees and piling branches: A folk explanation of the *citemene* cultivation of the Bemba of northern Zambia', *Journal of African Studies (Africa-Kenkyu)*, No. 53, pp. 1–19 (in Japanese with English abstract).

———— (2007) 'Path of money, path of food, and path of respect', in N. Kasuga (ed.) *Anthropology of Resources 05: Money and Resource*, Tokyo: Kobundo Publisher (in Japanese).

———— (2011) 'A reflection on innovation among the Bemba', in M. Kakeya and J. Itani (eds) *Regional Studies on Africa and Rural Development*, Kyoto: Kyoto University Press (in Japanese).

———— (2020) 'Making innovation socially inclusive: Lessons from the Bemba in Zambia', in G. Hyden, K. Sugimura and T. Tsuruta (eds) *Rethinking African Agriculture: How Non-agrarian Factors Shape Peasant Livelihood*, London: Routledge.

Tiffen, M., Mortimore, M. and Gichuki, F. (1994) *More People, Less Erosion: Environmental Recovery in Kenya*, Nairobi: ACTS Press.

Triomphe, B., Floquet, A., Kamau, G., Letty, B., Vodouhe, S. D., Ng'ang'a, T., Stevens, J., Van den Berg, J., Selemna, N., Bridier, B., Crane, T., Almekinders, C., Waters-Bayer, A. and Hocdé, H. (2013) 'What does an inventory of recent innovation experiences tell us about agricultural innovation in Africa?', *The Journal of*

Agricultural Education and Extension, Vol. 19, No. 3, pp. 311–324.
Williams, G. (1987) 'Primitive accumulation: The way to progress?', *Development and Change*, Vol. 18, No. 4, pp. 637–659.
World Bank (2007) *Enhancing Agricultural Innovation: How to Go beyond the Strengthening of Research Systems*, Washington DC: World Bank.

Part II

Connecting beyond Boundaries in Africa: Villages, Cities and Overseas

Chapter 5

Submarine Cable and African Fruits: Construction of an Information Network by Southern Hemisphere Fed-Farms

Atsuko Munemura

1. Introduction

1-1. Information and Global Knowledge in the Agricultural Sector

Imperfection of information poses a significant risk to entrepreneurs in developing countries. The export of agricultural products for foreign markets is a case in point. Producers require the development of technology that guides them regarding the species of crops they should choose, and how they should produce, pack and ship them, as well as when and how much they should provide to the market and which market. Innumerable examples demonstrate that information and communications technology (ICT) has successfully fulfilled these demands for individual farmers in the modern market, and information networks have attracted increasing attention in the agricultural sector with respect to long-distance trade, particularly between developed and developing countries.

Information usually proceeds unilaterally from its source. A recipient develops skills with which to be informed, (i.e., he/she must translate information that aligns with his/her own interests, which sometimes creates further communication downstream, like other producers or their market agencies). Newspapers are a rich source of the price-leading market and input availability, such as that of seeds, fertiliser, pesticides and other requirements, but they require each reader to be literate. Television and radio are more equitable for those who cannot access written sources, but the information they convey is not always relayed whenever their recipients desire it. In many cases in the agricultural sector, individual farmers seek to ship their commodities in the optimal season and to the most suitable place, based on satisfactory pricing (Mittal and Mehar 2013: 1–2; Streeten 2016: 34–52) and, in cases of perishable products such as fruits, they must consider how best to maintain freshness (before the fruits have ripened). The farther they are from a leading market, the more urgently they require a range of options with respect to production and shipping, based on accurate knowledge.

Regarding this challenge, Greenwald and Stiglitz (2014) noted that market failure occurs when 'learning' itself requires 'further learning' and that incentives to acquire knowledge are not equal between developed and developing countries, and large corporations and small enterprises, as well as, perhaps, the industrial and agriculture/craft sectors.[1] Developing (or sometimes hoarding/transmitting) knowledge is easier within a large firm than across small enterprises: first, because the former can invest more in the process from research to development, including intellectual property rights (i.e. preserving knowledge); second, because the former can internalise the external information that has already been generated by learning, but the latter cannot; and third, because densely concentrated industrial clusters can use their linkage to influence incentives to learn and advance while, by contrast, small-scale agriculture or individual producers must bear the cost of transmitting information to their dispersion (Greenwald and Stiglitz 2014). Thus, reducing the cost of learning for individual producers has been and continues to be a domain that an institutional approach can influence through the formation of export-marketing cooperatives (Stiglitz 1989: 202), although governments have occasionally relied on compulsory membership to avoid free-rider problems. In the case of agricultural cooperatives, this problem arises from the preference of affiliations to allow others to invest funds at the time of the formation of the cooperative bodies without investing themselves (Giannakas et al. 2016: 372). Furthermore, their operating principle differs from that of consumer bodies, which can combine multiple market channels with those of the producers; this requires each participant to make a full managerial contribution (Sato 1989: 14–15). In the 1920, the Union of South Africa (South Africa) attempted to instigate such a cooperative movement, but failed to sustain it.

This study explains why agricultural cooperatives, alone, in a single country were historically not enough to ease the imbalance in the amount of available commercial information, but, in the case of a successful model, the cooperatives of different Commonwealth countries were once connected in a horizontal alliance. At that time, they were connected with one another not because they were part of the British Empire but due to the geographical proximity of the Southern Hemisphere. This chapter sheds light on this well-organised agricultural business aimed at adjusting the seasonality of fruits at the London market and shows that its linkage worked as an 'external informant' for individual producers in South Africa. In this country, the first steps toward centralised market control under their government dates back to the inter-war period, particularly at the time of enactment of the Marketing Act of 1937: however, before that, a spontaneous commercial conglomerate had already been formed among fruit farmers as their own information network.

The focus on the early 1920s, as shown in the next section, prompts the question of what shaped an information network that supported colonial fruit farmers amidst volatile agricultural pricing in the absence of centralised governmental control policies. Submarine cable technology between London and Cape Town emerged as the earliest key global vehicle for producers. However, if we simply approach this case as proof of the widespread hegemony of the British Empire, we overlook other aspects of agricultural history during the inter-war period. This section examines a colonial fruit business using cable communication and the multifaceted producers' cooperatives across Commonwealth countries.

1-2. Connected Cables and Connecting Information Networks

Information can be distributed in two ways: it can be broadcast all at once or dispatched from point to point. A communication vehicle suitable for the latter method, the submarine cable, had been developed since the mid-19th century mainly in the Atlantic Ocean, when United Kingdom (UK) telecommunication companies took the lead in laying cable all over the world in competition with France and partially in cooperation with the United States (US). Cable communication is superior in speed, coverage, reliability, cost and security. In the 1920s, due to innovative technology allowing signals to be relayed via different interchanges, cable technology was more sophisticated in its accuracy and speed than ever before, offering the availability of transmitting services over 24-hour periods, regardless of weather conditions. Therefore, cable communication has been utilised for military, diplomacy and even commercial purposes, such as railroads, shipping lines, and mail order, as well as mass communication (Headrick 1991: 4–5, 196–200).

Beginning in the late 19th century, a submarine cable was gradually constructed around the African continent, at times inefficiently, but then the scramble for Africa among European powers hindered the provision of enterprise by means of telegraph services. By 1886, with the exception of a blank area between Cape Town and Durban in South Africa, Africa's coastline had been surrounded by relatively short submarine cables provided by different companies, sometimes with two cables overlapping. At the southern tip of Africa, the long connection from Cape Town to Cape Verde across the Atlantic Ocean was completed in 1901, in addition to innumerable short coastline connections on the continent. In these circumstances, Cape Town enjoyed an exceptional geographical advantage since its long connection had only six interchanges before its terminus at Porthcurno in the UK (Headrick 1991: 61, 90). In particular, once the cable companies installed new automatic transmission technology that corrected corrupted signals, the speed and accuracy of long-distance telegraphy increased (Headrick 1991: 198). This promoted several excellent examples of the commercial use of cable communication during the 1920s, but agricultural business was not part of this movement.

Since the first case in New York in 1810, agricultural

cooperatives have developed, particularly among the fruit and dairy industries in the US, but hard data are scarce[2] (Federico 2008: 168). In South Africa, a turning point in cooperative policy came after the implementation of apartheid in response to criticism that the Cooperative Societies Act of 1922 restricted bodies to be subsidised to white farmers only (Coleman (ed.) 1983: 59; Giliomee 2009: 77–79; Ortman and King 2007: 24), which led to a revision of the meaning of 'cooperative' in the Cooperatives Act of 2005 (Ortman and King 2007: 25; RSA 2005: 2). The Act of 1922 recognised 81 bodies in 1922 and 377 over the next decade with more than 70,000 memberships with both limited and non-limited liability.[3] Historically, these bodies have fulfilled three types of functions: (1) the credit, purchase and sale of agricultural inputs and equipment, (2) the purchase, storage and subsequent sale of agricultural commodities, and (3) transport services (Abbott 1987: 234; Ortman and King 2007: 22).

As to (2) – the sales channels that the cooperatives made use of – the history of this movement makes little mention of the pre-Second World War period, except for the Marketing Act of 1937. The Act was designed to maintain domestic prices for agricultural commodities that were higher than those on the world market conditions for protection (Feinstein 2005: 141). The Department of Agriculture obtained a single channel on price and a monopoly to distribute agricultural commodities through 23 marketing boards, with the Inspection Committee specialised for market research. The boards were government-monitored bodies that fixed the price and acted as 'secondary cooperatives', purchasing products from cooperatives and markets, both locally and internationally (Tinley 1954: 36–39; Du Toit 1975; Jeeves and Crush 1997: 11; DTI 2012: 31). This section clarifies their marketing history in the 1920s through a core question: 'What approach to the informing network provided colonial fruit producers with knowledge of volatile global agricultural prices "before" the construction of the control-board system?'

Furthermore, more pertinent in relation to the specific question at hand, 'How did South African cooperatives face "global middlemen", such as fruit agencies in London, in the 1920s?' To investigate the South African approach to global knowledge of this nature, this chapter emphasises that they were much more than mere organisations but, rather, developed to become effectively a sequence of bodies connecting the London market, global agencies such as United Fruits and colonial fruit producers via submarine cable communication. Thereby, they even benefited from knowledge of North America, which demonstrates the extent to which the cooperatives were exposed to externalities (although among white businessmen's ties) to improve 'learning'. We will then focus on a unique federation of cooperatives in South Africa, New Zealand and Australia, the Overseas Farmers Federation of Co-operative & Co. (the Fed-Farms), in the early 1920s.

1-3. Methodology

This chapter highlights three historical materials because the Fed-Farms network did not simply trace the control-board idea of the British Empire, but was also part of the Commonwealth countries and other groups. According to the Cooperatives Act of 1922, the Fed-Farms was not an agricultural cooperative but a federation of cooperatives[4] as well as a kind of 'further global federation'. It included three branches of Commonwealth countries in the Southern Hemisphere, but simultaneously accepted an unignorable outsider, US businessmen, in the fruit trade. This linkage to 'externality' drove the fruit export industry of the Western Cape ahead, in addition to the Western Cape having advantageous geographical accessibility to London's deciduous fruits market compared to that of Australia and New Zealand. Analysis of their business history highlights the rich information that individual producers in the Western Cape obtain via this submarine cable network. Here, different types of materials pertaining to the Fed-Farms contributed to this outcome from three perspectives, as indicated below.

First, the National Archives of South Africa (Pretoria) preserves a considerable volume of records on the beginning of the Fed-Farms, from 1919–1923. They include a memorandum of the first meeting of the Fed-Farms together with accountant reports and the company history. The first section sheds light on how the three countries cooperated to construct their unique business network. Although this relationship was highly likely to be preferred by the British Empire, with regard to 'who supported who' under this global federation, more detailed consideration must be given in that cooperation among the three included a tense but accommodative relationship when working for South Africa as an 'external informant' in actuality.

Aside from the Fed-Farms' purpose, another issue should be considered: why South African farmers belonged to this federation. This brings us to another point: a mediator in South Africa, the Co-op Deciduous Fruits Exchange of South Africa Ltd. (the Exchange). The *Eric Rosenthal Collection* of the National Library of South Africa (Cape Town) includes information on this cooperative (and its successor, the Deciduous Fruits Board). Thus, the second section simultaneously explains why South Africa took part in the Fed-Farms from the domestic perspective.

Third, the Fruits Exchange printed their industrial newspaper, *The South African Fruit Grower (The SAFG),* from 1921. This monthly newspaper reported agricultural price trends like other newspapers, but it included a unique column called the 'Agent Report', which conveyed information about different price trends 'cabled' by different global fruits agencies in London. The final section explores the roles of the Fed-Farms in this cable communication with agencies who wrote the price information that would be summed up on the column of the Exchange. Thereby, this chapter explores how market knowledge accumulated on the information network of cable communication, providing fruit producers with rich sources of information.

2. Tracking Institution for Exported Fruits of South Africa

2-1. Developing the Fruits Market before the Second World War

During the inter-war period, UK trade dramatically transformed its long-standing free-trade policy into the intra-regional inward trade of the British Empire. Although the importance of discriminatory tariff protection remained low at this turning point, the vertical trade relationship between colonial markets and London was steadily strengthened, with Commonwealth countries in particular. Regarding the UK trade volume, it dominated 48 per cent of trade between 1938 and 1948. In particular, with respect to the agricultural trade, after the Ottawa Conference in 1934, an estimate indicated that the preferential margin on the UK imports from these countries rose from 3 per cent to 12 per cent in the period between 1929 and 1937 (Kindleberger 1989; Anderson and Norheim 1993: 92–95; Anderson 2014: 291–292).

The largest volume of fresh fruit from colonial and non-colonial countries in Europe and elsewhere (such as Argentina) was imported into the UK. The public consumed 128 million dollars' worth of fruits annually before the Second World War, and this figure doubled until 1947. The top trading partners were Mediterranean countries such as Italy and Palestine. During the inter-war period, new participants were included from regions surrounding the Atlantic Ocean: the US, Canada, Spain and the Canary Islands, France, the Netherlands, and South Africa. For pear and citrus fruit exports, the fruit industry in the south of the Western Cape was as competitive as that of the Netherlands, Italy and Palestine, taking advantage of the opposite supply calendar in London.[5]

Increasingly varied European species of peaches, pears, apricots, plums and other fruits had been planted in the south of the Western Cape since the 1870s as new immigrant farmers spread to rural Paarl, Groot Drankenstein and elsewhere. A rector, Rev. C. Leghe in Stellenbosch, sent the first fruit box to London in 1891 (Pickstone 1917: 290). In the 1919–1920 season, 20,000 tonnes of fresh fruits were produced, most of which were set aside for domestic markets and transported via the South African Railways, while the remaining one tenth of produce was exported via the Union Castle line.[6] The UK increasingly emerged as the largest consuming market together with a significant amount of domestic demand. Beside the UK, other consumers of South African fruits varied during the 1930s because London functioned as a hub market for re-export to continental Europe, including Switzerland, Germany, France and Belgium.

The fruits (later from other rural areas including Natal) came to be known as the 'Goldland' brand since the Exchange vigorously advertised single standardised brands throughout the 1920s.[7] While the total quantity shipped to the UK increased over the next decade, the percentage with London as the destination market decreased from 98 per cent to 76 per cent, and by contrast, continental Europe developed to become the second largest destination (see Table 1). The Department of Agriculture reported the long-distance shipment process in 1932 as 'individual fruit growers nominated their own overseas sales agents and *the most attention to the bilateral contract was paid under the co-ordination by the Fed-Farms*'. New market commodities 'were promised at London parity price: the prices realised on the London market for other shipments at the same time'.[8] But the report did not fully explain about the price-stabilising machinery for agricultural commodities, in particular, what motivated each farmer to advance to distant markets in a very short period in the early 1920s.

If their contracts were literally based on the fixed leading market price, information failure between London buyers and each exporter could be exacerbated in the absence of an effective vehicle to inform individual shippers of global price fluctuation. When introducing the Control Board in 1937, the Department of Agriculture criticised this contract method and faced deadlock regarding the failure to ensure 'adequate control and proper recording'. However, contrary to their criticisms, the report admitted that individual farmers had been exempted from their 'own' risks associated with shipping fruits to new markets, such as the individual efforts to seek ad hoc fruits agents through mail service.[9] In other words, these contracts via the Fed-Farms had such two-sided generalisation including a problem as a contract institution before 1929. Below, we will see how the Fed-Farms were designed for a system of contract co-ordination to minimise the time gap from shipping to the fruits being unpacked.

2-2. Promoting Fruits from the Southern Hemisphere, 1919–1922

The idea of the Fed-Farms was arguably discussed almost

Table 1. England and other markets of South Africa, 1929–1938

	England		Continental Europe		North America		South America		East and West Africa		Middle East and Eastern Asia	
	ton	%	ton	%	ton	%	ton	%	ton	%	ton	%
1929	39,014	98.0	9	0.02	0	0	541	1.36	212	0.53	17	0.04
1930	30,633	96.1	151	0.47	248	0.78	442	1.39	248	0.78	3	0.01
1931	40,895	99.1	3	0.01	0	0	205	0.50	124	0.30	22	0.05
1932	56,636	99.4	49	0.09	67	0.12	78	0.14	26	0.05	77	0.14
1933	69,164	95.6	1,227	1.70	0	0	113	0.16	272	0.38	334	0.46
1934	66,237	88.4	3,888	5.19	1	0.00	87	0.12	447	0.60	348	0.46
1935	85,694	86.1	5,866	5.89	0	0	42	0.04	1,103	1.11	968	0.97
1936	66,316	79.8	7,040	8.47	230	0.28	191	0.23	1,784	2.15	541	0.65
1937	82,360	83.6	6,593	6.69	1,128	1.15	79	0.08	1,299	1.32	462	0.47
1938	73,862	76.1	10,582	10.90	375	0.39	18	0.02	1,133	1.17	499	0.51

Source: Union of South Africa (1939: 24).

simultaneously in several countries, but an exploration of the situation in Australia and New Zealand lies beyond the scope of this chapter. In Johannesburg, in June 1919, F. W. Patten, who was later appointed as the secretary as well as the acting manager of the Fed-Farms South Africa, sent a letter to the Secretary for Agriculture, F. R. Smith of the Department of Agriculture, requesting a call for a cooperative conference.[10] In his letter, the cooperative business was introduced as not only an investee of agricultural finance, as the government intended, but also as a marketing institution, reporting that 'the birth of the Fed-Farms South Africa commenced *the era of research*'.[11] At Bloemfontein on 28 January 1919, the conference appointed a Western Cape fruits farmer, H. E. V. Pickstone, as a delegate for South Africa, because he was the advocate of the 'federal body' of entire cooperatives.[12] In London in June 1922, the first meeting of the Fed-Farms between two commonwealth countries was held, New Zealand (F. R. Bushell as delegate) and Australia (M. M. Ibott and P. A. Badcock), while H. E. V. Pickstone from South Africa sent a letter of greeting due to his absence. The conference agreed to extend the activities of the business to promoting products from the Southern Hemisphere and to seek means of horizontal cooperation among the three, particularly regarding partition of the expenditure for its settlement.

Pickstone and others were the first members to enter the Fed-Farms office on Fenchurch Street, London (the South African office was settled in Cape Town[13]), and they worked more actively than representatives from the other two countries in which 'no one knew what was going to happen'.[14] According to the accountant's report, these three countries paid the expense of the commencement from the earnings of each of them (the commission for dealing in wheat, dairy and fruit products transacted from their home countries). Their incomes were: Australia 32,393 pounds, New Zealand 7,195 pounds and South Africa 1,889 pounds for twenty-one months until June 1922, and on their balance, Australia 14, 281 pounds, New Zealand 3,170 pounds and South Africa 1,889 pounds. At that time, South Africa fortunately enjoyed an increase in London fruit prices, with peaches averaging 20 shillings per box, and grapes 30 shillings per ten-pound box but the boom broke over the two subsequent seasons (Standler 1983: 19). Thus, in the early years the Fed-Farms discussed the mutually dependent relationship with the other two countries. First, New Zealand bore the communication fee on behalf of Australia in the first half-term of 1921, when the latter made a large loss of as much as 2,257 pounds. During the next half-period, Australia recovered, with 2,160 pounds, and thereafter loaned funds to New Zealand when the latter lost 111 pounds on its business as a result. The turnover reached two million pounds over the twelve months of 1921, and three-quarters of their income came from Australia's earnings, thanks to the prosperity of the butter industry in particular.

After this complicated accounting process in the early days, to maintain fairness in initial expenditures, the Fed-Farms took both the profit and loss of each country into account and resolved that the stake should be divided, with half to Australia and the other half shared between New Zealand and South Africa at 25 per cent each. South Africa made a loss of 557 pounds in the latter half of 1920, a loss of 421 pounds in the early half of 1921 and a loss of 749 pounds in the latter half of 1921. H. E. V. Pickstone was almost excluded from the discussion by an executive member in London, but was in a position to bear the initial cost fairly, based on the datum line that the other two required.[15]

This background demonstrates the problematic management of the Commonwealth's cooperative body, particularly the difficulty with respect to the fair division of expenditure. In the two years after this system was initiated, the Fed-Farms were subdivided into several specialised sections for different agricultural commodities. Besides the executive members, they included departments for grain, fresh fruits, wine, coffee, dried and canned fruits, dairy and other commodities, including wool, with chief managers for each. The fresh fruits section included five producers' cooperatives and a distributive one from the three countries (the US fruits cooperative was later included), each of which had an office with a testing room.

The Fed-Farms management was above their national units and, moreover, the executives agreed on independence from London interests at the first conference. Rather, their tie was based on their own necessity; sometimes, the connection went beyond their initial purpose of 'promoting fresh fruits from the Southern Hemisphere'. The most remarkable instance was the joint trade with a Seattle company with the 'same objective' as the Fed-Farms. The executives endeavoured to strengthen their trade by lengthening their operating period, taking the different seasons of the US into account. Because the fruits section was open for only five or six months of the year in 1922, they stabilised their business across the whole year through joint trade.[16] Additionally, if the US companies raised the volume that the Fed-Farms handled, their committee estimated that they could save one shilling per case in their freight costs on shipping.

F. Capell, who started three farms with a single common exporting company, the Fruits Export Corporation of Seattle, was appointed the chief manager of the fruits section. The executives valued him, in that his company was in a position to get in touch swiftly with the key office of the distributing network; in other words, his mission was to build a distribution channel in London for green apples and dried and processed fruits.[17] The Fed-Farms' principal purpose was actually initiated by several minds, shaping a connection between colonial exporting countries and the UK. However, the efficiency of their openness contributes to the final point of this section: what the Fed-Farms 'cabled' to South Africa.

2-3. Collecting Machinery in South Africa

A fruits nursery manager, H. E. V. Pickstone, was appointed as a delegate for South Africa despite seeming to be an insignificant character among the Fed-Farms executives. This key farmer was introduced to the Fed-Farms via H. S. Jager, a general manager of the fruit market agent, T. J. Poupart in London, after the concept of utilising the seasonal gap was shared among the executives. Initially, Pickstone was a son of an English immigrant to the US after the civil war, a farmer from California and a technical manager at Rhodes Fruit Farms owned by Cecil Rhodes (Rotberg 1990: 639–640). Even after his retirement in 1921, he remained at a fruit nursery in Groot Drakenstein, Western Cape, until his death in 1931. He not only trained dozens of young American managers from California but also provided interested local fruit farmers with 'standard' knowledge about Californian fruits.[18]

In 1917, Pickstone's article, 'The Cape Fruits Industry', *Journal of the Royal African Society*, raised the issue of the developing export industry as the most attractive goal because of the absolute reversal of the fruit seasons between continental Europe and the US (Pickstone 1917: 293). At the same time as the Fed-Farms were launched, Pickstone organised a fruit exporting company, the Exchange, that included 14 regional growers' unions (of varied regional associations). H. S. Jager helped him through his other career as a fruit buyer in Constantia, Western Cape. The Exchange was itself designed to work as a 'federal body' of local producers' cooperatives as expressed later: 'our cooperative movement is a democratic one, one man, one vote, where our members retain freedom of thought, a most valuable asset, freedom of speech, entire absence of recrimination, and best of all, no graft'.[19]

However, it ultimately became neither a nationwide association nor representative of all regional organisations. His plan was intended to include local cooperatives of every kind of fruit under a single centralised distribution. On 19 April 1922, 100 producer delegates gathered for 'a citrus conference' at Johannesburg. Pickstone urged participants to bear 30,000 pounds maintenance cost for a space at London docks, arguing that the expenditure was worthwhile for shipping as much as 50,000 pounds of fruits in the future.[20] However, his proposal was refused, largely due to accusations that he had ignored the interests of the citrus industry in Transvaal. Those producers wondered why they were not allowed to use the nearest and most convenient ports for their regions. An interview in *The Rand Daily Mail* let him concede that 'the decision of the majority that it was inadvisable also to register a citrus exchange covering the whole of South Africa as it was considered that additional machinery created would in no way advance the interest of citrus growers and considerably would add to the expense'.[21] Thereafter, the Exchange grew dependent on citrus exports that they handled, yet Western Cape bodies separated themselves from the existing Exchange in the late 1920s.

On the other hand, the Fed-Farms began to commit to the Exchange (of Western Cape), as *The SAFG*, the Exchange's newspaper, advertised them as multinational cooperative bodies in January 1923. In addition to the Exchange, the fruits section of the Fed-Farms included the New Zealand Cooperative Fruits Companies, the Port Huon (Australian) Cooperative Fruits Growing Companies, Tasmanian Orchardists Cooperative Companies and the American Fruits Cooperative Companies.[22] Of these, South African fruit shipments dominated what the Fed-Farms dealt with, with the exception of Australian apples. Australia and New Zealand had much longer shipments time involving the challenges associated with mixing hard fruits (apples and citrus fruits) and soft fruits (pears, peaches and plums).[23] On the other hand, the Western Cape was fortunate in being closer to London than the others when transporting perishable fruits, similar to Mediterranean perishable products.

The green fruits section at the London office collected extensive information regarding the amount and price of fruits from every local market in the UK. They contacted South African agents hourly via telephone and telegram to ascertain which markets were over-supplied or short of stock as well as those ports with heavy arrivals near at hand. This communication was followed by a succeeding procedure on inbound cargoes: when they arrived in London from Southampton by railway, fruits were examined immediately with the objective of determining whether their condition rendered them suitable for travel, often resulting in last-minute alterations. The office then followed up each market as to price and final result and, ultimately, the account sales, and reported to the various shippers. Theoretically, this could cause them to allocate consignments to the most suitable destinations.

3. Inventory Control by Farmers

3-1. State Control or Information Network

In the period following 1920, export to the UK rose temporarily by 200,000 boxes, reaching six times the usual amount in 1925, but thereafter gradually decreased until 1927. Meanwhile, the average price per box of deciduous fruits fluctuated in the first half-decade of the 1920s before converging on almost 4.9 pounds (1.0 US dollar) in the latter half (see Figure 1). This meant that the South African fruit industry developed in the UK market, but underwent extreme instability immediately after the First World War. Until 1932 when white farmers increasingly benefited from agricultural subsidy after the gold devaluation of their currency, both politicians and bureaucrats have scarcely recognized the need for direct regulating policy on the price stabilization and marketing (Jeeves and Crush 1997:10). In other words, exports of deciduous fruits were in far more dire straits than the optimistic outlook that their government had portrayed since the early 1930s.

Nonetheless, the Department of Agriculture looked back on this industry prior to introducing the control board in 1937, criticising its existing market administration. The report in 1934 criticised fruit growers' inability to comprehend the actual cost of export to European countries other than to the UK because of the absence of 'proper control'.[24] P. Viljoen, the Secretary for Agriculture asserted that,

> if these powers (marketing, the regulation of supplies according to requirements and uniformity in the products) are to be given to the (control) boards, we will definitely change our present system of marketing agricultural products. There would be a complete changeover and free competition as regards the wholesale selling of the products would be practically removed (Richard 1932: 477).

However, the control board's plans to administer a large proportion of these individual deals were not revealed to those with related interests, and the South African Federated Chamber of Industry was particularly bewildered (Richard 1932: 477).[25] Some were afraid that the newly established control board would impair the function of existing farmers' marketing machineries among cooperatives. At the very least, the Bill for the introduction of the control board, since the early 1930s, was disputed with respect to whether the marketing machinery should be entirely managed by

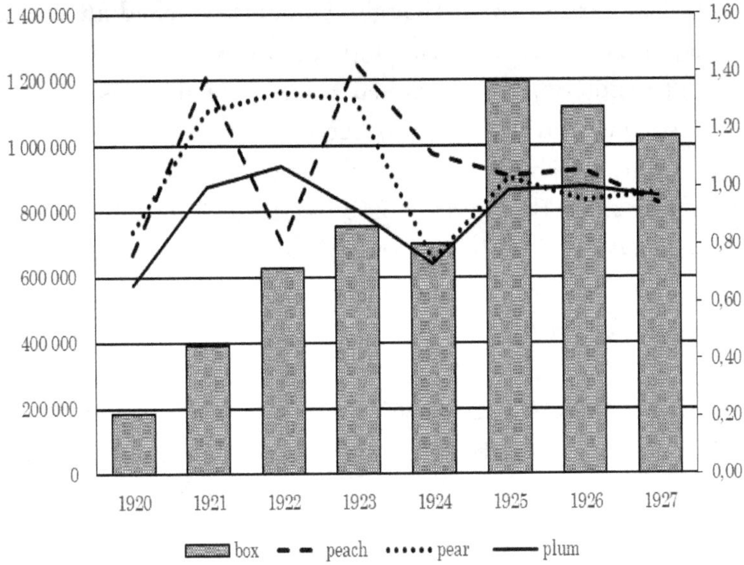

Figure 1. Exports to the UK: quantity (box) and average price per box (US dollars)

Source: Edited by the author from the Bureau of Foreign and Domestic Commerce, US Department of Commerce (1925: 470, 1928: 106).

the state.[26]

Contrary to the Department of Agriculture's criticisms, the cargo collection system had already been organised among cooperatives in the early 1920s. The development of long-distance transportation of fresh fruits between Cape Town and London prompted building infrastructure, including refrigeration facilities at the Table Bay Dock, and information networks utilising submarine cables for farmers. Meanwhile, problems arose in relation to regulating large amounts of cargo collected from every hinterland, and the Exchange improved these chaotic logistics that resulted from explosive increases in forwarding. For example, *The SAFG* notified all the senders of best practice in unifying packed boxes, sometimes introducing complements of fruits dealers (buyers) who opened boxes at London. Therefore, the Western Cape Exchange assumed the role of informing farmers of how every fresh commodity was dealt with at its actual destination.

The Fed-Farms, the Exchange's counterpart, cited an article on 20 May 1923 declaring that shipping from Cape Town was in excellent condition. The unnamed correspondent foresaw that this variety of qualified fruits would become commonplace in London in the future, which would affect the prices of 'home-grown' (UK) fruits. Thereafter, the number of boxes landed in each port had to be controlled based on regular returns of information.

The Fed-Farms expressed their unloading process as follows in a column of *The SAFG*:

> *Kenilworth Castle* landed 2,863 boxes of P[p]eaches and 84 boxes of N[n]ectarines, but both these items are now finishing. Plums are also finishing, the only one on the market now being Kelseys (a species of plum), the quantity brought by this boat being 3,781 boxes, while grapes amounted to 19,929 boxes and pears 31,303 boxes both being in excellent condition.

In this article, unlike the other regular 'agents' (mentioned later) who wrote for *The SAFG*, the Fed-Farms attached the condition about the other exhibitors, Australia and the US together. To take the example of raisins,

> The market and its features are unchanged. Little small business is being done but at low price. Practically all the South African (cargoes) are now clear. … Australian Sultanas (a species of plum): we have not heard of any business being done so far for new crop, but there have been offers at 88/0 CIF (price).[27]

This article embodied the Fed-Farms' horizontal perspective on exhibitors from different countries, informing the quantity of boxes, nominal price and CIF price (the price including the freight cost and insurance covered by sellers), although the mention of the CIF price was only to be partially noted.

3-2. Cabled from London, 1922

The perishable fruit season of the Western Cape is concentrated in the Southern Hemisphere's summer between December and

April. As much as 11,256 tons of fresh or processed fruits were sent to London between 1920 and 1922 (Standler 1983: 19). Cases of peaches, pears, plums and nectarines departed one after another with a slight difference in harvest seasons. In total, the shipping season lasted for more than six months (see Figure 2; when including citrus fruits exported after these products, the Table Bay Dock of Cape Town ingeniously succeeded in killing their offseason). The Union Castle line transported them on the regular service to Southampton, in the UK in almost three weeks. This city, which had been developed as a main hub for both the UK and continental Europe since the First World War, collected 70 per cent of imported goods from South Africa and received 500 million boxes of fruit a year by 1934 (Hyshlop 2017: 7).[28] When these cargoes started to be transported by rail to London, the Fed-Farms office began to deliberate different local fruit markets.

Thereafter, in South Africa, the 'Agent Report' in *The SAFG* consisted of relatively short sentences cabled from the regular five 'agent' companies: Gerald da Costa, G. E. Hudson, J. & H. Goodwin, T. J. Poupart and United Fruits. The general managers of these agents cabled these reports from London or another branch in Johannesburg. The articles conveyed information about the ship's name, date of unloading, each species of fruits and the minimum and maximum prices. They regularly informed readers of the interim report on the progress of their auction sales in London, but the reports themselves did not post the number of concluded contracts. However, the 'Agent Report' of *The SAFG* summarised the date of arrival, the variety of asking prices (the price each agent presented to London buyers) as a whole and the inventory clearance of cold storage on the ships, allowing individual senders to estimate how long it took from loading to unloading.

In Figure 3, the line shows the number of peach cases loaded at Cape Town, and the bar indicates the number of agents who offered the asking price in the 1923 season (which opened in November 1922 and closed in May 1923). It is clear that the busier season did not always attract more foreign agents to South African commodities. Surprisingly, some reports noted the arrival of ships but lacked the description by agents, which meant some cargoes

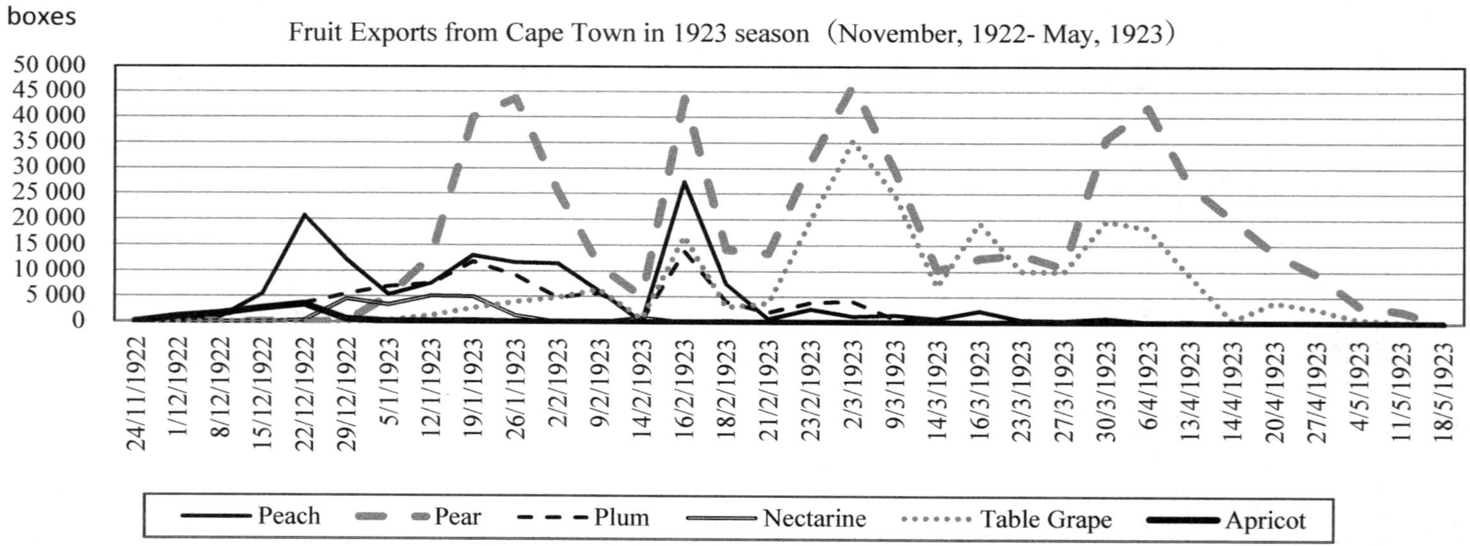

Figure 2. The number of boxes and the seasonal gap of Western Cape fruits, 1922–1923

Source: Compiled by the author from the 'Agent Report' in The SAFG, Vol. 10, January 1923, pp. 27–28; February 1923, pp. 58–60; March 1923, pp. 94–96; April 1923, pp. 130–132; May 1923, pp. 171–172.

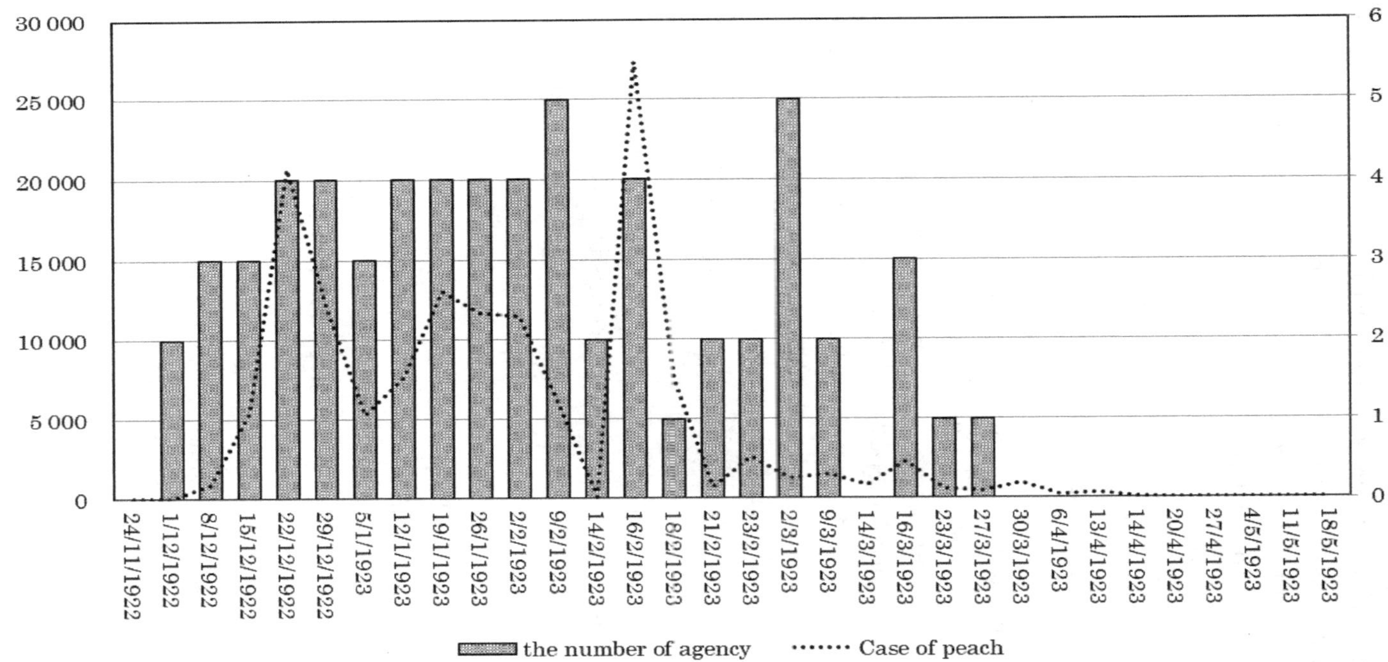

Figure 3. The numbers of exported peach boxes and the agents in charge, 1923 season

Source: Compiled by the author from the 'Agent Report' in The SAFG, Vol. 10, January 1923, pp. 27–28; February1923, pp. 58–60; March 1923, pp. 94–96; April 1923, pp. 130–132; May 1923, pp. 171–172.

missed any intermediation with buyers: on 30 March 1922, the *Edinburgh Castle* carried 939 boxes, but *The SAFG* subsequently report no tracking, and 2,393 boxes on four ships of 31 in total became untraceable. In this way, the trial run in the 1923 season experienced confusion because of a dramatic and unprecedented increase in exports. A disadvantage to the fresh fruits export industry was that refrigeration ships travelling to Southampton were loaded beyond their capacity due to the absence of good cold-storage systems at the dock (Siegfield 1983: 19).

3-3. What Did the Fed-Farms Report?

The 'Agent Report' regularly used fixed phrasing in *The SAFG* during the entire deciduous fruits season in 1923; for example, 'J. & H. Goodwin, Ltd. Cape Town, 3/1/23 (3 January 1923): cable advice received recently from our London Branch states that our *Briton* shipment arrived in good condition. And the price rulings at time of cabling were: peaches 10/0 (ten shilling per box) to 18/0, apricots 4/0 to 6/0, plums 10/0, plums Santa Rosa, (a species of plum) 6/0 to 10/0, Methley (a species of plum) 3/0 to 6/0'.[29] The five agents wrote columns based on telegraphs from London on every regular service of the Union Castle, and then the Exchange summarised this in a monthly report. For this reason, the cabled sentences became increasingly refined, consisting of relatively short sentences, as compared to previous messages. When giving an overview of several companies, all reports wrote an asking price at London in common, but some companies reported the grading or further sorting for local or continental European markets while others did not. Readers of *The SAFG* could differentiate each asking price on a single cargo through fixed short phrases and, thereby, this information gave shippers (fruits producers) the greater advantage.

The five graphs below indicate which agents offered, and how much they set on packs of shipped peaches during the first business season. The horizontal axis indicates the date every ship left Cape Town and the vertical bar shows the range between the minimum and maximum asking price. The highest season recorded 27,333 boxes of peaches brought by the *Arundale Castle,* on 16 February

1923; it received offers from four agents, with the exception of United Fruits. Of these, Gerald da Costa and T. J. Poupart offered 3.5 shillings per box at minimum, while J. & H. Goodwin and G. E. Hudson offered 0.5 shillings more per box. In terms of the maximum price, G. E. Hudson and T. J. Poupart offered 5.0 shillings per box while Gerald da Costa and J. & H. Goodwin offered 0.5 shillings more per box (see Figure 4, 5, 6, 7 and 8 on a given same date).

Additionally, in the 'Agent Report', columns by Fed-Farms began to appear from 20 March 1923. F. Capell, the manager of the fruits section, attached the nominal price for apricots, peaches, and pears alongside the grading information, such as 'Choice', 'Standard' and 'Second' at the end of cabling. The grading words 'Fancy (Extra Choice)', 'Choice', 'Standard', 'Second', and 'Pie', respectively, meant the highest quality, the second highest, standard, the second lowest and the lowest. This terminology was originally shared between the US fruits agents and London buyers in a system of 'forward contract', which cabled the prices of different graded fruits to shippers, enabling them to determine whether to forward them across the Atlantic Ocean.[30]

Besides this unique usage of forwarding phrases, the Fed-Farms' column conveyed more detailed information than others, 'Spot business is very quiet with quotation of peeled Extra Choice Californian (a species of peach) @ 65/0 (shilling), and America offering large quantities of the same grade @ 44/0 per cwt (hundredweight equivalent to almost 50 kg). CIF (price) for prompt shipment'. The cable from its writer, F. Capell, clearly informed the tone of the market by introducing terminology in relation to the Atlantic Ocean, contributing to the autonomous decision making of South African fruit producers.

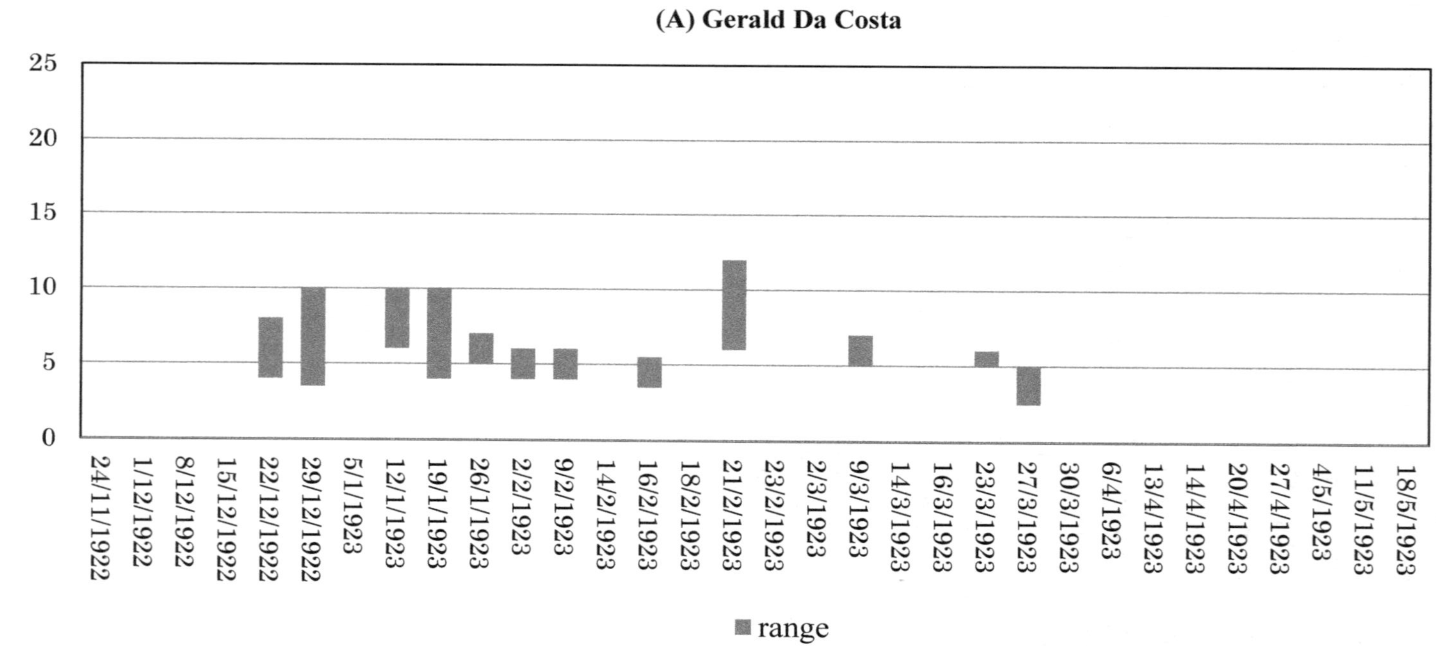

Figure 4. The range between minimum and maximum asking prices offered for peaches by Gerald da Costa, 1923 season
Source: Compiled by the author from each column of Gerald da Costa in the 'Agent Report' in The SAFG, Vol. 10, January 1923, p. 27; February 1923, p. 59; March 1923, p. 95; April 1923, p. 132; May 1923, p. 171.

(B) J. & H. Goodwin

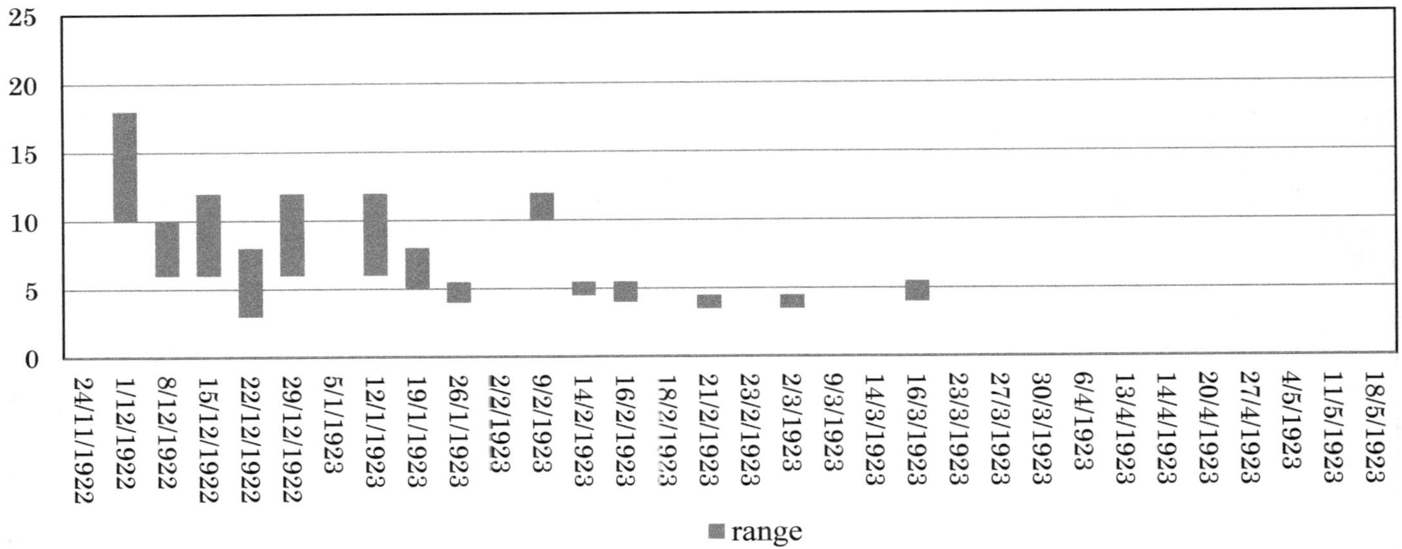

Figure 5. The range between minimum and maximum asking prices offered on peaches by J. & H. Goodwin, 1923 season

Source: Compiled by the author from each column of J. & H. Goodwin in the 'Agent Report' in The SAFG, Vol. 10, January 1923, p. 27; February 1923, p. 58; March 1923, p. 94; April 1923, p. 130; May 1923, p. 171.

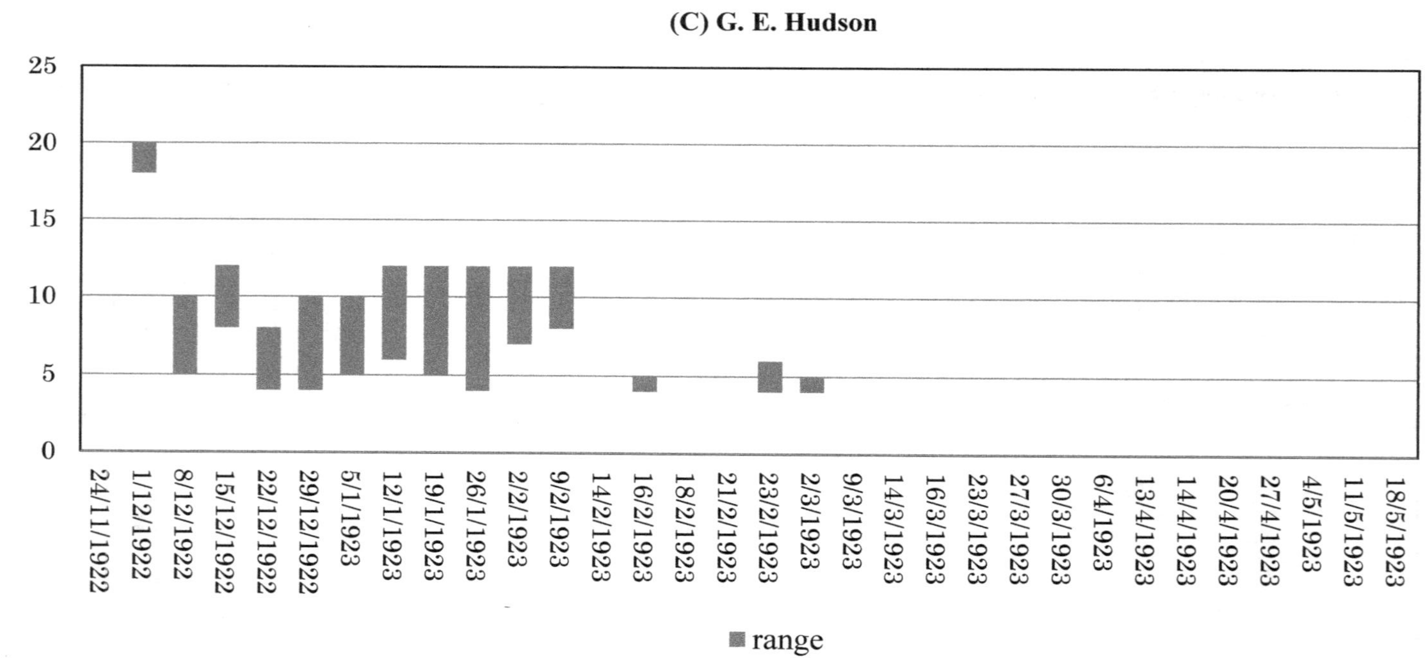

Figure 6. The range between minimum and maximum asking prices offered on peaches by G. E. Hudson, 1923 season

Source: Compiled by the author from each column of GE Hudson in the 'Agent Report' in The SAFG, Vol. 10, January 1923, p. 28; February 1923, p. 59; March 1923, p. 95; April 1923, p. 130; May 1923, p. 171.

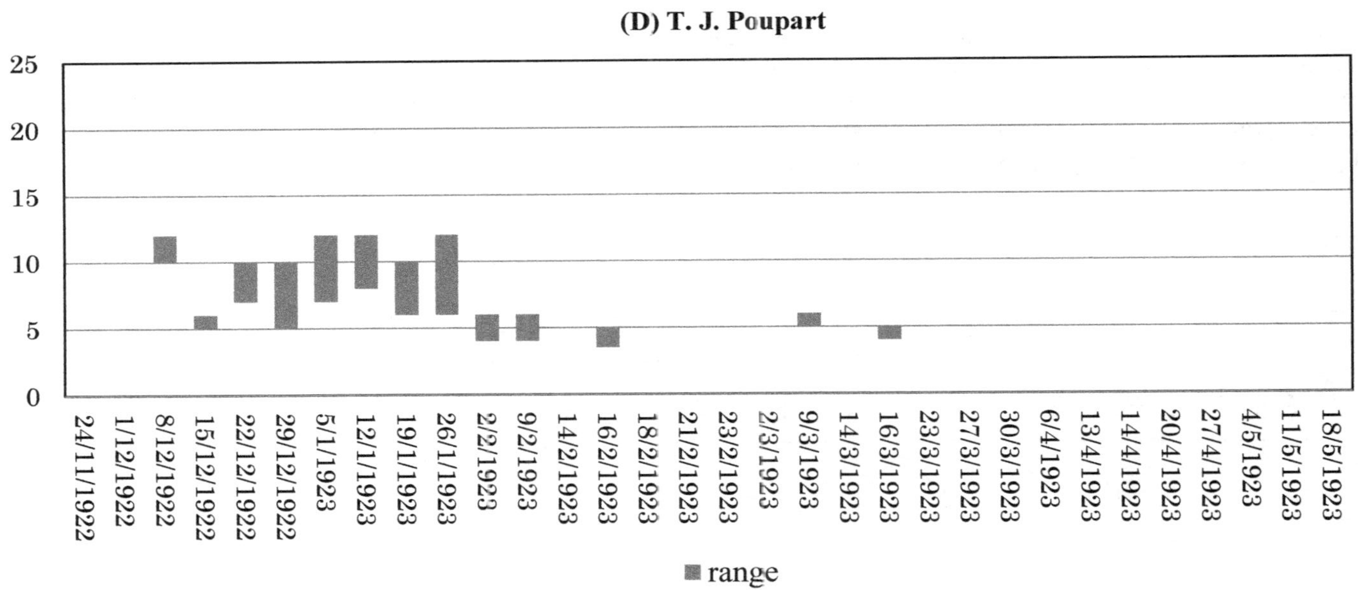

Figure 7. The range between minimum and maximum asking prices offered on peaches by T. J. Poupart, 1923 season

Source: Compiled by the author from each column of T. J. Poupart in the 'Agent Report' in The SAFG, Vol. 10, January 1923, p. 28; February 1923, pp. 58–59; March 1923, p. 94; April 1923, p. 131; May 1923, p. 171.

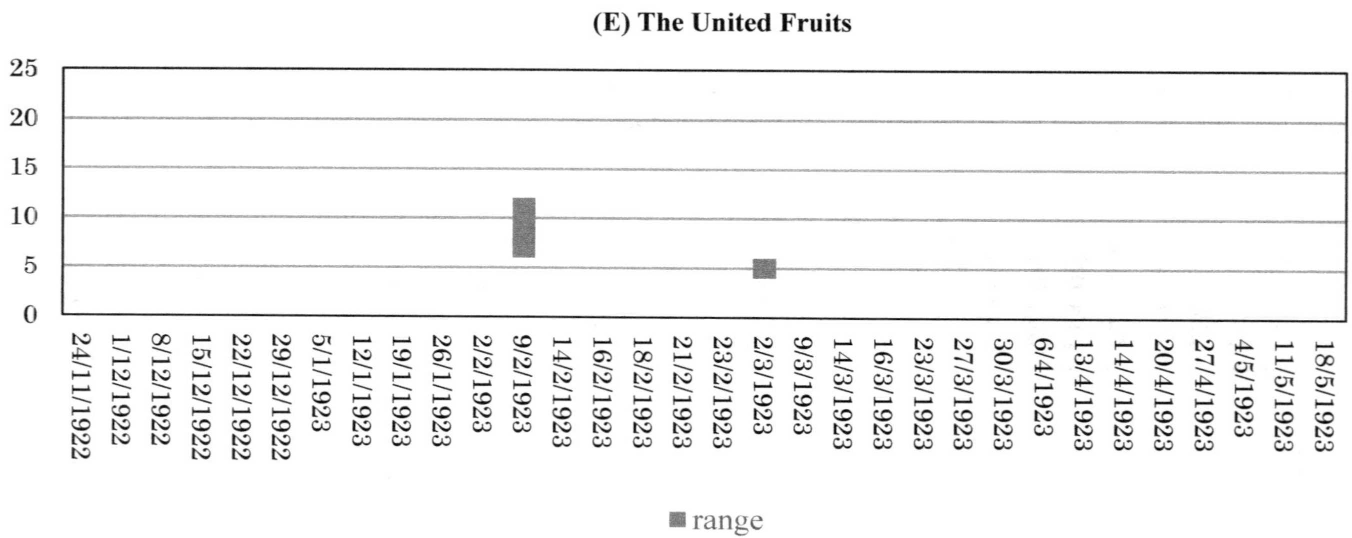

Figure 8. The range between minimum and maximum asking prices offered on peaches by The United Fruits, 1923 season
Source: Compiled by the author from each column of The United Fruits in the 'Agent Report' in The SAFG, Vol. 10, January to May 1923. The United Fruits adopted a unique format for its column as well as the Fed-Farms in that they did not mention which shipment was valued at London and which at further local markets, which affected negativity on this graph despite the fact that they actually wrote numerous columns on 'average price' alongside other agencies. Rather, the richest price information was shown in terms of citrus exports, which this agent continuously dedicated itself to through the 1930s.

4. Conclusion

In many African countries in the inter-war period, exports of agricultural commodities were an important way to earn sterling. For this purpose, local governments strengthened the monopolised market channel for African agricultural products, but on the other hand competitive products such as fruits were delivered for the UK and the Continental market by the active handling of private companies. The example of South Africa shows early participation in the mass consumer market at London before the Second World War, but the same development is being followed by African entrepreneurs in the 21st century, mainly because of advance in transport and communication technologies. In the context of 'African Potentials', the business history of indigenous white farmers sheds light on the critical understanding of the story of the hegemonic global vehicle, the submarine cable, i.e., knowledge of how they 'utilised' the technology of communication. Based on these successful examples, similar evaluations may apply to current African agricultural entrepreneurs, who have raised large earnings through contract farming for commercial companies in developed countries.

Looking back to 1929, just before its absorption into the Deciduous Fruits Board, the Western Cape Exchange had regular meetings to review their marketing scheme in South Africa. Once the issue in question had gone through the initial plan of promoting South African fruits on the London market, they began to adjust the grading standards for the domestic market. Fruits salesmen and dealers complained that they were able to collect only fruits that failed to satisfy the export criteria, implying that this industry had begun to be led by an export initiative.

In the Western Cape, the information network among farmers allowed them to advance into the European market as a top priority, followed by enrichment of their own domestic distribution. A participant in the Exchange, Molteno, a major apple farmer at Elgin, gave testimony as a member of the Grading Committee of Cape Town, saying that grading had become stricter every year since the distribution network in overseas markets had grown sophisticated.[31]

The meeting began to examine introducing an existing forward trade into domestic deals. In that plan, a 'market master' would be appointed from an exclusive agent of the Exchange, and he would supervise mail-order business between individual farmers.[32] Ultimately, this concept was never put into practice due to criticism by the Secretary for Agriculture that the industry lacked 'an appropriate control' over business between individual farmers and dealers.[33]

From the perspective of the South African fruits industry, what formed this information network before the construction of the single channel by the Department of Agriculture? The composition of Fed-Farms revealed that the interests of the three Commonwealth countries were shared in a form of conglomerate agricultural business after the end of the First World War. Furthermore, it did not exclude external interests such as F. Capell from the US. Rather, in light of the limited numbers of seasonal fruits from the north and south, their difference appeared to represent an opportunity to prolong their operation by minimising the cost of regular services on days when their cargoes were increased. In response to this expectation, Capell, an externality for the Fed-Farms, brought the conglomerate interests of the Southern Hemisphere to the existing terminology in cable communication for the fruits trade, upon which no other agent companies had ever relied in the 1920s.[34]

On the other hand, in the Western Cape, one point of this cable communication, the Exchange, drew local fruit producers and London agencies together in two respects. First, it joined the Fed-Farms, despite the fact that it did not represent any kind of national interest, as Pickstone had initially intended. A plan to make a single channel for the domestic market in the 1920s stirred competition between one that connected Table Bay Dock to London and the other that did not. Second, if it were not for the aggregator of frequent telegraphs from agents (the monthly 'Agent Report' in *The SAFG*), even the detailed cable communications from the Fed-Farms would be incomprehensible in the absence of translated knowledge on the potent global grading system in London. The information network in the form of point-to-point communication itself was never meant to be 'an appropriate control', as Viljoen, the Secretary of Agriculture invoked in arguing for the introduction of the control board in 1932. The export of 'colonial' products from south to north revealed the emergence of a system of inter-regional connectivity that could not be shaped and directed to a centralised national interest while its usage in the deciduous fruits trade could be grafted to 'a kind of federation of federations' during a period of global cooperative movement.

Endnotes

[1] They warn that the imperfection of information inhibits the late developing country from learning because spillover of technology is less than perfect. While the developed countries can limit dispensing of knowledge to late developing countries, the latter can be trapped by low-level equilibria that they may find status quo the optimal choice. (Stiglitz 1989: 198)

[2] According to Federico, the first cooperative in the U.S. was the sale body in New York while the first European one appeared from Norway in 1856. The first purchasing cooperative was organized in Switzerland in 1865, and the first rural credit body in Germany the 1850s. But the precise dating about these bodies is difficult because of 'somewhat pointless' (Federico 2008: 303). In South Africa in the 1880s, the credit body emerged in several districts for supporting wine and wheat farmers (Giliomee 2009: 69-79).

[3] Union of South Africa (1934) pp. 133–134.

[4] Union of South Africa (1934) p.137.

[5] *Fruits Trade World Directory 1947*, pp. 22, 24 and 31.

[6] Union of South Africa (1920) p. 584.

[7] Bureau of Foreign and Domestic Commerce, US Department of Commerce (1925) p. 470.

[8] Union of South Africa (1934) p. 440.

[9] Union of South Africa (1934) p. 441.

[10] *CD126/1*, 19 June 1919, 'Patten to Secretary'.

[11] *CD126/1*, 19 June 1919, 'co-operative marketing', p.1.

[12] *Eric Rosenthal Collection MSB 989* (3), 1920–1921, 'On Fed-Farms'.

[13] *KAB MOOC/6/9/5583*

[14] *CD126/1*, 24 August 1922 'report', pp. 150–151.

[15] *CD126/1*, 14 June 1922 'report', pp.14–17.

[16] *CD126/1*, 18 July 1922 'report', p.128.

[17] *CD126/1*, 18 July 1922 'report', p.131.

[18] Soon after arrival, Pickstone introduced a copy of a textbook, Wickson, E. J. (1889), *The Californian Fruits and How to Grow Them* (San Francisco: Dewey and Co., first edition), to a fruits jam maker in Wellington, a small town of Western Cape (Pickstone 1917: 290).

[19] *Eric Rosenthal Collection MSB 989* Vol. 4 'Record of a Life', pp. 9–10.

[20] *The Rand Daily Mail*, 20 April 1922.

[21] *The Rand Daily Mail*, 20 January 1922.

[22] *The SAFG*, July 1923, Vol. 10, p. 203.

[23] *CD126/1*, 'How it Operated'.

[24] Union of South Africa (1934) p. 261.

[25] Richard (1932: 477), in note 19, cited evidence from the S. A. Federated Chamber of Industries, 'No comment are offered upon the principle of the Bill, nor upon any of the directly governing the operation of that principle as affecting the regulation and marketing of agricultural products'.

[26] An economist C. S. Richard of Witwatersrand University was in agreement with this deliberation, raising four demerits on the idea of Agricultural Secretary Viljoen, saying that the Bill will promote neither (1) the interest of the country as a whole, nor (2) the ultimate interest of the producers, (3) the interests of consumers, as well as (4) existing wholesalers. He was also afraid, 'if the board fail, no machinery whatever will exist to market, [and] the farmer's [producer's] existing machineries will have been destroyed' (Richard 1932: 488–489).

[27] *The SAFG*, Vol. 10, May 1923, p. 172.

[28] Since the First World War, Southampton played the role of major port to handle imported food and war-related passengers on the Union Castle line. Also, the port was used for embarking British troops going to France, which advanced the city's key position for logistics all the more (Hyshlop 2017: 13–14).

[29] *The SAFG*, Vol. 10, January 1923, p. 27.

[30] Tanaka, H. (1926), p. 23.

[31] *Eric Rosenthal Collection MSB 989*, Vol. 4, No. 6, 21 August 1929, 'Deciduous Fruits Exchange Minutes'.

[32] *Eric Rosenthal Collection MSB 989*, Vol. 4, No. 6, 21 August 1929, 'Deciduous Fruits Exchange Minutes'.

[33] Union of South Africa (1934) p. 440.

[34] Though the same terminology can be seen in a column written by the United Fruits in 1930s, the author couldn't depict its exceptional character in the five global agents the Exchange intermediated because it mainly handled the different kinds of fruit from the area other than Western Cape.

Acknowledgements

This work was supported by JSPS KAKENHI Grant Number JP16H06318 and JP18H05693.

References

Abbott, J. C. (1987) *Agricultural Marketing Enterprises for the Developing World: With Case Studies of Indigenous Private, Transactional Cooperative and Parastatal Enterprise, CUP Archive Working Paper Series*, Cambridge: Cambridge University Press.

Anderson, K. (2014) 'Globalization and agricultural trade', *Australian Economic History Review*, Vol. 54, Issue 3, pp. 285–306.

Anderson, K. and Norheim, H. (1993) 'From imperial to regional trade preference: Its effect on Europe's intra- and extra-regional trade', *Weltwirtschaftliches*, Vol. 129, No. 1, pp. 78–102.

Bureau of Foreign and Domestic Commerce, US Department of Commerce (1925) *The Commerce Report*, Vol. 2, No. 21, Washington DC: US Department of Commerce.

——— (1928) *The Commerce Report*, Vol. 4, No. 41, Washington DC: US Department of Commerce.

Coleman, F. L. (ed.) (1983) *Economic History of South Africa*, Pretoria: HAUM.

DTI (The Department of Trade and Industry, Republic of South Africa) (2012) *Integrated Strategy on the Development and Promotion of*

Co-Operatives: Promoting an Integrated Co-operative Sector in South Africa, 2012–2022 (http://www.thedti.gov.za/economic_empowerment/docs/coops/legis_policy/Integrated_Strategy.pdf)(accessed: 15 December 2019).

Du Toit, C. M. (1975) 'Agricultural marketing management under the South African control board system', *Agrekon*, Vol. 14, No. 2, pp. 14–19.

Federico, G. (2008) *Feeding the World: An Economic History of Agriculture*, Princeton: Princeton University Press.

Feinstein, C. H. (2005) *An Economic History of South Africa: Conquest, Distribution and Development*, Cambridge: Cambridge University Press.

Giannakas, K., Fulton, M. and Sesmero, J. (2016) 'Horizon and free-rider problems in cooperative organizations', *Journal of Agricultural and Resource Economics*, Vol. 41, No. 3, pp. 372–392.

Giliomee, H. (2009) 'Aspects of the rise of Afrikaner capital and Afrikaner nationalism in the Western Cape, 1987–1915', in W. G. James and M. Simons (eds) *Class, Caste and Color: A Social and Economic History of South African Western Cape*, Cape Town: David Phillips, pp. 63–79.

Greenwald, B. and Stiglitz, J. E. (2014) 'Industrial policies, the creation of a learnin society, and economic development', in J. E. Stiglitz and J. Y. Lin (eds) *The Industrial Policy Revolution 1: The Role of Government beyond Ideology*, London: Palgrave Macmillan, pp. 43–71.

Headrick, D. R. (1991) *The Invisible Weapon: Telecommunication and International Politics, 1851–1945*, New York: Oxford University Press.

Hyshlop, J. (2017) 'Southampton to Durban on the Union Castle line: An imperial shipping company and the limits of globality c. 1900–1939', *Journal of Transport History*, Vol. 38, No. 2, pp. 1–24.

Jeeves, A. and Crush, J. (1997) *White Farms, Black Labour: The State and Agricultural Change in Southern Africa, 1910–1950*, Pietermaritzburg: Natal University Press.

Kindleberger, C.P. (1989) 'Commercial Policy between the Wars', in P. Mathaias and S. Pollard (eds) *The Cambridge Economic History of Europe*, Vol. 8, Cambridge: Cambridge University Press, pp. 161–

196.

Mittal, S. and Mehar, M. (2013) *Agricultural Information Networks, Information Needs and Risk Management Strategies Survey of Farmers in Indo-Gangetic Plains of India, Socioeconomics Working Paper 10*, El Batán: International Maize and Wheat Improvement Center.

Ortman, G. F. and King, R. P. (2007) 'Agricultural cooperatives: History, theory and problem', *Agrekon*, Vol. 46. No. 1, pp. 18–46.

Pickstone, H. E. V. (1917) 'The Cape fruits industry', *The Journal of the Royal African Society*, Vol. 16, No. 64, pp. 287–296.

Richard, C. S. (1932) 'The "new despotism" in agriculture: Some reflection on the marketing bill', *South African Journal of Economics*, Vol. 4, No. 4, pp. 469–504.

Rotberg, R. I. (1990) *The Founder: Cecil Rhodes and the Pursuit of Power*, Oxford: Oxford University Press.

RSA (Republic of South Africa) (2005) *Cooperatives Act No.14 of 2005, Republic of South Africa Government Gazette*, 2005, Vol. 482, Pretoria: Republic of South Africa.

Sato, M. (1989) *An Introduction of African Agricultural Cooperatives*, Tokyo: Nihon Keizai Hyoronsha (in Japanese).

Siegfield, S., (1983) *Tree of Life: The Story of Cape Fruits*, Cape Town: Saayman and Weber.

Standler, S. (1983) *Tree of Life: The Story of Cape Fruits*, Cape Town: Saayman &Weber (Pty) Ltd.

Stiglitz, J. E. (1989) 'Market, market failures, and development', *The American Economic Review*, Vol. 79, No. 2, pp. 197–203.

Streeten, P. (2016) *What Price Food?: Agricultural Policies in Developing Countries*, Cham: Springer.

Tanaka, H. (1926) *Fruits and Fruits Trade by Ford Fairford,* unpublished report, Tokyo: Toyo Seikan Co. Ltd.

Tinley, J. M. (1954) *South African Food and Agriculture in World WarII*, Stanford: Food Research Institute of Stanford University.

Union of South Africa (1920) 'Western province fruits crop', *Journal of Department of Agriculture, Union of South Africa*, Vol. January, p. 584.

——— (1934) *Report of the Commission to Inquire into Co-Operation and Agricultural Credit*, Cape Town: U.G. 16/34.

——— (1939) *Fruits Investigation Report No. 2: An Economic Survey of Certain Aspects of the Deciduous Fruits Industry in the Western Cape Province, 1937–1938, G.P.S.5314*, Pretoria: Department of Agriculture and Forestry, Union of South Africa.

Primary Sources

Eric Rosenthal Collection MSB 989, South Africa National Library, Cape Town.

Estate Paper of Pickstone, H.E.V. (KAB MOOC/6/9/5583), National Archives of South Africa, Cape Town.

Rhodes Fruits Farm Collection BC 1580, Special Collections Library, University of Cape Town.

Overseas Farmers Co-Operative Federations and Other Reports. 1922-1946 CD126/1, National Archives of South Africa, Pretoria.

Other Printed Materials

Fruits Trade World Directory: Year Book and Directory of the World's Fruits Trade, 1947–1948.

The Rand Daily Mail, 1921–1923.

The SAFG (The South African Fruits Growers), 1923–1924.

Chapter 6

Export-Led Industrialisation from Within: The Role of Mauritian Sugar Planters and Multi-Ethnic and International Collaboration

Kazuyo Ideue

1. Introduction: Beyond the Myth of FDI-Led Mauritian Industrialisation[1]

Mauritius is one of the few high-income countries in sub-Saharan Africa after the Seychelles, with a gross national income (GNI) per capita in 2019 of $12,900 in current United States (US) dollars. This is around eight times the average (1,555 US dollars) for sub-Saharan Africa. Furthermore, Mauritius has achieved high levels of human development. The Human Development Index (HDI) of the country in 2019 was 0.804, up from 0.62 in 1990. Mauritius has the highest HDI in sub-Saharan Africa. The country is also unique in the African context in that it regularly holds multiparty elections followed by peaceful democratic transitions (Tang et al. (eds) 2019). Mauritius stands out in Africa for its lively civic culture and relative social harmony (Bräutigam 1999).

The Mauritian experience has long attracted considerable attention from researchers due to its unique characteristics. However, in many ways the initial trajectory of political and economic development in Mauritius was not unusual in the African context (Bräutigam 1999: 154). For example, Mauritius was a typical primary commodity export-dependent country. Prior to industrialisation, in the 1960s, 90 per cent of Mauritian exports were sugar and sugar-related products. The population growth rate was more than 3 per cent and the unemployment rate exceeded 20 per cent. After its 1968 independence from Britain, the diversification of industry from a sugar export dependency and the creation of employment became pressing issues.

Almost immediately after independence, the new Mauritian government passed the Export Processing Zones Act in 1970 to promote the development of labour-intensive textile and clothing industries, and proactively attract foreign investors. The Export Processing Zone (EPZ) was established as a system of decentralised, bonded factories that could be located anywhere on the island. It, therefore, never created an enclave, and it provided employment opportunities in small towns and rural areas away from the capital (Bräutigam 1999: 148), although this is an option that may only be possible for a small country like Mauritius.

Since the implementation of the export-oriented industrialisation strategy, the Mauritius economy has experienced remarkable, sustained economic growth, which has been accompanied by important economic structural changes that were very unusual for Africa at that time. In just a few decades, the small African island state successfully transformed itself from an agro-based economy into an industrialised economy through deep internal structural changes (Tang et al. (eds) 2019: 184). By the mid-1980s, Mauritius had realised full employment, achieving the so-called 'Mauritian Miracle' (World Bank 1989).

The Mauritian experience has been compared with East and Southeast Asian development patterns, and those of other African countries. Researchers have offered different explanations for the country's success, including the initial conditions, openness to trade, foreign direct investment (FDI) and strong domestic institutions. In particular, studies regarding FDI have focused much attention on the role of foreign investors and their ideas. As Romer (1992) strongly argued, 'The only obvious candidate for explaining the success of Mauritius is the island's policy of supporting an EPZ, which made investment attractive to foreigners'. Much of the country's success is undoubtedly due to the establishment and promotion of the EPZ, which led to the successful diversification of the economy. The country even succeeded in attracting Asian investors to the EPZ, particularly from Hong Kong.

However, it should be stressed that foreign investors were not the only actors in Mauritian industrialisation, with local capitalists, entrepreneurs and catalysts who promoted collaboration between the capitalists and government, also being a driving force along with the government and factory workers. Local capitalists transferred sugar-industry-derived capital to various industrial sectors, such as textile companies, in the early stages of industrialisation. Those textile companies were essential drivers to promote the country's industrialisation. The catalysts took a leading role in public-private partnerships and in local-foreign capital joint ventures. The Mauritian 'miracle' would not have been successful without their input.

Sugar was once the engine of the country. Regarding the sugar industry, Roland Lamusse, a Mauritian economic historian, has stated: 'Today the old and weather scarred chimneys, which stand, haughty and derelict, in the middle of cane fields, bear witness to the struggle of past generations of sugar men, planters and labourers alike, who laid the foundations of our high-powered modern industry' (Lamusse 2011: 21).

The history of Mauritius is closely linked with the history of its sugar industry. Saylor examined the close collaboration between the Mauritian export-oriented sugar planters, known as the Franco-Mauritians, and colonial officials, which account for the growth of Mauritian state capacity during the 19th century. These mutual interactions promoted Mauritian state capacity and laid the groundwork for the country's relatively capable state (Saylor 2012).

The coordination between Franco-Mauritians and the government did not only occur in the 19th century. There are also examples of this coordination at the dawn of industrialisation. Around the end of the Commonwealth Sugar Agreement (CSA), which had lasted for nearly 25 years and allocated sugar quotas to all Commonwealth producers for entry into protected British markets, the new national unity government developed a strategy to position the country to enter the protected European market after independence in 1968 (Bräutigam and Diolle 2019). Finding a market for sole export and at a guaranteed price was a matter of life and death for the country and its people (Tsang Mang Kin 2010). To obtain a new market in Europe, the government dispatched many government–opposition joint overseas missions.[2] According to Bräutigam and Diolle, these missions created an opportunity for joint action on the part of the political and economic elites (Bräutigam and Diolle 2019).

Preferential entry into Europe opened the door for Mauritian sugar and for the export processing industries. Although the sugar industry benefited from extensive rents, these rents never became a resource curse because they were earned mostly by the sugar planters, partly collected by the government through the export tax, and used to build capacity and welfare in the state and in society (Bräutigam 2008: 158). Like many other African governments, Mauritius operated parastatals, marketing boards, price controls and subsidies for the major food staples. However, unlike most of other governments, Mauritius never allowed the exchange rate to become grossly overvalued, which would have substantially reduced the domestic value of sugar and manufactured exports. The public sector did not become the main channel of accumulation as it did in many African countries (Bräutigam 1999: 154).

The economic elites, i.e., the white, Franco Mauritian minority sugar estate owners and their allies, invested sugar capital in the new industrial sector immediately after the country's independence. From the beginning, half of the investment in EPZ factories has come from Mauritian investors (especially Franco-Mauritians and sugar interests). Incentives for local capital to invest in the EPZ were increased when the post-independence government imposed capital export controls that prevented the local sugar firms from remitting their profits to invest in sugar plantations in other countries, a common practice in colonial Mauritius (Bräugtigam

1999: 149).

This history prompted us to examine the trajectory of the emergence of the sugar capitalists and the liaison between the sugar capitalists, foreign investors and the government. Hence, in this chapter, we start to look back at the historical development of the sugar industry. Section 2 considers the relationship between the sugar industry and the colonial government, and Section 3 explores the characteristics of two sugar capitalist groups. Section 4 examines where the capital for the development of industrialisation originated from by focusing on the coordination with the government and the catalysts. Section 5 presents the conclusions.

2. Formation of the Colonial Economy and the Emergence of Sugar Capitalists

2-1. French Sugar Planters and the Reconciliatory Attitude of Colonial Officials

The origins of the Mauritian sugar industry date back to the early 18th century in the French colonial period, when La Bourdonnais (the French governor) actively encouraged the cultivation of sugar cane (Allen 1999). Sugar cane cultivation expanded across the island at this time. The industry was established as an export industry by the end of the 18th century. By 1822, in the British colonial period, the island was set upon a path of economic expansion and prosperity based on sugar (Lamusse 2011: 25). The French settlers remained as sugar planters, even during the British colonial period, and their descendants are now referred to as 'Franco-Mauritian'.[3] They established a position as elites, and developed both economic and political power throughout the colonial period.

When the British conquered Mauritius after the Battle of Grand Port with the French in August 1810, they preferred to administer the island rather than settle it. Mauritius became a Crown Colony (direct rule), where the power was concentrated in the hands of the governor, and was subject to close control from London. It was different from most of other British colonies in sub-Saharan Africa which were ruled indirectly via traditional rulers who were appointed by colonial powers as chiefs. The colonial governor received few directives from London and, therefore, had 'considerable discretionary authority' in policy making (Saylor 2012: 466).

On the other hand, the Colonial Office in London required the governor to minimise the expenses related to colonial operations and to establish a base themselves by seeking financial resources through commercial activities and taxation (Teelock 2009: 169–170). However, British investors paid little attention to Mauritius and the colony was seldom visited by the British because its position and possibilities were not widely known (Mauritius Royal Commission 1910: 13). Moreover, the British never settled in large numbers in Mauritius, and most of the plantations remained in the hands of white French planters (Salverda 2015: 36). Also, the sugar factories in Mauritius were not as well developed as those of Java and the Hawaiian Islands. Therefore, the governor in the early period of the British colonial rule was likely to be motivated to implement economic policies that were favourable for the French settlers, enabling them to cultivate sugar cane on the island, where economic viability was dependent on sugar exports.

From the outset, the rulers of the new Crown Colony adopted a reconciliatory attitude toward the colonists. They believed that easing the French settlers' resistance to the British depended on the terms of reconciliation and capitulation. The early British governors tended to shy away from the implementation of policies that might upset the colonists (Lamusse 2011: 26). The limited British interest in Mauritius was demonstrated by the fact that the terms of the treaty of capitulation guaranteed that the French colonists could preserve their customs, property, laws and religion. This accommodative approach by British can be explained by the fact that they recognised the well-organised community of planters as a valuable asset (Sornay 1950: 88, 262).

However, there were frequent conflicts between the Colonial Office and the Colonial Government, who had to run a colonial economy with limited foreign and local capital. For example, the financial assistance given to planters incurred the wrath of, and was disallowed by, the Metropolitan authorities. Lamusse stated:

> A particularly contentious loan was granted by Governor Colville to 'selected planters' in 1829. When the news reached the Colonial Office four to five months later, the Secretary of State did not sanction the loan. For his authorization of the loan of 1829, Colville was severely blamed by the Metropolitan authorities (Lamusse 2011: 136).

Moreover, for the maintenance of internal order and in pursuance of the British government policy of reconciliation and containment of the French colonists, a proclamation by Farquhar in 1817 established the *Commune* system, whereby a group of notables, i.e., 'Respected Inhabitants' was constituted to give advice to the Governor (Lamusse 2011: 28). Members were appointed by the Governor from a list submitted by the colonists. Another measure derived from the French colony, the *Militia,* was introduced to control the mobility of slaves and guard against slave rebellions (Lamusse 2011: 28). This gave a degree of political power to the white colonists and strengthened their social and economic influence on the island. This history was facilitated by the fact that the island had been uninhabited prior to the Europeans' arrival. For the remaining French settlers, there was no other option but to turn their attention to the development of the sugar industry and they shifted their focus from trade to sugar planting, while some of the wealthier settlers returned to France.

When Mauritian sugar was admitted to the British market on the same terms as sugar from the West Indies in 1825, the Franco-Mauritians lobbied British Officials to assist export production. In fact, with the granting of preferential sugar tariffs, the Mauritian sugar industry was established as an export industry and sugar production increased dramatically from 10,870 tons per annum in 1825 to 33,960 tons in 1830. The expansion of sugar production required sufficient labour supply, transportation systems to sugar factories and the resolution of the problems regarding the island's undiversified sugarcane stock (Saylor 2012: 466). In response, the sugar elites organised themselves through groups such as the Chamber of Agriculture and pressed the state for help resolving these barriers to expanded export production (Saylor 2012: 467). This situation was facilitated by the structure of colonial society and, as a consequence of this structure, the support and close cooperation between the British and Franco-Mauritians continued (Salverda 2015: 59).

2-2. Incorporation of Sugar Estates and the Emergence of Sugar Capitalists

The most significant change in 19th-century Mauritius was the dramatic expansion of the sugar industry and its gradual encroachment on society and the economy. The most important change was that of the ownership structure of the sugar estates. These factors shaped the evolution of the local plantation system in both its economic and social dimensions (Lamusse 2011).

The world sugar price dropped sharply during the 1860s due to the expansion of beet sugar and the rise of new sugar cane farming colonies. In response to these external shocks, the number of sugar estates between 1863 and 1903 declined by 70 per cent, from 255 to 80. This section explores the changes in the ownership structure of sugar estates from 1870–1960 in Mauritius. The data were obtained and calculated from *Histoire des domaines sucriers de l'île Maurice* (Rouillard 1979), which clearly records the historical ownership of sugar estates in Mauritius, including the name of the owner, the transfer date and the cultivation area. Based on these records, it is possible to classify ownership patterns into five broad categories:

individual, partnership, company, government and financial institutions.

According to the records, almost all of the sugar estates in Mauritius in the 1870s belonged to individual planters or partnerships. The number of sugar estates, which was almost 200 in the industry's heyday, declined to 150 in the latter half of 1880, 139 in 1900, and finally to 26 in 1960. On the other hand, by taking advantage of economies of scale, the sugar output per factory increased from 360 tons in 1868 to 960 tons in 1888, and then to 2,150 tons in 1903.

The centralisation of sugar estates was an important factor. The sugar estates took the form of a corporate organisation constituted by means of shares. This centralisation led to a subdivision of the ownership of individual (or partnership) estates and the amalgamation of estates under common management. This is a characteristic feature of the Mauritian sugar industry compared to other sugar colonies, such as those in Cuba, Hawaii and South Africa, where foreign capital played an important role in the development of the respective sugar industries.

The sugar manufacturing process generally involves two distinct operations: (a) the planting and harvesting of sugar cane, which requires agricultural technology, and (b) the processing of sugar cane into raw sugar and the processing of raw sugar into refined sugar, which requires the use of a manufacturing technology, such as juice extraction, pressing, purification, crystallisation and centrifugation. Most of the sugar estates were equipped with a simple sugar mill because the sugar content of cane decreases unless it is crushed and extracted immediately after harvest. In Mauritius, following centralisation, sugar manufacturing required sufficient capital to equip sugar planters with modern machinery. The *Report of the Mauritius Royal Commission 1909* explained this situation and the growth of sugar companies as follows:

> Modern developments are all in the direction of fewer and larger

factories with more efficient and expensive machinery, and in consequence require the expenditure of more and more capital. The tendency, therefore, is for the formation of limited companies with sufficient capital to provide the funds required for the manufacture of sugar on an economic scale while individual estate owners who do not possess the requisite capital will either become shareholders in such companies or will close their factories and devote themselves to cultivation only (Mauritius Royal Commission 1910: 20–21).

Before centralisation, the sugar estates in Mauritius belonged to individual planters or partnerships, which is a very simple ownership structure. This reliance on personalised ownership limited the financial resources available to sugar planters and made them dependent on short-term capital (Lamusse 2011: 135). However, once a sugar estate was incorporated and became a sugar company, its ownership structure underwent a fundamental change. In corporation theory, the shareholders own the corporation as a legal entity, and the corporation as a legal entity in turn owns its corporate assets, promoting capital accumulation in the company (Iwai 2002). This implies that even if the sugar planters did not possess enough capital to operate the sugar factory, incorporation would enable them to be involved in the management of the sugar estates, according to the amount of their investment.

Furthermore, incorporation resolved the issues related to the succession and persistence of sugar estates. Before incorporation, every owner had an equal right and an equal duty to any contract they maintained. This meant that whenever there was a departure of one of the co-owners (e.g., through internal dispute, illness or death) or the admission of a new co-owner, each contract had to be rewritten or at least the signatures of the remaining owners had to be updated (Iwai 2002). This generated various transaction costs. As the owners become more numerous or outside relationships become widespread and long term, these transaction costs quickly become prohibitively high. Incorporation could solve this transaction cost problem because incorporation unifies the various contractual relationships. Therefore, once a sugar estate was incorporated, outside sugar planters were encouraged to enter into contractual relations with the sugar company. This paved the way for Franco-Mauritians, as sugar capitalists, to become the dominant capitalist group on the island by exercising the ultimate ownership and control of the island's sugar companies.

3. The Characteristics of the Sugar Capitalist Groups

This section examines the sugar capitalist groups by analysing the ownership-control structure of sugar companies. Despite the ubiquity of these groups in the colonial period, little is known regarding the process of capital formation by them due to data limitations. In Mauritius, following the revision of the Company Act 1911, large associations or partnerships consisting of more than twenty persons were prohibited and required to take the form of an incorporated company (Council of Government 1912).

These incorporated companies were required to submit a statement, memorandum and list of articles related to the company. In this study, the historical Mauritian sugar companies' records were collected and the ownership-control structure was determined. The available data include shareholder lists, memorandums of the shareholder's meetings, memorandums of change in directorship, director's reports, financial statements and annual reports.[4]

3-1. A Case Study of Sugar Manufacturing by the Espitalier-Noël Family

Sugar production by the Espitalier-Noël family began in 1821 when Martial Henri René Noël, a son of Breton immigrants who had settled on the island, started cultivating his first acres of sugarcane in Moka.[5] After the admission of Mauritian sugar to the British market on the same terms as sugar from the West Indies in 1825, Martial Henri René Noël purchased land located in the centre of the island in 1827, named it 'Mon Désert', and started to produce sugar. He successively purchased L' Embarras Sugar Estate, and then, after the 1860s, he and other family members operated the Beau Bois Sugar Estate and Mon Désert Sugar Estate together.

When Mon Désert Sugar Estate was incorporated in 1882 as Compagnie Sucrière de Mon Désert, the neighbouring sugar estates, Helvetia Sugar Estate, St. Avoid Sugar Estate and Good Ground Sugar Estate, were centralised to the sugar company. Furthermore, L' Agrément Sugar Estate in 1885, Minissy Sugar Estate in 1920, and La Laura Sugar Estate and Pieter Both Sugar Estate in 1922 were also centralised to the Compagnie Sucrière de Mon Désert. At this time, the company was the second largest sugar producer on the island.

The ownership structure of the sugar companies became dispersed and complicated through the process of centralisation. For example, the number of shareholders of the Savannah Sugar Estate Company Ltd, invested in by the Espitalier-Noël family and other Franco-Mauritian families, reached 143. To rationalise the administration of the two sugar estates and develop business in emerging sectors, a holding company, Espitalier-Noël Ltd, was founded by the Espitalier-Noël family.[6] The family set up their own holding company to deal with 'organisational failure', which enabled them to be involved in the management and ownership of the sugar company.

The management structure of the holding company shown in Table 1 indicates that the Espitalier-Noël family occupied the management position for a long period. In addition, the ownership structure has remained virtually unchanged. Therefore, their activity can be defined as a family business according to Suehiro (1993), who defined a family business as 'a form of enterprise in which both ownership and management are controlled by a family kinship group, either nuclear or extended, and in which the returns remain inside that group, being distributed in some way among its members' (Suehiro 1993: 378). In addition, the shareholding of children or widows was managed by an attorney who was selected by the family members. This implies that the members were not allowed to manage shares at their own discretion; therefore, the invested capital was retained by the company.

Table 1. Directors of Espitalier-Noël Ltd, 1947–77

Director	1947	1957	1967	1977
Espitalier-Noël, Cyril				*
Espitalier-Noël, Daniel			*	
Espitalier-Noël, Edouard	*	*	*	
Espitalier-Noël, Hector				*
Espitalier-Noël, Hector Joseph Martial			*	
Espitalier-Noël, Jean	*	*	*	
Espitalier-Noël, Louis				*
Espitalier-Noël, Martial Louis	*	*	*	
Espitalier-Noël, Maurice			*	
Espitalier-Noël, Patrice				*
Espitalier-Noël, Philippe	*	*		
Espitalier-Noël, Roger			*	*
Chazal, Roger				*
Eynaud, P. Louis			*	*
Sauzier Raymond				*

Source: C648 *L'assemblée Générale Extraordinaire des Actionnaire de la Compagnie ENL Ltd., Report & Accounts.*

3-2. A Case Study of The Deep River Beau Champ Sugar Estates Co. Ltd

The Deep River Beau Champ Sugar Estate Co. Ltd is one of

largest sugar producers on the island, being ranked 6th out of 25 in terms of sugar production in 1953. The origin of the Deep River Beau Champ Sugar Estate dates back to 1949, with the merger of two sugar estates, the Deep River Sugar Estate Co. Ltd and the Beau Champ Sugar Estate Co. Ltd. Both sugar estates had been owned by Franco-Mauritian families for several generations.

The Deep River Sugar Estate Co. Ltd was started by two sugar planters during the British colonial period. The sugar estate was inherited by various owners over the period of a century and in 1912 it was incorporated. According to the shareholder structure in 1914, the Dalais family was the main shareholder.[7]

According to the memoirs of Pierre Dalais, who was in a management position within the company during 1949-63, the family started sugar production in 1912 when his father, Adrien Dalais, invested in the Deep River Sugar Estate with his friends as the main shareholders (Dalais 2010). Adrien had two roles: a manager and a *bailleurs de fond. Bailleurs de fonds* were usually local merchants or produce-brokers who possessed substantial liquid capital resources of their own and had good credit with the local banks. Their activities focused on providing planters with the short-term operating capital they did not have or could not raise elsewhere. They had a role in the local system of crop finance (Lamusse 2011).

The financial relationship between the planters and the *bailleurs de fonds* often led to the latter functioning as an estate's business manager, with the responsibility for providing the plantation with its needed supplies and money, as well as selling the annual crop (Allen 1999: 24; Lamusse 2011: 135). Interestingly, the relationship was not temporary, but was rather fixed and continuous. In the small white community of Mauritius, the planters and the *bailleurs de fonds* were closely bound together by the ties of intermarriage and long-standing family relationships (Allen 1999: 24). Therefore, based on this economic and social relationship with the sugar estates, which led to a decrease in transaction costs, Adrien Dalais was probably encouraged to enter into the management of the sugar company.

After the incorporation of the Deep River Sugar Estate, the company successively absorbed the neighbouring sugar estates, including Belle Rose Sugar Estate in 1919 and Etoile Sugar Estate in 1926. Furthermore, the area of cultivation expanded from 389 to 550 ha. However, the company's financial performance deteriorated due to the rapid fall in the world sugar price after 1927. Pierre Dalais, who was the manager of the estate, decided to seek a solution for this difficulty: 'What can I do? I, therefore, began to seek to expand and improve the family asset' (Dalais 2010: 16). He entered talks with the directors of the Beau Champ Sugar Estate Co. Ltd, which was located near the Deep River Sugar Estate Co. Ltd, to propose a merger.

The talks lasted for over a year, with both sugar companies finally merging in 1948, with the establishment of the Deep River Beau Champ Sugar Estates Co. Ltd. The new sugar company owned huge tracts of land and modernised its factory. The total assets of the company were 12,840,000 Mauritius Rupees, which was equivalent to roughly 2 per cent of the nation's GDP at that time. The main shareholders of the company were the holding companies of each sugar estate, with the Deep River Holding Co. Ltd holding 41 per cent and the Beau Champ Holding Co. Ltd holding 50 per cent of the new company's shares. The elected directors from the two holding companies jointly managed the new sugar company. The owners and management were Franco-Mauritian families, who had the authority to make the final decisions in all areas of the new company.

According to the articles of both holding companies, a board of directors consisting of ten members were selected from both companies (five members from each company) through a shareholder's meeting.[8] Based on the articles, we describe the management structure of both holding companies (Tables 2 and 3). In the Deep River Holding Co. Ltd, the members from the Dalais family held the management position for a long time, even after the beginning of industrialisation. The board members of the Beau Champ Holding Co. Ltd also consisted of Franco-Mauritians. Therefore, in the early industrialisation period, the Franco-Mauritians, who were the ultimate owners of the sugar company, continued to keep control over ownership and management.

Table 2. Directors of the Deep River Holding Co. Ltd, 1951–1975

Director	1951-68	1969-75
Dalais, Clément	*	*
Dalais, Henri	*	
Dalais, Pierre	*	*
Dalais, Paul	*	*
Dalais, Christian		*
Raffray, René	*	*

Source: C717, The Board of Directors, Dalais (2010).

4. The Source of the Capital Used to Build the Base for Industrialisation

4-1. Joint Collaboration with the Government

For countries that depend on the export of primary products, guaranteeing markets for export is crucial for their economic development. Mauritius concluded the CSA in 1951.[9] An examination of the export quotas under the CSA from the beginning of industrialisation in 1972 until 1974 (the end of the CSA) showed that Mauritius enjoyed the dual benefit of stable quotas and high prices. Its quotas were second only to those of Guyana.

The priority for Seewoosagur Ramgoolam, the first Prime

Table 3. Directors of the Beau Champ Holding Co. Ltd, 1951–1975

Director	1951-52	1953	1954-56	1957	1958-60	1961	1962	1963-64	1966	1968-71	1972-75
Adam, André	*	*	*	*	*	*	*	*	*	*	
Bovil, Joseph											*
Lagesse, Claude		*		*							
Lagesse, Cyril							*		*	*	*
Lagesse, Joseph	*		*		*	*		*			
Lagesse, Roland Rey											*
Leclézio, Claude						*	*	*	*		
Leclézio, Maxime										*	*
Maurice Doger de Spéville	*	*	*	*	*	*	*	*	*	*	*
Montocchio, Fernand Edouard	*	*	*	*	*						
Raffray, Maxime					*	*	*	*	*	*	
Robinson, George Henry	*	*	*	*							

Source: C718, The Board of Directors.

Minister of Mauritius, a Hindu politician, was to find a successor agreement to the CSA. Joseph Tsang Mang Kin, a former diplomat who was involved in the negotiations and formed delegations to European countries, recalled this moment in his memoir: 'Finding a market for our sole export and at a guaranteed price was a matter of life and death for the country and its people' (Tsang Mang Kin 2010: 25).

At that time, Britain had been refused entry into the European Economic Community (EEC). Mauritius now needed to fend for herself to take her sugar into the market. On 28 July 1969, soon after independence and on the eve of the signature of the Yaoundé Convention, which was a critical pillar for the post-independence government, a joint visit to Paris was made by Seewoosagur Ramgoolam, Veerasamy Ringadoo (Minister of Finance) and Gaëtan Duval (a Creole leader of the opposition party: *Parti Mauricien Social-Democrate* (PMSD)). The purpose of the joint delegation was to meet with the French government to obtain their support to access the EEC market. During the mission, Ramgoolam and Duval agreed to form a coalition government, a national unity government, which lasted for nearly four years (Tsang Mang Kin 2010: 46–47). At that time, the two leaders devised a strategy to position the country to enter the market.

Ramgoolam recognised that Mauritius had robust capitalist groups who were ready to invest to meet the 'Mauritian Challenge' of promoting export-led industrialisation, economic diversification and employment creation.[10] In that context, entry into the European market was crucial, with the assumption that the new government could reassure the opposition party of its intention to respect their property and foster investment (Tsang Mang Kin 2010; Bräutigam and Diolle 2019). The PMSD is a political party that represents the tiny white minority of Franco-Mauritian economic elites and their allies among the wealthier mixed-race Mauritians, and had a coalition with the MLP (Mauritius Labour Party), which represents the majority Hindu population and was led by

Ramgoolam. One of the conditions demanded by the PMSD for the coalition was a guarantee that the nationalisation of the sugar industry would never take place (Bräutigam 1999: 149). Unlike most other African governments, the Mauritian government has not established a large number of state-owned enterprises.

In February 1970, Ramgoolam led a joint delegation to the capital cities of the EEC countries. The purpose of the delegation was to facilitate contacts with them to allow Mauritius into the European market. 'None of these countries owed Mauritius a living and had no obligation towards a country that was not a colony of any of them at the time of her independence' (Tsang Mang Kin 2010: 43). The delegation comprised Veerasamy Ringadoo, Gaëtan Duval, Leckraz Teelock and Raymond Chasle, together with Guy Sauzier and Jacques Koenig from the private sugar sector. 'Those representatives from the sugar sector had all the information and had all the time to put in place its own strategy to serve its ends on the negotiations' (Tsang Mang Kin 2010: 94).

One of the delegation members, Sir Guy Sauzier, was from the Mauritius Sugar Syndicate (MSS) office in London. The MSS was formed by sugar planters in 1919 to increase their leverage in price negotiations (Storey 1997: 114). The MSS controlled the sale of sugar. By 1920, more than 70 per cent of sugar was sold through the MSS. By the time Mauritius signed the CSA in 1951, the MSS was marketing the entire crop. They deducted the tax and delivered it to the government, and this 'tax collector' role made them very conscious of their contribution to the revenue of the state (Bräutigam 2008: 142). Sir Guy Sauzier played an important role in persuading Britain and the European countries to sign the Sugar Protocol, and took the leading role in the subsequent sugar agreements. A former employee of the Mauritius Chamber of Agriculture, who was involved in the deal said, 'The industry was permanently represented in London by a famous Mauritian negotiator, Sir Guy Sauzier. He was so skilled, respected. … He helped conduct the very tough negotiations for the maintenance of the benefits of the soon to be defunct CSA'.[11] The joint mission successfully paved the way for the participation in Yaoundé Convention: 'It was given a most sympathetic hearing by the Heads of States who promised to do whatever they could to help Mauritius' (Tsang Mang Kin 2010: 55).

Claude Noël, a Franco-Mauritian 'who rose from modest origins to become managing director of a group of sugar estates, president of the Chamber of Agriculture, and a prominent private sector leader',[12] also played an important role as a catalyst between the sugar sector and the government in the subsequent sugar protocol negotiations. A Franco-Mauritian described him as 'a prominent figure of the industry' and 'a great negotiator'.[13] He was particularly trusted by Ramgoolam and urged Ramgoolam and Duval to form a government of national unity. Ramgoolam also needed to shore up support in his own party for the rapprochement with the capitalists who dominated the economy (Bräutigam and Diolle 2019: 54–55). He acted as a key go-between in the negotiations between Ramgoolam and Duval, conveying the strong desire of the private sector for a coalition government to succeed (Bräutigam and Diolle 2019: 55). As Claude Noël noted, 'One wing of the government tried to pressure Ramgoolam not to sign the convention. The private sector worked hard to explain the consequences of this to the politicians' (Bräutigam and Diolle 2019: 70). Ramgoolam, as a Fabian socialist, also recognised that to gain preferential access to European markets for Mauritian sugar was crucial to achieve his social goals (Bräutigam and Diolle 2019: 38).

The negotiations finally came to an end and the Yaoundé Convention was succeeded by the Lomé Convention. The Convention and Sugar Protocol were signed on 28 February 1975, under which the negotiated sugar price in Mauritius diverged 145 per cent from the market price between 1975 and 2000, a larger deviation than that enjoyed by any other African or Caribbean country (Herrmann and Weiss 1995). Thus, the Mauritian sugar industry was scarcely impacted by the end of the CSA. Rather, it continually acquired market access for sugar exports at higher prices than the global free-market price and enjoyed the blessing of preferential trade agreements for a quarter of a century starting in the 1950s. Tsang Mang Kin noted:

> Our team of diplomats and experts, together with our ACP colleagues worked conscientiously day and night to get the best deal for our countries. We had no doubts in our minds that the benefits to be obtained from EEC would spread to the whole Mauritian population. This clearly meant that such benefits were not only to be shared with the sugar sector, the sugar barons, the land and plantation owners, the big and small planters and the sugar camp dwellers, but also with all the other sectors of Mauritian economy (Tsang Mang Kin 2010: 89).

The convention, which paved the way for capital accumulation in the sugar industry as well as the development of the EPZ, might not have been made without an inclusive collaboration, including multi-ethnic groups, and joint lobbying efforts.

4-2. Investment in the EPZ

The conclusion of the preferential sugar agreement brought in billions of rupees to Mauritius. It facilitated further capital accumulation in the sugar estates. At the eve of industrialisation, there were only 25 sugar companies in the country. The sugar industries' contribution to the national income consisted of 'compensation of employees' (43.4 per cent), 'planters' incomes' (19.9 per cent), 'undistributed profits' (15.4 per cent), 'dividends etc' (12.2 per cent), 'direct taxes' (8.14 per cent) and 'cyclone and drought insurance fund' (0.9 per cent) (Meade et al. 1961). Most of the income from sugar has been in the form of planter's income and undistributed profits, with the income distribution in the industry being severely skewed.

A calculation of the annual dividend rates of the Deep River

Holding Company and the Beau Champ Holding Company showed that they paid out 11 per cent of dividends on average during 1971–1979.[14] Similarly, the Espitalier-Noël family's holding company, ENL, paid out 22 per cent of dividends on average during the same period, with a dividend of 38 per cent during the sugar boom. While the holding companies increased their amount of capital, ownership and control were not separated.

While the conclusion of the Lomé Convention brought in billions of rupees to the country's economy, the convention opened new guaranteed markets for the products from the EPZ (Tsang Mang Kin 2010: 90). Soon after the EPZ was established, the sugar capitalists founded 'investment companies'.

4-2-1. Investment in the EPZ and Collaboration with International Investors

The Espitalier-Noël family, who were the first to invest in the EPZ, founded a family investment company, the General Investment & Development Co. Ltd (GIDC). The primary shareholder of the investment company was the ENL holding company (53.8 per cent), which was also managed by the Espitalier-Noël family. The articles of incorporation state its objective as: 'Make any kinds of investments and capital investments acting as capitalists, financiers, concessionaires and merchants, and undertake, conduct, and execute all financial, commercial, agricultural, manufacturing and general industrial operations'.

Following this, we examined the investment in the EPZ by the group, which included all Espitalier-Noël-related capital. As can be seen in Table 4, the group invested in multiple textile and sewing-related companies. Six of these EPZ companies were based in Hong Kong and were joint ventures with multinational textile and clothing companies, including Textile Industries Ltd (sewing), Mauritian Woollen & Worsted Mills Ltd (spinning), International Fashions Ltd (retail), United Knitters Ltd, Alliance Knitters Ltd and

Table 4. Shareholder composition of EPZ firms in which the ENL Group invested

Shareholder	Country	EPZ firms							
		L.S.P Ltd. (1970)	Textile Industries Ltd. (1971)	Mauritian Woollen & Worsted Mills Ltd. (1972)	Beta Industrial Ltd. (1972)	International Fashions Ltd. (1974)	United Knitters Ltd. (1974)	Alliance Knitters Ltd. (1976)	Maurice Knitters Ltd. (1976)
Textile Alliance Ltd.	Hong Kong		73.3%	19.4%		16.7%	16.7%		
Afasia Ltd.	Hong Kong							40.0%	43.3%
Managers of Afasia and Textile Alliance	Hong Kong			58.3%		50.0%	50.1%	20.0%	10.0%
Joseph Z.Z. Lee	Hong Kong		6.7%						
Ah-Chuen, Moilin	Mauritius		2.0%						
GIDC	Mauritius	33.3%	7.5%	12.5%	5.0%	11.2%	13.4%	5.3%	6.5%
ENL affiliated companies			7.5%	3.9%	5.0%	11.1%	15.9%	29.8%	36.8%
Mauritius Commercial Bank	Mauritius			3.2%				5.0%	3.3%
Others	Mauritius	33.3%	3.0%	2.6%	90.0%	11.1%	4.0%		
	South Africa	33.3%							
Total	Hong Kong	0.0%	80.0%	77.8%	0.0%	66.6%	66.8%	60.0%	53.3%
	Mauritius	66.7%	20.0%	22.2%	100.0%	33.4%	33.2%	40.0%	46.7%

Source: C1809, Shareholder List; C1977, Shareholders in the Textile Industries Ltd.; C2057, Shareholders List; C2060, List of Shareholders; C2283, Shareholders List; C2282, Shareholders List; C2644, List of Shareholders of the Alliance Knitters Ltd.; C2643, Shareholder.
Note: The year in parentheses indicates the year in which the company was established. The numbers in the table indicate the percentage of shares owned by the shareholders as of the establishment of the company.

Maurice Knitters Ltd (knitted goods). It has been claimed that thesecompanies created one-fifth of the jobs in the EPZ as of 1984 (Hein 1988: 21).

The scale of the Espitalier-Noël family's investments indicates that they did not actively invest in these joint ventures to own and control them. In fact, as revealed in Section 3, the ENL holding company, which is the parent company of the GIDC, maintained the ownership and control exclusively for a long period. This implies that there was a limit to their investment capital as they had kept a family-based ownership structure. In fact, the ENL holding company opened some of their shares to the public to finance investment in the EPZ and other sectors. Thus, they became a 'Public Limited Company' instead of a 'Private Limited Company'. This move expanded their capital from MRU 7.92 million to MRU 14.25 million in 1971, soon after the EPZ was established. The director of the company, Maurice Espitalier-Noël explained this decision:

> This step which ranks as a milestone in the history of your company was prompted by an increasing awareness that in the context of the economy of a developing country, no country, if the basis of its foundations is not widened to enable new financial resources to be tapped whenever available, may be able to achieve a pattern of sustained growth over a number of years and thereby help, in a small measure though, to meet what may accurately be termed 'The Mauritian Challenge'. It is very encouraging in this respect to note that the company which was hitherto a Private Limited Company with shares solely owned by the Espitalier-Noël family has, since its going public, attracted the interest of over 75 shareholders who are now members of the company (C648: ENL Ltd, Director's Report 1970).

This suggests that they attempted to respond to the 'Mauritian Challenge', which was understood as the future desirable development course for the country to follow. The end of the CSA and the conclusion of the successive trade agreement became an opportunity for the family to diversify its businesses from sugar.

The directors of ENL holdings, Hector Espitalier-Noël and Maurice Espitalier-Noël, were assigned as the managers of the Mauritian side of the business in joint ventures. The formation of joint ventures enabled local investors to bring their opinions to the table in the decision-making process with foreign investors. They were the Chinese-Mauritians, Jean Ah-Chuen and Joseph Lee, the minority shareholders in Textile Industries Ltd in Table 4, who played an important role in attracting investors from Hong Kong. Soon after independence, Ah-Chuen invited numerous delegations of entrepreneurs from Hong Kong, supported by his eldest daughter, Marie-Madeleine, and her husband, Joseph Lee. Joseph Lee also had a career in textile chemicals and was appointed the Honorary Consul of Mauritius to Hong Kong 'as a reward for services rendered and also as a platform to promote more investment opportunities' (Berthelot 2013: 80).

Jean Moilin Ah-Chuen was the first Chinese Mauritian to be nominated to the Legislative Council in Port Louis in 1948. He was also the president of the Chinese Chamber of Commerce and a local government minister representing the interests of the city of Port Louis, where many ethnic minorities lived (Bräutigam and Diolle 2019: 34). The prime minister, Ramgoolam, asked Ah-Chuen 'if Madelein and Joseph Lee could attract Hong Kong textile entrepreneurs to invest in factories in Mauritius' (Berthelot 2013: 80). Ramgoolam knew that Ah-Chuen had extensive connections in Asia. 'He [Ah-Chuen] held big receptions here in Mauritius and there in Hong Kong and Taiwan to gather them and to attract them' (Berthelot 2013: 68). Following this, Joseph accompanied some thirty textile entrepreneurs for a prospective visit to Mauritius, and some of them actually established EPZ textile firms (Berthelot 2013: 80).

According to Ly Tio Fane-Pineo and Lim Fat, in the early stages of industrialisation, the workers in the EPZ factories found it difficult to adapt to the rigid discipline of industrial production because they had been used to the flexible working hours in agriculture and they could not easily maintain the set working hours (Ly Tio Fane-Pineo and Lim Fat 2008: 271–273). As a result, the first EPZ firms faced enormous difficulties in reaching a normal productivity. 'The Mauritian entrepreneur had to train all his workers from scratch and during the long training period, he might have by then lost most of his capital or even gone bankrupt' (Ly-Tio-Fane Pineo and Lim Fat 2008: 273). Despite these early drawbacks, huge amounts of foreign and local capital flowed into the EPZ. In particular, the creation of joint ventures with foreign investors could be attributed, in the most part, to the efforts made by the Chinese-Mauritian catalysts.

4-2-2. The Transition from Sugar to Textiles as the Driving Force of the EPZ

The Franco-Mauritian sugar capitalists of the Deep River Beau Champ sugar company also established their investment company, Commercial & Industrial Enterprises Ltd (CIEL), the year after the EPZ was established. The share capital of the investment company was paid by the Deep River Beau Champ sugar company. Five board members of the investment companies were assigned from the Deep River Sugar Estate, while seven were assigned from the Beau Cham Sugar Estate. The purpose of the company was the same as that of the ENL group.

Table 5 shows the CIEL Group's investments in EPZ firms as of 1978. Floreal Knitwear Ltd, which was founded in 1971, financed 73.5 per cent of its share capital from CIEL, 3.5 per cent from the Dalais family and 1.5 per cent from the CIDL investment company.[15] In total, the capital related to the sugar industry was responsible for about 80 per cent of the total investment of Floreal Knitwear Ltd. Initially, Floreal Knitwear Ltd was founded by Hong Kong capitalists, but CIEL bought out over half of its shares soon after it was established to enable it to make a fully-fledged entry

Table 5. Shareholder composition of EPZ firms in which the CIEL Group invested

Shareholder	Country	EPZ firms			
		Floreal Knitwear Ltd. (1971)	Floreal Textile Ltd. (1972)	Lords & Cashmere Ltd. (1976)	Ferney Spinning Mills Ltd. (1978)
Oriental Pacific Export Ltd.	Hong Kong	15.1%	15.1%		
Managers of Oriental Pacific Export Ltd.	Hong Kong	4.6%	4.6%		
CIEL	Mauritius	73.5%	73.5%	87.2%	88.6%
CIDL	Mauritius	1.5%	1.4%	1.6%	1.4%
Société du Maraise	Mauritius			4.1%	3.7%
Société d'Arlonville	Mauritius			2.9%	
Société de la Pigeonniere	Mauritius				2.6%
The members of Dalais family	Mauritius	3.5%	3.6%	2.4%	2.1%
Others	Mauritius	1.9%	1.9%	1.8%	1.6%
Total	Hong Kong	19.7%	19.7%	0.0%	0.0%
	Mauritius	80.3%	80.3%	100.0%	100.0%

Source: C1871, Shareholders List; C2053, Shareholders List; C2722, Shareholders; C2982, Shareholders List.
Note: The year in parentheses indicates the year in which the company was established.

into the textile and clothing sector. Floreal Textile Ltd, a company in the sewing industry, was also founded primarily with CIEL group capital in 1972. Furthermore, the CIEL group bought out Lords & Cashmere Ltd from the other shareholders in 1976, and it was also the primary investor in Ferney Spinning Mills Ltd, a company in the cotton-spinning industry that was founded in 1978 with 100 per cent Mauritian capital. This led to vertical integration within the group.

The managers of the holding company of the Deep River Beau Champ sugar company served also as the managers of these EPZ firms, although they appointed foreigners for roles that required specialised knowledge and skills. For example, Ferney Spinning Mills Ltd hired their 'Spinning/Dyeing Director' from Hong Kong. Collaborating with foreign investors was essential for the capitalists who had been based in the sugar industry to supplement the managerial resources that were lacking at the beginning of industrialisation such as managerial expertise in the textile and clothing industries, production techniques and overseas market networks.

These four CIEL group-affiliated EPZ firms created 12.3 per cent of the new jobs in the EPZ in the early period of industrialisation (Hein 1988: 21–22) and were responsible for 25 per cent of total knitwear and clothing product exports (Lamusse 1989: 26). In the late 1990s, the CIEL group's Floreal Knitwear Ltd became the world's second-largest producer of Woolmark's pullovers, which is just one example of how the group developed a central role as the driver of Mauritius's textile industry. CIEL group-affiliated textile companies employ 18,000 employees as of 2021 and support CIEL Textile Ltd, which is the island's largest textile company, with affiliated cotton-spinning, knitting, dyeing and sewing factories.

5. Conclusion

Sugar capitalists emerged in Mauritius through the centralisation of sugar estates during the British colonial period. Due to the historical development process of the sugar industry, both the ownership and management of the sugar companies were concentrated in Franco-Mauritian families, and the establishment of a holding company facilitated a hierarchical ownership structure. When the export-oriented strategy was implemented in 1970, the sugar-based capitalists directly transferred part of the capital accumulated by sugar exports to different sectors. In our case study of two sugar capitalist groups, it was found that they invested in textile companies in EPZ. These companies were the driving force of Mauritian industrialisation.

At the time of independence, most other African countries implemented nationalisation of European companies that were established during the colonial period. What the Franco-Mauritian sugar capitalists most feared was the nationalisation of the sugar estates. On the other hand, the new government needed to establish a compromise with the business class that would prevent capital from leaving Mauritius (Bräutigam and Diolle 2019: 22). At the same time, job creation was crucial for the government. By leveraging the capital in the sugar industry, the government sought to realise a mutual benefit. Instead of nationalisation of the sugar estates, they regulated the capital outflow and created strong incentives for EPZ companies; thus, actively promoting domestic investment in the EPZ. They created stability and credibility for the sugar sector and supported their investment into the new sector and its industrialisation.

In Mauritius, the political and economic elites are separated, with each having different stakes in the country. However, a cooperative relationship was built around sugar production. Although politico-economic elite collaborations discussed in this chapter were not a story of ordinary African people, those elites are also indigenised Africans and the events were ways to show potential for an African society to realise export-oriented industrialisation through mobilising resources including capital accumulated locally. No doubt, however, reforms to reduce socio-economic disparities caused by oligopolistic capitalist development is now the next 'Mauritian Challenge'.

Endnotes

[1] Part of this chapter is based on author's previous work, Ideue (2020).

[2] In Mauritius, the post-independence coalition was forged by bringing the opposition into a government of national unity between 1969–1973 (Bräutigam and Diolle 2019).

[3] In general, the term 'Franco-Mauritians' refers to 'Mauritians of French descent'. In Mauritius, however, the term is used to refer to 'whites of European descent who were born and raised in Mauritius' or 'white descendants of French or British colonial settlers'. It should be noted, then, that the term is used neither in a single sense nor in a fixed way, but in a multifaceted and variable way, and has been used fluidly over the whole history.

[4] The file number (C***) is attached to each company's files that are stored in the company registry office in Mauritius. In this study, when referring to the company's data, we mention only the file number and the name of the documents.

[5] ENL website (https://www.enl.mu/en/group/about-us/our-story) (accessed: 4 April 2020).

[6] ENL website (https://www.enl.mu/en/group/about-us/our-story) (accessed: 4 April 2020).

[7] C12, *Shareholder's list 1914*.

[8] The articles of association of the Deep River Beau Champ Sugar Estates Co. Ltd were not filed at the registration office.

[9] The quotas in the treaty were classified into standard and agreed-price quotas. The former is the general framework for exports, and

the latter, which comprises part of the former, is subject to both the agreed price and preferential tariffs (Hoshino 1983: 59).

[10] According to Bräutigam and Diolle, the coalition government had four goals to achieve a success of development: to signal to the other ethnic groups that Mauritius was not a purely Hindu country; to ensure political stability; to build the confidence and encourage economic cooperation of the 'sugar barons'; to encourage foreign investment with the hope that this would generate employment (Bräutigam and Diolle 2019: 27).

[11] Through interview, 19 February 2019, Mauritius.

[12] Bräutigam and Diolle (2019: 30–31).

[13] According to the person, 'I guess that the Noël and the Espitalier-Noël are somehow related. What I do not know is when the prefix Espitalier was added', through online interview, 23 June 2020.

[14] The calculation was based on the companies' profit and loss statements and balance sheets, obtained from the corporate registry office in Mauritius.

[15] The CIDL investment company is an investment company (Compagnie d'Investissement et de Développement Ltée.) established mainly by the Franco-Mauritian Lagesse family.

Acknowledgements

This work was supported by JSPS KAKENHI Grant Number JP16H06318, JP20K20049 and K. MATSUSHITA FOUNDATION Grant Number (13-G04).

References

Allen, R. B. (1999) *Slaves, Freedmen and Indentured Laborers in Colonial Mauritius*, Cambridge: Cambridge University Press.

Berthelot, L. (2013) *Sir Jean Étienne Moi Lin Ah Chuen (1911–1991)*,

Port Louis: Stream Heart.

Bräutigam, D. (1999) 'The "Mauritius Miracle": Democracy, institutions and economic policy', in R. A. Josepheds (ed.) *State, Conflict and Democracy in Africa*, Boulder: Lynne Rienner Publishers, pp. 137–162.

———— (2008) 'Contingent capacity: Export taxation and state-building in Mauritius', in D. Bräutigam, O.-H. Fjeldstad and M. Moore (eds) *Taxation and State-Building in Developing Countries: Capacity and Consent,* Cambridge: Cambridge University Press, pp. 135–159.

Bräutigam, D. and Diolle, T. (2019) 'Coalitions, capitalists, and credibility: Overcoming the crisis of confidence at independence in Mauritius', in V. T. Tang, T. M. Shaw and M. G. Holden (eds) *Development and Sustainable Growth of Mauritius,* London: Palgrave Macmillan, pp. 17–67.

Council of Government (Mauritius) (1912) *A Collection of the Ordinances Passed by the Council of Government during the Year 1911*, Port Louis: Government Printing Office.

Dalais, P. P. (2010) *Pierre P. Dalais 1906–1999 : Sa famille,son travail*, Port Louis: Precigraph.

Hein, C. (1988) *Multinational Enterprises and Employment in the Mauritian Export Processing Zone, Multinational Enterprises Programme Working Paper No. 52*, Genève: International Labour Organization (ILO).

Herrmann, R. and Weiss, D. (1995) 'A welfare analysis of the EC-ACP sugar protocol', *The Journal of Development Studies*, Vol. 31, No. 6, pp. 918–941.

Hoshino, T. (1983) 'The transformation of the world sugar market in the 1970s and the Caribbean', *Ajia Keizai*, Vol. 24, No. 6, pp. 56–73 (in Japanese).

Ideue, K. (2020) 'The relationship between sugar capital and industrialisation in Mauritius: Focusing on the ownership and dominant structure of sugar-based capitalists and their investment to the industrial sectors', *Social System Study*, Vol. 41, pp. 43–70 (in Japanese with English abstract).

Iwai, K. (2002) 'The nature of the business corporation: Its legal structure and economic functions', *The Japanese Economic Review*, Vol. 53, Issue 3, pp. 243–273.

Lamusse, R. (1989) *Adjustment to Structural Change in Manufacturing in a North-South Perspective: The Case of the Clothing Export Sector in Mauritius, ILO International Employment Policies Working Paper No. 27*, Genève: International Labour Organization (ILO).

———— (2011) *The Supremacy & Twilight of the Mauritius Sugar Industry*, Beau Bassin: Osman Publishing.

Ly Tio Fane, H. and Lim Fat, E. (2008) *From Alien to Citizen: The Integration of the Chinese in Mauritius*, Rose Hill: Editions de l'Ocean Indien.

Mauritius Royal Commission (1910) *Report of the Mauritius Royal Commission 1909,* London: Her Majesty's Stationery Office.

Meade, J. E. and Others (1961) *The Economic and Social Structure of Mauritius: Report to the Governor of Mauritius*, London: Methuen and Co. Ltd.

Romer, P. M. (1992) 'Two strategies for economic development: Using ideas and producing ideas', in L. H. Summers and S. Shah (eds) *Proceedings of the World Bank Annual Conference on Development Economics 1992*, Washington DC: World Bank, pp. 63–116.

Rouillard, G. (1979) *Histoire des domaines sucriers de l'île Maurice*, Port-Louis: The General Printing & Stationery Co.

Salverda, T. (2015) *The Franco-Mauritian Elite: Power and Anxiety in the Face of Change*, New York and Oxford: Berghahn Books.

Saylor, R. (2012) 'Probing the historical sources of the Mauritian miracle: Sugar exporters and state building in colonial Mauritius', *Review of African Political Economy,* Vol. 39, No. 133, pp. 465–478.

Sornay, P. (1950) *Isle de France, Ile Maurice*, Port Louis: The General Printing and Stationery Company.

Storey, W. K. (1997) *Science and Power in Colonial Mauritius*, Rochester: University of Rochester.

Suehiro, A. (1993) 'Family business reassessed: Corporate structure and late-starting industrialisation in Thailand', *The Developing Economies*, Vol. 31, Issue 4, pp. 378–407.

Tang, V. T., Shaw, T. M. and Holden, M. G. (eds) (2019) *Development and Sustainable Growth of Mauritius*, London: Palgrave Macmillan.

Teelock, V. (2009) *Mauritian History: From Its Beginnings to Modern Times,* Moka: Mahatma Gandhi Institute.

Tsang Mang Kin, J. (2010) *Sir Seewoosagur Ramgoolam, the Rare Diplomat: Mauritius on the World Stage*, Rose Hill: Editions de l'Ocean Indien.

World Bank (1989) *Mauritius, Managing Success*, Washington DC: World Bank.

Chapter 7

The Potential Created by Mobility: Social Ties with Strangers in the Migration History of One Family in Northwestern Zambia

Masaya Hara

1. Keep Moving

My host father, Mr Lewis,[1] and I travelled to Mwinilunga District from Mufumbwe District in North-Western Province, Zambia, in August 2019 (Figure 1). The purpose of this journey was to visit K Village in Mwinilunga, which was the home village of Mr Lewis's mother, and to visit Mr Willard, specifically, who is Mr Lewis's maternal cousin. Mr Willard is the village headman of K Village. Mr Lewis and Mr Willard both belong to the Lunda people. Lunda society is matrilineal. It is important for the Lunda to visit the home village of their own mother; however, Mr Lewis had never been to his mother's home village. He did not know the location and history of K Village. The reason was that Mr Lewis's parents and Mr Lewis had kept moving throughout their lives. Many people living in sub-Saharan Africa continually move between different areas to sustain their livelihoods (Potts 1995; van der Geest 2010).

The Bantu-speaking peoples have engaged in slash-and-burn cultivation in miombo woodlands, which extend widely across the southern edge of Central Africa's Congo Basin since they settled in the area. They have also engaged in hunting and fishing, and gather mushrooms and caterpillars, achieving self-sufficiency using natural resources. They repeatedly move between miombo woodlands and other open, richly resourced woodlands (Hara 2020). Northwestern Zambia is also an area of miombo woodlands and is home to Bantu-speaking peoples, such as the Lunda, Kaonde and Luvale.

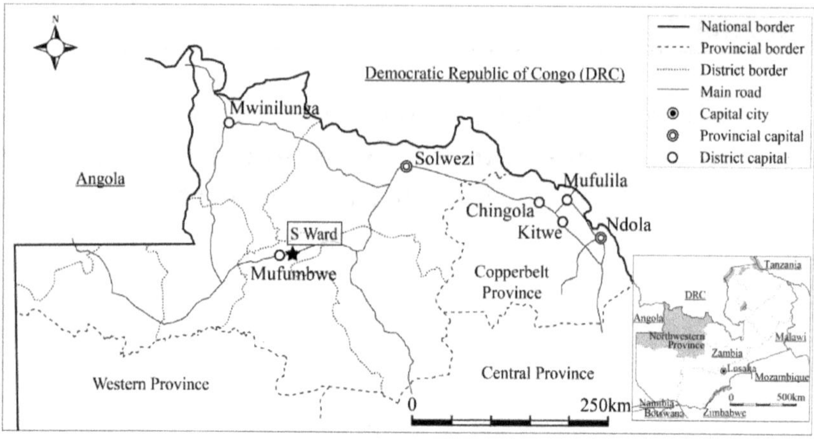

Figure 1. Map of North-Western Province, Zambia

Source: Author.

Labour migration from rural to urban areas and mining centres has been ongoing since the operation of copper mines during the 1920s in the colonial period in Northern Rhodesia (present-day Zambia). Compared with other sub-Saharan African countries, the population of Zambia is more heavily concentrated in urban areas (Potts 2005). When Zambia achieved independence in 1964, 22 per cent of the total population lived in urban areas, but by 2018 this figure had increased to 44 per cent (World Bank 2020). People in Zambia have moved between rural and urban areas since the colonial period.

Since the colonial period, people living in rural Zambia have moved to urban areas for economic reasons, typically, to earn a cash income and achieve a better quality of life. Migration is easy today because of well-developed infrastructure. Migrants tend to maintain relationships with their relatives in rural villages as a prop for their urban lives (Ogura 1991; Cliggett 2003). Rural people expect their urban relatives to introduce them to job opportunities and places to live. After migration to urban areas, urban dwellers regard their home villages as sanctuaries in the event their circumstances deteriorate. Rural dwellers also expect financial support from their urban relatives. The urban–rural reciprocity of kinship is not only a one-way movement of people, money and goods from urban to rural areas, but also involves the movement of food from rural to urban areas (Frayne 2004). When people move between rural and urban areas in Africa, they tend to rely on their relationships with relatives (Frayne 2007; Njwambe et al. 2019).

On the other hand, some retired mine workers have migrated back to rural areas from mining centres, with assistance from friends, churches or workplaces in the Zambian Copperbelt. These migrants had no relatives who were reliant on them and avoided jealousy and disputes over money in their home villages (Ferguson 1999). The urban born population has been increasing in recent years. In this situation, relationships with relatives in rural and urban areas have tended to become weaker.

This chapter is focused on the migration history of Mr Lewis's family, whose origin was in Portuguese West Africa (present-day Angola), and examines how they maintained their livelihood by moving between dwelling places. Mr Lewis lives in M Village of S Ward in Mufumbwe District, North-Western Province, Zambia. K Village, which is the birthplace of Mr Lewis's mother, is located in Mwinilunga District in northwestern Zambia (Table 1). According to the personal migration history of each member of Mr Lewis's family, they have moved between dwelling places and have relied for assistance not only on their relatives but also friends and strangers. They moved and lived by building social ties with various people.

Table 1. Properties of the villages

Village	Location in 2019	Year of building	Place of origin
K Village	Mwinilunga District	before 1935	Portuguese West Africa (Angola)
I Village	S Ward in Mufumbwe District	1985	S Ward
M Village	S Ward in Mufumbwe District	1993	S Ward

Source: Author's interview.

This chapter is also focused on a person who a member of Mr Lewis's family relied on for assistance with his migration and life after migration and considers the potential for supporting his subsistence. Potential migrants rely on specific individuals when they migrate to a new dwelling place. These individuals are referred to as *chinsahu* in the Lunda language. In this chapter, we call them guarantors. The original meaning of the word *chinsahu* is evidence and guarantee. Having a *chinsahu* guarantees a migrant's character and background to community members. The guarantor introduces migrants to their new communities and certifies that they will live there without any problems. The role of a guarantor is not an official government appointment. Any person can become a guarantor if he or she is trusted by a migrant and the local community. The guarantor is only selected on the strength of personal relationships.

2. Migration and Economic Fluctuation in Zambia

This section provides an overview of the social and economic trends of Zambia since the colonial period. Social and economic conditions had a direct impact on the migration of Mr Lewis's family. There was only limited economic development in Northern Rhodesia when the area was ruled by the British South Africa Company (BSAC). However, large copper deposits were developed in the present-day Copperbelt Province in the 1920s and several copper mines then began to operate in the late 1920s (Roberts 1976: 186). Some small-scale farmers living in rural areas moved to urban and mining areas for work after the introduction of a poll tax by the colonial government in the 1900s (Heisler 1974: 37). Migration from rural to urban areas had been common before Zambia's independence.

After Zambia achieved independence in 1964, Zambia experienced an economic boom due to the high copper price in the world market. Although the number of migrants to urban areas had been increasing before independence, after independence it increased rapidly (Ogura 1991). The wages offered to urban and mine workers were much higher than an agricultural income. In the 1970s, the average income of an urban household was four times that of a rural household (ILO and JASPA 1977: 288). After independence, male workers migrated to urban areas with their families, with the intention of settling in the city.

Zambia then experienced an economic crisis after the sharp fall in the world copper price. This was triggered by the oil crisis in the mid-1970s and there was no recovery during the 1980s. The Zambian government accepted a Structural Adjustment Programme (SAP) from the International Monetary Fund (IMF) and the World Bank due to a deterioration in the national financial situation in 1978. The SAP had a severe negative impact on the daily lives of the Zambian people. Commodity prices soared (including those of daily necessities and food, particularly maize flour as a staple food), real wages decreased and the quality of life for urban dwellers declined (Ogura 1991). Some poor urban dwellers, including the unemployed and retired people returned to rural areas (Ferguson 1999). Urban dwellers moved to rural areas and began to work as farmers when they could not earn a cash income in urban areas. In rural areas, they could grow food for self-consumption and sell any excess produce.

In 1991, the first general election was held after the establishment of a multi-party democracy in the previous year. The United National Independence Party (UNIP), which was led by Dr Kenneth Kaunda, who had taken control of Zambian development since independence, lost the election. The Movement for Multiparty Democracy (MMD) won the election and Mr Frederick Chiluba's government was established. President Chiluba restarted the SAP and oversaw its rapid progression despite the previous administration having abandoned the project in 1987. All government subsidies were abolished and national enterprises were privatised. The unemployment rate increased and people's livelihoods deteriorated. The population outflow from urban areas progressed (Potts 2005). Life in urban areas has been vulnerable since the colonial period.

The Zambian economy has since recovered because the copper price has risen, due to the increased demand for mineral resources and the offsetting of financial obligations since 2001. People returned to urban areas and began to earn a cash income by working in the formal or informal sectors. However, Zambia has recently experienced another economic depression due to a fall in the copper price in 2015. Several large mines in Zambia suspended the employment of mine workers and gave workers indefinite holidays. The Zambian economy has fluctuated with the world copper price. People in Zambia decide to move between rural and urban areas in accordance with the economic situation.

3. The North-Western Province as a Frontier in Zambia

The North-Western Province is recognised as a remote area by most Zambians. A population census of the North-Western Province in 2010 revealed a population density of 5.8 people per square kilometre, which was the lowest of all Zambian provinces (CSO 2012). There are five main ethnic groups of Bantu-speaking peoples in the Province: the Lunda, Kaonde, Luvale, Chokwe and Luchazi. The population of each ethnic group is small, and their societies are fluid. The North-Western Province has been left behind in terms of economic development due to its remote location (Crehan 1997).

The provincial capital city of the North-Western Province is Solwezi. Solwezi is adjacent to the Copperbelt Province, which has seen the establishment of several mines since the 1920s. Although there has been little development in Solwezi due to its remoteness, two large mines have operated in the area since the 2000s. Solwezi has experienced an economic boom and the population of northwestern Zambia has increased. Mwinilunga is the second largest town in the North-Western Province and is located approximately 250 kilometres west of Solwezi. It is located near the border with Angola and is the centre of the Lunda territory.

Mr Lewis lives in S Ward, which lies within the territory of the Kaonde traditional chief. The Lunda, Luvale, Chokwe and Luchazi are also inhabitants of S Ward. In 2012, the population of S Ward consisted of 1,320 people, living in 243 households spread among 23 villages (Hara 2017). Each village had approximately 10 households. Some non-Kaonde migrants arrived from other villages and towns after the 1970s (Hara 2017, 2020). A number of migrants secured paid work in mines or cities.

4. The Migration of K Villagers across the International Border

Mr Lewis's family tree is shown in Figure 2. The central person in this chapter is Mr Lewis, who was born in 1974. His parents were born in Mwinilunga District and were also married there. After their marriage, they lived in several cities before moving to S Ward in Mufumbwe District.

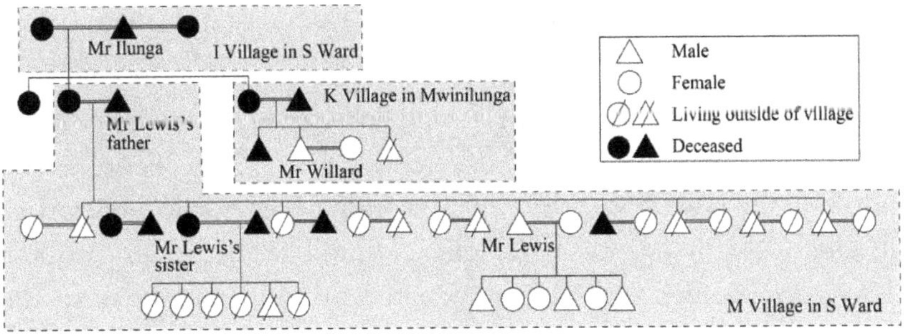

Figure 2. Mr Lewis's family tree in 2019

Source: Author's interview.

K Village, which is the home village of Mr Lewis's mother, was located in Portuguese West Africa (present-day Angola). The village consisted of a village headman, his nine siblings and their wives and children. The members of K Village emigrated to the environs of Mwinilunga in Northern Rhodesia from Portuguese West Africa in 1936. Nine of the siblings were male and one was female. The woman's second daughter was Mr Lewis's mother. The name K Village was retained for the new settlement after their migration.

According to Mr Willard, who knows the history of K Village, the Portuguese colonial government imposed compulsory labour on 'natives' without remuneration at the time the members of K Village migrated to Mwinilunga. He said that the British colonial government required labour for public infrastructure in Northern Rhodesia and, unlike the Portuguese government, offered remuneration in the form of cash or clothes. The members of K Village felt dissatisfied with their unjust treatment on the part of the Portuguese colonial government and migrated to Mwinilunga to improve their lives.

Mr Willard was born in K Village in 1959. Most of the villagers who migrated from Portuguese West Africa had died by 1970. Most of the villagers who remained moved to urban areas or other provinces to find jobs or get married. Mr Willard was married to a woman born in a neighbouring village in 1982. He is K village's headman, and his wife and children have only lived in Mwinilunga since the 2010s.

The Portuguese colonial government imposed low wages and taxation on 'natives' in 1910 (Clarence-Smith 1979). People were not provided with a wage when working for public enterprises (Clarence-Smith 1979: 33). Trading, visiting relatives and business across the border had been conducted by local people since the colonial period in the borderland near Mwinilunga (Pesa 2019). The BSAC administration had controlled the Mwinilunga area since 1906, but it did not identify the location or basic data of each village near Mwinilunga until 1920 (Pesa 2019: 66, 73). The administration of Mwinilunga was not successful, and the K villagers were not the only local people to migrate to Mwinilunga from Portuguese West Africa.

5. A Split in the Village: Mr Ilunga's Search for a New Dwelling

Mr Lewis's maternal grandfather, Mr Ilunga, was born in 1917. He died in S Ward in 1995. Although Mr Ilunga lived in K Village, he left in 1946 to work in Kitwe in the Copperbelt Province, returning in 1960 after losing his job. He attempted to become a village headman but lost to his sibling and then moved to S Ward in Mufumbwe in 1985.

Mr Ilunga and his siblings competed for the seat of village headman in 1985. His siblings were dissatisfied with the way his return was handled, so one of his siblings seized the position. K Village, which originated in Angola, was a historic village with a long history. For Lunda men, serving as the headman of a historic village is a proud achievement. Supposedly, the dissatisfaction of Mr Ilunga's siblings over his return was rooted in their jealousy of his experience in urban areas and the wage work he performed.

After losing the contest, Mr Ilunga had to leave the village. He visited Mufumbwe District to look for a new dwelling because he heard it had many wild animals that could be hunted for food. In November 1985, he happened to meet a Luvale man, Mr Samukonga, who lived in S Ward. They came to know each other well. Mr Ilunga informed Mr Samukonga that he wanted to migrate to S Ward and build a new village.

They visited the senior headman of S Ward the following day and informed him that Mr Ilunga wanted to live in S Ward and build a new village. The senior headman allowed his migration and permitted him to build a new village. Mr Ilunga built I village. The senior headman is appointed by the local chief in Kaonde society and has the responsibility of allocating land for cultivation and building, resident registration and the arbitration of conflicts. Mr Ilunga immigrated to S Ward officially because Mr Samukonga had introduced him to the Kaonde senior headman of S Ward.

Mr Ilunga went back to K Village in Mwinilunga to re-unite with his two wives, his younger sister and seven children. They immigrated to S Ward the following week. First, they stayed at Mr Samukonga's house. Mr Samukonga gave them a daily meal immediately after their migration. One month after migration, Mr Ilunga had built a new house where he lived with his family. They purchased food, such as maize, cassava, beans, fish and chicken from their neighbours. They often worked at neighbouring farms and received cassava roots as a reward. Mr Ilunga was given cassava seed stems as a welcome gift by Mr Samukonga and began to cultivate cassava at his farm.

Mr Ilunga lost the campaign for village headman and arrived at S Ward of the Kaonde territory following his encounter with Mr Samukonga of the Luvale. He had no relatives and friends in S Ward. He spoke with a stranger (Mr Samukonga) living in S Ward and became friends with him as well as building other relationships in the area. They helped his migration to S Ward. Mr Samukonga was the guarantor for Mr Ilunga. In this case, a stranger played the role of a guarantor and mediated between a migration applicant and the local community. For this migration applicant, a stranger became a friend and then a guarantor. After achieving migration, the migrant built social ties with other local dwellers.

6. Migration between Rural and Urban Areas: Migration of the Urban-Born Mr Lewis to a Rural Village

Although Mr Lewis could trace his origins to K Village in Mwinilunga, he was born in 1974 in Mufulila, which is a mining centre in the Copperbelt Province. His father worked for a timber company there. His parents were born in villages in Mwinilunga District and moved to the Copperbelt for work.

In 1980, in the middle of the economic crisis, Mr Lewis's father left the timber company due to an employment adjustment. He began to farm to secure food for his family and travelled to seek new dwellings. He found a good area to establish a village with farming potential in Chingola District. This was the first time he had visited the area. He visited the local chief and explained his situation. The local chief allowed his family's migration. According to Mr Lewis, his father migrated to the village in Chingola District to avoid the jealousy of his relatives regarding his urban experience. He avoided going back to his home village in Mwinilunga.

Mr Lewis went to his older sister's home in Solwezi town to help her run the house in 1988. When her husband became ill and retired from work as a driver in 1989, she decided to farm. She visited her maternal grandfather, Mr Ilunga (see previous section), in S Ward to explain the loss of her cash income. He allocated her land for cultivation. She migrated to S Ward with her husband, children and Mr Lewis in May 1991.

Mr Lewis's father visited S Ward from Chingola District to see Mr Lewis's sister's family in 1993. In S Ward they ate game meat and fish every day because there were many wild animals in the local area. After a short stay in S Ward, Mr Lewis's father decided to move to S Ward with his wife and children. After migration to S Ward, he built his village, which was named M. Mr Lewis moved to M Village and was allocated a field for cultivation by his father. Shortly thereafter, Mr Lewis married a woman from a neighbouring village in 1994. His mother died in 2013 and his father died in 2017. Mr Lewis secured his livelihood in M Village in 2019, where he now lives.

Mr Lewis's seven siblings and his nieces and nephews have moved to cities for work and marriage opportunities since the 2000s. Mr Lewis has invited them to M Village and offered them the opportunity to experience the farm and housework of village life during school vacations. He also invited his sick sister to S Ward and helped her with daily life. Mr Lewis in M Village was a caring big brother to his siblings who were born in urban areas.

When Mr Lewis and his father moved to S Ward in the 1990s,

Zambia was experiencing an economic crisis and the nation was in a state of confusion. The price of agricultural products rose suddenly and both urban and rural dwellers became poor (Kodamaya 2011). People in Zambia attempted to secure subsistence by various means.

7. The Potential Created by Mobility: Building Social Ties with Strangers

Mr Lewis and I were able to meet Mr Willard, who is Mr Lewis's cousin, in Mwinilunga on the day following our departure. Mr Lewis and Mr Willard were connected through mobile phone communication. A friend of Mr Lewis studied at high school in Mwinilunga. The friend happened to meet Mr Willard and realised that he was a relative of Mr Lewis. Mr Lewis's friend knew Mr Willard's phone number and gave it Mr Lewis. During the journey they were able to contact each other on their mobile phones. They met at Mr Willard's house and, for more than five hours, they talked about the history of K Village, their families and their current lives. Mr Willard gave Mr Lewis a warm welcome and treated him to lunch and snacks. Mr Willard gave Mr Lewis two fowls before departure. Although they had only just met for the first time, they agreed to rely on each other as relatives and promised to meet again.

Mobility is an important way to secure subsistence in Africa. While kinship plays an important role in rural–urban migration and in the daily lives of migrant populations (Frayne 2007; Njwambe et al. 2019), this chapter shows that factors other than kinship also play an important role in migration. Each member of Mr Lewis's family migrated and subsisted with support from individuals who were not relatives.

The K villagers escaped from the inhumane policies of the Portuguese colonial government and migrated to Northern Rhodesia to make a better life. Migration offered K Villagers the potential to overcome the severe conditions of daily life. It is not unusual for slash-and-burn cultivators to move to better surroundings on a regular basis (Oyama and Kondo 2007; Hara 2020). It is likely that the members of Mr Lewis's family had no relatives in Mwinilunga when they migrated to Northern Rhodesia. It is not clear how they found a suitable location to establish dwellings in Mwinilunga, but it is likely that they did so by building a relationship of trust with a guarantor in the local community.

When Mr Ilunga, Mr Lewis's maternal grandfather, had to leave K Village in Mwinilunga due to conflict with his siblings, he moved to S Ward in Mufumbwe District where he had no relatives or friends. Only with the assistance of Mr Samukonga, whom Mr Ilunga met for the first time in S Ward, was he able to immigrate. Mr Ilunga and Mr Samukonga met in S Ward and developed a close friendship. Mr Samukonga introduced Mr Ilunga to the senior headman of S Ward and other members of the local community. A migration applicant needs a guarantor who will provide a connection between the migrant and the local community. Guarantors are not part of any official government system and are not influenced by the local chief. The guarantor plays the role of supporting migrants on the basis of a close personal relationship. A migrant needs to build a close friendship with a potential guarantor who is a stranger to him or her. After getting to know each other, the migrant will expand his or her social ties in the community through the guarantor's support.

Migration with the assistance of a guarantor is popular in northwestern Zambia. For example, there was a case in which drinking companions in an urban bar helped migration applicants to migrate to a rural village. The migrants moved to new locations by relying on their own social ties not only with relatives but also with close friends, colleagues and even strangers. Any person in a local community can become a guarantor if he or she is trusted by a migration applicant. A guarantor also confirms that a migration applicant has a suitable character. It is important for migrants to build close relationships with strangers, even if they meet by chance, as they may be potential guarantors. As Mr Samukonga became the guarantor for Mr Ilunga in S ward, the social ties that were built light-heartedly functioned to sustain mobility and subsistence for the migrant in a vulnerable economic, social and political situation in Africa.

Mr Ilunga built social ties with neighbours through food bartering and hosting relatives, such as Mr Lewis, after their migration. For migrants, a person who was initially a stranger can become a friend and then a reliable friend in their daily life during and after migration. The social ties of migrants expand through migration and might have the potential to sustain subsistence for his or her family after migration.

Mr Lewis, his parents and his siblings lived in an urban area for a long time before migrating to S Ward with Mr. Ilunga's assistance. While many urban dwellers in Africa rely on their home villages and relatives as a form of insurance against urban life (Ferguson 1999; Cliggett 2003; Njwambe et al. 2019), Mr Lewis's father did not return home because he wanted to avoid his relative's jealously. This is not an uncommon phenomenon – people who experience urban life and its wage work tend to move to new villages after giving up urban life because there is a tendency that they will be isolated and excluded by their relatives back home (Ferguson 1999). Even if they do not earn an income in the city, village relatives still tend to think that urban migrants have a lot of money. For rural villagers, the urban experience is glorious. Urban dwellers returning home have to give their relatives and friends money, food and clothes from city, whether they have it or not. Not bringing anything may mean they cannot live in peace once back in the village.

Mr Ilunga and Mr Lewis's father had to leave their home villages to survive. People in these situations need to rely on strangers as potential guarantors to restart their lives in a new place. In this case, it was difficult for Mr Lewis and his siblings, who were born in urban areas, to rely on their parents' home village in Mwinilunga. It was a strange environment for them. M Village, which was built by Mr Lewis's father and sustained by Mr Lewis, should have been a sanctuary for Mr Lewis's siblings living in urban areas.

The encounter with Mr Lewis and Mr Willard was realised through the mediation of Mr Lewis's friend. This social tie was also built by mobility. The interrupted kinship was re-established because they had kept moving. Mobility is important for overcoming difficult situations in daily life by seeking a better life in a new location. The social ties made with strangers through the process of migration also provide the potential for ensuring subsistence. Building and expanding social ties with strangers can have a strong positive effect on the quality of life for migrants and their families, ensuring that people in turbulent African societies can secure their place in a community and live well. The migration history of Mr Lewis's family showed that mobility and social ties with strangers, who can later act as guarantors, have the potential to secure people's subsistence against the vulnerable economic and social situation in Africa.

Endnote

[1] The names of all persons referred to in this chapter have been changed to preserve their anonymity.

Acknowledgements

This chapter was financially supported by the Japan Society for the Promotion of Science (JSPS) KAKENHI grant numbers 13J02843, 16H06318 and 19K20552 and a Sasakawa Scientific Research Grant from the Japan Science Society.

References

Clarence-Smith, W. G. (1979) *Slaves, Peasants and Capitalists in Southern Angola 1840–1926*, Cambridge: Cambridge University Press.

Cliggett, L. (2003) 'Gift remitting and alliance building in Zambian modernity: Old answers to modern problems', *American Anthropologist,* Vol. 105, No. 3, pp. 543–552.

Crehan, K. (1997) *The Fractured Community: Landscapes of Power and Gender in Rural Zambia*, Berkeley: University of California Press.

CSO (Central Statistical Office) (2012) *Zambia 2010 Census of Population and Housing: Population Summary Report*, Lusaka: Central Statistical Office.

Ferguson, J. (1999) *Expectations of Modernity: Myths and Meanings of Urban Life on the Zambian Copperbelt*, Berkeley: University of California Press.

Frayne, B. (2004) 'Migration and urban survival strategies in Windhoek, Namibia', *Geoforum*, Vol. 35, Issue 4, pp. 489–505.

———— (2007) 'Migration and the changing social economy of Windhoek, Namibia', *Development Southern Africa*, Vol. 24, No. 1, pp. 91–108.

Hara, M. (2017) 'Regional food security to cope with agricultural policy changes in north-western Zambia', *Japanese Journal of Human Geography*, Vol. 69, No. 1, pp. 9–25.

———— (2020) 'Coexistence of multiple ethnic groups practicing different slash-and-burn cultivation systems adapted to field conditions in miombo woodlands in northwestern Zambia', *TROPICS*, Vol. 28, No. 4, pp. 75–89.

Heisler, H. (1974) *Urbanisation and the Government of Migration: The Inter-relation of Urban and Rural Life in Zambia*, London: C. Hurst and Company.

ILO (International Labour Office) and JASPA (Jobs and Skills Programme for Africa) (1977) *Narrowing the Gaps: Planning for Basic Needs and Productive Employment in Zambia*, Addis Ababa:

International Labour Office.

Kodamaya, S. (2011) 'Agricultural policies and food security of smallholder farmers in Zambia', *African Study Monographs, Supplementary Issues*, Vol. 42, pp. 19–39.

Njwambe, A., Cocks, M. and Vetter, S. (2019) 'Ekhayeni: Rural-urban migration, belonging and landscapes of home in South Africa', *Journal of Southern African Studies*, Vol. 45, No. 2, pp. 413–431.

Ogura, M. (1991) 'Rural-urban migration in Zambia and migrants ties to home villages', *The Development Economies*, Vol. 29, No. 2, pp. 145–165.

Oyama, S. and Kondo, F. (2007) 'Sorghum cultivation and soil fertility preservation under *bujimi* slash-and-burn cultivation in northwestern Zambia', *African Study Monographs, Supplementary Issues*, Vol. 34, pp. 115-135.

Pesa, I. (2019) *Roads through Mwinilunga: A History of Social Change in Northwest Zambia*, Leiden: Brill.

Potts, D. (1995) 'Shall we go home? Increasing urban poverty in African cities and migration processes', *The Geographical Journal*, Vol. 161, No. 3, pp. 245–264.

———— (2005) 'Counter-urbanisation on the Zambian Copperbelt? Interpretations and Implications', *Urban Studies*, Vol. 42, No. 4, pp. 583–609.

Roberts, A. (1976) *A History of Zambia*, London: Heinemann Educational Books Ltd.

van der Geest, K. (2010) 'Local perceptions of migration from north-west Ghana', *Africa*, Vol. 80, No. 4, pp. 595–619.

World Bank (2020) 'Urban population (% of total population) Zambia', World Bank Open Data (https://data.worldbank.org/indicator/SP.URB.TOTL.IN.ZS?locations=ZM) (Accessed: 14 February 2020).

Chapter 8

Urban Developments, the Diminishing Agricultural Land and the Significance of Urban Backyard Gardens in the City of Lusaka, Zambia

Godfrey Hampwaye, Garikai Membele and Linda Namakando

1. Introduction

By 2050, close to 70 per cent of the world's population is projected to be living in urban areas and will number over 6.7 billion people (Bocquier 2005; United Nations 2018). In particular, Africa's urban population is growing at a very high rate. The urban population increased from 27 per cent in 1950 to 40 per cent in 2015 and is projected to rise to 66 per cent by 2050 (United Nations 2014). Rural urban migration is one of the major causes of the rapid increase of urbanites in most cities in the Global South (Lall et al. 2006). The population of Zambia increased from 7,759,117 in 1990 to 9,885,591 in 2000, 13,046,508 in 2010 and is now estimated to be over 18 million (Central Statistical Office 2011). Over 44 per cent of the country's population lived in urban areas in 2018 (Plecher 2020). Urban agriculture in Zambia is neither embraced in policy nor in urban development planning processes (Simatele et al. 2012).

The high rate of urbanisation in cities in the Global South has brought a lot of environmental, cultural, social and economic impacts (Thuo 2013). The rapid increase of the urban population has also exerted a lot of pressure on urban land use. Land use changes, especially in the Global South, have adversely affected people's food security due to the fast rate at which agricultural land is diminishing in preference for other land uses such as industrial, commercial and residential uses (Wang et al. 2016). These land use changes also adversely affect local traders or marketeers who rely on the availability of assorted farm produce for their livelihood, as well as to support urban food security by ensuring that there is easy access to affordable food especially for the urban poor. Notwithstanding, the significance of agriculture in urban settings in Africa is still an issue of debate (Hampwaye et al. 2007).

Lusaka city, like any other city in the Global South, is experiencing high urban growth. Between 2000 and 2010 the city had the highest growth rate in the country at 4.7 per cent. Urban Agriculture has been a significant characteristic of Lusaka's land use, which can be traced as far back as the 1920s (Hampwaye et al. 2007). The rapidly growing population of Lusaka is on the verge of changing the narrative because agricultural land is diminishing at unprecedented levels. Diminishing agriculturl land is made worse by the Lusaka City Council's lack of interest in reducing the rate at which agricultural land is diminishing. The planning authority has also not taken time to assess the impact of the loss of agricultural land on the livelihood of food traders and the urban poor in the city.

Remote sensing and Geographical Information Systems (GIS) provide a powerful suite for analysing the spatial and temporal dynamics of land cover and land use (Herold et al. 2003; Dewan and Yamaguchi 2008). Remote sensing data provide multi-temporal data on the processes and patterns of land cover and land use while the GIS is valuable for analysing and mapping the patterns (Treitz and Rogan 2004; Yuan et al. 2005). Information derived from remote sensing and GIS has been very helpful for decision making and guiding policy interventions (Treitz and Rogan 2004).

Based on the field research conducted in Makeni, remote sensing data and GIS and interviews with key informants and marketeers from a local community market, this chapter explores the impact of land use change, particularly of agricultural land conversion to other uses, on the livelihoods of the residents of Lusaka, especially the marketeers who depend on buying crops from the surrounding small-holder farms in Lusaka.

The chapter is structured in such a manner that it starts with the introduction, which essentially contextualises the discussion, before moving to the description of the the city of Lusaka as the study area. This section describes the study area by giving the geographical location, climate and socio-economic features. The chapter then examines trends of land use change in peri-urban areas, followed by a section on materials and methods which outlines the materials used and describes how data were collected and analysed. The next section focuses on agricultural land reduction in the Makeni area of Lusaka. Before finally presenting the discussion and conclusion, the chapter discusses the role of backyard gardens in improving livelihoods in urban areas, especially in Lusaka. It is argued that some of the residents are innovative and seize the opportunity of utilising backyards to grow food crops mainly for comsumption.

2. Lusaka: Capital City of Zambia

Lusaka is the administrative and capital city of Zambia. It is located between longitudes 22°–34° east and latitudes 9°–18° south. Figure 1 shows the location of the study sites in the city of Lusaka. The population growth in Lusaka greatly influences the settlement and its development dynamics. The population of Lusaka increased from 769,353 in 1990 to 1,084,703 in 2000. In 2010, the population increased to 1,747,152 (Central Statistical Office 2012). In 2010, Lusaka had an annual average growth rate of 4.9 per cent. The population is currently estimated to be close to three million people. More than 70 per cent of people in Lusaka live in informal settlements comprising only 20 per cent of the city's residential land (World Bank 2002).

Daily mean temperatures for Lusaka range from about 8°C in the cold season to about 34°C in the hot dry season. Lusaka experiences

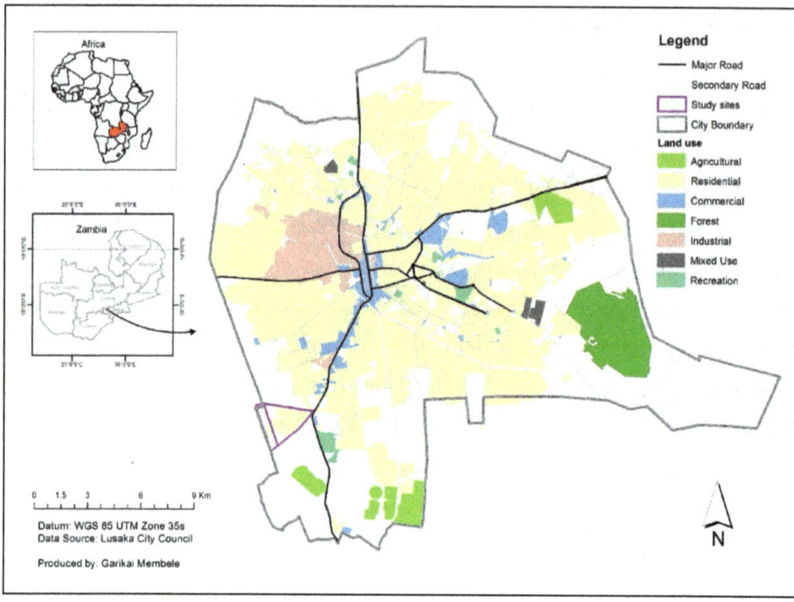

Figure 1. Location of study site in Lusaka District
Source: Research by authors in 2020.

a subtropical climate that has three seasons. The cool dry season is from April to mid-August, the hot dry season is from mid-August to mid-November and the warm wet season is from mid-November to mid-April. The average annual rainfall in Lusaka is 803 millimetre of which 95 per cent falls in the warm wet season (Nkhuwa et al. 2006). The topography of Lusaka is generally flat. It has an elevation ranging from 1,200 metre to 1,300 metre above sea level.

3. Trends of Land Use Change in Peri-Urban Areas

The worlds's uban population has been projected to increase and comprise close to 70 per cent of the world's population numbering over 6.7 billion people by 2050; about 90 per cent of this increase is said to take place in Asia and Africa (Bocquier 2005; United Nations 2018). Rural urban migration is one of the major causes of the rapid increase of urbanites in most cities in Africa (Lall et al.

2006). The rapid population increase in Africa has contributed to peri-urban expansion, leading to competition for limited land resources (FAO 2011; Appiah et al. 2019). It has also led to rapid conversion of large prime agricultural land in peri-urban areas to urban land use (Appiah et al. 2019). Population increase in African cities has also led to the sub-division of prime agricultural land into small uneconomical units. Generally, increased agricultural production in many African countries is usually achieved through the use of more land and not intensification (FAO 2017). Therefore, reduced farm sizes undoubtedly mean reduced production in most African countries. Howerver, Antwi (2020) proposes an integrated soil fertility managent system to ensure crop production all year round and improved crop yield in Ghana.

Gitau (2018) revealed that agricultural land is reducing at an alarming rate in many African cities as it is being converted to built-up areas. In Kenya, agricultural land reduced from 8,430 hectares in 1995 to 4,377 hectares in 2018 entailing that 4,053 hectares of prime agricultural land had been converted into built-up areas within a period of 23 years (Gitau 2018). In Ghana land use/land cover maps show a decline in agricultural land, mainly due to the high demand for land for settlement development (Antwi 2020). Naab et al. (2013) submit that demand for land for industrial and commercial use in Ghana has further contributed to decreased agricultural land. This has led to low agricultural productivity and food insecurity in peri-urban areas.

Appiah et al. (2019) argued that the diminishing of agricultural land is critical in determining the amount of food produce. In Kenya, food production has been threatened due to changes in land use which have seen large amounts of agricultural land being converted into urban land uses such as residential, commercial and industrial uses (Musa and Odera 2015; Gitau 2018). The rate at which agricultural land is being converted to other urban land uses surpasses the ability of the current available land to provide food for the growing population in most African countries.

The impact of changes in land use on food production is a major concern and has been a subject of many studies recently. For instance, analysis of the conversion of other land cover categories to built-up land conducted in Anyigba Nigeria by Tokula and Ejaro (2012) showed that agricultural land lost a lot of land to built-up areas and this had implications on food production, food security and maintenance of the biodiversity. The development of the State University in Anyigba for instance saw a rise in the demand for land for residential and other developments. Most agricultural land was converted to residential in order to build houses for the university staff and also for those that offered business services to the university. Within a period of two years, agriculture land visibly reduced in size around the town. This led to shortages of local farm produce and a rise in food prices. Similar implications were observed by Ogechi and Hunja (2014) in Kisii County, Kenya, where food production decreased by 29 per cent over five years due to diminishing agricultural land.

Zambia, like other African countries, is affected by conversions of agricultural land. Urban agriculture has been an important part of city life in Lusaka. However, the importance of agriculture has reduced over the years as agricultural land is giving way to urban development. As Lusaka's built-up area is expanding, it is also taking up agricultural productive land, leaving little scope for long term practice of urban agriculture (JICA 2009). Agricultural land in the city of Lusaka is mostly in the peri-urban areas to the south, west and east of the city. These areas include Makeni in the south of the city, Ibex hill to the east of the city and Lusaka west in the west. The total area of agricultural land in Lusaka decreased from 397 square kilometre in 2000 to 285 square kilometre in 2009. Residential development and some industrial development have taken over agricultural land in Lusaka (Simwanda and Murayama 2017).

JICA (2009) further states that residential areas in Lusaka including formal settlements, informal settlements and rural smallholdings have drastically increased shares from 35 per cent to 50 per cent out of the total land area of the city. Meanwhile, large pieces of land zoned as agricultural land in urban fringes has been decreased from 47 per cent to 14 per cent (JICA 2009).

Geographical distribution of land use change is identified in the areas along Kafue Road which indicates incidences of land use change from agricultural to industrial, and urban sprawl of residential areas in the southern and eastern parts of Lusaka on agricultural land. Built-up area has increased its share from 43.5 per cent to 63.7 per cent out of the total land area of Lusaka city and most of these developments took place on former agricultural land (JICA 2009).

The majority of farmers in Lusaka City are small-scale farmers, presently producing cabbages, tomatoes, baby corn, beans, rape, Chinese cabbage, eggplants, peas and tomatos as fresh vegetables for city consumers and home consumption, while commercial farmers have settled outside the Lusaka city, Chongwe and Chisamba districts, with large capital investment to manufacture domestic and export-oriented products. In Zambia, and specifically Lusaka, the implications of diminishing agricultural land and food production as well as the impact on food security and generally on people's livelihoods deserve critical consideration.

4. Materials and Methods

4-1. Data Used

The United States Geological Survey Earth Explorer (URL: https://earthexplorer.usgs.gov/) was used to obtain Landsat satellite images for 1990, 2000, 2010 and 2017. Much care was taken to ensure that the images had less than 5 per cent cloud cover and that they were acquired within the same season. Table 1 shows the description of the satellite data used in this study.

High resolution satellites namely Quickbird (0.6 m spatial resolution) and Aerial photographs (0.2 m spatial resolution) obtained from the Survey Department were used in this study. Vector data in the form of plot boundaries covering the study sites (farms which were originally plot number F/50a and F/401a) in Lusaka were sources from the Survey Department.

Table 1. Satellite data used in the study

Year	Satellite	Resolution (m)	Path/Row	Observation date
1990	Landsat 5 TM	30	172/071	25 September 1990
2000	Landsat 7 TM	30	172/071	14 October 2000
2010	Landsat 7 TM	30	172/071	15 October 2010
2017	Landsat 8 OLI/TIRS	30	172/071	30 August 2017

Source: Research by authors in 2020.

4-2. Methodology

Atmospheric correction was conducted on all the images and geo-referencing was also done to orient the images to UTM zone 35 south and to the local datum Arc 1950. The vector data covering the entire extent of farms F/50a and 401a was used to clip the Landsat scene to obtain the areas of interest. Bands 1–5 and 7 for Landsat 5 and 7 TM and bands 2–7 for Landsat 8 OLI/TIRS were used to generate the composite images for 1990, 2000, 2010 and 2017 respectively. Land cover/land use change was analysed using unsupervised classification. The K-means clustering algorithm was used to classify the Landsat satellite images into agriculture and built-up land classes. The K-means classifier executes the land cover land use classification based on similarity of samples and classes centres are grouped through iteration until the best clustering results are obtained. Unsupervised classification was used because the study areas is generally small (419 hectares) and homogenous hence prior knowledge was not required (Phiri and Morgenroth 2017). The formula below was used for this purpose:

$$j_j = \sum_{x \in s_j(l)} \left\| x - z_j(l+1) \right\|^2 \quad (1) \qquad \text{and} \qquad z_j(l+1) = \frac{1}{N_j} \sum_{x \in s(l)} x \quad (2)$$

Here j_i is the clustering criteria of error sum of squares and N_j is the sample number contained in S_j which is the clustering class j, and j = 1,2,3…k

In the absence of a high resolution image for 1990, a Google Earth image for the 1990s was used to assess the accuracy of the 1990 classification while the Quickbird images for 2000 and 2010 were used to assess the classification for 2000 and 2010 respectively. The 2016 aerial photography was used on the 2017 image.

The land use maps were processed in ArcGIS 10.5 to obtain the rate at which agricultural land diminished from 1990 to 2017, including the size of land available for agriculture.

Data were further collected using both quantitative and qualitative methods. Quantitative data were collected using the interview schedule technique administered on marketeers at a local market, whereas qualitative data were obtained through an interview guide with key informants. The marketeers basically provided information on the impact of agricultural activities on the study area. In terms of data analysis, qualitative data were analysed using content analysis while quantitative data were analysed using descriptive statistics, including tables and graphs.

5. Agricultural Land Reduction in Makeni

In terms of land conversions in the Makeni agricultural area, two farms (Farm 50a and Farm 401a as indicated in Figure 2) were selected and studied to provide evidence for the extent of agricultural land reductions in Makeni area and Lusaka as a whole.

For Farm 50a, it should be noted that it was originally 108 hectares while farm 401a was 311 hectares. The attribute-based analysis conducted in a GIS shows that the smallest plots on farms 50a and 401a are 540 square metres (36 metre x 15 metre). The first subdivision was done in 1972 with an area of 19,500 square metres (100 metre x 195 metre).

In the late 1990s smaller plots for residential use began to be subdivided. The largest plots are on Farm 401a with an area of 403,237 square metres while the second largest is 124,559 square metres. The reduced land sizes generally entail reduced agricultural productivity (Figure 2).

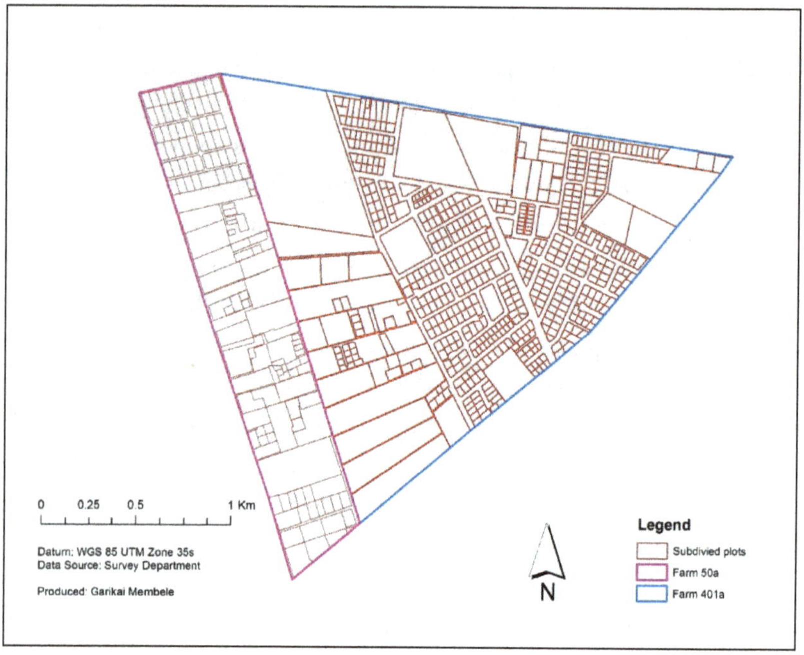

Figure 2. Subdivision in Farm 50a and Farm 401a

Source: Research by authors in 2020.

Furthermore, an assessment of the rate of land use/land cover change in the study area shows that the land available for cultivation in the study area (455.53 hectares) in 1990 reduced by 7 per cent in 2000. There was a further reduction of 38 per cent from 2010 to 2017. This is due to the rapid increase in hectares built-up area. When compared to the other years analysed, built-up increased significantly in 2000 from a paltry 7 hectares in 1990 to 40 hectares in 2000 (Table 1 and Figure 2).

It is evident from Table 2 that the major threat to agrictural land in the City of Lusaka is the built-up area. Whereas the agricultural land declined steadily from 1990 to 2017, built-up land use rapidly increased during the same period (Figure 2, Figure 3 and Table 2). Therefore, the implication is that built-up area is replacing agricultural land in Lusaka. Such decline in agricultural land has implications for food production, food security and livelihoods of the residents in the city.

Clearly, the decline in the available land for agricultural purposes has consequences in terms of food production in the city. As for crop production, the findings show that among the property owners interviewed, 90 per cent agreed to producing vegetables such as cabbages, rape and pumpkin leaves on their farms before the year 2000. Only 10 per cent of respondents were not productive prior to the year 2000. However, at the time of fieldwork, only about 20 per cent of the respondents were still productive on the available pieces of land.

Consequently, crop production declined as alluded to by the respondents (50 per cent) who stated that there has been a reduction in crop production in Makeni due to a reduction in agricultural land. The study findings reveal that 20 per cent of the respondents recorded an increase in agricultural production while 30 per cent felt indifferent, implying that nothing had changed between 1990 and 2017.

Reduced agricultural production entailed difficulties for the local traders of horticultural products between farmers and the local

Table 2. Land use change dynamics 1990–2017 in hectares

Land cover	1990	2000	change (%)	2010	change (%)	2017	change (%)
Crop land	455.53	422.02	-7.4	369.41	-12.5	230.67	-37.6
Built-up	6.85	40.37	489.3	92.97	130.3	423.67	355.7

Source: Remote sensing analysis by authors in 2020.

markets. It should be stated that the Makeni area used to be a source of products for the surrounding markets such as Chawama, John Laing, Soweto and Makeni Simoson (Figure 4).

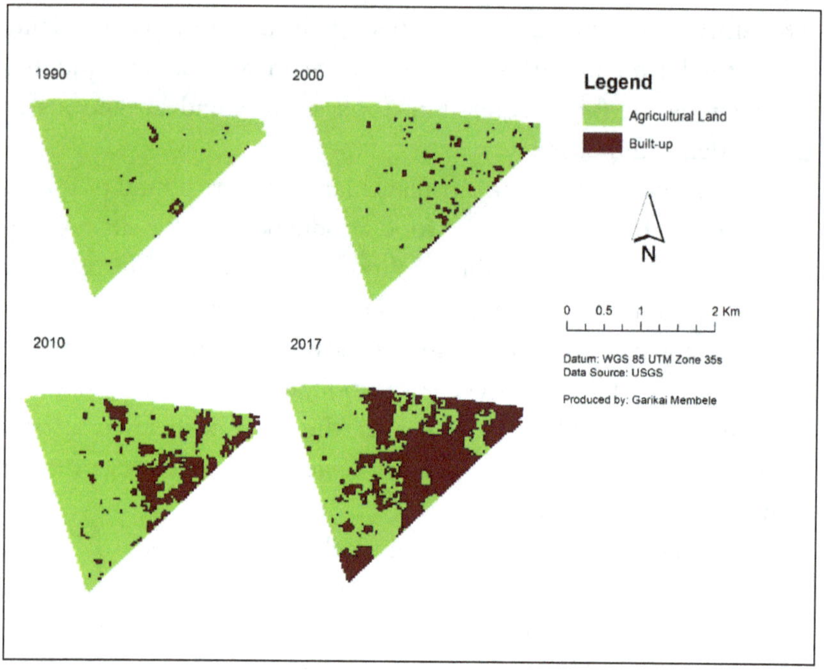

Figure 3. Multi-temporal reduction of agricultural land use
Source: Research by authors in 2020.

The scenario has, however, changed since 1990 as the importance of Makeni has adversely changed. Those who were purchasing their agricultural produce for sale by farmers outside Lusaka who bring their produce to Soweto were only 16.7 percent in 2000 and 50 per cent in 2005. In 2017, there was an increase of up to 70 per cent of the traders getting their produce from Soweto (farmers outside Lusaka). There is also a corresponding reduction on those who are buying agricultural produce from Makeni area. This implies that there is a direct relationship between decreasing agricultural land

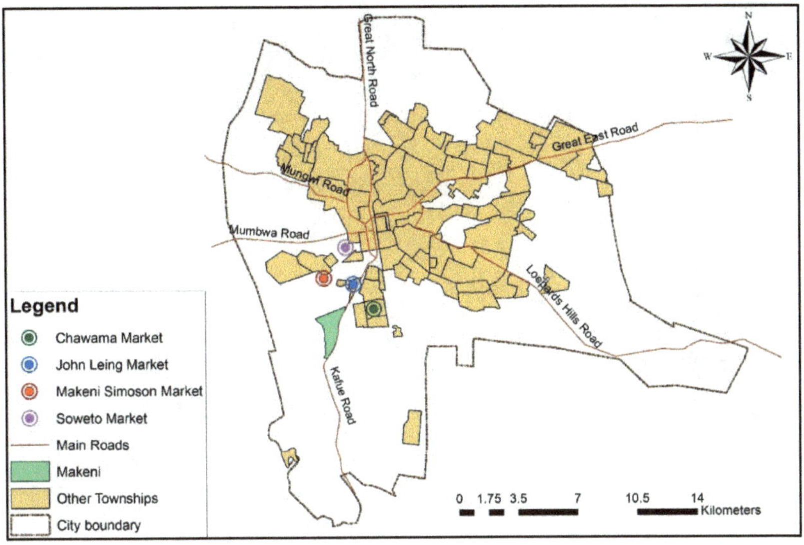

Figure 4. Local markets around Makeni

Source: Research by authors in 2020.

and reduced food production, because the two have been reducing synonymously over the years as evidenced from the decreasing number of traders getting agricultural produce from Makeni. Before 2017, it is stated that the agricultural food production in Makeni was sufficient for the surrounding markets to purchase and farmers could still sell part of the produce to places far from their immediate surroundings.

The major sources of agricultural produce coming outside Lusaka include such places as Kabwe, Chibombo, Chisamba, Chongwe and Chilanga (Figure 5). These sources have increasingly become sources of agricultural products in Lusaka over the years and this means an extra cost of food due to transportation of the agricultural products over to long distances.

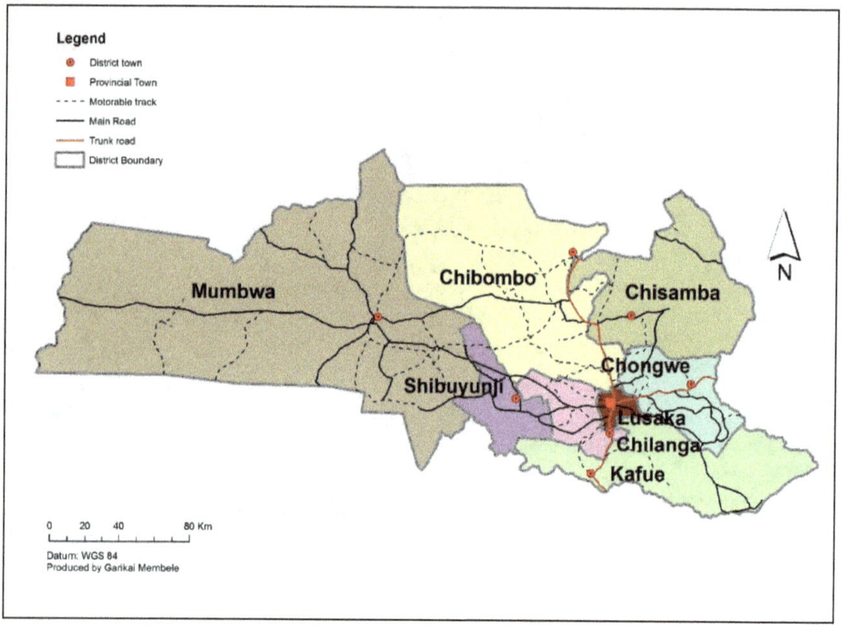

Figure 5. Sources of agricultural produce outside Lusaka
Source: Research by authors in 2020.

6. Roles of Backyard Gardens in Improving Livelihoods in Lusaka

The local people in Lusaka especially the urbanites have responded to the increasing food insecurity in the city by enganging in urban agriculture (Thornton et al. 2010). This is being done through backyard gardens also called on-plot gardens. The urban poor are also growing crops on open spaces in the city, mostly bare institutional land, road reserves, dambos and river banks. These open spaces are, however, increasingly diminishing due to the fast urban developments taking place in the city. According to Hampwaye et al. (2007) and Nel et al. (2009), urban agriculture is a very important survival strategy for the urban poor in Lusaka, especially for women and the youth.

Hampwaye et al. (2009) conducted a study with 400 households in Lusaka and three other cities namely Ndola, Kitwe and Kabwe. The study findings show that backyard gardens significantly contributed to total household income, cheaper food and minimum nutrition requirements for most people in the four cities. In addition the same study findings indicated that close to 60 per cent of households in the four cities were engaged in backyard cultvation. They also found that 80 per cent of the crops produced in the backyard gardens were consumed at the household level (own consumpation). For Lusaka in particular, the study findings demomstrated that households consumed 80 per cent to 100 per cent of the crops they produced in the backyard gardens. Furthermore, close to 50 per cent of the householsd in these cities sold their livestock (mainly broilers) to earn extra income. Hampwaye et al. (2009) further found that backyard gardens contributed 42 per cent of total household income in the four towns. Hence it is argued that backyard gardens are an important survival strategy for the combating of food insecurity in the city, which has largely been caused by unprecedented conversion of agricultural land to other land uses.

Although backyard gardens are important in Lusaka, the Lusaka City Council does not seem to have a clear policy supporting backyard gardens and urban agriculture in general. However, backyard gardens are tolerated albeit crops like maize are considered breeding grounds for mosquitoes which cause malaria. There are also concerns about poor handling of agricultural chemicals (Hampwaye et al. 2007).

7. Discussion

It is an undeniable fact that urban developments are taking away land which was originally planned for agriculture in the peri-urban areas of Lusaka. This is based on the GIS analyses of the area between 1990 and 2017, which shows that most of the land for agriculture has been converted into built-up area, especially residential and commercial land uses. This analysis was confirmed by a key informant from Lusaka City Council who stated that 'there has been two distinct types of land use changes in Makeni from either agriculture to residential and agriculture to commercial and there was no record of land use change from residential or commercial to agricultural' (Key informant No. 1, 19 August 2017).

As JICA (2009) noted, there has been a significant reduction of agricultural land, especially in the urban fringes from 47 per cent to 14 per cent in 2009 due to the expansion of settlements, both informal and formal. This finding is in tandem with findings from studies of other cities in the Global South (FAO 1999, 2017, 2019; Gitau 2018; Njiru 2016; Musa and Odera 2015; Tokula and Ejaro 2012; Van Dijk et al. 2012). It is categorically clear that agricultural land is under immense pressure as the city grows and more land is needed for other land uses, which seemingly tends to yield higher returns. In explaining the causes of land use conversions from agriculture to other uses, a key informant from the Ministry of Local Government in Zambia revealed that 'population growth, housing deficit, real estate business, shortage of agricultural inputs and low returns and profitability of agricultural land, are the main causes of reduced agricultural land in Lusaka' (Key informant No. 2, 15 August 2017).

Apparently, the Lusaka City Council and the Lusaka Provincial Planning Authority do not control but are only facilitating these land use conversions. At this rate at which agricultural land is diminishing, sooner than later all the agricultural produce for the city of Lusaka will come from the outside districts with serious implications on the cost of food for ordinary residents owing to high transport costs. Cheelo et al. (2019) found that the proportion of income spent on food among the poor in Lusaka is very high. It is estimated that about 47 per cent of poor people's income in Lusaka is spent on food (FAO and RUAF 2019).

One of the implications of a reduction in agricultural land in the study area has been a corresponding reduction in agricultural produce from within the city. A reduction in food production due to loss of agricultural land has been noted in many other studies in the world (Antwi 2020; Gitau 2018; Rondhi et al 2018; Njiru 2016; Zambia Land Alliance 2011; Quasem 2011; JICA 2009). Consequently, issues of food insecurity emerge as residents find it difficult to access food. As explained by several authors, loss of land for agriculture has led to decline in food production (Muṣeleku 2013; Quasem 2011; Tokula and Ejaro 2012). This has not, however, been the case in China. According to the studies by Jiang et al. (2013), the reduction in agricultural land did not lead to a decline in food production. To the contrary, food production increased due to intensification and application of chemicals. In the case of Makeni in Lusaka, the majority of the traders who used to buy and sell agricultural produce are no longer able to. Antwi (2020) has suggested an integrated soil fertility management system in Ghana to improve crop yields but the extent to which this can work is a discussion for another day due to the fact that in future there may be even no or very little land to cultivate around major cities.

These traders, therefore, shifted their attention to other sources outside the city to buy the agricultural products. These outside sources, however, are quite distant from Lusaka to the extent that the farthest could be approximately 200 kilometres from Lusaka. The implication of sourcing the produce from distant places hinges around the final retail price of the produce for the residents and the profitability levels of the business as well its viability. The challenges of accessing merchandise produced from far away sources affects the livelihoods of both the traders and the residents. The residents are particularly adversely affected owing to their inability to afford this produce being sold at exorbitant prices due to the high transportation costs. FAO and RUAF (2019) estimated that over 60 per cent of food sold in Lusaka is not produced within the city. The significant increase of built-up land from 1990 corresponds to the increase in population in the city. By 2000, about one-third of the urban population was living in Lusaka and the population was growing at about 4 per cent per annum and between 2000 and 2010, the annual growth rate was at 5 per cent per annum (Mulenga 2013).

The poor have, however, devised mechanisms and responded in order to reduce the impact of the increased transport and food prices in the city. The urban poor have maximised the production of crops in their backyards (Hampwaye et al. 2009). Hampwaye et al. (2009) have contended that the backyard gardens significantly contribute to households' total income, access to cheaper food, minimum nutrition requirements and poverty reduction in general.

8. Conclusion

In conclusion, the study has demonstrated that, indeed, as a result of urban developments, such as industrial growth, expansion of settlements and general urbanisation, land which was originally planned for agriculture in Lusaka, in general, and Makeni, in particular, is under threat. Analyses by GIS techniques and findings from other studies such as those done by JICA (2009) have confirmed that there has been a significant reduction in agricultural land in Lusaka over the years.

Resulting from this scenario, there have been negative effects on the food production, and food access by most residents, especially the urban poor. The major food sources for the city are currently in the surrounding districts which entail that food prices have been adjusted upwards due to transport costs as some sources are located farther away from Lusaka. Therefore, many of the low income residents of the city have challenges in accessing this food.

Apart from food insecurity, the traders are also impacted negatively as the customers experience affordability challenges. For the traders, this is their livelihood and any disruption in their business poses a serious hindrance to their source of income. When most of the produce was sourced locally, the prices were relatively low and therefore affordable by most people in the city. It is therefore critical for the planners to consider the importance of food for the city when considering converting agricultural land use to other uses. Further, the planning authority should consider incentives to existing farmers in the city to minimise the rate at which agricultural land is diminishing in preference to other uses. Available farmers in the city should also be engaged to explore and consider intensive methods of farming to increase food production in the city. Overall, agricultural land conversions in the city of Lusaka have contributed to food insecurity among the low income residents and deprived traders of the opportunity to grow their businesses. The municipality should encourage backyard gardens in the city as they are an important survival strategy for the urban poor, especially for the women and the youth, instead of considering them as health hazards. Educational campaigns can be conducted to educate households engaged in backyard gardening on better and safer ways of growing crops and rearing livestock in the city (Hampwaye et al. 2007, 2009).

Acknowledgements

This work was supported by JSPS KAKENHI Grant Number JP16H06318.

References

Antwi, M. (2020) 'Integrated soil fertility management as a potential for Ghana's development: The geospatial approach', in Y. Ofosu-Kusi and M. Matsuda (eds) *The Challenge of African Potentials: Conviviality, Informality and Futurity*, Bamenda: Langaa RPCIG, pp. 115–142.

Appiah, D. O., Asante, F. and Nketiah, B. (2019) 'Perspectives on agricultural land use conversion and food security in rural Ghana', *Sci*, Vol. 1, No. 1 (https://doi.org/10.3390/sci1010014.v1) (accessed: 17 November 2020).

Bocquier, P. (2005) 'World urbanization prospects: An alternative to the UN model of projection compatible with the mobility transition theory', *Demographic Research*, Vol. 12, pp. 197–236 (https://doi.org/10.4054/demres.2005.12.9) (accessed: 22 December 2020).

Central Statistical Office (2011) *2010 Census Population and Housing Preliminary Report*, Lusaka: Central Statistical Office.

——— (2012) *2010 Census of Population Summary Report*, Lusaka: Central Statistical Office.

Cheelo, C., Mckee, D., Sanni, M. and Cheelo, M. (2019) *Affordability of Protein-Rich Foods: Evidence from Zambia*, Lusaka: Southern African Institute for Policy and Research.

Dewan, A. M. and Yamaguchi, Y. (2008) 'Land use and land cover change in Greater Dhaka, Bangladesh: Using remote sensing to promote sustainable urbanization', *Applied Geography*, Vol. 29, Issue 3, pp. 390–401 (https://doi.org/10.1016/j.apgeog.2008.12.005) (accessed: 18 November 2020).

FAO (Food and Agriculture Organization of the United Nations) (1999) *Spotlight Issues in Urban Agriculture Studies Suggest that up to Two-Thirds of City and Peri-Urban Households are Involved in Farming*, Rome: FAO.

——— (2011) *The State of the World's Land and Water Resources for Food and Agriculture: Managing Systems at Risk*, Rome: FAO (http://www.fao.org/3/a-i1688e.pdf) (accessed: 18 November 2020).

——— (2017) *The Future of Food and Agriculture: Trends and Challenges*, Rome: FAO (http://www.fao.org/3/a-i6583e.pdf) (accessed: 19 July 2020).

——— (2019) *FAO Framework for the Urban Food Agenda Leveraging Sub-National and Local Government Action to Ensure Sustainable Food Systems and Improved Nutrition*, Rome: FAO (http://www.fao.org/3/CA3151EN/ca3151en.pdf) (accessed: 1 July 2020).

FAO and RUAF (Resource Centres on Urban Agriculture and Food Security) (2019) *Assessing and Planning the City Region Food System - Lusaka Zambia*, Food and Agriculture Organization of the United Nations and RUAF Foundation (http://www.fao.org/3/ca6078en/CA6078EN.pdf) (accessed: 18 November 2020).

Gitau, J. M. (2018) 'Analysis of land use land cover change and its implication on peri-urban agriculture: Case study; Kiambu Sub-county in Kiambu County, Kenya', Doctoral dissertation, University of Nairobi (http://erepository.uonbi.ac.ke/handle/11295/104228) (accessed: 20 August 2020).

Hampwaye, G., Nel, E. and Ingombe, L. (2009) *The Role of Urban Agriculture in Addressing Household Poverty and Food Security: The Case of Zambia, GDN Working Paper No. 19*, GDN (Global Development Network).

Hampwaye, G., Nel, E. and Rogerson, C. M. (2007) 'Urban agriculture as local initiative in Lusaka, Zambia', *Environment and Planning C: Government and Policy*, Vol. 25, Issue 4, pp. 553–572 (https://doi.org/10.1068/c7p) (accessed: 18 November 2020).

Herold, M., Goldstein, N. C. and Clarke, K. C. (2003) 'The spatiotemporal form of urban growth: Measurement, analysis and modeling', *Remote Sensing of Environment*, Vol. 86, Issue 3, pp. 286–302 (https://doi.org/10.1016/S0034-4257(03)00075-0) (accessed: 18 November 2020).

Jiang, L., Deng, X., and Seto, K. C. (2013) 'The impact of urban expansion on agricultural land use intensity in China', *Land Use Policy*, Vol. 35, pp. 33–39 (https://doi.org/10.1016/j.landusepol.2013.04.011) (accessed:

28 December 2020).

JICA (Japan International Cooperation Agency) (2009) *Development Plan of Lusaka Plan Framework Integrated development of Greater Lusaka* (https://openjicareport.jica.go.jp/pdf/11932845_02.pdf) (accessed: 18 November 2020).

Lall, S. V, Selod, H. and Shalizi, Z. (2006) *Rural-Urban Migration in Developing Countries: A Survey Of Theoretical Predictions And Empirical Findings, Policy Research Working Papers Series 3915*, Washington DC: World Bank (https://doi.org/10.1596/1813-9450-3915) (accessed: 15 November 2020).

Mulenga, C. (2013) *The State of Food Insecurity in Lusaka, Zambia, AFSUN Food Security Series No. 19*, AFSUN (African Food Security Urban Network) (http://www.afsun.org/wp-content/uploads/2016/06/AFSUN 19.pdf) (accessed: 28 December 2020).

Musa, M. K. and Odera, P. (2015) 'Land use land cover changes and their effects on food security: A case study of Kiambu County-Kenya', *Kabarak Journal of Research & Innovation*, Vol. 3, No. 1, pp. 74–86 (http://ojs.kabarak.ac.ke/index.php/journal1/article/view/62)(accessed: 28 December 2020).

Museleku, E. K. (2013) 'An investigation into causes and effects of agricultural land use conversions in the urban fringes: A case study of Nairobi-Kiambu interface', Doctoral dissertation, University of Nairobi (accessed: 21 July 2020).

Naab, Z. F., Dinye, R. D. and Kasanga, R. K. (2013) 'Urbanization and it's impact on agricultural lands in growing cities in developing contries: Case study of Tamale in Ghana', *Modern Social Science Journal*, Vol. 2, No. 2, pp. 256–287.

Nel, E., Hampwaye, G., Thornton, A., Rogerson, C. M. and Marais, L. (2009) *Institutional Responses to Decentralization, Urban Poverty, Food Shortages and Urban Agriculture, GDN Working Paper No. 36*, New Delhi: GDN (Global Development Network).

Njiru, E. B. (2016) 'Evaluation of urban expansion and its implications on land use in Kiambu County, Kenya', MA thesis, Kenyatta University (https://ir-library.ku.ac.ke/bitstream/handle/123456789/14936/Evaluation%20of%20urban%20expansion%20and%20its%20effects%20in%20landuse%20in%20Kiambu%20County.pdf?sequence=1) (accessed: 15 July 2020).

Nkhuwa, D., Xu, Y. and Usher, B. (2006) 'Groundwater quality assessments in the John Laing and Misisi areas of Lusaka', in Y. Xu and B. Usher (eds) *Groundwater Pollution in Africa*, London: CRC Press, pp. 239–251.

Ogechi, B. A. and Hunja, W. E. (2014) 'Land use land cover changes and implications for food production: A case study of Keumbu Region Kisii County, Kenya', *International Journal of Science and Research (IJSR)*, Vol. 3, No. 10, pp. 752–758 (https://www.ijsr.net/archive/v3i10/T0NUMTQ5OQ==.pdf) (accessed: 28 December 2020).

Phiri, D. and Morgenroth, J. (2017) 'Developments in Landsat land cover classification methods: A review', *Remote Sensing*, Vol. 9, No. 9 (https://doi.org/10.3390/rs9090967) (accessed: 18 November 2020).

Plecher, H. (2020) 'Zambia: Urbanization from 2008 to 2018', Statista (https://www.statista.com/statistics/455963/urbanization-in-zambia/#:~:text=Urbanization in Zambia 2018&text=Urbanization means the share of,in urban areas and cities) (accessed: 18 November 2020).

Quasem, M. A. (2011) 'Conversion of agricultural land to non-agricultural uses in Bangladesh: Extent and determinants', *The Bangladesh Development Studies*, Vol. 34, No. 1, pp. 59–85.

Rondhi, M., Pratiwi, P. A., Handini, V. T., Sunartomo, A. F. and Budiman, S. A. (2018) 'Agricultural land conversion, land economic value, and sustainable agriculture: A case study in East Java, Indonesia', *Land*, Vol. 7, Issue 4, pp. 1–19 (https://doi.org/https://doi.org/10.3390/land7040148) (accessed: 22 December 2020).

Simatele, D., Binns, T. and Simatele, M. (2012) 'Urban livelihoods under a changing climate: Perspectives on urban agriculture and planning in Lusaka, Zambia', *Journal of Human Development and Capabilities*, Vol. 13, No. 2, pp. 269–293 (https://doi.org/10.1080/19452829.2011.645029) (accessed: 18 November 2020).

Simwanda, M. and Murayama, Y. (2017) 'Integrating geospatial techniques for urban land use classification in the developing sub-Saharan African City of Lusaka, Zambia', *ISPRS International Journal of Geo-Information*, Vol. 6, Issue 4, No. 102 (https://doi.org/10.3390/ijgi6040102) (accessed: 18 November 2020).

Thornton, A., Nel, E. and Hampwaye, G. (2010) 'Cultivating Kaunda's plan for self-sufficiency: Is urban agriculture finally beginning to receive support in Zambia?', *Development Southern Africa*, Vol. 27, Issue 4, pp. 613–625 (https://doi.org/10.1080/0376835X.2010.508604) (accessed: 18 November 2020).

Thuo, A. (2013). 'Impacts of urbanization on land use planning, livelihood and environment in the Nairobi rural-urban fringe, Kenya'. *International Journal of Scientific & Technology Research*, Vol. 2, Issue 7, pp. 70–79.

Tokula, E. A. and Ejaro, S. P. (2012) 'Dynamics of land use/land cover changes and its implication on food security in Anyigba, North Central, Nigeria', *Confluence Journal of Environmental Studies*, Vol. 7, pp. 42–52 (https://works.bepress.com/cjes_kogistateuniversity/15/http://www.journalhome.com/cjes) (accessed: 21 December 2020).

Treitz, P. and Rogan, J. (2004) 'Remote sensing for mapping and monitoring land-cover and land-use change–An introduction', *Progress in Planning*, Vol. 61, Issue. 4, pp. 269–279 (https://doi.org/10.1016/S0305-9006(03)00064-3) (accessed: 18

November 2020).

United Nations (2014) *World Urbanization Prospects: The 2014 Revision*, New York: Department of Economic and Social Affairs, United Nations.

——— (2018) *2018 Revision of World Urbanization Prospects*, New York: Department of Economic and Social Affairs, United Nations.

Van Dijk, M., Hilderink, H., Rooij, W., Rutten, M., Ashton, R., Kartikasari, K. and Lan, V. (2012) *Land-Use Change , Food Security and Climate Change in Vietnam: A Global-To-Local Modelling Approach, LEI report 2013-020*, The Hague: LEI Wageningen UR (https://edepot.wur.nl/250651) (accessed: 10 August 2020).

Wang, Z., Chai, J. and Li, B. (2016) 'The impacts of land use change on residents' living based on urban metabolism: A case study in Yangzhou City of Jiangsu Province, China', *Sustainability*, Vol. 8, No. 10 (https://doi.org/10.3390/su8101004) (accessed: 18 November 2020).

World Bank (2002) *Upgrading of Low Income Settlements Country Assessment Report: Zambia*, Washington DC: World Bank (http://web.mit.edu/urbanupgrading/upgrading/case-examples/overview-africa/country-assessments/reports/Zambia-report.html) (accessed: 15 November 2020).

Yuan, F., Sawaya, K. E., Loeffelholz, B. C. and Bauer, M. E. (2005) 'Land cover classification and change analysis of the Twin Cities (Minnesota) metropolitan area by multitemporal Landsat remote sensing', *Remote Sensing of Environment*, Vol. 98, No. 2-3, pp. 317–328 (https://doi.org/10.1016/j.rse.2005.08.006) (accessed: 18 November 2020).

Zambia Land Alliance (2011) *Social Impacts of Land Commercialization in Zambia: A Case Study of Macha Mission Land in Choma District*, Lusaka: International Land Coalition.

Chapter 9

The Non-Agricultural Informal Sector in Madagascar: Assessing the Potential to Shift from a Logic of Survival to a Logic of Development

Herinjatovo Aimé Ramiarison

1. Introduction

Many experts and scholars believed that sub-Saharan African countries (SSACs), during the early stages of their independence, enjoyed more growth prospects than did Asian countries. Two decades later, the economic performance of the former has been disappointing and has continued to be so whereas that of the latter has been phenomenal and has resulted in successful structural transformation (World Bank 1993). Consequently, since the late 1980s, strategies and priorities in SSACs have shifted from targeting development to ensuring survival. Indeed, poverty alleviation has been at the centre of all policy actions undertaken in this region at both the national and international levels. The development trajectories observed in many SSACs have followed a neoliberal approach under the guidance of international partners and donors (e.g., the IMF, World Bank, EU, UN and its affiliated organisations), with Asian experiences offering evidence of the success of this mainstream view. Thus, liberal policies have been recommended for SSACs, while official development assistance (ODA) disbursement has been conditional on structural reforms and free-market policies (UNCTAD 2000). Unsurprisingly, many SSACs have followed these recommendations and implemented reforms. SSACs' major partners attach particular importance to promoting foreign direct investment (FDI) as a means of fighting poverty and achieving major development goals. This assumption has been widely argued in economic literature, stemming from the neoliberal view and evidenced by the successful experience of the Asian newly industrialised economies (NIEs) and emerging economies (Amirahmadi and Wu 1994; OECD 1998; Findlay 1978). It is widely agreed that FDI plays a key role in the development of countries where local firm capacity is low and where government incentives are ineffective and insufficient. In addition, FDI embodies capital, markets and technology, which are the key ingredients for growth, entrepreneurship development, productivity, skills and innovative capacity and income security (Wang and Blomstrom 1992, McFetridge 1987). According to the neoliberal perspective, FDI will ignite the modernisation process and help to achieve structural transformation. However, three decades of FDI promotion policy have not yielded significant economic performance in many SSACs, as it has done in East Asia and in other regions. Indeed, in spite of high economic growth, particularly in the capitalist or modern sectors, the majority of SSACs still have a large subsistence informal economy that continues to expand independently. For example, in Madagascar, while the economy experienced high growth after the 2002 political crisis, the informal economy, in terms of employment, grew in size from 73 per cent in 2002 to 89 per cent in 2005 (Rakotomanana and Rakotoasimbola 2019).[1]

Such unexpected outcomes call into question the neoliberal approach to development fuelled by theories of modernisation (Lewis 1954; Rostow 1960; Chen 2012; Harris and Tadaro 1970). According to this mainstream view, the traditional or informal sector is expected to disappear gradually during the growth and modernisation process as policies focused on promoting growth in the capitalist sector and higher wages in the manufacturing sector attract informal workers. This approach has four major implications regarding the informal economy.

First, the proliferation of the informal economy is the result of the failure of the capitalist sector to create further sufficient employment opportunities to absorb the unlimited labour supply (Chen 2012; Lewis 1954; Harris and Todaro 1970).

Second, the informal economy is temporary in nature. It is thus considered to be a logic of survival initiative taken by individuals when job opportunities in the formal sector and government support are lacking.

Third, as a solution, the government needs to focus its policies only on promoting growth in the capitalist sector and on establishing legal institutions (rules and regulations) and other incentives to encourage entrepreneurship and investment under the market principle (De Soto 2000).

Fourth, the informal economy is illegal and must be formalised according to the rules and regulations in force.

Consequently, national and international decision makers have always believed that by concentrating their efforts and resources on economic growth and by emphasising law enforcement (i.e., sanctioning and expelling informal firms not legally registered), they could attend to the double objectives of ending the proliferation of the informal economy and achieving development and structural transformation. However, as previously stated, economic policies based on this mainstream view have failed to develop SSACs' economies. Rather, they have accelerated the unexpected development of the informal economy. Thus, this neoliberal vision, which considers productive employment as a transversal element resulting automatically from economic growth, is losing traction in SSACs, prompting experts and researchers to reconsider the informal economy with the aim of successfully transitioning to a formal economy. In other words, it is necessary to depart from this mainstream view and direct more attention toward the real economy in SSACs, the informal economy, which is the daily life economy of a large majority of the population. The informal economy is usually characterised by high vulnerability, poverty and low income, low productivity, precarious working conditions, lack of social protection and rule of law, and several constraints related to access to capital, markets and training (BIT 2017). These factors constitute structural barriers restricting informal actors – and thus the large majority of the population – from improving their wellbeing and keeping them in highly vulnerable situations. As mentioned earlier, the informal economy has developed independently of the formal economy and has allowed millions of people to survive and attain individual achievement, which constitutes a source of happiness for the actors involved. Despite these structural barriers, the informal economy's survival capacity indicates that it possesses huge potential that must be investigated to appreciate how such potential can be effectively exploited to realise a more successful transition toward formalisation. For all these reasons, the informal economy merits considerable attention with respect to a country's economic development. It is within this context that the present research is undertaken in the case of the non-agricultural informal sector in Madagascar.

This chapter aims to explore the potential of Madagascar's informal economy, particularly the non-agricultural branch, for achieving inclusive development. More precisely, the chapter will assess this potential and the likelihood that the shift in the nature of activities from subsistence to real entrepreneurship will be achieved, by highlighting the sector's existing strengths and opportunities and by analysing current constraints. The analysis will focus particularly on the potential of the non-agricultural informal economy to mobilise domestic *capital*, to create and to develop domestic *markets* and to develop and diffuse *technology* and know-how. In doing so, the chapter will argue that policy incentives targeting productivity growth in the non-agricultural informal sector will be more likely to offer effective alternative ways to promote FDI as a means of achieving inclusive development.

2. Potential in Terms of Capacity to Mobilise Domestic Savings for Capital Accumulation

Like the majority of SSACs, Madagascar is a poor country in which the vast majority of the active population are in the informal economy, which continues to expand. Madagascar's informal economy is characterised by the abovementioned structural barriers, leaving a vast majority of the actors in poverty and without any social protection or fundamental rights. Owing to the paucity of professional development prospects, most are unable to increase their income significantly and get out of poverty. Although the unemployment rate is low, jobs are considered precarious.[2] Indeed, atypical forms of employment – for example, part-time jobs, the absence of contracts, labour sub-contracting, working from home – are ubiquitous (INSTAT 2013b). According to the 2012 employment survey, eight out of ten workers are affected by inadequate employment and paid less than the legal minimum wage, whereas the ratio of salaried workers is only 10.1 per cent of the total, excluding the majority from any social protection schemes.[3] The same survey indicated that, in the non agricultural informal sector, average monthly income stands at MGA (Madagascar ariary) 85,900, the equivalent of USD 39 or 61.35 per cent of the minimum wage, whereas median wage is MGA 57,000 or USD 26.[4] This notwithstanding, the informal economy in Madagascar has real potential that should be investigated and exploited, particularly for the non-agricultural informal sector.

One such potential is the capacity of the non-agricultural informal sector to mobilise capital. In economic literature, it is widely argued that capital accumulation is crucial to a country's economic growth and development in that it facilitates increased production, the ultimate purpose of which is to attain optimal satisfaction of the population's needs. As such, capital accumulation yields several socioeconomic benefits, including value added (VA) creation, job creation, the importance of which depends on the nature of accumulated capital, income opportunities for the population, increased demand and supply and real entrepreneurship, among others. Capital is typically mobilised and accumulated (investment) in the presence of market conditions or incentives that allow such accumulation to be profitable. Thus, the profitability of investment is the driving force behind capital accumulation. With respect to the non-agricultural informal sector, its potential to mobilise capital may be appreciated in various ways.

2-1. Important Stock of Capital Coming Essentially from Individual Savings

The 2012 employment survey estimated the existence of 2,268,900 individual production units (IPUs) in this sector, with manufacturing (excluding mining), commerce and service taking the lion's share at 43.1 per cent, 34.4 per cent and 18.3 per cent, respectively (Table 1).[5] Although manufacturing represents a significant share of IPUs and 33.8 per cent of the total workforce, it accounts for only 19.3 per cent of the stock of capital, whereas commerce and services in total take the lion's share (67.5 per cent or MGA 1,388.2 billion). More than half of IPUs in manufacturing (or 18.8 per cent of total IPUs) are in textiles and clothing (T&C), followed by construction (5.5 per cent of total IPUs), food (4.4 per cent of total IPUs), wood (3.4 per cent of total IPUs) and others (3.2 per cent of total IPUs). The importance of T&C is also observed in terms of capital, as it accounts for 61.8 per cent of the manufacturing's capital at MGA 246 billion (or USD 108 million).[6] As 72 per cent of the IPUs in the non-agricultural informal sector are self-employed, individual savings financed 95 per cent of the sector's total capital, which is valued at MGA 2,058 billion (USD 910 million). For such important stock of capital, self-financing accounts for 87.5 per cent, with a higher ratio in the manufacturing sector, especially in the food (97.1 per cent), T&C (93 per cent), wood (95 per cent) and construction (96.8 per cent) industries. Loans represent only 1.7 per cent, with informal sources accounting

Table 1. Distribution of IPUs by sector and by area (%)

Sector	All areas	Urban	Rural	Total
Primary Sector	4.2	13.6	86.4	100
Forestry	4.2	13.6	86.4	100
Manufacturing	43.1	20.9	79.1	100
Mining	7.8	13.3	86.7	100
Food	4.4	32.9	67.1	100
Textile & clothing	18.8	16.9	83.1	100
Wood	3.4	20.1	79.9	100
Other manufacturing	3.2	30.3	69.7	100
Construction	5.5	30.7	69.3	100
Commerce	34.4	31.8	68.2	100
Service	18.3	47.5	52.5	100
Repair	1.6	54.7	45.3	100
Transportation	4.6	45.8	54.2	100
Housework	3.7	42.4	57.6	100
Other services	8.4	49.3	50.7	100
Total	100	29.2	70.8	100

Source: INSTAT (2013b).

for more than 70 per cent of loans. IPUs are rated as very high risk by formal lending institutions and are less likely to benefit from loans granted by the latter. Access to credit is not considered to be a serious issue by the majority of IPUs, meaning that few of them are interested in borrowing and/or are conscious of its utility.[7] Another reason that credit access is less relevant to IPUs is the fact that existing formal credit schemes do not match their particular needs, rendering the credit institutions useless for the vast majority of IPUs. Therefore, they must run their businesses without credit, having successfully done so for many years. For this reason, credit access is not a serious issue. The average life span of an IPU is approximately 10 years. By mobilising only individual savings, they can ensure their survival and achieve their business goals.[8] Moreover, the investment ratio is 8 per cent, most of which is undertaken by more experienced IPUs, with younger IPUs preferring to take fewer risks and focus mainly on the profitability of their recurrent activities.[9] The informal economy is thus an important lever with which to mobilise individual savings for capital accumulation with the aim of increasing production and income.

However, it is worth noting that the average stock of capital per IPU and investment per IPU are very low, standing respectively at MGA 956,300 (USD 435) and MGA 268 900 (USD 122).[10] By sector, it is the service sector that has the highest level of capital per production unit, with transportation standing at MGA 5,119,600 per IPU (Table 2). Average capital per IPU in the manufacturing and T&C sectors is lower than the average, in spite of their importance in terms of numbers and job creation. Given the importance of self-financing, low capital per IPU is explained by low per-capita income in the informal economy. This situation constitutes a serious obstacle to the development of the non-agricultural informal sector; on the one hand, this may partly explain why informal workers' income remains at the subsistence level and, on the other hand, it may lock them in a vicious circle of low capital, low production, low income and low savings. This cycle could be broken by the availability of a credit scheme that fits the needs of the informal actors. For example, in rural microenterprises (MERs) in basketry, customers give advanced payment for large orders, thereby presenting an opportunity to increase income and, therefore, to increase capital stock. If a similar scheme or other adequate incentives for borrowing were to be made available in the informal economy, IPUs would be able to increase individual income. Given the informal economy's high potential to mobilise domestic savings for capital accumulation, capital stock and investment will increase, thereby breaking the vicious circle.

As will be analysed in the following sections, IPUs' small sizes also place serious limits on the profitability of their activities.

Table 2. Capital, productivity of capital and labour by sector

Sector	Apparent productivity of labour and capital			Capital/IPU (MGA 1,000)
	VA/L1 (MGA 1,000 per month)	VA/L2 (MGA 1,000 per month)	(VA/K)	
Primary Sector	78	0.5	0.2	749.9
Forestry	78	0.5	0.2	749.9
Manufacturing	73	0.5	0.2	623.8
Mining	57	0.4	0.2	561.2
Food	105	0.8	0.2	827
Textile & clothing	45	0.4	0.1	583.9
Wood	68	0.5	0.1	989.4
Other manufacturing	62	0.4	0.2	739.2
Construction	150	1.0	0.8	330.1
Commerce	182	1.1	0.3	857.9
Services	161	1.1	0.1	2,054.1
Repair	232	1.6	0.5	669.8
Transportation	245	1.7	0.1	5,119.6
Housework	51	0.5	0.3	253.1
Other services	148	1.0	0.2	1,497.5
All sectors	125	0.9	0.2	956.3

* VA: Value Added; VA/L1: Value added per number of workers; VA/L2: Value added per hour.

Source: INSTAT (2013b).

2-2. Contribution to Economic Growth

Despite the limitation of financing, in making full use of mobilised domestic savings, the non-agricultural informal sector contributes considerably to the country's growth. Indeed, it accounted for 24 per cent of Madagascar's GDP in 2012, a figure higher than that of the formal secondary sector (14.6 per cent). By sector, 46 per cent of VA derives from commerce while the manufacturing and service sectors' shares are 29 per cent and 22 per cent, respectively, of the total VA created.[11] Nonetheless, the return on capital or VA per unit of capital is very low at 0.2 (Table 2), meaning that the incremental capital output ratio (ICOR) in the non-agricultural informal sector is 5–0.5 higher than the national average (4.5). Unsurprisingly, labour accounted for 91 per cent of the VA created in this sector. This high level of ICOR may indicate that capital is less productive there and that innovation initiative is lacking. As stated earlier, the small amount of capital invested may also explain this low capital productivity. Therefore, efficiency gain is very low.

To illustrate, the case of MERs in basketry or basketwork using vegetable fibres in the region of Analamanga (Antananarivo) indicates the positive relationship between capital size and performance in terms of productivity and, therefore, efficiency gain.[12] A study undertaken by the Ministry of Agriculture and Livestock in 2008 classified MERs into three categories (Table 3):[13]

- Vulnerable MERs, which are characterised by small size, low capital, the secondary nature of the activity and, thus, a short-term business vision.

- Developing MERs, which are more profit-oriented, with larger sizes in terms of employees and capital.

- Advanced MERs, which are much larger, employing nearly 100 workers and, more importantly, with more capital. They have an advanced entrepreneurship culture and a more long-term vision.

According to the study, 90 per cent of MERs are either vulnerable or developing whereas none of the MERs, even among the advanced ones, can afford to buy modern equipment, particularly looms for semi-finished goods and sewing machines for finished goods.

Like most informal actors, MERs are self-financed. However, they can increase the scope of their activities thanks to advance pay-

Table 3. Characteristics of basketry-producing MERs by category

	Vulnerable MER	Developing MER	Advanced MER
Size of employment	1 to 5 workers who are family members	1 to 30 workers who are family members and from outside the family circle	1 to 100 workers who are family members and other permanent workers
Size of equipment	One piece of traditional equipment	Several pieces of traditional equipment	Several pieces of traditional equipment
Income-generating activity	Vegetal fibre transformation is the single income-generating activity	Vegetal Fibre transformation is the main income-generating activity	Vegetal Fibre transformation is the single income-generating activity
Status of agricultural activity	Agricultural activity is for subsistence	Agricultural activity or other non-agricultural activity is secondary	No other activity
Status of the transformation activity	Vegetal fibre transformation is a secondary activity	Vegetal fibre transformation is a full-time activity	Vegetal fibre transformation is a full-time activity
Vision	Short-term vision	Mid-term or long-term vision	Long-term vision

Source: MAEP (2008).

ments from their customers for large-quantity orders. Finance schemes of this nature have allowed some of them to gradually shift from a vulnerable production unit toward a real entrepreneurship -driven production unit.

As Table 4 illustrates, the difference in capital size explains the performance divide among MERs. Advanced and developing MERs are, respectively, 2 and 1.5 times better equipped with traditional looms than vulnerable MERs. For the fabrication of finished goods, an advanced MER has 2.5 times more sewing machines than a vulnerable MER. This difference in production capacity is also reflected in the quantities of raw materials and other intermediate goods used by each category of MER. For example, the quantity of thread balls used by developing MERs is more than twice that used by vulnerable MERs (Table 4). Differences in capital endowment yield differential performances among MERs. This is first observed in terms of labour productivity, which is much higher in developing and advanced MERs, meaning that well-equipped MERs are at least able to double their labour productivity compared to MERs with low capital endowment (Table 4). The difference in performance is more remarkable in terms of VA produced by MERs. VAs produced by a developing MERs and advanced MERs are 7 and more than 100 times that of a vulnerable MER, respectively (Table 4). This situation may reveal the existence of efficiency gains stemming from improved know-how, effective learning, good organisation and real entrepreneurship. Indeed, it is specified in the study that basketwork is a secular ancestral art and that basketry know-how has passed from generation to generation over several centuries, allowing a long learning process period. Moreover, as some of the products are exported to Europe, the USA and China, producers are exposed to the requirements of international quality standards, forcing them to be more efficient. This demand for efficiency can extend even to vulnerable MERs due to clustering, whereby

Table 4. Equipment, intermediate goods, raw materials, output and value added by category of basketry MER

Category		Vulnerable MER	Developing MER	Advanced MER
Equipment, tools and raw materials (Average quantity per MER)	Thread (balls)	60	138	480
	Needles	10	12	80
	Glue	70	172	600
	Chisels	2	2	40
	Dyeing (kg)	8	10	65
	Buckets	6	8	40
	Traditional loom	1	1.5	2
	Sewing machine	1	1.5	3.5
Output & value added (NVA)	Annual output per MER (Qty)	574	3,444	47,642
	Monthly VA/worker (MGA 1,000)	128	261	303
	Number of MERs	1,904	2,380	476
	Annual VA produced (MGA 1,000)	6,076,730	52,679,777	149,273,067
	Average VA per MER (MGA 1,000)	3,192	22,134	313,599

Source: MAEP (2008).

developing MERs subcontract their production to vulnerable MERs. As Tables 2 and 4 illustrate, labour productivity among vulnerable MERs (MGA 128,000 or USD 57 per month) is higher than the average in manufacturing within the non-agricultural informal sector (MGA 73,000 or USD 32 per month).[14] Moreover, several factors work in favour of efficiency gain; namely, the existence of supporting projects related to environmental protection, the local production of small equipment, the existence of training schemes, and the creation of clusters in rural areas.

Nonetheless, profits are rarely reinvested owing to the low level of income for the majority of MERs. For the non-agricultural informal sector, data from the 2012 employment survey point to several possibilities to improve the current productivity of capital and, consequently, the income in this sector. However, such possibilities were not exploited due to several constraints. This issue will be discussed below.

2-3. Fiscal and Employment Issues

Although the IPUs are living at subsistence level, as stated above, they still pay taxes of around 2 per cent of their VA or the equivalent of USD 43 million per year.[15] Furthermore, they are expected to pay up to MGA 6,700 per month in tax, or double that which they currently pay (INSTAT 2013b). While this situation demonstrates the IPUs' willingness to honour their fiscal obligations as good citizens, it may also indicate the possibility of increasing production and income, in turn indicating the possibility of improving the return on capital, as mentioned earlier.[16] However, they doubt transparency regarding the government's use of tax revenue. Three out of four IPUs expressed a wish that tax revenue be used to build infrastructure (roads, marketplaces, water supply, etc.) in their own territories and to finance basic human needs, particularly in health and education (INSTAT 2013b). This situation is consistent with their high level of vulnerability, such that their access ratios to basic services are extremely weak (for example, 10.3

per cent for water, 8.4 per cent for electricity), whereas 80 per cent of them do not have a place to undertake their activity or do it at home (INSTAT 2013b). Moreover, 99.9 per cent have no social protection, and their education levels are very low.[17] Therefore, another possibility to increase the profitability of their activities, or the productivity of the capital, is the effectiveness of fiscal decentralisation and the prioritisation of public expenses in favour of economic infrastructure building and basic human needs. This has the double effect of reducing the vulnerability and improving the wellbeing of the informal actors while giving the government an important source of tax revenue thanks to the increase in production and income, contrary to the neoliberal vision's claims. Therefore, a shift from subsistence mode to real entrepreneurship becomes more likely. As will be discussed below, the low education level of the workforce and the lack of training are two further major constraints affecting productivity. Therefore, if measures aimed at dealing with the above-cited constraints are available, they will enhance the likelihood that the shift toward real entrepreneurship will be successfully realised. Therefore, rather than considering informal actors to be outlaws or scapegoats, the government should listen to them and provide the appropriate incentives to sustain their activities.

Moreover, the informal economy is the country's largest source of paid work, accounting for 93.6 per cent of total employment (Bonnet 2019). Given that the average size of the IPU is 1.4 persons, the non-agricultural informal sector creates more than three million jobs, or three times the number of jobs created by the formal sector, meaning that the capital there is not labour saving but is consistent with the needs of massive job creation and thus an important means of achieving inclusive growth. Most informal workers are self-employed, accounting for 72 per cent of IPUs. More importantly, this huge potential for job creation is further strengthened by the key roles of female workers, who account for 58 per cent of the total, and young workers with an average age of

35 years old. Women play a crucial role in sustainable development in terms of food security and household welfare.[18] Nonetheless, the high proportion of female and young workers may also reveal a situation of high vulnerability in the sector. Furthermore, low levels of education and poor access to training opportunities in the sector exacerbate the vulnerability of the situation. Average schooling is 4.6 years (see note 17), with much lower figures in the manufacturing sector, most notably in mining (3.1 years) and T&C (3.6 years). Moreover, on-the-job training (OJT) is the principal mode of learning used by the majority of the workforce (68.7 per cent), with much higher proportions in the service sectors, such as household services (91.1 per cent) and commerce (81.4 per cent).[19] Only 27 per cent of workers in small enterprises have received training, with a higher ratio in the manufacturing sector, including T&C (46.2 per cent), wood (44.1 per cent) and other industries (43.9 per cent).[20] Unsurprisingly, average income per capita stands at subsistence level, while female workers earn half what their male counterparts earn (Table 5). Low levels of education and poor access to training can negatively affect labour productivity, thereby constituting a serious obstacle to the creation of decent and productive jobs. Such situations also limit IPUs' capacity to innovate and will undoubtedly affect the origin of overall weak productivity, keeping the sector at subsistence level. The empowerment of women and youth workers will undoubtedly favour higher return on capital, further increasing the contribution of the non-agricultural informal sector to growth and sustainable development.

2-4. Earning Opportunity Coupled with Entrepreneurship Culture

The potential to mobilise capital is appreciated through the earning opportunity offered by the non-agricultural informal sector to its population, evidencing its potential role in poverty reduction and wealth distribution. Indeed, a large proportion of IPUs (70.8

Table 5. Average monthly income per person, by area, gender and institutional sector (MGA)

		Public administration	Formal enterprises	Informal enterprises	Informal enterprises in agriculture	Associative enterprises	All
Area	Urban	329,200	217,800	103,700	39,200	168,400	102,900
	Rural	189,200	142,000	73,100	33,800	94,900	43,600
Gender	Male	274,400	218,500	119,700	47,300	133,100	73,100
	Female	228,000	145,600	60,500	19,700	107,300	36,400
All		260,100	187,300	85,900	34,500	124,700	55,600

Source: INSTAT (2013a, 2013b).

per cent) in all branches, except for repair services, are located in rural areas (Table 1). Rural areas, in which subsistence agriculture is the main activity (75 per cent of the population), are also where poverty rates (i.e., the percentage of population under the national poverty line) is the highest (77.3 per cent), and where the average monthly income for agricultural activity is very low at MGA 33,800, or USD 15.[21] Since agricultural production is seasonal, a positive complementary relationship exists between the two activities – agricultural and non-agricultural – given the crop calendar and the passage of the lean period. As such, farmers are also simultaneously producers of non-agricultural goods. The non-agricultural sector is thus seen as an important source of earning opportunities for poorer rural households because it allows them to at least double their income. Indeed, the average monthly income of non-agricultural IPUs in rural areas is MGA 73,100 or USD 32.4 (Table 5).[22] However, it is still a subsistence income, given that the average household size is 4.5 persons. However, several facts indicate the likelihood of further income increases.

The first is the main motivation for establishing an IPU. The lack of salaried jobs is not the main motivation (incentive), as is assumed by neoliberal thought.[23] In other words, it is not necessarily the logic of survival that pushes a person to undertake informal activity; rather, it is the income increase (a deliberate choice) that is cited by 46 per cent of IPU leaders as the major incentive, whereas the difficulty in finding salaried jobs is ranked second at 22.4 per cent, confirming the assumption that the informal economy has developed independently of the formal economy (Rakotomanana and Rakotoasimbola 2019). It also suggests that nearly half of the IPU's leaders are motivated by a business logic or logic of development in setting up their production units. This reflects the relative profitability of their activity although the overall profitability ratio remains low. Income increase is mostly cited as the main incentive in sectors such as forestry (59 per cent), food industry (57 per cent), mining (54 per cent) and commerce (50 per cent), whereas family tradition (35.1 per cent) is the reason most frequently cited by IPUs in T&C (Rakotomanana and Rakotoasimbola 2019).

The second is the possibility of increasing production capacity. When asked about the kind of support they need for the development of their business, the majority singled out access to large-quantity orders from customers, meaning that they estimate themselves to have the capacity to meet demands emanating from major clients (mainly public institutions through procurement and large firms in the formal sector) with the currently available capital and equipment.[24] Figures on the sustainability of their activities come in support of this assumption. The average age of non-agricultural IPUs is 10.3 years, with a higher figure (18.5 years) for IPUs who are characterised by the intergenerational transfer of specific know-how. They are IPUs in the branch of transformation (example of basketry mentioned earlier) and T&C, which have undergone a long learning period, the outcome of which is probably business efficiency and, therefore, significant potential to increase production capacity. Moreover, 52 per cent of IPUs are more than 10 years old, whereas 25 per cent of IPUs in T&C have existed for more than 25 years. The permanent and durable nature of their activities reflects the presence of a large and permanent business network that favours increased production capacity. The IPUs must be given access to adequate incentives for borrowing and market opportunities.

The third is entrepreneurship culture. According to a study undertaken by Rakotomanana and Rakotoasimbola (2019), 82 per cent of the IPU leaders are true entrepreneurs whose goal is to maximise profit and minimise costs. When they encounter difficulties, such as a fall in market demand, their strategy reflects a truly entrepreneurial attitude. Indeed, 61.8 per cent will choose to diversify their activities, improve the quality of their products or reduce their profits.

The fourth is their survival capacity amid fierce competition and crisis, partly reflecting the existence of entrepreneurship culture. As will be discussed in Section 3, the free market prevails in the informal economy and competition is very fierce. Withstanding such fierce competition over long periods requires resources, strategies and good organisation, exemplifying the real potential of the informal economy to cope with vulnerability and secure subsistence resources. Therefore, modern economic theory has failed in overlooking such potential that allows the actors to survive and go beyond to thrive. IPUs in the non-agricultural informal sector are thus established according to their actors' own business logic. As such, they have their own operating mode, organisation, investment coordination mechanisms and income distribution systems, all of which have facilitated their survival despite multiple crises.

However, their gains remain small as they encounter difficulties and constraints related to the market, training and skill development, low production and weak demand, and administrative control and sanctions. Despite these constraints, informal IPU leaders trust in their capacity and in their operating mode and, consequently, remain optimistic regarding their futures. Indeed, 69.6 per cent believe that their activity has a future, with a higher ratio in manufacturing (70.6 per cent), particularly in wood manufacturing (79.1 per cent), and in IPUs that are more than three years old (70.8 per cent). Moreover, more than half of the IPU leaders want their children to take over their activities. Again, the ratios were higher in the manufacturing branch (58.2 per cent), wood (65.5 per cent) and T&C (62.1 per cent). In this regard, the non-agricultural informal sector is therefore seen as an effective model for social insertion.

Strong perceived optimism on the part of the large majority of the IPU leaders, with all the arguments mentioned above, reveal a real growth potential in the non-agricultural informal sector. The latter, particularly the manufacturing branch, is thus set to play a leading economic role in the near future.

3. Potential in Terms of Capacity to Develop a Large Market

Generally speaking, the market plays an important role in economic growth as the free intercourse of supply and demand facilitates and creates trade which, in turn, encourages production, efficiency and innovation. More production means more job creation and higher aggregate demand. Additional benefits offered by the free market include business efficiency, innovation and higher productivity. In a free market regime, firms must compete against one another and consequently tend to do whatever is necessary to lower costs and thus increase productivity. In addition, the permanent search for efficiency and competitive edge encourages firms to innovate by creating new products and using new technology. Innovation will further increase productivity and efficiency. Thus, developing a large and free market is essential for the growth and development of activities in all economic sectors (primary, secondary and tertiary). Another potential of the non-agricultural informal sector is its capacity to develop a large free market.

The inward-oriented character of the activities in this sector exemplifies its potential. Indeed, the IPUs are able to create a market independently within the informal economy. As previously stated, the informal economy develops independently of the formal economy and therefore enjoys a large domestic market, in terms of population, where demand and supply are mostly from the informal economy itself. Indeed, 21 per cent of the demand is issued from the trade within the informal economy, whereas 71 per cent derives from the final consumption of households whose income is also essentially derived from the informal economy, or around 80 per cent (INSTAT 2013b). Furthermore, IPUs essentially buy inputs and intermediate goods from within the informal economy. Only 29 per cent of their needs are supplied by the formal economy (INSTAT 2013b). In terms of value, the volume of transactions is estimated to be MGA 14,721 billion or USD 6.7 billion.[25] The large market has stimulated production and created millions of jobs, facilitating the survival of tens of millions of people. However, trade volume could be further increased if the constraints to the profitability of the activities stipulated in the previous section were eliminated. The increase in profitability is a double-edged sword acting on both supply and demand. It will allow efficiency gain and, at the same time, increase income for informal workers.

In addition, efficiency gain can be further strengthened as the market is characterised by nearly perfect competition, leading to a Pareto-efficient allocation of economic resources.[26] First, only 2 per cent of IPUs say that they have no direct competitor, while 98 per cent assert that they work within a highly competitive environment. Actors in the informal economy are, particularly, in competition with one another. The market is atomised and saturated by goods and services that are of almost the same quality, giving more bargaining power to customers. Products are thus homogeneous and interchangeable, and a mere increase in price on the part of a firm would force the customer to change supplier.[27] The large majority of IPUs think that their competitive power lies within the sector's average, revealing the severity of the competition (Table 6).

The main strategy that IPUs employ to survive this situation is price alignment.[28] Indeed, more than three quarters of IPUs consider their prices to be the same as those of their competitors, meaning that they are price-takers. This environment is very close to the situation of perfect competition visualised in neoliberal theory (Arrow and Debreu 1954; Debreu 1972; Arrow 1959). As such, it should necessarily result in greater efficiency as competitive pressure encourages economic agents to be more productive and more efficient to survive amidst competition. In other words, they must increase productivity through innovation and other means that will lead to cost reduction and quality improvement. However, this is not always the case for IPUs. They regard competition as a constraint rather than an incentive for productivity growth. Thus, when asked about the major constraints affecting the growth of

Table 6. Percentage distribution of IPUs' perception compared to their competitors, by sector (%)

Perception of IPU	All	Primary sector	Manufacturing sector	Commerce	Service sector
Selling price					
Above average	3.8	2.3	3.2	5.1	3.5
Average	76.2	86.3	73.9	78.6	69.8
Below average	20.0	11.4	22.9	16.3	26.8
Total	100	100	100	100	100
Costs					
Above average	7.2	2.0	5.8	11.3	5.5
Average	76.7	78.9	74.2	76.8	79.8
Below average	16.2	19.0	20.0	11.9	14.7
Total	100	100	100	100	100
Quality of goods					
Above average	17.4	16.6	21.1	14.5	15.9
Average	78.8	82.0	74.3	82.0	79.6
Below average	3.8	1.5	4.6	3.5	4.5
Total	100	100	100	100	100

Source: INSTAT (2013a, 2013b).

their businesses, they single out the lack of demand (57 per cent of responses) and the excessive competition (52 per cent of responses). Owing to the lack of incentive for productivity growth through innovation and to the use of less productive technology, capital is less productive, as noted above. The low share of capital allocated to the purchase of machines and equipment (11.8 per cent of the total) and the high share of 'used capital', which largely comprises buildings and cars (87 per cent), also explain capital's low productivity. Even in manufacturing, machinery and equipment account for only 12.9 per cent of the sector's total capital. The situation is exacerbated by the low level of education and poor access to training discussed earlier, thereby allowing less and less room for innovation initiatives to thrive. Such a situation constitutes a major impediment for the non-agricultural informal economy to take full advantage of the large domestic market, which is characterised by nearly perfect competition.

The non-agricultural informal economy brings a large domestic market with nearly perfect competition, whose outcome could be economic efficiency. However, this has not yet come about owing to three major constraints, namely, the low level of capital – particularly machinery and equipment – low education levels and the lack of necessary skills. This allows less room to accommodate innovation and productivity gain. Efforts are required to increase further the sector's contribution to Madagascar's development.

4. Potential in Terms of Capacity to Upgrade and to Diffuse Technology

The essential role of technological progress in economic growth is widely recognised by several experts and economists and has been argued in many economic studies. Indeed, the use of new technology or technology transfer coupled with effective learning facilitates technical change (McFetridge 1987). The latter is an important factor in efficiency gain as it improves the product or production process. In other words, it allows increased productivity and reduced production costs. Output growth generated by technical change will therefore offer a major earning opportunity for both producers and workers via productivity gain. Technical change is often embodied in knowledge accumulation via the use of new technology, the learning process, invention, innovation and diffusion of knowledge through the production sector.

As discussed earlier in the chapter, the non-agricultural informal sector has overall low productivity and low capital stock. This situation may explain the low level of income per capita for the vast majority of informal workers. However, as in the case of basketry discussed earlier and as is demonstrated by the strong optimism of most IPU leaders, it is possible to achieve a relatively high level of profitability. This situation is partly explained by the effectiveness of knowledge transfer and effective learning in some branches of the non-agricultural informal sector.

Effective knowledge (technology) transfer and effective learning can first be appreciated by the existence of years-old know-how accompanied by long periods of learning as well as by exposure to international markets. This is the case, for example, in basketry, wherein the heritage of secular technology and the intergenerational transfer of specific know-how permits relatively high efficiency gain and gives way to permanent innovation via product diversification. Some products even become relatively famous and are exported to the markets of advanced economies. Furthermore, it is unsurprising that IPUs characterised by intergenerational technology transfer have existed for longer periods (18.5 years on average) than others, meaning longer learning periods and consequently relatively higher labour productivity. For example, labour productivity in basketry is 1.75 times that of the manufacturing sector (Tables 2 and 4). T&C is another example of intergenerational transfer of specific know-how such that 25 per cent of IPUs in this branch have existed for more than 25 years, and textile goods, such as silk products and embroidered goods, are exported to American and European markets.

IPUs are conscious of the importance of technology in their activities and invest effort in acquiring more productive machines and other equipment. According to the 2012 employment survey, the purchase of new capital is rare, as used capital accounts for 59.4 per cent of the total capital stock. Data on the structure of the capital stock show that buildings and cars have the highest share (see Section 3), while 68.8 per cent of buildings and 61.3 per cent of cars are used. However, as far as 'machines' and 'equipment' are concerned, IPUs prefer to buy new ones. Indeed, the share of new machines and new equipment is 88.9 per cent and 80.6 per cent, respectively. This elevated awareness of the value of more productive technology is not well capitalised due to lack of financial resources, as IPUs have no other sources of income.

Training is another aspect of appreciating knowledge transfer. As discussed in previous sections, OJT is the principal mode of learning in the non-agricultural informal sector and therefore the main channel of knowledge transfer. Several vocational training schools (public and private) operate countrywide, and the government, through the Ministry of National Education, has implemented a vocational training policy through several projects and with the support of international donors. It appears that workers in the informal economy do not benefit from these projects: only 2.4 per cent reported having acquired knowledge and skills from a vocational training school, limiting the level of technological capacity in the sector and, therefore, innovation. Likewise, training in a small formal enterprise is insignificant in the non-agricultural informal sector (27 per cent of workers). However, training in a small formal enterprise is relatively more important in manufacturing, particularly in T&C (46.2 per cent), wood transformation (44.1 per cent) and other industries (43.9 per cent), making manufacturing the most promising sector in terms of technological capability and innovation, probably leading to efficiency gain.

As OJT is the most widely used channel for knowledge transfer, it is also considered an effective means of learning and constitutes a lever for innovation, particularly for IPUs, which have higher levels of entrepreneurship skills. Indeed, amid fierce competition, as discussed above, the majority of IPUs opt for price alignment, while nearly half of them choose to diversify their products or improve their quality.

Therefore, technological change will be more likely to occur in the non-agricultural informal sector. Manufacturing is the most promising branch because it is where (1) intergenerational transfer of know-how takes place, (2) the greatest use of new capital is observed, and (3) the proportion of workers receiving formal training is relatively high. As nearly half of IPUs undertake diversification and quality improvement, they are potential innovators and should be supported to allow further efficiency gain. It also worth noting that informal workers' low levels of education constitute a major obstacle to more effective technological change.

5. Conclusion

Madagascar's informal economy is an informal economy of exclusion. The exclusion factors are not limited to macroeconomic factors and the high cost of formalising activities. The structural barriers mentioned above also exert an influence. These factors keep informal actors and thus the vast majority of the population in a situation of high vulnerability. The ignorance of the political decision makers with respect to this situation explains why various earlier attempts to combat the proliferation of informal activities in the country have failed. Informal employment continues to grow while informal actors tend to consider their activities to be permanent. It is thus necessary to adopt a different perspective on the situation. Rather than prioritising economic growth and the strict application of regulations, it would be wiser to prioritise the exploration of how these actors might be assisted in making their activities more profitable for them. Indeed, the informal economy – more particularly, the non-agricultural informal economy – is rich in potential, which may be an important lever of development if it is effectively exploited. This potential mainly includes the non-agricultural informal sector's capacity to (1) mobilise individual savings for capital accumulation, the outcome of which is significant in terms of its contribution to GDP, job creation, additional earning opportunities for poor farmers, tax revenue, survival strategies, organisation and entrepreneurship; (2) develop a large domestic market characterised by nearly perfect competition the outcome of which will be efficiency gain; and (3) foster technical change through an intergenerational transfer of know-how. In this sense, non-agricultural informal activities may be an effective alternative means of promoting FDI to achieve inclusive development. Given such potential, the non-agricultural informal sector, particularly the manufacturing branch, is set to contribute significantly to Madagascar's development in the future.

Unfortunately, the real potential of the non-agricultural informal sector is poorly understood by modern economic theory and political decision makers. Consequently, the large majority of its population is still living at the subsistence level, as policy measures have failed to exploit this potential. However, as argued in this chapter, the outcome stemming from this potential may be further increased if the available supporting incentives are used in a way that will effectively exploit this potential. Therefore, it is time to acknowledge that the poor are not the problem; rather, they are the solution, as they have their own means of socioeconomic existence that must be understood by the government.

Endnotes

[1] The country's growth rate increased from -13 per cent in 2002 to 5 per cent in 2005, mainly driven by the secondary and tertiary sector (more than 6 per cent).

[2] Employment is considered precarious if it fulfils one of the following criteria: absence of written work contracts, absence of wage slips, wages below legal minimum wage or absence of social protection coverage.

[3] The data used in this chapter are taken from the 2012 employment survey undertaken by the Institut National de la Statistique (INSTAT or the National Statistical Office; INSTAT 2013a, 2013b). Therefore, the source for the figures stated in the chapter is the 2012 employment survey, unless otherwise specified.

[4] The average exchange rate in 2012 was USD 1 = MGA 2,196.37 (Source: Central Bank of Madagascar).

[5] INSTAT (2013b).

[6] The average exchange rate in 2012 is USD 1 = MGA 2,196.37

(Source: Central Bank of Madagascar).

[7] According to the 2012 employment survey, 16.3 per cent of IPUs consider access to credit to be the main difficulty.

[8] A significant proportion (46 per cent) of IPUs are primarily motivated by increased income when setting up their enterprises.

[9] This is the ratio of the total amount of investment (MGA 382.5 billion) to the total VA of the sector. However, the ratio increases to 12 per cent if only the total VA created by the IPUs that have prior experience of investment is taken into account.

[10] Average official exchange rate for 2012 is 1 USD = 2196.37 MGA (Source: Central Bank of Madagascar).

[11] The informal economy as a whole (agricultural and non-agricultural) contributes nearly half of the country's GDP (MEP 2015; INSTAT 2013a, 2013b).

[12] Examples of basketry goods are bags, shopping bags, mats, tablecloths, hats, curtains and decorative objects.

[13] MAEP (2008).

[14] The 2008 exchange rate is USD 1 = MGA 2,255 (Source: Central Bank of Madagascar).

[15] The 2012 average exchange rate is USD 1 = MGA 2,196.37 (Source: Central Bank of Madagascar).

[16] This situation may also indicate an underutilisation of capital due to lack of skills, high transaction costs and fierce competition (see section on market potential).

[17] A worker in the non-agricultural informal sector has 4.6 years of schooling on average.

[18] Women usually spend a larger proportion (90 per cent) of their earnings on their families (especially on the health and education of their children) than men do (35 per cent) (Source: Clinton Global Initiative: Empowering Girls and Women) (Notes of ECOSOC. https://www.un.org/en/ecosoc/phlntrpy/notes/clinton.pdf).

[19] It is noteworthy that it is in repair services that average schooling is the longest (7.8 years) and the proportion of workers who learned their trade at vocational schools is the highest (21.6 per cent against 2.4 per

cent for the overall sector).

[20] The branches in the manufacturing informal sector are mining, food, textiles and clothing, wood and other industries.

[21] As many as 75 per cent of the active population are in subsistence agriculture whereas the poverty rate in rural areas stands at 77.3 per cent (MEP 2015).

[22] The 2012 average exchange rate is USD 1 = MGA 2,196.37 (Source: Central Bank of Madagascar).

[23] According to neo-liberal assumptions, which are the extension of the dual model of A. Lewis, informal employment is a temporary situation for those waiting for an opportunity offered by the formal sector. In that sense, it is an imposed situation as a logic of survival, but not a freely chosen option (Chen 2012; Lewis 1954; Harris and Todaro 1970).

[24] The access to 'big orders' comes as the first support required by the informal actors, with 53 per cent of answers (INSTAT 2013b).

[25] According to the 2012 employment survey, total output stood at MGA 7,472 billion (INSTAT 2013b).

[26] A perfectly competitive market is characterised by: (1) atomicity or the existence of many buyers and sellers, making all producers price takers; (2) undifferentiated products, making them interchangeable for the customers; (3) fluidity, meaning that a firm can enter and exit the market easily; (4) perfect information about the products; (5) free mobility of factors of production.

[27] Nearly 80 per cent of IPUs think that the quality of their products is within the average of the sector whereas more than three-quarters think that they are within the average of their competitors in terms of price and business costs (ENEMPSI).

[28] Other strategies, such as the diversification of activities (34.3 per cent), the amelioration of product quality (15.6 per cent) and the reduction of profit (11.9 per cent) are also used by IPUs in cases of low market demand.

Acknowledgements

This work was supported by JSPS KAKENHI Grant Number JP16H06318.

References

Amirahmadi, H. and Wu, W. (1994) 'Foreign direct investment in developing countries', *The Journal of Developing Areas*, Vol. 28, No. 2, pp. 167–190.

Arrow, K. J. (1959) 'Toward a theory of price adjustment', in Abramovitz, M. (ed.) *The Allocation of Economic Resources*, Stanford: Stanford University Press, pp. 41–51.

Arrow, K. J. and Debreu, G. (1954) 'The existence of an equilibrium for a competitive economy', *Econometrica,* Vol. 22, No. 3, pp. 265–290.

BIT (Bureau International du Travail) (2017) *Recommandation (N°204) sur la Transition de l'économie informelle vers l'économie formelle 2015: Guide à l'intention des travailleurs*, Genève: ILO.

Bonnet, F. (2019) 'Aperçu statistique de l'économie informelle en Afrique', in F. Lapeyere and S. Barussaud (eds) *La formalisation vue d'en bas: Enjeux pour la transition vers l'économie formelle*, Louvain-la-Neuve: Academia l'Harmattan.

Chen, M. A. (2012) *The Informal Economy: Definition, Theories and Policies, WIEGO Working paper No 1*, Cambridge: Harvard Kennedy School.

De Soto, H. (2000) *The Mystery of Capital: Why Capitalism Triumphs in the West and Fails Everywhere Else*, New York: Basic Books.

Debreu, G. (1972) *Theory of Value: An Axiomatic Analysis of Economic Equilibrium*, New Haven: Yale University Press.

Findlay, R. (1978) 'Relative backwardness, direct foreign investment, and the transfer of technology: A simple dynamic model', *Quarterly Journal of Economics*, Vol. 92, No. 1, pp. 1–16.

Harris, J. R. and Todaro, M. P. (1970) 'Migration, unemployment and development: A two sector analysis', *American Economic Review*, Vol. 60, No. 2, pp. 126–142.

INSTAT (Institut National de la Statistique) (2013a) *Le Marché du Travail à Madagascar en 2012 dominé par le phénomène de sous-emploi massif, Enquête Nationale sur l'Emploi et le Secteur Informel (ENEMPSI) 2012 Tome 1*, Antananarivo: INSTAT.

——— (2013b) *Le Secteur Informel à Madagascar en 2012: Poids économique et social importants en déconnexion avec le système formel, Enquête Nationale sur l'Emploi et le Secteur Informel (ENEMPSI) 2012 Tome 2*, Antananarivo: INSTAT.

Lewis, W. A (1954) 'Economic development with unlimited supplies of labour', *Manchester School*, Vol. 28, No. 2, pp. 139–191.

MAEP (Ministère de l'Agriculture, de l'Elevage et de la Pêche) (2008) *Etude de Cas Programme Pays Madagascar : Analyse de la Filière Artisanat à base de Fibres Végétales dans la Région Analamanga*, Antananarivo: MAEP.

McFetridge, D. G. (1987) 'The timing, mode and terms of technology transfer: Some recent findings', in A. E. Safarian and G. Y. Bertin (eds) *Multinationals, Government and International Technology Transfer*, London: Croom Helm, pp. 135–150.

MEP (Ministère de l'Économie et du Plan) (2015) *Plan National de Développement 2015–2019*, Antananarivo: MEP.

OECD (Organisation for Economic Co-operation and Development) (1998) *Foreign Direct Investment and Economic Development: Lessons from Six Emerging Economies*, Paris: OECD.

Rakotomanana F. H. and Rakotoasimbola J. J. (2019) 'Les travailleurs indépendants dans le secteur informel non agricole à Madagascar', in F. Lapeyere and S. Barussaud (eds) *La formalisation vue d'en bas: Enjeux pour la transition vers l'économie formelle*, Louvain-la-Neuve: Academia l'Harmattan.

Rostow, W. W. (1960) *The Stages of Economic Growth: A Non-Communist Manifesto*, Cambridge: Cambridge University Press.

UNCTAD (United Nations Conference on Trade and Development) (2000) *The Least Developed Countries 2000 Report, Aid, Private Capital Flows, and External Debt: The Challenge of Financing Development in the LDCs*, Geneva: UNCTAD.

Wang, Y. and Blomstrom, M. (1992) 'Foreign investment and technology transfer: A simple model', *European Economic Review*, Vol. 36, No. 1, pp. 137–155.

World Bank (1993) *The East Asian Miracle: Economic Growth and Public Policy*, New York: Oxford University Press.

Part III

Development and Survivals in African Cities

Chapter 10

Horizontal Development and Knowledge-Sharing in an Industrial Cluster: Open-Air, Informal Sofa Manufacturing in Nairobi, Kenya

Motoki Takahashi, Masumi Owa and Kazuyo Ideue

1. Introduction

From the early 21st century until the mid-2010s, the countries of sub-Saharan Africa (hereinafter, Africa) achieved relatively high economic growth. International demands, mainly for resources and primary commodities, increased, as did domestic consumption. Compared to the high rates of economic growth in the mining, agriculture and service industries, however, the manufacturing growth rate has been relatively sluggish.[1] In Africa, although industrialisation has not yet reached the high-technology-intensification that comes with developments in heavy and chemical industries, a phenomenon of 'negative deindustrialisation' has seemingly emerged, wherein the relative proportion of manufacturing has dropped amidst increasing reliance on agriculture and mining (Takahashi 2016; Rodrik 2018).

Judging from the historical trajectory of socio-economic development in the industrialised Western and East Asian nations, reducing large-scale poverty in Africa depends on the promotion of import substitution and export-expansion through industrialisation i.e. development of manufacturing, the diversification of exported products, increasing value added, long-lasting increases in foreign exchange revenue and resulting reductions in the international trade balance deficit, wide-ranging technological innovations, and widespread employment. Contrary to Rodrik's vision (2018), economic development and structural shifts without industrialisation probably could not be effective pathways for Africa to move forward. Such a scenario would not offer the opportunities needed to increase foreign exchange revenue, spread technological innovation and create new jobs.

Assuming that industrialisation is essential for Africa's economic transformation, observing and analysing current conditions are initially needed to design future visions. Political and business leaders in Africa and Japan anticipate that foreign direct investment will have a significant impact, symbolised by the slogan 'investment rather than aid', a concept receiving increasing attention since the 2008 International Conference on African Development (TICAD). Foreign direct investment undeniably helped kickstart industrialisation in East Asian countries (other than Japan and South Korea). Domestic capital, however, cannot be ignored in understanding how industrialisation in East Asia has contributed to job creation and rise in the technological level of society as a whole.

It is likely to be the same for Africa. So-called 'industrialisation from below' or 'industrialisation from within' (see Chapter 6), has to come from local African capital and enterprises. From there, long-lasting development and poverty reduction across the socioeconomic spectrum can be envisioned. In other words, sustainable, inclusive development in Africa means that nobody will be left behind.

Several actors have played a part in Africa's industrialisation. For example, there are state-owned enterprises and locally incorporated foreign companies, as well as formal firms started with capital accumulated from other sectors (such as agriculture and services). Micro-, small- and medium-sized (MSM) manufacturers, the majority of which are informal, have also played a role, and this chapter focuses on them for the following three reasons.

First, it appears that MSM manufacturers have rapidly increased their overall scale of production in recent years. Second, informal MSM manufacturers receive little involvement or support from governments and foreign corporations. They are spontaneous and, thus, we can expect them to offer ideas for a more sustainable and locally rooted vision of development than that which is determined by forces from above or outside. Third, despite the importance of the issues already outlined, there are far fewer statistical data and research findings available on informal MSM manufacturers than formal economic activities.

MSM manufacturing activities have expanded in Africa. It is often the case that although the scale of activities undertaken by these enterprises remains small, their numbers, as well aggregate production, appear to be increasing. Most of these enterprises have remained informal.

Before discussing the policy responses to the wide variety of problems related to informal MSM manufacturing in Africa, we must first understand why enterprises continue to remain small-scale and informal.

This chapter examines sofa production as an example of MSM manufacturing that has evolved on the streets of Nairobi, Kenya. Like other spontaneously developing MSM manufacturing enterprises, sofa production enterprises have followed the aforementioned pattern of remaining relatively small in scale, increasing in number and staying informal.

To the best of our knowledge, limited research has been done on small-scale sofa production in Africa, and current conditions remain practically unknown. While some research exists on furniture in general, there are few studies on informal, small-scale enterprises, such as those analysed in this chapter.

To shed light on current conditions regarding sofa production, we focus on how the processes of sofa production are carried out and consider how these processes are affected by internal factors, such as technology and organisations, and external factors, such as governments and markets. In the latter half of this chapter, we discuss why the scale of sofa vendor activities in Nairobi has remained small despite their increasing number. The concept of 'vendor' used in this chapter includes two elements: 'masters', who control the sofa manufacturing processes by engaging in work directly, and *showroom* (shop) owners, who own showrooms but are not directly engaged in production. The second objective of this chapter was to consider why the expansion of this industry follows the trajectory outlined above.

In Section 2, we discuss the framework and methods used in this chapter. We reflect on prior research and outline our own viewpoint in terms of how best to understand 'informality' in the context of development. In Section 3, we describe the general state of sofa manufacturing in Nairobi and identify the key characteristics of the X area, which was the subject of our investigation. In Section 4, we describe each step of the production process based on our research in X. We explain how sofas are made and how the supply chain provides parts. In Section 5, we discuss the responsibilities and attributes of the various actors involved in sofa production. In Section 6, we focus on the interrelationships between actors in terms of division of labour. Finally, in Section 7, we suggest tentative answers to the questions posed by this study.

2. Research Standpoint and Investigation Methods

2-1. Characteristics of Informal Economic Activities in Africa

Most definitions of the term 'informal sector' focus on the relationship between an economic activity and an entity and the government. This chapter employs the most common definition, which is: 'Economic activity, or an aggregate of economic actors, conducting business without being registered with, and thus not being regulated by, the government.'

Until the 1960s, the strategy of development in Kenya was primarily government-led, and the informal economy was largely seen as detrimental. The 1972 International Labour Organization (ILO) employment report (ILO 1972) was the first to question this perception. An investigative group[2] dispatched to Kenya conducted a joint study together with Kenyan researchers and 'discovered' that, thanks to its efficiency, the informal sector actually played important roles in various aspects of the Kenyan economy, including job creation. The ILO Kenya Report marked a turning point. Attitudes toward the informal sector gradually began to change. There were increasing doubts over government-led development and disappointment at stagnation in large formal corporations, not only in Kenya but also in the rest of Africa and developing countries from the 1980s through the 1990s (Bangasser 2000: 2). Thus, Kenya is a prime country in which to consider the relative impact of the state and characteristics of the informal sector.

In recent years, the ILO has reconsidered its 'Kenya Report'. While the importance of the informal sector was a new 'discovery' for investigators from developed countries, for Kenyans, it was a self-evident part of daily life that Kenyan researchers had already noted by the time of the 1972 mission (Bangasser 2000: 11).

From the perspective of the general public, the so-called informal sector is an important aspect of economic life since it encompasses the majority of daily economic activities. While it is difficult to describe quantitatively due to the nature of the sector, the following data are telling. As shown in Kenya's *Economic Survey* (KNBS 2019), more than four-fifths of all income opportunities in Kenya are generated by the informal sector (including in rural areas), and the informal sector created 6.8 times the opportunities of the formal sector for the five years from 2014 to 2018. Even in Nairobi, where the relative importance of the formal sector far surpasses other parts of the country, half of the population resides in densely populated areas where informal economic activities occur – that is, in the so-called slums and other low-income residential areas.

Informal economic activities are an important part of the daily lives of African people across strata, especially the low-income groups. Much discussion has focused on the particular characteristics of the different types of activities. Keith Hart, a pioneer in economic anthropological studies of Africa's informal economy, emphasised in his study of Ghana that, in the informal economy, people do not adhere to a specific economic activity. Rather, the sector is characterised by fluidity as people change their means of livelihood according to their circumstances. There is little continuity for individual businesses in such a situation, and they cannot be expected to develop in the sense of expanding the scale of their activities (Hart 1973). The relative ease with which the informal market (ILO1972; Bangasser 2000) can be entered and left has led to fierce competition. In the informal sector, initial investments are minimal, and it is not necessary to complete a complicated government registration process. These characteristics show that it is easy to move capital, labour and other resources from low-profitability to high-profitability ventures and that a relatively high rate of efficiency has been achieved. While the formal sector is characterised by industrialisation that is capital-, import- and technology-intensive and, thus, not well suited to the limited resource endowments of African countries, the informal sector conserves capital and imports and usually appears to operate at the appropriate technological level. The informal sector can, in these senses at least, be regarded as efficient.

In recent years, however, criticisms have emerged of the observation that it is easy to enter or exit from the informal market. According to one critique, the informal economy has high barriers to entry in the form of concepts such as 'territory' (Takeuchi 1998: 68–69). The minibus industries in South Africa and Kenya are cases in point, in which competition surrounding bus routes has involved violence and exploitation. Thus, entry and competition in the informal economy cannot be entirely characterised as positive and vibrant.

This chapter is focused on the sofa industry in Nairobi, Kenya, as a means to examine some of the issues that have been raised in the literature about the informal economy: the informal economy in Africa plays an important role in people's daily lives; it is fluid and lacks continuity; actors are small in scale; entry to and exit from the informal market is relatively easy with notable exceptions; and the use of resources such as capital, imported goods and technology is appropriately conserved.

2-2. The 'Problematics' of Informality as Seen from the Perspectives of Developmentalist Views and 'Organisation Theory'

The development of the informal economy in Africa is due more to the total number of enterprises than the scale of activities of each enterprise. Since enterprises are small in scale, their activities tend to remain informal. MSM enterprises often cannot effectively manage the cumbersome costs of the formal sector, such as registering as an incorporated firm.

Informal activities are, accordingly, on the rise. This is an inconvenient truth for people who think that integration of informal activities to the formal sector through government regulation is an essential step for national economic development (ILO Governing Body 2015). The informality of MSM enterprises makes it difficult for governments and observers to grasp fully the circumstances and gain a clear picture of their activities, which hinders the formulation of pertinent policies. Legitimate and fair taxation is extremely difficult, and government regulation of, and assistance for, labour protection, environmental conservation and health and hygiene are often obstructed (Swaminathan 1991). Informal entities cannot be formally contracted, so they receive none of the rights and are subject to none of the obligations under formal law, and their transactions with formal entities are limited. An especially significant problem is the difficulty these entities face when seeking credit from commercial banks (ILO Governing Body 2015; De Giorgi, et al. 2018; Mahadea and Zogli 2018; cf. Swaminathan 1991).[3]

The small-scale nature of most informal enterprises means that only a small number of people deal with them regularly and that their internal organisation is simple. Why not expand? The answer may be related to neo-institutional economist Oliver Williamson's theory on the emergence of economic organisations, for which he was awarded the Nobel Prize in Economics. This theory explains the development of hierarchical organisations, instead of markets, from the perspective of efficiency.

Williamson begins his argument with the example of pin manufacturing, as touched on by Adam Smith. Producing a small product, such as a pin, requires at least 18 technical processes. Smith emphasised that if these processes are divided among many workers, rather than being completed by a single worker, productivity would increase dramatically as a positive result of the division of labour. But Williamson focused on the question of why so many workers remain within a single company. Given that each worker has specialised skills, why do they not become independent operators, buying and selling parts amongst each other, making the pins through the aggregate efforts of different individual labourers (Smith 1993: 12–13; Williamson 1983: 50–51).

According to Williamson, a horizontal collection of specialists linked through the market would become a vertically integrated enterprise with chain of command structures in cases where it is necessary to respond to the following three problems:

1. costs of buffer inventories for each specialist that arise from needing to fill gaps between supply and demand;
2. various costs resulting from disagreements and conflicts that arise due to the high number of transactions;
3. obstacles to production due to unforeseen circumstances, such as the sudden absence of workers.

Hierarchical organisations that concentrate decision making functions to 'a boss' for each operation can address these problems better than a market system (Williamson 1983: Chapter 3, especially pp. 50–51).

Below, we provide a brief explanation of the above argument on the genesis of a corporate organisation, or 'a firm', incorporating our own interpretation.

First, from the viewpoint of downstream Enterprise B, for instance, is it beneficial for upstream Enterprise A to keep plenty of buffer inventory of A's products? Or, is it more secure for B itself to keep buffer inventories of the products? The answer seems to be that it is best for both enterprises to maintain as little inventory as possible. In a hierarchical corporation, since production activities are carried out systematically at each part of the production process based on commands from the boss, gaps between supply and demand in each process (i.e., buffer inventories) are less likely to be large.

Second, in the case of products with many parts, if there is no precise agreement between Parts Suppliers A, B, and C and Assembler D about the size, shape and price of each part, it will be impossible to complete the finished product. Discrepancies between products from different production processes, as well as conflicts, may arise. In hierarchical firms, many of which are relatively large and formal with production carried out according to a centralised plan and commands from bosses, it is not necessary to reach an agreement between specialised workers at every part of the production process, thereby reducing discrepancies and conflicts.

Third, a firm must be prepared for unexpected contingences, such as workers suddenly becoming unable or unwilling to work or essential parts not being delivered on time, by hiring more than the minimally required number of workers. The larger the firm, the greater its labour and inventory. Even in the face of unexpected circumstances, a firm need not rely on uncertain procurement through the market for every single item; production can then proceed more smoothly.

Implied in Williamson's argument is the idea that since production carried out by hierarchical firms is more efficient than subdivided specialists linked through market transactions, it is likely that the latter mode of production will be eradicated by competition. Unlike traditional economics approaches, Williamson emphasised that opportunistic behaviour could arise by which one party tries to impose the burden of inventory costs on the other, and discrepancies in information (i.e., information asymmetry), as to what to supply and receive emerge. Opportunistic behaviour and information asymmetry were not a feature of traditional neo-classical economics theory but are common in neo-institutional economic theory.

Developmentalists who hope formalisation of as many MSM enterprises as possible, would expect Williamson's argument seemingly predicting scale of enterprises becoming larger enough to bear costs involved in formalisation. Yet, one should not forget that Williamson indicated that under the said three conditions (or problems), we can predict that increase in size of a firm could be expected. Perhaps because relevant enterprises and actors can overcome the problems without expansion of each, the eradication of the production mode linked through market transactions does not seem to be taking place in a wide-range of Africa's informal economy – at least, not in the informal sofa manufacturing enterprises in X. As we noted, the number of enterprises is increasing, and they are failing to expand their scale of production and organise into larger formal firms. If Williamson's style of production expansion through forming hierarchical corporations can be called 'vertical development', then perhaps the mode of production expansion examined in this chapter is 'horizontal development'. Why is horizontal, rather than vertical, development taking place in X?

2-3. Research Method

This study was conducted primarily through fieldwork. We chose the X area of Nairobi, the capital city of the Republic of Kenya, as our research site. X is located in a relatively low-income residential part of the metropolitan city and is known for its agglomeration of sofa producers and sellers. Within X, there are 55 sofa showrooms in a limited area of several thousand square metres. If we include associated workshops and shops selling other kinds of furniture (such as beds, wardrobes) and coffins, there are as many as approximately 300 buildings along the streets in the X cluster (Figure 1). Many of the 'buildings' in which sofa manufacturing and sales take place are simple structures with roofs and walls made of corrugated metal, which would perhaps be better called 'shacks'. Shops in X are called *showrooms*. A majority of the showrooms face a sub-arterial route with workshops located on the back side. Workers engage in most of their tasks under open-air conditions without roofs,[4] stopping when it rains. Sofas are exhibited outside, in front of showrooms, to catch customers' eyes.

Figure 1. Sofa-manufacturing Cluster X in Nairobi, where 55 shops are standing side by side

We carried out field research four times, as described below.

In March 2018, we conducted simple structured and unstructured interviews with four sofa vendors and 13 workers.

In August 2018, we conducted structured interviews with 36 sofa vendors. We asked the vendors about the profiles of their 169 employees (workers and salespeople). We observed differences in the products and production processes of Clusters Z and Y (see below) as compared to X. We interviewed two shopkeepers and two workers in Z and one showroom owner in Y.

In February 2019, we conducted semi-structured, in-depth interviews with 10 senior sofa vendors, 15 workers, 23 salespeople (shopkeepers), one bandsaw owner and one designer. We inquired about the history of X, the relationships among its various actors and the acquisition and transfer of technical knowledge.

In September 2019, we conducted in-depth interviews with eight showroom owners and one sewing enterprise owner. We observed differences in products and production processes between Clusters W (see below) and X. We interviewed one showroom owner in W.[5]

Most of the workers in X are more proficient in Kiswahili than English. Since we are not proficient enough in Kiswahili to discuss complicated topics, we hired three graduates of Kenyan universities as research assistants.

3. Sofa Manufacturing in Nairobi and the Positioning of X

3-1. Sofa Manufacturing Cluster Differentiation in Nairobi

We learned from our interviews and observations that several informal furniture and sofa manufacturing clusters exist within Nairobi. The four main clusters include one in a high-income residential area (Cluster Z), one in the city centre (Cluster Y), another close to an industrial area (Cluster W) and X.

The area that Cluster Z sits in was part of the European residential area during the colonial period, where the wealthy African population of Nairobi resides. As in X, the products made in Cluster Z include other furniture, such as beds and chairs. However, Cluster Z differs from X in that it is also a cluster for metalworking. Perhaps because many of the customers in Z live in large residences, sofas made there tend to seat far more people – sometimes 10 or 15 – than those made in X, which seat five or seven in most cases. Compared to the sofas made in X, the sofas in

Z are more complex to manufacture, with sturdier frames and more parts. Sofa seats made in Z are padded with flexible cushioning using rubber bands, which is quite different from sofas made in X (explained later). In other words, sofas take more time and effort to produce in Z, and the price is correspondingly higher. Production processes are carried out both outside and inside, with structures stronger and more durable than those made in X.

As in X, the target customer in Cluster Y tends to be from lower income strata. Cluster Y is also the hub for the distribution of various materials and commodities for a number of manufacturing sub-sectors in which MSM enterprises are leading actors. There are numerous small business operators whose work involves sawing the lumber brought in from forests in the country and in foreign countries. Most sofa vendors in other clusters procure lumber from Y. Mr J, an elderly vendor, who is both a showroom owner and a master of sofa manufacturing in X said that, until quite recently, he ordered sawmillers in Y to cut up the parts for his sofa frames (from an interview with Mr J in February 2019). According to Mr M, another elderly showroom owner and sofa manufacturing master in X, sofa manufacturing in Y is older than in X (interview with Mr M in February 2019). When he was younger, Mr M worked in Y, where he mastered the skills necessary for every process of sofa manufacturing. X has been dependent on Y as a source of materials and knowledge for production methods.

In contrast to Z, X is located in the former African residential area from the colonial period. X is adjacent to one of the biggest 'slums' in Nairobi where low-income people reside. Sofas manufactured in X differ from those made in Z in that they fall within a lower price range. Unlike Z, X's customers come from lower income strata.

Cluster W is located near the so-called industrial area. Most people living around Cluster W fall within a middle-income bracket. Sofas made here are sold at a higher price range than those in X, and the manufacturing methods are rather similar to those in Z.

Unlike X, the work in W is not done entirely under open-air conditions. Vendors set up tents so that work can continue in the rain with the inside remaining entirely visible.

3-2. A Brief History of X

In X, enterprises related to sofa manufacturing and sales are concentrated in a very small area. Following Kenyan independence in 1963, this area was established as a residential district composed of modern houses and apartments targeting the middle class. The houses and apartments constructed at the time are still in use today, but some parts, such as the outer walls, have deteriorated. The gutters used for drainage are frequently stuck with accumulated garbage until cleaners come by to remedy the problem.

According to Mr J, when he and his two older brothers first got into sofa manufacturing and sales in X in 1982, there were only five or six other sofa showrooms in the area. After completing primary school (a seven-year course at the time), Mr J studied at a vocational training school where he learned carpentry and the methods of sofa manufacturing. Importantly, according to him, he applied the size specifications he learned at the vocational training school to the sofa parts to start the business. From then on, his applied size specifications have become the standard among all masters and workers in X. Mr J has taught countless people, free of charge, how to make sofas following these specifications. Some of them went on to work for him while many left, and some moved to other areas entirely. We heard similar stories from other elders, such as Mr M, about teaching without compensation (from interviews with Mr J and Mr M in February and September 2019).

According to Mr J, sofa manufacturing methods did not change much until recently. Several years ago, a domestically 'invented' (according to several interviewees) electrical bandsaw was introduced to X, which resulted in several changes. Before then, manufacturers either relied on sawmillers in Cluster Y to cut the lumber for sofa frame components using large foreign-made bandsaws, or they did it themselves by hand. But since the development of a simple, Kenyan-made electrical bandsaw and its arrival in X, it is no longer necessary to go to Y. Mr J said that electrical bandsaw owners sometimes receive requests from sofa vendors to make frames for them (from an interview with Mr J in February 2019).

Ms S, the wife of an electrical bandsaw owner and wood distributor, now runs a business in X. She started the business with her husband several years ago. In addition to selling lumber obtained from trees that her husband and his workers fell at the production site, skilled employees in her enterprise cut wood in accordance with customers' orders using the electrical bandsaw in X, which they then use to make sofa frames. For a charge, some sofa manufacturers are permitted to use the electrical bandsaw themselves if they are familiar with it. Ms S said that the number of electrical bandsaws in X has been gradually increasing, and as of February 2019, she believed there to be around 14 or 15 in use (from an interview with Ms S in February 2019). When we returned in September the same year, there was more lumber piled in front of Ms S's shop than there had been in February, suggesting that demand for her services was increasing. Another sofa showroom owner and manufacturing master named Mr H was commissioning different sawmillers (most likely electrical bandsaw owners) to make his sofa frames, as Mr J had described (from an interview with Mr H in September 2019).

Mr J said that sofa manufacturing in X had become faster and easier since the introduction of the electrical bandsaw. He thinks it is a good thing that so many manufacturers have been able to start a business, including people he had taught. He is very happy to earn the gratitude and respect of people he has taught sofa manufacturing methods to, and he is proud that he has never asked for anything in return (from an interview with Mr J in February 2019).

If Mr J's memory is correct, the number of showrooms rose

from just a few in the early 1980s to 55 by the end of the 2010s. The stores that are currently in operation are all small in scale and have a small number of employees. Thus, the sofa manufacturing and sales business in X has followed a process of horizontal development.

4. The Sofa Manufacturing Process and Supply Chain

Based on our observations, sofa manufacturing in Kenya consists of the following processes:

1. Design (determining the size, shape and pattern)
2. Logging and production of other materials (metal pieces, such as nails; materials such as cloth and leather; and cushioning)
3. Sawing parts for the frame
4. Assembling the frame
5. Sewing the cover (upholstery)
6. Attaching the cushions and other parts to the frame
7. Attaching the cover and finishing the sofa
8. Selling the final product

Below, we explain each of these phases in more detail.

1. Design

To manufacture a sofa, it is necessary to plan the size and layout, the number of people it will seat (in X alone, there are many variations; some sofas seat one to three people and some five to seven), the overall shape and structure of the frame, and the colour and shape of the cover. The size and shape of frames and covers should match.

Although the structure of the frame is basically the same for all sofas, there are different models to choose from in terms of the shape and size of the backrest and armrests. Models come in and out of fashion. It is becoming common to copy designs from other showroom owners, manufacturers or images on the internet.

Since the structure of the frame basically does not change, the parts tend to become standardised. Although the shape of each part and component varies according to models, a certain common understanding has emerged due partly to the copying process mentioned above. Thus, the size and shape of the components are becoming loosely standardised.

The most difficult aspect of the design is determining the shape and size of the sofa frame and the external cover in advance so that they will match once put together.

When working on the design, it is necessary to imagine the frame broken down into its constituent parts and to understand the size and shape of the different components that are required. There are likely to be some shared standards for these components. According to the story told by Mr J, this standardisation originated from the size specifications he had learned (interview with Mr J in February 2019).

The cover should be sewn as a three-dimensional object so that its shape will fit the frame. It is necessary to project this three-dimensional image onto a flat material in order to determine what parts and processes are necessary.

The manufacturing masters, including Mrs J, M, and H, and/or showroom owners who oversee production processes, determine the structure of the various sofas, decide how many people they will seat, and choose the colour and pattern of the cover through consultation with each customer. They must take customers' demands and preferences into account throughout the design process.

Specialised 'designers', who are commissioned by sofa vendors, have appeared in recent years. Mr B, a freelance 'designer', learned carpentry, woodworking and design at a vocational training school. He mainly works for a middle-aged showroom owner and manufacturing master, Mr C.

2. Logging and production of other materials

Lumber used in sofa manufacturing is logged from various forested areas within Kenya and the Democratic Republic of Congo. The wood is commonly mahogany or pine. Ms S and her husband sell lumber logged from the forests of Kirinyaga County, a mountainous region not far from Nairobi.

Nails are important materials in sofa manufacturing. We observed that all the nails used in X were made in China, as were the cloth and leather materials. Domestically produced Kenyan sponge was used for the seat cushions.

Medium-density fibreboard (MDF) is commonly used for the base of the seat cushion (as mentioned, in Z, this portion of the sofa uses flexible cushioning with rubber bands). Most MDF is reused from scaffolding at construction sites, which is pervasive in Nairobi because of the construction boom. It used to be free, but there is now a cost involved to obtain it due to growing demand.

Second-hand scraps of cloth are used inside the backrest instead of cushioning.

3. Sawing (cutting the lumber)

The wooden parts of the sofa frame are cut from original pieces of lumber according to the shape of the sofa and the number of people it is designed to seat.

The lumber is cut in Cluster Y or X using an electrical bandsaw. The Kenyan-made bandsaw described by Mr J and Ms S has become increasingly popular in recent years. However, it relies on a used foreign-made motor; only the body and the outer frame are manufactured in Kenya. These bandsaws are most often produced in the K area, which is a metalworking cluster located within walking distance of X.

As mentioned by Mr J and Ms S, sawing is usually done by an electrical bandsaw owner at the request of showroom owners and/or manufacturing masters. Alternatively, bandsaw owners sometimes allow others to use the saw for a charge.

4. Making the frame

Frame making does not vary much, although adjustments may be necessary depending on design details and model, notably the desired shape and size. There are several shapes and sizes for backrests and armrests, but the width and depth of each seat are generally fixed. The angle between the seat, which is mostly even with the ground and the backrest, is generally fixed at around 100 degrees. This is seemingly the most difficult part of the sofa to make.

Frames are made using a hammer and spikes. Mortise and tenon joints are not applied. In Z, a wood reinforcer is used when two wooden parts are joined, but in X, such reinforcements are not used.

Workers usually make frames according to the instructions of a vendor. In some cases, such as orders by Mr H, bandsaw owners make frames for showroom owners and/or manufacturing masters.

5. Sewing the cover

The fabric is cut with scissors, following the design decided by showroom owners and/or manufacturing masters, and sewn together with a sewing machine. Some manufacturing masters have their own sewing machines and task their employees with the sewing, but independent sewing enterprises are also used.

Japanese and Chinese-made machines are commonly used and, in many cases, are procured second hand. Many are believed to have been previously used in formal garment factories.

6. Attaching the cushions and other parts to the frame

For the backrests, used grain bags are tightly packed with cloth scraps, then smoothed and shaped so that they will not lose their form during use. Many short nails are used to fix the bags firmly to the frame. A certain amount of skill is needed to drive many nails in accurately in a short period of time.

Armrests are furnished with sponge cushioning, for which short nails are used to attach the parts.

7. Attaching the cover and finishing the sofa

The cover sewn in 5 is attached to the body made in 6 (Figure 2). For the cover to fit the body, the original design is very important. Seat cushions, usually covered with the same design with the body, are then placed on it, and the sofa is complete. Many short nails are used to fix the cover to the body.

Figure 2. Two sofa-finishing workers in Cluster X are attaching a cover to the backrest

8. Sales

Completed sofas are transported to showrooms, usually facing the sub-arterial road, to be sold. Almost all shops are staffed with shopkeepers who directly negotiate prices with customers and consult about models with clients in cases of order-made sofas, and less often, ready-made sofas are sold on the spot. In most cases, showrooms deliver the sofas at their own expense. It is also very common for customers to visit showrooms and order a sofa based on their own preferences with particular specifications. Some showrooms prepare a catalog with a collection of photos of sofas that they can make.

In X, the price of a five-seater set (usually composed of two single-seaters and one triple-seater) ranges between 10,000 Kenyan shillings (KES) and 50,000 KES.[6] This variation reflects the fact that the amount of work involved depends on the model.

There are significant differences in showrooms in terms of the number of sets sold. Some showrooms may sell less than one set per week, while others may sell an average of five per week. Most showroom owners agree that sofa sales are unstable and hard to predict (from interviews conducted in August 2018).

5. Attributes of the Main Actors Involved in Sofa Manufacturing and Sales

5-1. Actors Involved in Sofa Manufacturing and Sales

Focusing on Cluster X, the actors involved in sofa manufacturing and sales can be divided into the following types:

a. Manufacturing masters
b. Showroom owners
c. Frame-making workers
d. Sofa-finishing worker
e. Sewers
f. Shopkeepers
g. Designers
h. Electrical bandsaw owners

a. The manufacturing masters direct the entire sofa production process from 1 to 8, excluding 2 (the production of materials). In our study, all masters were male, had prior experience as workers in sofa production and were also showroom owners. Elderly masters in X, such as Mr J and Mr M, take care of almost the entire sofa-construction process by themselves. Masters are generally responsible for directing every aspect of production but, in some cases, such as that of Mr H (who is a master), the frame-making is commissioned to other actors (bandsaw owners). Quite a few masters use the services of a specialist to sew the covers.

b. Showroom owners are either male or female. Most male shop owners are masters. None of the female showroom owners are masters, and they have no work experience or training in processes 4, 6, or 7. Some have sewing experience. Approximately 66 per cent of sofa vendors, which we have defined as including showroom owners and/or masters, are male.

Showroom owners initiate and directly (in the case of masters) or indirectly control the entire production process of each sofa made in X, starting with the design and placement of orders.

Manufacturing masters and showroom owners (sofa vendors) tend not to have many assets apart from their showrooms. Only 44 per cent of sofa vendors own machinery in addition to their showrooms (from interviews in August 2018). Based on our observations and interviews, only a few sofa vendors had their own electrical bandsaw.

c. Frame-making workers and d. sofa-finishing workers are loosely differentiated and, based on our observations, are all men. Both actors complete their part of production according to the master's or showroom owner's design. These workers are paid by masters and/or showroom owners for their tasks on a piecework basis (fixed amount fee-for-service). In many cases, payments are fixed per task.

e. Sewers use a sewing machine to sew sofa covers in accordance with the vendor's design. Based on our observations, more women than men do this task. In X, we found only one example of an independent sewing enterprise who took orders from masters or showroom owners to sew covers (from interviews in September

2019). Their payment is also on a piecework basis.

f. Shopkeepers, rather than showroom owners themselves, meet customers, decide on the final price and complete sales. Thus, on behalf of sofa vendors, shopkeepers sometimes manage this important process. They are paid by employers based on a certain proportion of the final price.

g. Designers either assist with or manage the design, which is the most important part of the entire sofa production processes.

h. Electrical bandsaw owners can be involved in sofa production in three ways. They may employ frame-making workers with bandsaw operating skills to manufacture frames in accordance with specifications, cut the wooden components as designed without making frames, or lend their bandsaw to masters to make the frames themselves.

5-2. Attributes of Actors

As shown in Table 1, the average age of sofa vendors in our case was 36 years. The oldest vendor (Mr J) was 66 as of February 2019, and the youngest, who is a male showroom owner but not a master, was 22. The average age of sofa vendors was higher than that of workers and shopkeepers.

Seventy-eight per cent of sofa vendors have completed a secondary level of education or above. Similarly, 79 per cent of shopkeepers completed a secondary level of education. However, the proportion is only about 46 per cent of workers, revealing a gap between their educational levels and those of the sofa vendors and shopkeepers. On the other hand, every interviewee, including the least educated workers, had received some degree of schooling, implying the importance of basic school education for manufacturing development (Cramer et al. 2020: Chapter 7).

The average length of time that sofa vendors had been in business was approximately ten years. This may be different from the common perception of an informal enterprise as described, for example, by Hart (1973).

Table 1. Age and educational backgrounds of sofa vendors, salespeople and workers

	Average age	Primary graduate	Secondary dropout	Secondary graduate	Higher than secondary	Total
Sofa vendors	36.1	6	2	24	4	36
Workers	30.5	11	3	11	1	26
Shopkeepers	30.0	3	1	12	3	19

Source: Compiled by the authors from August 2018 and February 2019 interview data.

Ethnicity plays a role in Kenyan politics and society. We asked about each person's ethnic origin, either directly or via interviews (during interviews in August 2018). Kamba people comprised 60 per cent of the total number of actors in X. For example, Mr M is a Kamba. Kamba people are said to be traditionally well-skilled in carving and other woodwork, and it is said that they are more likely to be involved in the woodworking industry, including leadership roles. The prevalent myth of Kamba's innate superiority in woodworking is not supported by facts. Mr J, one of the initiators of sofa manufacturing in X, belongs to the Luhya ethnic group (about 14 per cent), followed by Luo (11 per cent).

Of the sofa vendors, 14 per cent had received formal training. Of the remaining sofa vendors, 36 per cent answered that they had received only informal training (on-the-job training, or OJT) from 'friends' (30 per cent) or 'brothers' (6 per cent), in all cases free of charge. Female showroom owners had received no training related to sofa manufacturing except in relation to sewing (from interviews in August 2018).

None of the workers had received formal vocational training. Rather, they learned free of charge from acquaintances or relatives by doing OJT for several months (from interviews with workers in March 2018 and February 2019). Approximately 59 per cent of sofa vendors trained their staff themselves (from interviews in August 2018). This means that 'friends', as an answer to our question of who teaches sofa manufacturing skills may include masters. One can call such a way to teach skills and knowledge to junior people, free of charge, as apprenticeship.[7]

6. Division of Labour and Interrelationships among Actors in X

We focused mainly on what kind of relationships sofa vendors (who are presumably running the sofa manufacturing and sales processes) have been built with other actors. We considered whether the relationships between vendors and each of the other actors are similar to those described by Williamson as conditions for a firm to be organised. That is, has a permanent chain of hierarchical centralised command developed, like that between large enterprise management and its employees or subsidiary companies?

6-1. Relationships between Sofa Vendors

Among sofa vendors in X, it can be observed that there are cooperative relationships in terms of knowledge sharing. This leads to a common understanding of the basic structure of a sofa, the shape of each model and the shape and size of parts required for each model and the number of persons sofas are to seat. Soon after a sofa vendor acquires knowledge of a new model on the internet or from others and adopts that model, the same model is likely to appear at other nearby vendors through a process of imitation.[8] We have confirmed that sofa vendors in Cluster X are able to produce at least 13 models. Such knowledge sharing is also supported by much of the work being done under open-air conditions and shops standing side-by-side in a narrow industrial cluster.[9]

Also, some sofa vendors seem to be so kind as to allow others' learning knowledge of sofa production through imitation under open-air or transparent conditions. According to Ms K, a female shop owner in Cluster W, where models and production processes are quite transparent to each other among different vendors as well as X, altruistic attitudes emanating from friendship allow imitation by vendors in the same cluster. This is similar to what Mr J told us about his teaching of size and shape specifications.

Nevertheless, knowledge sharing of new models is not enjoyed by everyone. Mr J only knows five models, not 13. The reasons might be that he is too old to have easy access to information, especially on the internet, and/or that he belongs to a minority ethnic group in X (Luhya). On the other hand, Mr M, another elder, said that he was able to differentiate his products from other vendors' so that he could respond to the particular demands of individual customers even though the model category used may be the same as that of other vendors. While Mr J's business appears to be in decline, Mr M speaks confidently of his thriving business. We are unsure if Mr M's success can be attributed to his ethnicity, that is Kamba.

Vendors essentially have equal, or horizontal, relationships with each other, with mutual competition. Dominant/subordinate relationships, such as that of a parent company and a subsidiary, were not described by any of the vendors.

6-2. Relationships between Sofa Vendors and Part Manufacturers

For imported materials, such as nails, spikes and cover fabrics, the relationship between sofa vendors and manufacturers is indirect.

Some products, such as the lumber and sponge used in the seat cushioning and armrests, are generally procured directly or indirectly from domestic producers. These producers have equal status to fellow traders in the market.

Vendors' relationships with electrical bandsaw owners include renting or commissioned cutting of wood parts and frame making. These relationships are equal through market transactions but have only recently emerged due to the recent introduction of the electrical bandsaw. The relationship between sofa vendors and the sewing enterprise is also equal and based on market transactions.

6-3. Relationships between Sofa Vendors and Workers/ Shopkeepers

Perhaps the most important set of relationships among actors in X are those between sofa vendors and workers and shopkeepers. In our fourth field research, we conducted in-depth interviews with masters/showroom owners, salespeople, workers and shopkeepers involved in frame making, sofa finishing, sewing and sales.

Frame making costs vendors between 1,000 KES and 15,000 KES per frame, with finishing costs around 1,000 KES to 10,000 KES. When one person does both the frame making and finishing, remuneration for frame making is combined with the finishing. If frame makers are employed by bandsaw owners, payment by sofa vendors for frame making is paid to the bandsaw employer rather than directly to the frame maker.

It costs vendors between 500 and 8,000 KES to have a cover sewn. This remuneration range stands regardless of whether workers employed by vendors who own a sewing machine complete the work in-house or commission it to the independent sewing enterprise.

Except for one shopkeeper, none of our interviewees received payment at a permanent, fixed monthly amount. Payment from vendors is on a commission basis. It appears common to receive 5 per cent of the sale price.

Considering the large differences in remuneration paid to workers on a piecework basis, we can presume that sofa vendors do not usually pay workers and shopkeepers at a uniform rate or amount. When we asked workers and shopkeepers about additional employment benefits that they received, nothing particular was mentioned except for the expectation of possible future assistance in times of emergency.

All the workers we interviewed were free to work for more than one master/showroom owner. A majority of the workers said that they were employed by a specific master/showroom owner, but this is probably not an employment relationship in the usual sense. All of the shopkeepers, except for one, worked for specific sofa vendors (that is, a specific shop) and were obligated to maintain confidentiality about sales.

The instructions given by sofa vendors for each specific design must be followed, even if there is no real employment relationship in the usual sense.

7. Discussion and Conclusion

The first objective of this chapter was to shed light on the current state of informal, open-air sofa production in Nairobi, Kenya. We believe we have achieved this objective through our discussion, though perhaps only to a limited extent.

The second objective was to understand why some of the informal economic activities in Africa follow a path of horizontal development, wherein the number of vendors increases even though the scale of each enterprise does not. This scenario is contrasted against a vertical path of development in which numerous activities are conducted by a single hierarchical firm that continues to expand in scale as developmentalists may expect.

It is understood that Williamson identified the following workplace requirements as a basis for vertical development:

1. The need to reduce buffer inventory costs.
2. The need to avoid the disagreements and conflicts that accompany trading large numbers of parts.
3. The need to respond to unexpected circumstances, such as sudden absence of workers.

If masters/showroom owners in Cluster X are responding to these requirements without growing as individual enterprises or developing vertically, or if the needs listed above do not exist, then horizontal, rather than vertical, development seems to be taking place.

Sofa vendors in X do their best to avoid having extra sofas (and parts) as buffer stock, partly because there is little space in their shops. Moreover, as durable goods with substantial prices, sofas are a large investment for customers, which means that sofa vendors operate on an order-made basis and that sales can be unstable and unpredictable. Since sofa vendors generally do not place orders with part manufacturing enterprises until they receive orders from a client, it is unlikely that actors will hold excessive stock on hand at any step of the process, provided that no errors have been made along the way.

Since each sofa vendor controls the individual production processes for each product in X according to their specific designs and instructions, disagreements and discrepancies over quantities and types of parts can, to a certain extent, be avoided. Misunderstandings are further avoided by the shared knowledge among sofa vendors and workers who learn about sofa manufacturing free of charge from masters and other senior workers. This means that finished products and their components tend to be standardised and knowledge on them shared.

Although it is necessary to update common knowledge about shapes and sizes of parts as new sofa models emerge, commonality is maintained day-to-day through repeated imitation among vendors and the workers who work for multiple vendors. It is significant that sofa manufacturers in X implicitly collaborate with each other. Mutual collaboration makes it possible for a vendor to manufacture a product with standardised specifications, regardless of who they hire to do the work. According to Gereffi et al. (2005), who specialise in supply chain studies, this type of standardisation occurs without the vertical organisation of a firm with a boss at the top; it is sufficient that each step of the process is connected through transactions on the ad-hoc contract basis in the same cluster (Gereffi et al. 2005). Therefore, sofa production in X does not need to follow a centralised chain of command through a hierarchical firm or firm group that is permanently managed and controlled by one sofa vendor as the boss.

When unforeseen circumstances arise, such as worker absences due to accidents, sickness or other problems, vendors in X can respond flexibly because of their use of piecework payment (fixed amount fee-for-service) and their freedom to choose and contract with multiple counterparts. Even if a worker with whom a vendor has a strong relationship is unable to work due to an emergency, work can still be done by other workers (implying that, problematically, workers are substitutable), and extra workers need not be permanently employed.

Sofa manufacturing in X does not follow a pattern of vertical development by which a small number of enterprises expand. Instead, it maintains a pattern of horizontal development. By remaining small in scale, sofa vendors avoid bearing the financial and non-financial costs associated with larger formal enterprises, such as merger negotiations, processing fees involved with registration and corporate taxes, and enduring jealousy and grievances from competing vendors. We have pointed out that remaining small in scale, however, means that economies of scale are difficult to realise.

It is important to note that horizontal development offers employment opportunities for numerous sofa vendors and associated workers. Almost all the workers who responded to the February 2019 survey said that their salary was high enough to live on with their families. At the same time, most of them aspired to become sofa vendors and have shops of their own. These aspirations do not seem unachievable since horizontal development accommodates the entry of new vendors relatively easily.

The foundation of this kind of horizontal development is the shared knowledge and understanding between sofa vendors and workers about sofa manufacturing. This includes both old and new models and the sizes and shapes of their parts.

Horizontal development in X, characterised by the expansion that accompanies the sharing of knowledge and benefits, represents one form of African Potential. Stakeholders in X, an open-air industrial cluster, have been realising steady and long-lasting expansion of production and employment without bothering to make hierarchical centralised organisation by the three problems of inventory costs, possible mutual disagreements and sudden absence of workers, as indicated by Williamson.

On the other hand, we have to indicate that despite its benefits, noticeable gaps have recently begun to emerge between sofa vendors that may be linked to limitations in knowledge sharing due probably to differences in age and ethnicity. We hope to discuss this and other related issues following further research.

Endnotes

[1] Annual average growth rates of mining, agriculture and services from 2000 to 2015 are 18.2 per cent, 5.0 per cent and 5.9 per cent, respectively. On the other hand, that of manufacturing is as low as 3.9 per cent (calculated by the author based on data from World Bank 2020).

[2] The group was one of several Comprehensive Employment Missions that visited countries across the world in the 1970s. The mission to Kenya in 1972 was the first one to Africa, and its report was famous for re-evaluating the contribution of the informal sector to employment and people's livelihoods due to its efficiency (Bangasser 2000: 6–11).

[3] Lince (2011) indicates that there are cases where formalisation makes former vendors lose command over their own life and conflict with the government.

[4] In Kenya, informal manufacturing and other economic activities are generally called '*Jua Kali*'. *Jua Kali* literally means 'hot sun' in Kiswahili. It symbolises characteristics of a number of informal economic activities which take place under open-air conditions.

[5] Through the four time field researches, the authors, with other researchers, have obtained data on 36 sofa vendors (or their proxies), one designer, one independent tailor, one bandsaw owner, 119 workers and 44

shopkeepers. These figures do not necessarily correspond to the number of samples who could answer each of our questions.

[6] As of September 2020, one Kenyan shilling was equivalent to approximately 0.0092 US dollar.

[7] Bas (1989), a staff member of ILO, appreciates merits of apprenticeship as a way to transfer working skills and knowledge. Yet, he also argues that it lacks theoretical aspects and thus should be complemented by formal vocational education. His argument represents the ILO's standpoint to pursue formalisation of the informal sector.

[8] Swaminathan (1991) suggests that absence of regulation on intellectual property rights may hinder innovation in the informal sector as it leads to imitations. The informal sofa manufacturers in X, however, take advantage of such absence and make their innovations in the form of introduction of new models from websites of furniture vendors in Western countries and other vendors in X and Nairobi.

[9] In a different condition where enterprises cannot easily observe other vendors' production process, knowledge is hardly imitated by neighbours. Matsubara finds that in a leather shoemaking cluster in Addis Ababa, Ethiopia, where enterprises are allocated different rooms in a building by the local authority, they do not imitate others' designs (models). She also finds that in a cluster in Nairobi, shoemakers, working under roofs but with workshops being small and open, share designs and exchange knowledge with each other. The situation of shoemakers in the Nairobi cluster is very similar to that in sofa manufacturers in X. These three examples imply that knowledge sharing among clusters varies depending on conditions of places and probably characteristics of societies and countries. In short, knowledge sharing in a cluster is circumstantial (Takahashi and Matsubara 2021).

Acknowledgements

This work was supported by JSPS KAKENHI Grant Number JP16H06318 and JP17H02235.

References

Bangasser, P. E. (2000) *The ILO and the Informal Sector: An Institutional History, Employment Paper,* Geneva: International Labour Organization.

Bas, D. (1989) 'On-the-job training in Africa', *International Labour Review,* Vol. 128, No. 4, pp. 485–496.

Cramer, C., Sender, J. and Oqubay, A. (2020) *African Economic Development: Evidence, Theory, Policy,* Oxford: Oxford University Press.

De Giorgi, G., Ploenzke, M. and Rahman, A. (2018) '"Small firms" formalisation: The stick treatment', *The Journal of Development Studies,* Vol. 54, Issue 6, pp. 983–1001.

Gereffi, G., Humphrey, J. and Sturgeon, T. (2005) 'The governance of global value chains', *Review of International Political Economy,* Vol. 12, Issue 1, pp. 78–104.

Hart, K. (1973) 'Informal income opportunities and urban employment in Ghana', *The Journal of Modern African Studies,* Vol. 11, No. 1, pp. 61–89.

ILO (International Labour Organization) (1972) *Employment, Incomes and Equality: A Strategy for Increasing Productive Employment in Kenya,* Geneva: ILO.

ILO Governing Body (2015) *Formalization of the Informal Economy: Area of Critical Importance (GB.325/POL/1/1),* Geneva: ILO.

KNBS (Kenya National Bureau of Statistics) (2019) 'Economic survey 2019', KNBS (https://www.knbs.or.ke/?wpdmpro=economic-survey-2019) (accessed: 31 October 2020).

Lince, S. (2011) 'The informal sector in Jinja, Uganda: Implications of formalization and regulation', *African Studies Review,* Vol. 54, No. 2, pp. 73–93.

Mahadea, D. and Zogli, L. K. J. (2018) 'Constraints to growth in informal sector activities and formalisation: A case study of Ghanaian slums', *The Southern African Journal of Entrepreneurship and Small Business Management*, Vol.10, No.1, pp.1–9.

Rodrik, D. (2018) 'An African economic growth miracle?', *Journal of African Economies*, Vol. 27, Issue 1, pp.10–27.

Smith, A. (1993) *An Inquiry into the Nature and Causes of the Wealth of Nations*, Oxford: Oxford University press.

Swaminathan, M. (1991) *Understanding the 'Informal Sector': A Survey, WIDER Working Paper*, Helsinki: WIDER (World Institute for Development Economics Research).

Takahashi, M. (2016) 'Current state and quality of African economies', in K. Kitagawa and M. Takahashi (eds) *Contemporary African Economies: A Changing Continent under Globalization,* Tokyo: African Development Bank, pp. 91–131.

Takahashi, M. and Matsubara, K. (2021) 'Human resource development in production sites of manufacturing in developing countries: Cases of Kenya and Ethiopia', in S. Yamada and I. Ohno (eds) *Industrial Human Resource Development in Developing Countries*, Tokyo: Nihon Hyoronsha (in Japanese).

Takeuchi, S. (1998) 'Traders and capital accumulation: Imperfect foodstuff markets: The case of Congo', in J. Ikeno and S. Takeuchi (eds) *Re-examining the Informal Sector in Africa*, Chiba: The Institute of Developing Economies, pp. 57–100 (in Japanese).

Williamson, O. E. (1983) *Markets and Hierarchies: Analysis and Antitrust Implications,* New York: Free Press.

World Bank (2020) *World Development Indicators* (https://databank.worldbank.org/source/world-development-indicators) (accessed: 21 October 2020).

Chapter 11

West African Traders and Their Interactions with 'Aliens': Focusing on the Careers of Traders in Today's Ghana

Hitomi Kirikoshi

1. Introduction

In the 1990s, people from Asia started entering and investing in Ghana's markets (Anarfi 2010). In 2015, of the 896,524 people who entered Ghana, 41,032 were Asians. By nationality, 18,144 were Indians (representing 2.0 per cent of total entries in that year), 15,891 were Chinese (1.8 per cent of all entries) and 6,998 were Lebanese (0.8 per cent of all entries) (Ghana Immigration Service 2015). Of these, Chinese immigrants are particularly notable for how they have rapidly penetrated Ghana's retail industry. Muslim traders in West Africa have recently started shipping vast volumes of Chinese-made goods to inland arid areas, meaning that the residents of these areas have more opportunities than ever to encounter Chinese products. Consequently, China's presence has grown in the West African hinterland, just as it has elsewhere in Africa.

Muslim traders in West Africa buy Chinese goods – including plasticware, clothing, bicycles and electrical appliances – in Kumasi (Ghana's second largest city), and then ship them to the inland arid areas. Often, they ship these goods with other cargo (such as agricultural produce) along traditional trade routes. These routes emerged during a period of trade between the Ashanti Kingdom and Hausa Kingdoms in the 18th and 19th centuries. Numerous towns developed along the routes that became trade stations where traders would sojourn. The ethnically diverse traders served as middlemen, facilitating the swift shipment of goods along the trade route, which at times stretched over 2,000 kilometres.

Centuries ago, long distance trade routes in West Africa were primarily used for transporting high-value goods such as salt, gold and leather, which could justify the heavy costs associated with transporting a caravan. Long distance travel was prohibitively costly for an individual trader, so the transport process was divided into sections, with groups of traders each managing a section of the process. To ensure seamless transactions between the traders and the swift shipment of goods, traders provided each other and consigned one another to sell goods. These practices were predicated on trust between the traders (Lovejoy 1980: 33–35).

The inland arid areas of West Africa had long been in contact with the Islamic world through the Trans-Saharan trade, which exposed the areas to Islamic influence. Developed by Muslim traders, the Trans-Saharan trade was based on Islamic ties and established practices suited to West African commerce, which included a lingua franca and certain organisational characteristics (Lydon 2009: 57–59). Even today, Muslim traders remain as the key players in long distance trading in West Africa, with trading practices retaining many features of the historic Trans-Saharan trade. Thus, in the course of the region's trading history, the Muslim traders of West Africa built trust-based relationships transcending ethnicity and region, through which they were able to expand their trade networks.

The trade of kola nuts, a luxury item in West Africa that this chapter focuses on, is based on such trust-based relationships. The basics of the trading practice were first developed by Mande traders and later adopted in the 18th century by Hausa traders, who had grown in power. That same practice continues to be followed today: traders assess the trustworthiness of a potential trading partner based on what is known in the Hausa language as *gaskiya*. If a trader judges a person to be trustworthy (has *gaskiya*), the trader will enter into credit transactions, such as consignment and credit sale, with them.

In its common usage, *gaskiya* means truth, honesty or fairness. In a trading context, to demonstrate *gaskiya* is to prove that one can be trusted as a trading partner. This chapter explores the career paths of individual West African traders to examine how such traders have forged connections with traders from outside the region ('aliens'), focusing on the ways in which they establish a trustworthy reputation based on the concept of *gaskiya*.

2. Survey Overview

The data for this chapter come from fieldwork that I conducted continuously from 2013 to 2018 and from 19 February to 1 March, 2019 in the Republic of Ghana (see Figure 1). Specifically, it was conducted in Kumasi, the capital of the Ashanti Region, and in two villages in the Eastern Region. The first village (Village F) is in the Kwahu West Municipal District, and the other (Village S) is in the Kwahu East District. Even compared to the rest of Ghana, these villages have hot, moist climates and the vegetation consists of semi-deciduous broadleaf forests. The climate is ideal for cultivating kola trees (*Cola nitida*). Indeed, the environs of Kumasi are characterised by kola production area. Located around 80 kilometres west of Village F, Kumasi hosts Ghana's largest market for kola. Kola is produced in Village S, stored in Village F and is then shipped to inland arid areas such as Niger and northern Nigeria. Both villages were originally inhabited by members of the Akan people from Kwahu and Asante, but they have now been joined by members of the Hausa people, as well as by members of the Kusasi people, a group in northern Ghana.

Kumasi rose to prominence in the 17th century as the capital of the Ashanti Kingdom. Today, the city serves as a regional economic hub and is home to major markets, one of which is the Kumasi Central Market (or Kejetia Market), the largest marketplace in West Africa. Another is the Asawase Market, which is used by numerous Muslim traders.

During the fieldwork, I conducted interviews with Muslim traders who handled Chinese-made goods. This chapter analyses data from three of the informants: a woman in her fifties who lived in Kumasi and two men in their thirties. All three were Kusasi people from

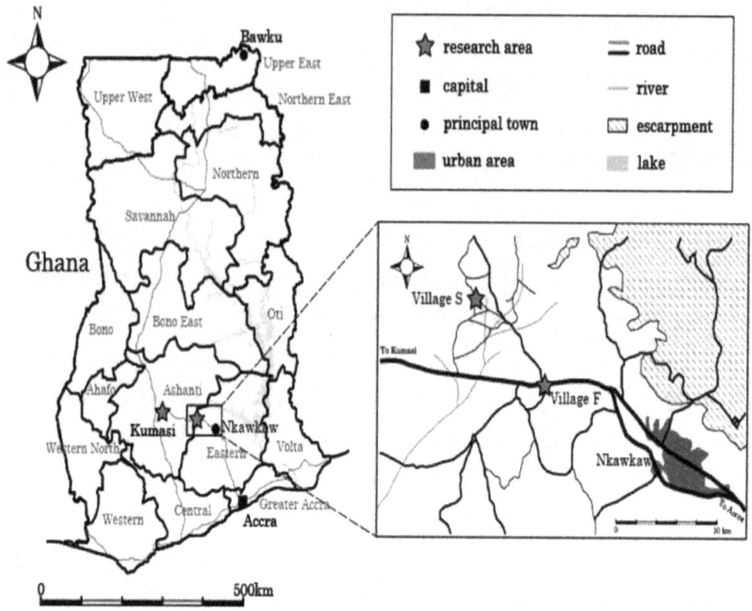

Figure 1. Research areas

Bawku in the Upper East Region of Ghana.

Many Kusasi people migrate to southern Ghana in pursuit of cash income. Historically a trading people, the Kusasi have a long history of trading with the Hausa. Bawku is a frontier town situated near the border between Burkina Faso and Benin. As such, the town is well known as a gateway for immigrants from all over West Africa. Many Kusasi travel to and from markets in various parts of Ghana to trade a wide variety of goods, and they often facilitate the kola trade between non-Ghanaian traders (such as Hausa traders) and Akan producers.

In this chapter, I discuss the results of the interviews I conducted in 2019, referring to the fieldwork on the kola trade I conducted from 2013 to 2018. An individual employed in the kola trade had introduced me to the three informants, as they were traders who engaged with Chinese people. During the 2019 fieldwork, I also had the opportunity to interview a Chinese man who ran a printing business in Kumasi. The original plan was to interview a number of Chinese residents, but I could only interview one due to certain restrictions on meeting Chinese people (which I will discuss later). Each interview was conducted in Hausa (the lingua franca in the kola trade) and English.

3. The West African Kola Trade and the Building of Credit and Trust

3-1. Kola: A Luxury Item in West Africa

Kola has been traded over long distances in West Africa since ancient times. Grown in the forested areas of southern Ghana, kola is consumed primarily in West Africa's arid inland regions. Kola nuts are the fruits of trees of the genus *Cola*, which belongs to the family Malvaceae. The area I conducted my research in is dominated by *Cola nitida*. The nuts, which contain caffeine and theobromine (Lovejoy 1980: 2–5; Tachie-Obeng and Brown 2001), are chewed and used as a stimulant to help people to focus and fight drowsiness.

In the late 17th century, the Ashanti Kingdom rose to prominence in what is now southern Ghana. Key commodities traded in the kingdom were enslaved persons, gold and kola. Kola was shipped primarily to the Hausa Kingdoms, which covered a stretch of territory corresponding to today's southern Niger and northern Nigeria. The product was special because it was produced only in the forested southern areas, despite the fact that its main area of consumption was in the northern arid areas. In forested southern areas, kola is perceived as mystical. It is consumed in small amounts for ritualistic purposes rather than on a daily basis. The product was also notable for having to be kept fresh, even when transported over long distances of 2,000-plus kilometres. Hausa traders developed an expansive trading territory, stretching from the forested areas in the south to the Sahara in the north, and from the Ashanti Kingdom in the west to Chad Lake in the east. Across this territory, they established trust-based relationships with different ethnic groups, culminating in a network that transcended the boundaries of the nation-state (Lovejoy 1980: 33–35).

Because kola products spoil if exposed to heat and moisture, their transportation over long distances required considerable labour and expense, which increased their value. Consequently, the products commanded formidable social and ceremonial value in the inland arid areas as symbols of wealth and power (Abaka 2005: 126–128).

Kola remains highly prized in inland arid areas with large Muslim populations. People in these areas crack the nuts with their fingers and then chew them like chewing gum for 10 to 30 minutes. Chewing the nuts in this way alleviates hunger and drowsiness, and men and women alike use it during everyday tasks like farming, housekeeping and studying for exams. Some people chew as many as three to five nuts a day, costing them the equivalent of 0.60 to 1.00 US dollars. At the time of my fieldwork in 2012, a single kola nut fetched around 100 West African CFA francs (0.20 US dollars) in Nigerian markets. In Niger, an adult male typically consume one kola nut every one to three days, spending 2.00 to 5.00 US dollars a month. In addition to personal consumption, the nuts are still used as tributes to traditional chieftains, gifts for house calls and offerings in festivals and ceremonies.

3-2. Today's Kola Trade and Shipment Process

In the fieldwork's target areas, each commodity had its own distribution system, and each of the key trading cities had markets that specialise in a certain commodity. There would, for example, be a crop market, a livestock market and a materials market. These markets had their respective commodity sections, and transactions would be segregated by commodity. In Kumasi's wholesale market, people used the English word 'business' to describe each of the trades. The trade in millet, for example, was known as the 'millet business'. Each 'business' had its own transactional procedures and distribution system.

Although each commodity had its own distribution network, traders would often hop from one 'business' to another or engage in multiple 'businesses' at the same time. During the 19th and 20th centuries, traders in West Africa rarely specialised in a single commodity (Clough 1985; Lynn 2002). This trend persists today in West Africa, such that the distribution networks for different commodities are intertwined.

While both men and women are engaged in trade, men are more likely to trade in commodities that must be transported over long distances, while women are more likely to deal in crops involving much shorter distances (Hart 1988; Clark 1994). Male traders are typically around the age of 40 or more and female traders tend to be mothers. Traders often employ young men aged 10 to 40 years as assistants, who help to ensure smooth trading by undertaking processes such as purchasing and transport. A young man who assists traders in northern Ghana, northern Nigeria, or elsewhere in the inland arid regions is known in the Hausa language as *yaro*, meaning 'young man' or 'junior'. *Yaro* commonly refers to an apprentice, junior or someone who is close to but has not yet reached adulthood.

A *yaro* is not yet a business owner, but is a valued member of a trade. This is reflected in the following statement: 'To ensure success as a trader, you must hire a reliable youth as your *yaro*.' Young men may assist in the distribution of any commodity, and many do so to gain skills in fundraising, commerce and trading. Young, unmarried women rarely become *yaro*.

In Village F, the kola trade is known as the 'kola business'. Today, the kola shipment process consists of buying kola in the village, removing the nuts from their pods, booking cargo and shipping. Harvested kola is assembled in a pickup point known as a *shago* and is then shipped in bulk to Lagos, Nigeria, or Niamey in Niger. Kola is also transported from southern forested areas to northern arid areas via trade routes that date back to the 18th and 19th centuries. These routes form the basis of West African long-distance trade today. Upon arrival at their destination, the nuts are brought to a distribution point (also called a *shago*) and then sold wholesale to markets. Each pickup point and distribution point has a single owner and is frequented by multiple kola traders.

The process of shipping cargo from the pickup point to the distribution points is known as the '*shago* system' in Village F. In the 19th century, traders from the inland arid areas were forbidden to set foot in the Ashanti Kingdom. Thus, Hausa and other traders would buy the kola from Asante traders at the Salaga Market, which was located on the eastern part of the kingdom (Wilks 1975: 267; Lovejoy 1980: 64–69). The *shago* system differs from this historic practice in that traders from the inland arid areas purchase the kola directly where it is produced. To distinguish between today's kola trade, which is based on this *shago* system, and the historic kola trade, I will refer to the former as the 'kola business'.

Broadly speaking, the kola business has two possible shipment methods: (1) traders can sell directly to distributors, or (2) they can sell indirectly via the pickup and distribution point owners. I focus on the second method, as it is now the more popular of the two.

First, traders procure kola nuts from a local buyer. The traders then pack the nuts in cement sacks. The package is called *aowu*. The traders then delegate a *yaro* to get the goods from the local buyer to the pickup point. Next, the traders entrust the owner of the pickup point with the storage, management and sale of the kola nuts. Meanwhile, the *yaro* removes the nuts from their husks, divides two *aowu* worth of kola nuts into three portions, wraps the contents in leaves and then repackages them in sacks.

The sacks containing the repackaged kola are called *tafiya*, meaning 'cargo for shipment'. The leaf wrapping helps protect the contents from jolts in transit and from drying out. After 500 to 1,000 *tafiyas* are assembled at the pickup point, the owner arranges for a large trailer to transport the cargo to its destination. At the destination town, the cargo is received by a *yaro* who works for the owner of the pickup point. One at a time, the *yaro* delivers the cargo shipment to each distribution point that does business with the owner of the pickup point and collects payment from the owners. He then deposits the sum of all payments into the account of the owner of the pickup point. Upon receipt of payment, the owner then pays the traders. The traders receive the sale price minus the storage and shipping fees. The owners of the distribution points then sell the kola to wholesalers, who in turn ship the goods to markets in various locales.

This *shago* system enables traders to swiftly ship the kola, which is vulnerable to heat and dryness. The system relies on *gaskiya* since smooth, trust-based transactions are crucial.

3-3. Kola Traders and Gaskiya

Since kola is such a high-value item, traders rely on trust relationships, which they determine based on the person's *gaskiya* (Kirikoshi 2018). *Gaskiya* is an ethical concept, which describes a prized trait among the Hausa (Adamu 2001; Aminu 2003). The word is used broadly across West Africa, not just in Hausa society; it is featured in the title of a newspaper in northern Nigeria[1] and in the name of a political party and radio station elsewhere.[2] Many young people strive to enter the kola business, believing that if they can demonstrate *gaskiya* and build a reputation of trustworthiness, they can gain the prestige that can unlock a wide range of commercial opportunities.

How is a person's *gaskiya* judged in different situations? One might, for example, judge that a *yaro* has *gaskiya* on the basis that he prudently managed a highly perishable kola cargo on the fortnight leading up to a shipment. Similarly, the owner of a pickup point might be judged to have *gaskiya* if he/she, when passing on the takings, reports to the trader the exact number of sacks sold rather than trying to short-change. In other words, judging someone's *gaskiya* involves considering whether he/she has accurately and faithfully reported information and accomplished his/her duties.

Because *gaskiya* is so highly valued in commerce, the kola business is seen as a gateway to a career as a trader in West Africa. Many young people use the kola business as an opportunity to learn negotiation skills and commercial techniques, which they then use to venture into other businesses. As a result of this practice, *gaskiya* criteria are shared among traders who start out in the kola business and then move on to other businesses.

4. Trading Partners of West African Traders

Ghanaians typically refer to people from other African countries as 'strangers' and to people who come from outside Africa as 'aliens' (Malki 2013). Adopting this distinction, I use the word 'strangers' hereafter to refer to traders from Nigeria and other African countries and the word 'aliens' to refer to traders who hail from outside the continent.

Though West African retailers and wholesalers buy many of their wares from Chinese traders, Ghana also has frequent visitors from Lebanon and India, with whom many West African traders claim they rarely trade.

4-1. Lebanese and Indians in Ghana

Isaac Xerxes Malki offers valuable insights into the role the Lebanese have played in Ghanaian politics. According to Malki (2013), Lebanon was plagued by sectarian strife in the 1860s. Many émigrés migrated to West Africa via North and Latin America. The Lebanese population in the Gold Coast started appearing in census data in 1892. Indians, in contrast, began migrating to Ghana and elsewhere in West Africa following the 1947 partition of India.

The Lebanese population initially dominated trade in textiles, motorbikes, spare parts, timber and construction materials. Seeking to shift Ghana's economy away from dependence on cocoa production, Kwame Nkrumah announced a programme of industrialisation, in which the Lebanese population were to play an active part starting in the late 1950s. By the end of the 1960s, the Lebanese had become a major presence in the economy, running small-scale finance and wholesale operations and owning major holdings in industrial sectors.

During Nkrumah's industrialisation programme, the Lebanese were branching out from manufacturing into retail and wholesale. They were also enjoying a flourishing business with West African traders – businesses based on trust relationships. Said one Lebanese who was a retailer at that time, 'West African traders use local language and customs to gain the upper hand over their rivals [including Lebanese].' Some Lebanese businessmen even employed West Africans as workers.

However, Nkrumah's call for a policy of Africanisation changed this state of affairs. Tax privileges for Lebanese became restricted to the manufacturing sector (a sector that would contribute greatly to industrialisation), and Lebanese were discouraged from venturing into industries traditionally run by Africans, such as timber production, retail and bakery. As the Lebanese expanded their economic clout in the 1960s, Ghanaians viewed these 'aliens' with an increasingly hostile eye, believing that Ghanaian retailers were losing out in direct competition to Lebanese, Syrian and Indian competitors. This perception made the position of aliens in Ghana increasingly precarious.

Animosity towards Lebanese became more open during the tenure of Ghana's second prime minister, Kofi Abrefa Busia. Enacted in 1969, the Aliens Compliance Order stipulated that non-nationals without a residence permit could not stay in the country for longer than 14 days. Although the order applied to all non-nationals, including those from other African states, it was clear that Lebanese and Syrians were the intended targets. Ghana then enacted the 1970–1971 Aliens Compliance Order Act, which led to the closure of 60 per cent of wholesale, retail and manufacturing operations owned by foreign residents. The initial targets of the legislation were Lebanese and Indians, but the effects also extended to Nigerians. Consequently, many Ghanaian traders who depended on Lebanese and Nigerian financiers were forced to close. Likewise, many Ghanaians who worked for foreign employers lost their jobs.

Thus, although West Africans have had a long history of transactions with Lebanese and Indians, Ghana's post-independence governments created a more hostile climate for resident aliens and foreigners. Even today, few Lebanese or Indians engage in retail or wholesale.

4-2. Chinese in Ghana

According to Ho (2008), the earliest Chinese migrants to Ghana began arriving in the late 1940s and early 1950s. They were of Hong Kong origin and worked as employees in Chinese-owned factories in western Ghana. Nkrumah requested that the Chinese work in the coastal region between Accra and Tema, which resulted in the creation of a large harbour and an industrial sector in Tema in 1961. This facilitated the establishment of Chinese factories in eastern Ghana. Most of the Chinese in Ghana were bachelors or had left their families behind in Hong Kong. Eventually, in the 1960s and 1970s, they brought their families over from Hong Kong.

Chinese migration to Ghana started to rise in the late 1990s, with many of the Chinese immigrants entering the retail trade (Kohnert 2010). Many of them came from mainland China (Ho 2008). The reason why Chinese people have managed to penetrate retail and establish trading relations with West Africans, in all likelihood, is that Chinese imports have proven extremely popular with the public, in both urban and rural areas. In the Makola Market, the largest market in Accra (Ghana's capital), there are many Chinese-owned shops that sell clothing and daily necessities. By contrast, no Chinese shops can be found in Kumasi, a city frequented by traders from many different locations. My interviews with West African traders in 2019 revealed that many Chinese traders have set up small offices in mixed-use buildings in Kumasi, but that only a few West African traders can access them to conduct business.

As of ten years ago, half of the 30 shops along Zongo Lane in Accra (a figure that includes illicit retailers) were reported to be

Chinese-owned (Liu 2010). Today, most of the shops in Zongo Lane are Chinese shops (Dankwa and Amoah 2019). Their legality is not certain. The informants told me that a surge in illicit retailers in Accra had prompted a crackdown on Chinese traders in Kumasi. The West African traders claimed that Kumasi's tougher approach has made it hard for Chinese traders to open a shop in the city.

I met the Chinese informant 'L' in Kumasi when conducting research in 2019. Born in Qingdao, L started running a printing business in Kumasi in 2012. He took the business over from his uncle, and most of his employees had worked there since his uncle owned it. L also had new employees, but they were recruited by other Ghanaian employees (L did not select them personally). The office was located near the centre of Kumasi, and L's living space was situated on the same site. He ate most meals in his living space but had lunch, which he cooked with a female employee, in the office. Because he was under police surveillance, L rarely ventured outside except to buy groceries. He would only leave Kumasi when he needed to go to Accra to travel abroad. All orders from Ghanaian clients were received by Ghanaian employees; L never interacted with any Ghanaians aside from his employees. He claimed that, despite Kumasi having a sizeable Chinese population, West Africans cannot easily establish connections with them due to police surveillance.

Under the 1994 Ghana Investment Promotion Centre (GIPC) Act, foreigners can only establish an enterprise involving the purchasing and selling of goods if they invest foreign capital of at least 300,000 US dollars and employ at least ten Ghanaians. The unintended consequence of these exacting requirements was a rise in illicit retailing and small-scale mining, leading in 2007 to the arrests of Nigerians, Indians, Germans and Dutch people (Kohnert 2010).

In 2012, Ghanaian traders put intense pressure on the government to enforce the laws regulating trade by foreigners in Ghanaian markets. A number of shops operated illegally by foreigners were subsequently shut down. This was followed by the amendment of the GIPC Act in 2013 (Obeng 2018). Today, investment activities in Ghana are governed by the GIPC Act 2013 (Ghana Investment Promotion Centre Act, 2013, Act 865), which demands 500,000 US dollars from foreigners who establish enterprises without partnering with Ghanaians. Ghana has recently tightened its restrictions on alien and stranger traders, making it harder than ever for West African traders to establish connections with them.

These interventions have, however, failed to yield the anticipated outcomes. Obeng (2018) describes cases in which Ghanaians have used their nationality to facilitate Chinese investment by claiming partnership with Chinese entrepreneurs, despite lacking a personal financial stake in the venture. This practice is popular with foreign investors because it reduces initial capital requirements and simplifies numerous related processes, such as business registration, tax clearance and filing VAT returns. Obeng (2018) states that this practice, known as 'fronting', remains common despite being criminalised because the offence is difficult to prove. Given the history of Chinese migration to Ghana, which dates from the 1960s, the Chinese in Accra would be expected to have strong connections with Ghanaian collaborators. Therefore, a certain number of illegal retailers in Zongo Lane may have evaded arrest.

5. Careers of West African Traders

As we have seen, Kumasi's crackdown has made it difficult for West African traders in the city to deal with non-West African traders. Nonetheless, West African traders do desire to establish connections with Chinese people and procure large quantities of their goods. My 2019 fieldwork revealed that only a few traders, known as '*mai-gida*', could directly negotiate with the Chinese, and that other traders could only sell the wares by working for the *mai-gida*. Many individuals who work for the *mai-gida* are young *yaro*. Junior traders leverage the networks they forge in the trade of kola (and in the trade of other items over long distances) to create opportunities for meeting *mai-*

gida, who can trade with the Chinese. Presented below are case studies illustrating the career paths of two junior traders and one *mai-gida.*

A junior trader, 'S' (a male in his thirties), was employed in the kola business and in an enterprise involving the wholesale of second-hand bicycles. He also engaged in the onion business. After completing junior secondary school in 2002, S moved to Kumasi and got a job as an assistant in the kola business through an introduction by a relative. In 2004, S started working concurrently as an assistant for a wholesaler of second-hand bicycles. In 2012, he entered the onion business as a trader, not an assistant.

The second-hand bicycle wholesaler for whom L worked imported bicycles from China and Japan. S got the job through a personal connection he forged during his time in the kola business. He had told the person about his interest in bicycle wholesaling, and that person then introduced him to a *mai-gida* who dealt in second-hand bicycles. S visited the *mai-gida,* a Ghanaian in his fifties, repeatedly to pitch his services as an assistant. The *mai-gida* had started out in the kola business and then ventured into bicycle wholesaling, where he procured bicycles from a Hong Kong trader and a Japanese enterprise.

S said that he gained valuable trading skills from his time in the kola and second-hand bicycle businesses. Having entered the onion business in 2012, he started heading out to negotiate with suppliers himself. His aspiration was to become a *mai-gida* who procured motorbikes directly from China.

A junior trader, 'R' (a male in his thirties) and a resident of Village F, wholesaled mobile phones and was engaged in the kola business. After completing senior secondary school in 2005, R entered the kola business through an introduction by his father, himself a kola trader. That same year, not long after entering the kola business, he started wholesaling mobile phones after doing a kola transport to Nigeria. While there, he visited mobile phone shops in Lagos, one by one, requesting approval to sell the phones in Ghana. One of the shops he visited was that of an Igbo man who procured mobile phones from China via his Chinese wife. The man visited the kola markets a number of times to see how R worked and, after judging him to have *gaskiya*, agreed to give R approval to sell the phones in Ghana. R's aspiration was to expand his personal network through the wholesale trade and, eventually, to deal directly with a Chinese trader.

A *mai-gida*:,'H' (a woman in her fifties), wholesaled artificial flowers in Kumasi, where she was a resident. At the time of the interview, she had one shop in Kumasi's Central Market and another elsewhere in the city. To procure her wares, she would first check the products on the website of her Chinese supplier and then order them by telephone. She then travelled to China once a month to inspect and procure the goods at the supplier's site.

H started her career in the 1980s in the onion business. She had transactions with onion traders, who engaged in the kola trade concurrently, in Bawku. In 2000, she started wholesaling bicycles and motorbikes through a contact she made in the onion business. This contact was a trader who had experience dealing in onions, kola and bicycles. With the contact's support, H started importing bicycles and motorbikes from China. While trading in all three products, H gained recognition for her talent, and many traders approached her with new business propositions. An important one came in 2003, when a Hausa trader whom she had met in the motorbike trade introduced her to a Chinese artificial flower company. This prompted H to switch to artificial flower wholesaling, being the first person in Kumasi to do so. The business took off, thanks in part to the many hotels and restaurants opening in Kumasi around the same time. Demand for artificial flowers continued to rise, and H's business grew so much that she was eventually running two large shops.

The three cases above illustrate a common career path for junior traders: building a network of contacts through the kola business that leads to dealing in imported goods. According to the informants, a critical element in this career path is for one's *gaskiya* to be recognised by a *mai-gida*, and the kola business is a good way for this to happen. R described the kola business as a way to confirm a person's *gaskiya*.

Although she did not engage in the kola business herself, H made a contact in the business and this contact was instrumental in her switching from the onion business to the bicycle and motorbike business.[3] Although H never actively used the kola business as an opportunity to demonstrate her *gaskiya*, her *gaskiya* was recognised in the course of her interactions with kola traders, which bolstered her reputation. Like the two junior traders, H forged a personal network in the course of her engagements in long-distance trading in West Africa. Through this network, her *gaskiya* became known far and wide, which eventually unlocked a trade route from China. But it took her nearly twenty years to transition from onions to bicycles.

6. From Intraregional to Interregional Trading

Even today, kola traders sojourn at many of the trading stations that historically developed between the Ashanti and Hausa. During their stays, traders keep a close eye on market trends and exchange information – increasingly via mobile phones – about kola price trends, the amount of kola they has managed to sell, promising junior traders, currently prevailing trades and international commerce.

For West African Muslim traders who want to expand their business and deal with aliens, starting out in the kola business provides the best shortcut. Kola trading involves a vast commercial network in West Africa, and transactions in the business are based on trust relationships, which themselves are predicated on certain criteria concerning the person's *gaskiya*. Engaging in the kola business enables a trader to forge a broader network of contacts, potentially unlocking a desired career path. It is also important in terms of *gaskiya*, which is so highly valued among West African traders; maintaining a successful kola business will itself demonstrate one's *gaskiya* (Kirikoshi 2018).

As noted previously, it is by no means rare for a kola trader to deal in other commodities. The junior traders, S and R, for example, engaged in multiple businesses. It was thanks to this tendency that someone like H, who never personally engaged in the kola business, could nonetheless forge contacts and thereby gain opportunities to demonstrate her *gaskiya* to West African traders far and wide, which resulted in business propositions. Given the propensity for female traders to deal in agricultural produce traded over shorter distances, H may never have crossed paths with the kola trade. But her case illustrates that if traders manage to demonstrate *gaskiya* and trading skills to kola traders, they can latch on to kola business networks, build a good reputation and find new avenues for business success.

Many junior traders (*yaro*) in the kola business use the business as a gateway into an increasingly expansive trading milieu. As traders expand their activities, their *gaskiya* rating carries over from one business to another. In this way, the notion that *gaskiya* is critical to success as a trader becomes a widely held belief.

7. *Mai-gida* Negotiations

H's case illustrates a career path of starting in a West African trading business, establishing connections with kola traders, and then using those connections to venture into another business. According to someone who knows H well, although she started out in the women-friendly onion business, her ability to demonstrate *gaskiya* to the traders she met allowed her to gain widespread recognition for her trading talent, which explains her advancement from the onion business to bicycle and motorcycle wholesaling to artificial flower wholesaling.

The practice of dealing directly with alien traders is restricted to just a few traders who have business talent. These traders are some of the people known as *mai-gida.* Not every *mai-gida* can deal directly with alien traders, but they need the qualities of popularity and leadership based on *gaskiya* and excellent negotiation skills cultivated through extensive experience as *mai-gida.* These qualities must be highly valued by West African merchants, especially those who act as intermediaries, in order to gain the trust of alien traders. In other words, the intermediaries must be able to introduce them with confidence or they will not even have access to alien traders. An intermediator is also a person who gained the trust of alien traders through a series of honest transactions (*gaskiya*).

Alien traders residing in Kumasi have small offices located in mixed-use or apartment buildings. The locations of these offices are disclosed to only a few trustworthy *mai-gida*; assistants of *mai-gida* are not permitted to meet aliens directly. Hence, junior traders like S and R must first accumulate experience in the services they perform for a *mai-gida* and gather information about aliens before they can get a chance to meet one. Junior traders employed by a *mai-gida* strive to gain the knowledge and skills necessary for negotiating with an alien. If the *mai-gida* permits the trader to deal with an alien, the trader may potentially inherit the trading relationship in the future. As was the case of the Chinese businessman L, one might be able to trade with an alien if the alien is introduced via a Ghanaian (African) intermediator who already deals with him/her.

Recognised as they are to trade directly with aliens, *mai-gida* are described as individuals who have proven their *gaskiya* in trading activities within West Africa. The only people who enjoy the right to negotiate with aliens as a *mai-gida* are those who have traded within West Africa and who have demonstrated the *gaskiya* necessary to garner respect as a skilled trader.

The role that *mai-gida* play today in trade negotiations resembles that of their historical namesake. In the 18th and 19th centuries, '*mai-gida*' referred to the proprietor of an inn located at a trade station.[4] Because these *mai-gida* would sojourn at trade stations for long periods of time, they needed to maintain amicable relations with the host community. To do so, they required leadership skills to ensure that traders using the stations would likewise be accepted by the host community. In other words, the kind of person suited to being a *mai-gida* was one who commanded the trust of the host community and who, as a leader, could direct trust-based transactions between different traders (Curtin 1984; Lovejoy 1980). Relating this to present-day interactions, the kind of person suited to dealing directly with aliens as a *mai-gida* is one who possesses outstanding talent as a trader (*gaskiya,* leadership and negotiation skills) and who commands widespread trust. The go-between role that the *mai-gida* have played in transactions between West Africans and aliens has helped cement commercial norms in the transactions between the two and contributed to stable trading relations.

Since gaining independence, Ghana has pursued industrialisation and adopted legislation under the banner of home-grown economic development and national social protection – ideals that accorded with Nkrumah's Africanisation policy and socialism (Malki 2013). Under these policies, aliens – particularly those engaged in retail and wholesale enterprises – have faced heavy government restrictions and surveillance. The government's severe attitude toward aliens and strangers is demonstrated by the exclusionary policies of the 1970 Aliens Compliance Order Act – which targeted Lebanese and Indians – and the surveillance of aliens and strangers mandated by the 1994 GIPC Act (Kohnert 2010; Malki 2013). Yet, in reality, numerous Ghanaian retailers have received support from aliens and strangers, and many Ghanaians are employed by aliens. Touted as necessary for national social protection, the legislation has, ironically, ended up depriving many Ghanaians of trading opportunities and jobs.

With surveillance growing ever stricter, aliens and strangers who fall outside the government's requirements increasingly find themselves unable to enjoy legal protection. Without the backing of the law, they have no other option than to trust in their counterpart's word of honour that they will fulfil their side of the agreement. Ghana boasts an abundance of global retail and wholesale activities, but on the flipside, aliens and strangers operate in a space outside the government's legal protection, where they enjoy no firm legal guarantees as retailing enterprises. Through the practices of the *mai-gida*, a product of historic commercial activities, West African Muslim retailers and wholesalers have made up for this guarantee deficit and thus helped sustain the economic activities of individual traders.

8. Conclusion

Long distance trading in inland West Africa has a long history involving numerous ethnic groups and regions in which people have actively interacted with outsiders. Now the march of globalisation is strengthening connections between West Africa's trading milieu and the outside world.

According to data recorded in the 19th century, the caravans that traversed long distances across the Sahel consisted of as many as 1,500 traders and bearers and 2,000 asses. Transporting cargo by caravan required vast expenditures in labour and defence. Reflecting this expense, the commodities traded inland were primarily high-value items such as rock salt, leather, and kola, passing from one trader to another until they arrived at the destination. This practice entailed trust-based transactions between traders. Large-scale caravans also relied upon individuals known as *mai-gida* to support a smooth sojourn in the host communities along the way. The *mai-gida* play a similar role in today's trading milieu by facilitating trust-based transactions with aliens.

My fieldwork reveals that by continuing these time-honoured trading practices, West African traders continue to establish connections with other regions through trust-based trading relationships. The *mai-gida* play an important role in connecting West Africa's trading milieu with the wider world by upholding West African customs and, as go-betweens, demonstrating *gaskiya* to their counterparts. Further research would be helpful in identifying the criteria or methods that aliens use to determine who to deal with and the processes by which they come into contact with *mai-gida.*

Endnotes

[1] Founded in 1939, the Nigerian newspaper *Gaskiya ta fi kwabo* is the oldest Hausa-language newspaper. During World War II, *Gaskiya ta fi kwabo*

played a role in communicating information about the war effort to Nigerians (Philips 2014).

[2] One of the political parties in Niger is called *Rassemblement Social Démocratique, RSD-Gaskiya*, or the Social Democratic Rally. Ghana's Brong-Ahafo Region (today's Bono Region and Bono East Region) has a radio station called Gaskiya FM (SONIDEP 2016; Ghana Media Info n/d).

[3] The kola and onion businesses are closely related. Because onions are produced in arid inland areas (mainly in Niger) and shipped to southern Ghana, kola traders will often take a cargo of onions back with them when they transport kola to the arid areas. The frequent back-and-forth trips among kola and onion traders explain why S was able to expand from the kola to the onion business.

[4] In the Hausa language, *mai* means a patron of something, while *gida* means a house, compound, family or buildings. Hence, *mai-gida* generally means the owner of a house or the head of a household. The word is widely used among the Hausa, who typically use it to refer to a shopkeeper. It is a common occurrence for a shopper to call the shopkeeper a *mai-gida.*

Acknowledgements

Grants-in-Aid for Scientific Research of the Japan Society for the Promotion of Scientists (JSPS KAKENHI Grant Numbers JP16K21411, JP16H06318, JP17H04506, JP18H03439, JP19KK0031, JP19K20517) provided support to conduct this fieldwork.

References

Abaka, E. K. (2005) *Kola is God's Gift: Agricultural Production, Export Initiatives & The Kola Industry of Asante & the Gold Coast c.1820–1950*, Athens: Ohio University Press.

Adamu, A. U. (2001) 'Tarbiyar Bahause, Mutumin Kirki and Hausa prose fiction: Towards an analytical framework', *Hausa Literature*

Debates Series, Vol. 9, pp. 1–14.

Aminu, M. L. (2003) 'The Hausa code of world - life: A paremiological exposition', *African Studies Association of Australasia and the Pacific 2003 Conference Proceedings – African on a Global Stage: History, Economics and Culture*, pp. 1–21.

Anarfi, J. K. (2010) 'Immigration into Ghana since 1990', *Workshop on Immigrant Integration in Ghana*, University of Ghana, Accra, 8 December 2010.

Clark, G. (1994) *Onions are My Husband: Survival and Accumulation by West African Market Women*, Chicago and London: The University of Chicago Press.

Clough, P. (1985) 'The social relations of grain marketing in Northern Nigeria', *Review of African Political Economy*, Vol. 12, No. 34, pp. 16–34.

Curtin, P. D. (1984) *Cross-Cultural Trade in World History*, Cambridge: Cambridge University Press.

Dankwa, K. O. and Amoah, P. A. (2019) 'Gauging the dispositions between indigenes, Chinese and other immigrant traders in Ghana: Towards a more inclusive society', *Asian Ethnicity*, Vol. 20, No. 1, pp. 67–84.

Ghana Immigration Service (2015) *Annual Report 2015*, Accra: Ghana Immigration Service.

Ghana Media Info (n/d) (http://www.ghanamedia.info/radio-stations/gaskiya-fm/) (accessed on 15 September 2020).

Hart, K. (1988) 'Kinship, contract, and trust: The economic organization of migrants in an African city slum', in D. Gambetta (ed.) *Trust: Making and Breaking Cooperative Relations*, Oxford: Basil Blackwell.

Ho, C. G.-Y. (2008) 'Living transitions: A primer to Chinese presence in Ghana', *The China Monitor*, Vol. 26, pp. 9–11.

Kirikoshi, H. (2018) 'Youth business development in West Africa: Building and spreading of trust through the Kola trade', *Africa Report*, Vol. 56, pp. 22–35 (in Japanese).

Kohnert, D. (2010) *Drivers of Change or Cut-Throat Competitors?*

Challenging Cultures of Innovation of Chinese and Nigerian Migrant Entrepreneurs in West Africa, Munich Personal RePEc Archive Paper No. 23132, Munich: University Library of Munich.

Liu, J. J. (2010) 'Contact and identity: The experience of "China goods" in a Ghanaian marketplace', *Journal of Community & Applied Social Psychology*, Vol. 20, No. 3, pp. 184–201.

Lovejoy, P. E. (1980) *Caravans of Kola: The Hausa Kola Trade, 1700–1900*, Zaria: Ahmadu Bello University Press.

Lydon, G. (2009) *On Trans-Saharan Trails: Islamic Law, Trade Networks, and Cross-Cultural Exchange in Nineteenth-Century West Africa*, Cambridge: Cambridge University Press.

Lynn, M. (2002) 'The West African palm oil trade in the nineteenth century and the "crisis of adaptation"', in R. Law (ed.) *From Slave Trade to 'Legitimate' Commerce: The Commercial Transition in Nineteenth-Century West Africa (African Studies, Series No. 86)*, Cambridge: Cambridge University Press.

Malki, I. X. (2013) 'Productive aliens: Economic planning and the Lebanese in Ghana, c. 1930–1972', *Mashriq & Mahjar*, Vol. 1, No. 1, pp. 85–114.

Obeng, M. K. M. (2018) 'Chinese traders in Ghanaian markets: A bag of threat and opportunities', *Review of Social Studies,* Vol. 5, No. 1, pp. 45–70.

Philips, J. E. (2014) 'The early issues of the first newspaper in Hausa *Gaskiya ta fi Kwabo*, 1939–1945', *History in Africa*, Vol. 41, pp. 425–431.

SONIDEP (Société Nigérienne des Produits Pétroliers) (2016) 'Cheiffou Amadou candidat du RSD Gaskiya soutiendra le président Issoufou au second tour de l'élection présidentielle du 20 mars 2016', 20 March 2016 (http://www.tamtaminfo.com/cheiffou-amadou-candidat-du-rsd-gaskiya-soutiendra-le-president-issoufou-au-second-tour-de-lelection-presidentielle-du-20-mars-2016/) (accessed: 6 September 2017).

Tachie-Obeng, E. and N. Brown (2001) *Cola nitida & Cola acuminate:*

A State of Knowledge Report Undertaken for the Central African Regional Program for the Environment, Oxford: Oxford Forestry Institute, Department of Plant Sciences, University of Oxford.

Wilks, I. (1975) *Asante in the Nineteenth Century: The Structure and Evolution of a Political Order*, Cambridge: Cambridge University Press.

Chapter 12

Struggles of Young Bike Taxi Men in West Cameroon: Rethinking a 'Bamiléké's Survival Strategy' toward the New Era

Makiko Sakai

> 'They, Sardinards, the politicians in our country always soak in the olive oil comfortably like sardines. On the contrary, we, tontinards, poor gays, put our pittance into the tontines for rotating money ourselves and survive!' (TR, a bike taxi man, 25 years old, June 2019, in Dschang city)

1. Introduction

Since 2015, I have conducted field research in Dschang, Department of Menoua, West Region of Cameroon, where the main ethnic groups, Bamiléké, are dominant. I have been interested in the small-scale economic activities of vegetable vendors, and the periodic market system based on the traditional chiefdoms in this area. During my stay, I realised the importance of the role of bike taxis which provide the transport service between the cities and rural areas, where the condition of the roads is poor. For this reason, in 2019, I conducted an inquiry and research interviews among the young bike taxi men in Dschang. Just after the field research, a strike of bike taxi men occurred in Dschang at the end of July 2019,[1] which illustrates their frustration and their trial-and-error attempts to break the conflictual relation with the authority in future. This event brought me to a reflection about the youth's actions in the face of the authorities; if this kind of manifestation could open a possibility of dialogues for so-called democracy overcoming ethnical conflicts, or open a Pandora's box, namely violence.

The Bamiléké people have a reputation of their 'entrepreneurial spirit' and economic success (Dongmo 1981a, 1981b; Warnier 1993) using their own form of economic structure 'tontine' or Rotating Saving and Credit Association (ROSCA) (Henry et al. 1991). Many of them have immigrated to the big cities and enjoyed economic success around the world. Their social structure, highly hierarchised and based on the traditional chiefdoms and ancestor worship, developed a solid structure of solidarity composed of and supported by their financial management system. Their crisscrossing solidarity is characterised by the hatred of and contempt for President Paul Biya, whose origin was an ethic group, the Beti, of the Central South of the country, and his hangers-on, namely the governmental authorities. The opening citation shows this stereotyped conflictual relation between the Bamiléké and the governmental authorities.

Although the Bamiléké entrepreneurship spirit has been appreciated as a good example of African Potentials, their strong sense of belonging to their ethnic identity may deepen conflicting feelings and cause the ethnical division of the country. In this chapter, through my research among the bike taxi men in Dschang, West Region, I would like to consider if the traditional 'Bamiléké' potentiality can be renewed and be opened toward the neighbours and the authorities beyond the ethnic frameworks. However, as it is impossible to reach a conclusion in a short chapter here, I propose, modestly, to open a possible discussion on this matter.

In today's globalising world, the increasing gap between rich and poor is a common problem that must be solved. The critical economic crisis can be observed everywhere in Africa. The emergence of bike taxis in the 2000s has been considered as helping the youth to escape impoverishment, as many have said (for example, Kumar 2011; Lombard and Ninot 2012; Olvera et al. 2007, 2012; Olvera et al. 2016). Actually, the fragility and instability of the bike taxi as an occupation seem to reflect to a radical structural change/degradation of the society; this option provides only temporary relief. It would be difficult to overcome the impoverishing situation using only Bamiléké means and logic, ethnically introverted solidarity.

In this regard, what kind of solutions are the young bike taxi men in Dschang seeking? Taking a hard look at reality at the coming to an end of Biya's dictatorial regime which lasted for 38 years, it is clear from the suffering in every respect, such as the Anglophone Crisis and Boko Haram's attack in the extreme north, that the violent options must be avoided by any means. At the same time, they practise different types of mutual help in daily life.

2. Encounter with Young Bike Taxi Men in Dschang

My research has found the issue of bike taxis in rural African cities to be one of the most important determinants of regional socioeconomics. Recent times have seen a remarkable increase of bike taxi activities in both urban and rural areas in sub-Saharan Africa as an organic initiative to tackling chronic youth unemployment. Considering their manifest impact on the local economy, this informal industry has become one of the important issues to be analysed in the social sciences. Most research on bike taxis has been conducted in big cities, leaving the rural situation relatively unexplored. To fill this gap, this research used more than 100 questionnaire results from Dschang – a mid-sized West Cameroonian city which exhibits both urban and rural qualities – to clarify the precarious realities of young Bamiléké bike taxi men.

The bike taxi phenomenon took off with the introduction in the 2000s of cheap made-in-China motorcycles following the creation of close diplomatic ties based on the Forum China African Cooperation (FOCAC) (Cissé 2012; Adisu et al. 2010; Zafar 2007). Since then, bike taxis have created low-barrier-to-entry vocational opportunities to young people who would otherwise suffer from chronic unemployment. Moreover, it has improved connections between rural and urban areas by facilitating the transfer of goods and people.

Despite the liberating image of bike taxis, the economic reality faced by their drivers in local cities is less appealing. It surprised us to learn that most bike taxi drivers consider their work a pastime or a stepping stone to another career. As research progressed, we realised the difference between the stable employment enjoyed by big-city drivers and the volatile demand for driving work in rural locales due to area limitations and the outsize impact of new competitors.

Furthermore, the crisis between 'Anglophones' and 'Francophones' in the North-West and South-West Regions has accelerated the proliferation of bike taxis in recent years. The sudden saturation of the market has brought about significant decreases in income for bike taxi men. During our field research in August 2019, we observed their frustration and anger at the mounting career uncertainty they faced. We hope that this chapter provides a basic foundation for discussing this issue.

3. Bike Taxi Expansion in Cameroon

3-1. Socio-Economic Situation

Half of sub-Saharan Africa's main cities (with populations of at least 100,000 people) host bike taxi operations, with the biggest expansions since 1980 in Nigeria, Togo and Ghana in the west, Cameroon, Central African Republic and Chad in central Africa, Uganda, Kenya and Rwanda in the East Africa and Angola in southern Africa (Pochet et al. 2017).

The bike taxi boom has many causes apart from accelerating urbanisation, with two demand-driven causes highlighted by Olvera et al. (2012: 5). The first is demand for cross-border transport, e.g., Niger–Nigeria, Kenya–Uganda, Togo–Burkina Faso. The second is a demand for alternative public transport in the wake of disruptive general strikes in big cities like Lomé and Douala as a result of Structural Adjustment Programmes in the 1990s.

Bike taxis in Cameroon are called *bandskins*, after a traditional dance from the Bamiléké region in the west, but started in the northern Grand Nord and Adamawa Regions during the 1980s. Poor border control in those regions, which share long boundaries with

Nigeria, enables rampant smuggling to this day, including bootleg motorcycles. It follows then that northern Cameroonian cities such as Maroua, Garoua and Ngaoundéré have become centres of bike taxi activity (Djouda Feudjio 2014: 100).

Bike taxis then spread east, through cities like Bertoua, Batouri and Yokadouma. In the 1990s bike taxis arrived in Douala, Litoral Region. The bike taxi booms in the capital Yaoundé (Central Region), in the western regional cities (Bafoussam, Mbouda and Dschang) and in the Anglophone Northwest Region (Bamenda) started later from about 2000, increasing rapidly thereafter.

Douala, the biggest commercial city in Cameroon, exemplifies the second bike taxi use case. The 1990s marked serious economic crises in several African countries brought about by Structural Adjustment Programmes (SAPs) which initiated the radical and immediate privatisation of multiple sectors as directed by the World Bank and International Monetary Fund (IMF). SAPs intervened in local politics in the name of good governance, making funding conditional upon the establishment of democratic assets such as multi-party systems and transparent elections.

Introducing a multi-party system into Cameroon which had hitherto enjoyed stability albeit under a one-party dictatorship created tension between the ruling and opposition parties as well as sowing nationwide political confusion. Moreover, liberalisation and privatisation impacted private citizens directly by leading to increased unemployment.

The Social Democratic Front (SDF) with its strong political foundation in Anglophone regions led opposition calls for a 'national conference on sovereignty' which were rebuffed by the ruling *Rassemblement Démocratique du Peuple Camerounais* (RDPC). The people – taxi drivers, students, teachers and merchants in particular – responded to the opposition's subsequent calls for general strikes, leading to violent clashes and further stagnation in the economy (Djouda Feudjio 2014: 100–101). Roitman (2005) analyses this civil disobedience movement, widespread in the whole territory of

Cameroon in beginning in 1990, in order to oppose state fiscal authority. This event was dubbed *opération villes mortes* by the opposition, on the one hand, and, on the other hand, *incivisme fiscal* by the government, accusing the participants of illicitness in failing in their civic obligations. It is noted that she examined this movement as a 'productive moment' (Roitman 2005: 8) which questioned the intelligibility of the regulatory authorities' exercise.

Due to the general strikes, the public transport service SOTUC (*la 'Société de Transport Urbains au Cameroun'*) was paralysed for six months, leaving people desperate for alternatives. A system of mutual aid arose from this deadlock. As privately owned motorcycles were the most mobile urban vehicles – able to navigate heavy traffic on clogged, poorly maintained roads – owners helped otherwise stranded family members and friends travel within the city during the roughly six months of turmoil, after which some naturally extended their services to others as private bike taxis.

Transport in major Cameroonian cities is problematic because of a combination of poorly maintained roads, hazardous conditions and increasing traffic, with the authorities being helpless to alleviate the worsening conditions. Flexible and manoeuvrable motorcycles are uniquely suited to these conditions and, as demand for bike-based transport increased, scores of unemployed youths re-purposed the bootleg bikes they had used to cart friends and family during the crisis in order to earn some money by meeting this demand. Thus, the bike taxi network developed rapidly to reinforce straining transport connections between the city centre and gridlocked suburban areas like Bépanda, Bonabéri, PK8 and Mabanda.

Buses are a potential competitor to bike taxis. The public bus service SOTUC was established in 1973 but closed in 1995 as a part of the privatisation measures introduced by the Structural Adjustment Programme (Kumar 2011: 8). It was replaced in 2001 by SOCATUR (*Société camerounaise de transports urbains*). Douala-based SOCATUR is privately owned by 35 Cameroonian investors, but despite – or because of – private ownership has so far been unable to provide a reliable bus service to the population.

3-2. Material Factors

People of little means wanting to start bike taxi services require easy access to cheap machines and petrol. In this regard, developing diplomatic and trade ties between China and African countries were the most significant factor.

China needs good relations with African countries to secure natural resources for industrial development. To that end, the three-yearly Forum on China–Africa Cooperation (FOCAC) was established in 2000 as the basis for multiple strategic partnerships. It aimed to boost trade, investment and aid within the framework of a south–south partnership with no stipulated conditionality, and implicit non-interference in domestic affairs. This approach differs from many partnerships between Africa and OECD countries, which often include requirements from the Western 'aid consensus'. China has entered into many trade conventions with African countries and has taken several measures to encourage trade and investment, such as establishing special categories of priority investment, including trade in motorcycles.

An article in *Jeune Afrique* on 8 November 2012, titled 'Chinese Motorcycles invade Douala' (*Les motos chinoises envahissent Douala*), reported that made-in-China motorcycles had overwhelmingly displaced traditionally popular motorcycles from Japan in Cameroon's biggest commercial city, Douala. Douala's city council reported that 95 per cent of the 40,000 motorcycles within its bounds – far beyond the 15,000 running in Yaoundé city – had been made in China. Demand for Japanese motorcycles is supported by the public sector and NGOs, particularly those running deep-pocketed development and foreign aid programmes without vehicle price limits.

As the numbers of imported Chinese motorcycles have grown since 2000, so did the number of bike taxis. A new Chinese-made motorcycle plus *carte grise* (registration certificate) costs CFA 400,000–500,000 (600–760 euros), far cheaper than a Japanese

Yamaha, Honda or Suzuki, which costs around CFA 950,000–1,200,000 (1,500–1,800 euros) in the 1990s. Japanese bike prices have since reduced to around CFA 800,000 (1,200 euros) at the time of writing. As Chinese motorcycles seemed to have depressed motorcycle prices in Africa, it is evident that their introduction facilitated the expansion of bike taxis.

In terms of motorcycle import pathways: in the case of Benin and Togo, those who went to Nigeria for temporary work often bought bikes abroad and rode them home (Olvera et al. 2012: 6). Most of Cameroon's imported motorcycles first arrived at the port of Douala, but a non-negligible number are smuggled across the Nigeria–Cameroon border. Bootleg motorcycles and petrol make it easier for entrants to start bike taxi driving.

It is also necessary to mention the emergence of young entrepreneurs called *feymen* who capitalised on the economic crisis to open shops for imported motorcycle sales, thereby contributing to bike taxi growth and influencing rural socioeconomics (Djouda Feudjio 2014: 102–103). *Feymen* in local language means to 'put the flame'. They import motorcycles, mainly via overland routes from Nigeria, the country with the biggest bike export share to the rest of West Africa.

4. Field Research Area: Dschang

Dschang, Menoua Department, West Region of Cameroon, lies in the Equatorial Monsoon climate zone, with an altitude of about 1,400 metre above sea level and an average temperature of 16–21C°. Dschang's population in 2005 was 285,764. Its main ethnic groups are Bamiléké. Bamiléké is not one ethnic group but an ensemble of several groups. High population density and a lack of farmland encourage Dschang locals to leave for bigger cities. Bamiléké people enjoy a reputation for being highly educated and entrepreneurial (Dongmo 1981a, 1981b; Warnier 1993). This region is characterised by mountainous areas situated around Mt Bamboutos, altitude 3,008 metre. From the colonial era to the late 1980s the main industry was the Arabica coffee production organised by a cooperative union (UCCAO). In the 1990s the coffee industry was destroyed by crashing international prices due to SAP-implemented trade liberalisation. Making the most of the favourable highland climate, local farmers shifted from coffee to grow vegetables like cabbages, potatoes, carrots, corn and various beans. Coffee trees, visible throughout the area until the end of the 1990s, have all but been replaced by vegetables or other crops, demonstrating how thoroughly farmers have exited coffee growing (Uwizeyimana 2009).

That is not to say that the change happened quickly. There was a slight time lag between the bust in coffee production and the boom in vegetable growing due to problematic transport connections between marketplaces in the cities and production areas in the peripheral highlands. Despite the rapidly urbanising West Region cities' increased demand for vegetables, farmers could not send large consignments because poor roads meant produce would spoil before they arrived. Bike taxis filled this transport gap with their ability to carry cargo across roads in disrepair, although in smaller quantities than four-wheeled vehicles.

5. What Has Been Happening in Anglophone Regions in West Cameroon?

By June 2019, the people evacuated from Anglophone regions had seemed to increase. The number of bike taxi men had been increasing everywhere. The crisis in Anglophone regions and the neighbouring West Region was getting more and more severe. Since my last visit one year before, there has been a kind of tense atmosphere in Dschang, otherwise no violence. But the residents in Dschang have showed their hospitality towards Anglophone displaced people and welcomed them into their places of residence. Actually, although Bamiléké and Anglophone people cannot be grouped in the same ethnicity with different languages, they share a certain similarity in the culture based on the ancestor worship and the chiefdom social structure. The historical separation in the colonial era into French and British trustees after the withdrawal of Germany in the World War I brought about a deep cleavage between them. Warnier (1993: 67), calling them 'sisters' or 'cousins', explained their closeness: if those regions had been governed together under the same state, Anglophone people might be called 'Bamiléké'.

The feud between the Anglophone and Francophone in Cameroon dates back to the end of German colonial rule (Konings and Nyamnjoh 2003: 10). Following the defeat in World War I, the region, which was a German colony in Africa, became trustee territories separated into British and French, and British territory was merged into Nigeria, a political and social system completely different from French territory. Upon the independence of Cameroon in 1960, a referendum was held in the area asking for attribution to Nigeria and Cameroon, and as a result, the northern part of the former British territory was assigned to the Allies of Nigeria and the southern part to Cameroon. The southern part of British territory is the current Northwest and Southwest states. In 1961, the two states were merged into Cameroon and became the federal republic state.

The reasons for the decision to join Francophone Cameroon taken by the Anglophone population were rather complicated. Although the people had lived for a long time under the British rule, using English, they felt rather closer to the West Cameroon people, the Bamiléké, in term of ethnicities and shared similar cultures based on the traditional chiefdom systems. But this explanation is not enough to understand the unification. According to Konings and Nyamnjoh (2003: 10), the Anglophone elite desired their own independence as the Southern Cameroons state, but internal 'ethno-regional power struggles between the Anglophone elite prevented them finding a compromise concerning the political future of the Southern Cameroons' namely independence. Furthermore, 'the anti-colonial Africa bloc in the United Nations, with the blessings of the United Kingdom, ruled out the possibility of sovereignty for the

Southern Cameroons, claiming that this option was economically unviable and politically undesirable (since it would promote a further "Balkanisation" of the continent)' (Konings and Nyamnjoh 2003: 10). Finally, the southern part of Anglophone regions decided to join Francophone Cameroon in the form of a federation, hoping to maintain the equal relationship in which their own cultural heritage and social system would be protected by the Cameroonian government.

But Ahamadou Ahidjo, the first president of Cameroon, and his successor Paul Biya, gradually changed over from the federation system to centralisation. As a result, the Francophone political elite dominated the Anglophone minority in the post-colonial state and tended to eliminate the Anglophone identity based on culture and institutional heritage. The Anglophone people found themselves marginalised by this 'recolonisation' by the government, which enlarged the cleavage between Anglophone and Francophone Cameroon.

The current crisis in Anglophone regions (North West and South West) was triggered by the elimination of English-language judges and procedures in Anglophone courts, as well as the erosion of the common law system more generally (CHRDA 2019: 9). In October 2016 in Bamenda, Capital city of North West Region, lawyers of those regions went on strike, protesting against those changes for the worse driven by the government. Later on, English-speaking teachers jointed the strike. Those actions were organised by the Anglophone Civil Society Consortium (CACSC) and the Southern Cameroons National Council (SCNC), exercising their rights to expression and peaceful assembly.

Although in the very beginning the protests expanded in a peaceful way, the national army suppressed them by the force and brought the situation to a regional conflict, filled with the suffering and fear, that resulted in thousands of deaths. The government's suppression and the shutdown of the Internet in both regions for several months intensified the conflict and triggered huge regional strikes.

Anglophone separatist groups proclaimed an independent state of 'Ambazonia' on 1 October 2017, worsening the situation. The government pushed forward with military intervention in the regions, which gave rise to grave consequences. The separatists demanded the release of the political prisoners in exchange for the hostage lawyers and teachers. The government intensified the military intervention with more severity, which resulted in more than 200 villages being attacked and mass displacement of those who had lost their property and livelihoods and been forced to flee from security operations and attacks that destroyed villages – 45 to 50 million people, an estimated 10 per cent of the population of the regions, evacuated and 30 to 35 thousand crossed the border to exile to Nigeria.

A large number of Anglophone people evacuated also to the neighbouring West Region. According to the humanitarian local NGO, APDEL's report (2018), the West Region received 32,000 displaced persons, and those of 12,000 people exiled to the Department of Menoua, where the population count is 285,000 (Cameroon Data Portal 2014).

The rapid growth in number of displaced people from Anglophone regions has intensified the social and economic tensions, and caused the social disorder in local society. Recent political developments have diminished bike taxi profitability. Many of these internally displaced refugees who had abandoned their fields, homes and shops took up bike taxi driving to quickly gain an income, increasing competition and driving down the prices of bike taxi services in Dschang. According to interviews with bike taxi men in June 2019, takings enjoyed by established drivers halved from CFA 5,000 to 2,500 per day – sometimes only CFA 10,000 in one day – since the conflict started and refugees entered the industry. Frustration among bike taxi operators is mounting, but local authorities still dependent on humanitarian aid programmes from the likes of the Red Cross and local NGOs are in little position to help. Despite the hospitality of the Dschang residents, the lasting economic crisis has become a heavy burden for them.

6. Reality of Bike Taxi Men in Dschang

In June 2019 our researchers visited 21 bike taxi 'camps' or 'stations' at crossroads throughout Dschang and asked bike taxi men to complete a questionnaire.[2] These camps are not merely locations but they also denote affiliations akin to an informal circle of drivers. Fifty-seven per cent of survey respondents belonged to a camp, with the unaffiliated remainder working solo. The questionnaires were initially only in French, but we soon realised that there were a significant number of drivers who had migrated in from Anglophone zones, and prepared English versions of the survey. Of the 114 sampled, 101 respondents answered in French and 13 in English, but this does not reflect the size of language groups because some Anglophone respondents used the French questionnaire. Very few bike taxi men initially agreed to participate in the survey, suspecting us of working for authorities like the police and Dschang city, towards which they bore distrust and discontentment. However, as some came to understand our independence and purely academic interest, participation gradually increased.

6-1. Characteristics of Dschang Bike Taxi Drivers[3]

Bike taxi drivers are overwhelmingly male and predominantly young. The majority are 25 to 29 years of age (52 per cent), with 30 to 34 years of age (13 per cent) being the second largest age bracket. The third largest age bracket was 20 to 24 years of age. Bike taxi men are well educated for their professions, with 58 per cent having completed secondary school (college and senior high school) and 33 per cent having achieved a tertiary qualification: 15 respondents held bachelor degrees, eight had achieved their masters and two were pursuing doctorates. In Dschang high youth education levels could be uniquely related to the town having been formed around a national university. Many respondents had pursued or were pursuing professional qualifications such as in electrical engineering, carpentry, garage mechanics, pastry-making and baking. Some were teachers in maternal schools, technical colleges and similar educational institutions.

About half the bike taxi drivers were single, with the remainder in monogamous or polygamous marriages/relationships. Regardless of marital status, 77 per cent of respondents bore the responsibility of financially supporting family members, with 62 per cent supporting between one and five persons and 20 per cent supporting up to 20 persons.

Only nine respondents (eight per cent) specified bike taxi driving as their sole profession. Most drove bike taxis alongside other work: 30 per cent were students, most likely at university, 18 per cent worked in agriculture, 10 per cent as merchants, 9 per cent as teachers, 5 per cent as finishing carpenters, with the remainder in diverse occupations such as confectioners and car mechanics. Six per cent of respondents worked more than two jobs. Most bike taxi men stated that driving bike taxis was not even their main occupation. Interestingly, there is little social segregation or hierarchy formation among bike taxi drivers according to educational level or primary occupation.

6-2. Motorcycle Ownership and Financial Support

Ninety-two per cent of surveyed drivers own their work motorcycles, with the rest purchasing their vehicle on instalment (French: *acheter en location*). Very few remain subcontracted to the motorcycle owners. This shows the majority of them intend to be economically independent, as possession of a motorcycle would provide certain stability in the uncertain daily life.

Sixty-five per cent of respondents started bike taxi driving rather recently: between 2015 and 2019. The entrants into bike taxi driving increased significantly in the last a few years. All of the respondents' motorcycles were made in China with an average price of CFA 450,000. Many understood and were appreciative that Chinese motorcycles had become affordable in recent years, thanks to the Chinese diplomatic engagement with Africa.

In terms of initial funding for motorcycles: 67 per cent of respondents reported being self-funded and 15 per cent received financial support from relatives or friends. Three per cent received bank loans and none received micro-finance loans. Eight per cent received financing by joining a tontine or ROSCA (Rotating Savings and Credit Association). The remaining 7–8 per cent raised a private loan by other means. Where self-funding is not possible, strong ties among family and friends are clearly the preferred financial support mechanism, while formal financial services are the lender of last resort.

6-3. Choice of Work Area: Urban versus the Rural Periphery

About half of drivers limit their work area to the city, with the rest working larger territories including peripheral rural areas. Providing long-distance services is more profitable than restricting driving to the city, but requires local knowledge of rural routes and current events, which can be a barrier to unfamiliar entrants. For example, funerals are considered important village events so drivers with local knowledge of impending funerals are advantaged when it comes to transporting people to and from their villages to assist with funerals on weekends. Knowledge of local eight-day periodic market schedules is also important (Hill 1966). For instance, demand for the transportation of agricultural products from farms in the periphery to the Dschang *Grand Marché* spikes during early mornings on market days. Similarly, drivers with local knowledge of market schedules for other cities are better placed to profit from the increased demand for farm-to-market transport on market days, and potentially fill otherwise unpaid return journeys with a fare. 'It is lucky if you could get another passenger return from and to Dschang. Income becomes double!' said a bike taxi man whose knowledge of the local calendar gave him an advantage in providing long-distance transport.

6-4. Savings

Among 114 cases, 91 people (84 per cent) save money and 17 people (16 per cent) do not. The types of savings vary: tontine (39 people), bank (18 people), microfinance (15 people), keeping at home (9 people), mobile money (7 people), trust someone with (9 people) and others (5 people). The largest number of people are saving as a form of tontine. The tontine is a variety of local financial systems, defined as 'an association formed upon a core of participants who make regular contributions to a fund which is given in whole or in part to each contributor in turn' , the so-called 'Rotating Organization for saving and Credit Associations (ROSCAs)' (Geertz 1962; Ardener and Burman (eds) 1995: 1). We can find the variety of tontine all over the world, but it is especially widespread in West Africa, and the Bamiléké land of West Cameroon was one of the most developed places even before the colonial era.

The *réunion* is a French term for a kind of regular meeting where the members contribute regularly their *cotisation* (tontine). Besides that, the *réunion* has several other functions such as acting as a school fee fund, health insurance and life insurance, etc. According to the 69 responses to the question about tontine activities out of 114 cases, there three people participate in three different tontines at the same time, 18 people take part in two tontines, and 47 people practise one tontine. The types of *réunions* vary and are organised based on different social relationships: family members, villagers of the same origin, neighbours in the residence area, groups of friends, associations for youth, associations for city residents from the same village, etc.

The most remarkable groups are the traditional dancing teams who are organised based of the chiefdoms, according to the types of dances: Medzong, Kwakwa, Samba, Sopdap, Kana and Mangassa. Fifteen people participate in the tontine of the dancing teams.

The Bamiléké social system always consists of the traditional chiefdom structure characterised by ancestor worship. The people have a strong sense of belonging in their chiefdom. The traditional dance groups are formed according to the different types of dance. For example, Medzong, the dance of warriors defending the chiefdom, is a highly hierarchical structure divided by age. The members are nominated by the Chief. The newcomers will be instructed by the elders in not only the dance but the social norms, on the one hand but, on the other hand, the structures of some other dancing teams are not divided into age groups.

Secondly, the associations (residents, villagers of the same origin, graduates of the high school, etc.) also provide tontine activities and their structure is fairly stable. These types of groups which are clearly different from simple friends' circles, modern or traditional, represent a solid and systematic social structure, diversified by participation of different generations and occupations.

It was rare to see a tontine among the bike taxi men. It seems that the economic fragility and lack of economic diversity are some of the reasons why the bike taxi men do not practise tontine among themselves.

6-5. Debt

Table 1 extracts 22 cases of debt of 100,000 CFA or more and classified the amount, lender and interest rate from the results of the inquiry. Let us see the purposes/reasons for debt of the bike taxi men. We distinguished the reasons into three categories:[4] according to the economic investment, social investment and non-investment (or consumption). The economic investment denotes such acts as the purchase of a motorcycle, investment in agriculture and livestock keeping, opening a shop, etc. which will surely make a profit if successful.

The social investments refer to, for example, the wedding dowry and funerals of family members. The school expenses for children usually might be categorised under economic investment, but this type of investment in the long term does not help directly in the repayment of the debt. So, here we expediently categorise it under social investment.

Among the 22 cases in the Table 1, 15 people reluctantly borrowed certain sums of money to deal with difficult situations, for example, illness of family members, funerals, accidents, etc. Those kinds of debt do not make any profit which could assure the repayment of the debt, on the one hand, while, on the other hand, there are seven cases where the debt was used for economic investment such as agriculture, livestock keeping, opening a shop or purchase of a motorcycle for starting the bike taxi business.

From whom have the bike taxi men borrowed the money? The most common case is the *réunion* ('meeting' in English) where the members organise a tontine activity (eight cases), especially they borrowed certain sums of money from the *Réunion* of the traditional dancing groups (Medzong or Kwakwa, etc.). The interests of the *Réunion*s are rather low, set from three to five per cent, maximum ten per cent. The next common case is from family members (five cases) and from friends (three cases). Some mentioned the purchase of goods by loan (No. 87 and 92). Among 22 cases, three people got a loan from a bank with a higher interest rate (25–31.25 per cent).

If we could distinguish the types of *Réunions* into horizontal small size (family, friends, etc.) and vertical and large size (associations and dancing teams, etc.), certainly, a circle of bike taxi men is in the former, as its volume of circulation of money is low and unstable. It may be one of the reasons why the bike taxi men do not like to practise tontine among themselves. It is worth noting that there is no case of financial support or contract of debt within Christian Church organisations. A bike taxi man said, 'No, no, it is impossible to do tontine with the Church, we only listen to the good stories of the Bible here.'

6-6. Roles of the 'Camps' or the Stops in the City

We saw that the majority of bike taxi men did not intend to organise any kind of association or union (*syndicat*) /guild through the interviews and inquiry survey. Before there were two unions of bike taxi men in Dschang. One of them was under the National

Table 1. Financial management of the significant debt cases (over 100,000 CFA)

No.	Sum of debt (Franc CFA)	Uses	Creditor	Interests (%)
5	150,000	medical fee for the wife	*Réunion* (dance)	5
25	300,000	help someone	family	2
32	480,000	funeral	bank	25
36	500,000	metal sheets for construction	*Réunion* (association)	10
37	300,000	?	wife	0
39	300,000	purchase of a motorcycle	bank	31.25
43	500,000	house construction	*Réunion* (association)	3
45	100,000	agriculture, livestock keeping	friends	3
47	102,000	medical fee for the wife	*Réunion* (dance)	3
61	150,000	wedding dowry	*Réunion* (dance)	3
78	400,000	medical fee for the wife	friends	2
79	1,500,000	investment in agriculture, motorcycle purchase	family	0
84	250,000	medical fee for the wife	brother	0
87	121,000	agriculture	neighbours and suppliers of agricultural materials	0
90	1,500,000	pastries shop (bankrupt)	a shopkeeper	0
92	700,000	purchase of a motorcycle	a bike seller	40
94	170,000	family problems	*Réunion* (dance)	5
97	650,000	daughter's entrance fee for the university	bank	31.25
100	250,000	pesticides	*Réunion*	5
112	300,000	medical fee for a family member	family	0
113	355,000	school expenses for children	*Réunion*	2.5
114	385,000	accident, medical fee, school expenses	friends	1

Source: The result of the inquiry of 2019 (Sakai 2020) compiled by the author.

Union '*Syndicat national des mototaxis* (*Synamotac*)'. Mr P. K., vice president of the *Synamotac* in Dschang, accepted my interview. According to him, from 2014 to 2015, he tried with some members to organise a Dschang branch of the National Union of bike taxis (*Synamotac*), but faced with distrust and indifference, he gave up the idea of establishing a union here. Younger generations consider the bike taxi activity as pastime job, tend to quit it as soon as possible and are not interested in committing themselves permanently to the union management.

Instead, the 'camps' or the station at the crossroads in the city offers them a kind of forum for loose network and belonging. Most of the respondents of the inquiry do not practise tontine with bike taxi colleagues, but keep a certain sense of belonging in the 'camps'. For example, in a camp named 'BB crossroad', situated in the north side of the City Market B, there is a kind of group of bike taxi men who organise a football team under the instruction of an elder in the 40s, called 'doctor'. He is a kiosk keeper of pharmacy in the BB crossroads and also cultivates a farm on the periphery of Dschang. The team BB play football matches against different football teams of camps in Dschang. I assisted them twice with their matches against Team 'I' at the pitch of the university.

This type of organisation provides them an opportunity to build a kind of interpersonal relationship. As I observed, it is interesting to remark that members' educational backgrounds differ, but their social order seems to consist of age groups. Whatever the grade at school, youngers call elders 'grand' with respect and are willingly called 'petit'. Their loose relationship has not been bound by politics or economics. The results of the inquiry showed that they have their own foothold in family ties, their chiefdom or associations of the same village of origin, etc. and they had not committed to the politics in their vocations. The question that arises is what kind of factors made it possible to organise a strike in August 2019.

7. Bike Taxis and Authority

Our researchers were surprised to discover that 42 per cent of bike taxi men were unlicensed and 59 per cent were uninsured. Only 36 per cent had registered their bike taxi work with municipal authorities leaving the remaining 64 per cent operating bike taxis without legal status because of financial difficulty, distrust of and dissatisfaction with authorities, and so on.

According to local authorities, registration of bike taxis is in fact increasing; from 276 registrations in 2008 to 778 in 2016, to remaining steady at around 750 in 2017 and 2018. Despite the jump in registrations the official data still does not reflect the over 2,000 bike taxis counted in the field. Registered vehicles are the tip of a bike taxi iceberg, the true size of which is impossible to grasp.

Dschang authorities have increased regulation of bike taxis purportedly to promote security, peace and order, including mandatory licensing, taxation, limiting passengers to one per voyage and mandating yellow vests. The cost of compliance encourages drivers to remain informal, risking conflict and even violence with officials. The person in charge of Dschang City's registration section is worried that poor driving and flouting regulations could cause severe accidents.[5]

In the face of this concern for public well-being the bike taxi men interviewed expressed deep distrust of and hatred towards local authorities and the police. Those who were registered had been forced to do so during a police campaign. Of the 744 registered bike taxis in 2018, 264 (35 per cent) had been registered during a week-long police crackdown running from 19 to 25 April. The number of registrations outside that campaign averaged less than ten per week.

The negative attitudes held by bike taxi drivers towards police stem from reports of police violence during registration campaigns and police demands for bribes to allow drivers caught unregistered to avoid registering. These bribes are often priced such that it is cheaper for drivers to pay the bribe and avoid conflict than to incur the costs that registration entails, but bribes are still seen as the preferential treatment of those with the available money.

According to Roitman (2005), who quoted the example of the situation in the north of the country, the origin of the conflictual relations between Cameroonian regulatory authorities and the population dates back to the French colonial era where the fiscal systems installed as a tool of deprivation of the local wealth. In this regard, it is impossible for the state to redefine its legitimacy because the structure of the state also depends upon the 'illicit' economic activities in the international borders and the 'bush'. The West Region has more or less the same political and economic structure based on the conflictual relations between the authority and the population inherited from the French colonial era, and strengthened in the independence process, which continues to exist today.

The Bamiléké solidarity has developed around the tontine system against the financial institutions and the government authority by the ethnic exclusion by the government. Their own financial system helped many Bamiléké's successes and fulfilled their economic ambition to rise in the world. But beside the successful persons, people on the bottom of the social scale, such as bike taxi men are always struggling to escape the poverty by practising different types of tontines or depending on personal relationships.

Bike taxis have undoubtedly benefited the local economy by giving young people an alternative to joblessness and by providing transport within and between urban and rural areas despite the less-than-ideal infrastructure, thus revitalising the commercialisation of agricultural products through the regional periodic markets. However, the bike taxi explosion has its downsides: bike taxi work is uncertain, and persistent tensions between drivers and authorities mean safety and violence concerns around the regulation of drivers will remain for some time. The current globalising situation does not allow the local societies to be locked in the ethnic logic. Here we see the limit of introverted ethnic solidarity defined by the hierarchical society.

8. Conclusion

A strike of bike taxi men occurred in Dschang in July in 2019, which illustrates their frustration and their trial and error to break the conflictual relation with the authority into the future. This problem can no longer be understood only from an economic aspect, but politics also plays a role. The form of strike as a political manifestation has been repeated many a time in history. However, the Cameroonian government seems to fear being accused of its illicitness in accumulating wealth and controlling the region by force if it may enter into democratic dialogues with opposition. As a consequence, the political strikes or demonstrations easily turn into the battlefield.

Their claim to the right to work in better conditions must be accompanied with the right of citizenship. If the state authority considers the appearance of the bike taxis as an alternative source of wealth to be accumulated by the regulation, in licit or illicit ways, as the French colony did, the authority may make the same mistake as that of *operation villes mortes* in 1990, where President Paul Biya had questioned this problematic as 'peace or wealth', ignoring the meaning of citizenship. As the result, the relationship between peace and wealth becomes unsettled.

It is important to see that both sides, or everyone, more or less depends upon the ambiguous zone, hiatus of the state system where the daily economic activities have not been determined as legal or illegal. The series of the democratic movements that faced the government constitute the path to the real democracy which demands that both sides assume their responsibilities in exchange for their rights as 'citizen'. In that sense, the notion of 'citizenship' reclaimed by the population may open a Pandora's box and shake the Cameroon's political and social structure from the bottom.

If the tension increases between the government army force that suppresses the people with arms and the separatists respond excessively, a story of 'ethnic division' and violence will be repeated again and again. At least, in Dschang there are no hostile attitudes toward Anglophone people by the local residents, who offer hospitality to their Anglophone 'cousins'.

Fortunately, the bike taxi's strike in Dschang came to a sort of favourable end and avoided a violent situation. The local authorities (the mayor of Dschang and the governor of Menoua Department), the representatives of bike taxi men and other transport companies took a seat at the negotiating table together on the same day of the strike. The demands of bike taxi side were negotiated: tax reduction and certain measures to prevent the domination of certain routes by medium transport companies. Although the tax reduction was refused by the authorities, as to the latter matter, the transport companies ended up by giving up the routes from the city centre to the long-distance bus stations and to limit their territory to between the peripheral stations and neighbouring cities for the sake of bike taxi operators. After the event, the mayor held a football tournament for the bike taxi's camp teams, and finally Team BB won the championship.

However, it is not easy to conclude for the moment whether their efforts towards compromise at the local level brought a radical change to the legend of Cameroonian politics in the future. It is important to observe the progress of the relations among the local stakeholders and the local host society's actions toward Anglophone neighbours. Regarding the bike taxi youth's situation, the Bamiléké's survival strategy, which consists in *sardinard* versus *tontinards* logic, must be renewed in different spheres beyond the ethnic limit to social and political commitment in order to prepare for the post-Biya era.

Endnotes

[1] Reported by our research assistants by e-mail.

[2] This questionnaire was part of a socioeconomic research project run by Makiko Sakai (Sociologist, Associate Professor, Tokyo University of

Foreign Studies – TUFS) and assisted by:

1) Metsagho Mekontcho Boris, PhD Student in Political Science, Faculty of Law and Political Sciences, University of Dschang.
2) Tchaba Zébazé Rostand, Masters Student in Animal Biology (Physiology), Faculty of Sciences, University of Dschang and Dschang Bike Taxi man.
3) Koagne Defo Boris Stéphane, PhD Student in Sociology (Sociology of Politics), Faculty of Humanities, University of Dschang.
4) Tchatchouang Pegmi Yves Serges, PhD Student of Geography (option: risk geography), Faculty of Humanities.

[3] The detailed result of the survey is available in Sakai (2020).

[4] It is expedient because in the reality it is difficult to distinguish between those three categories in clear way.

[5] Interview with Director, Registration Section, June 2019 in Dschang City.

Acknowledgements

This work was supported by JSPS KAKENHI Grant Number JP18K11806, JP16H06318, and conducted during my sabbatical leave from April to September 2019 thanks to Fondation France-Japon (FFJ) of EHESS which accepted me as a visiting researcher.

References

Adisu, K., Sharkey, T. and Okoroafo, S. C. (2010) 'The impact of Chinese investment in Africa', *International Journal of Business and Management*, Vol. 5, No. 9, pp. 3–9.

APDEL (Association pour la Promotion du développement Local) (2018) *Evaluation des besoins des déplacés internes dans le Département de la Menoua', Rapport d'évaluation*, Dschang: APDEL (https://www.humanitarianresponse.info/sites/www.humanitari

anresponse.info/files/assessments/apdel_rapport_eval_besoins_idp_menoua_2.pdf) (accessed: 23 December 2020).

Ardener, S. and Burman, S. (eds) (1995) *Money-Go-Rounds, The Importance of Rotating Savings and Credit Associations for Women*, Oxford and Washington DC: Berg Publishers.

Cameroon Data Portal (2014) (https://cameroon.opendataforafrica.org/bvrgzlb/caracteristiques-de-la-population-2014).

CHRDA (Centre for Human Rights and Democracy in Africa) and Raoul Wallenberg Centre for Human Rights (2019) *Cameroon's Unfolding Catastrophe - Evidence of Human Rights Violations and Crimes against Humanity*, CHRDA and Raoul Wallenberg Centre for Human Rights.

Cissé, D. (2012) *FOCAC: Trade, Investments and Aid in China-Africa Relations, Policy Briefing*, Stellenbosch: Centre for Chinese Studies, Stellenbosch University.

Djouda Feudjio, Y. B. (2014) 'Les jeunes benskineurs au Cameroun: Entre stratégie de survie et violence de l'État', *Autrepart*, Vol. 71, Issue 3, pp. 97–117.

Dongmo, J.-L. (1981a) *Le dynamisme Bamiléké (Cameroun): La maîtrise de l'espace agraire volume I, Thèse de doctorat*, Yaoundé: Centre d'édition et de production pour l'enseignement et la recherche.

———— (1981b) *Le dynamisme Bamiléké (Cameroun): La maîtrise de l'espace agraire volume II, Thèse de doctorat*, Yaoundé: Centre d'édition et de production pour l'enseignement et la recherche.

Geertz, C. (1962) 'The rotating credit association: A "Middle Rung" in development', *Economic Development and Cultural Change*, Vol. 10, No. 3, pp. 241–263.

Henry, A., Tchente, G.-H. and Guillerme-Dieumegard, P. (1991) *Tontines et banques au Cameroun: Les principes de la société des amis*, Paris: Karthala.

Hill, P. (1966) 'Notes on traditional market authority and market periodicity in West Africa', *The Journal of African History*, Vol. 7, Issue 2, pp. 295–311.

Konings, P. and Nyamnjoh, F. B. (2003) *Negotiating an Anglophone Identity: A Study of the Politics of Recognition and Representation in Cameroon*, Leiden-Boston: Brill.

Kumar, A. (2011) *Understanding the Emerging Role of Motorcycles in African Cities: A Political Economy Perspective, Sub-Saharan Africa Transport Policy Program (SSATPP) Discussion Paper No. 13*, Washington DC: The World Bank.

Lombard, J. and Ninot, O. (2012) 'From mobilities to transport: Diverse outlooks on West Africa', *EchoGéo*, No. 20, pp. 1–20.

Olvera, L. D., Plat, D., Pochet, P. and Sahabana, M. (2007) 'La diffusion des taxis-motos dans l'Afrique urbaine au sud du sahara', *XLIIIè colloque de l'ASRDLF (Association de Science Régionale de Langue Française), Les Dynamiques territoriales, Débats et enjeux entre les différentes approches disciplinaires.*

———— (2012) 'Motorbike taxis in the "transport crisis" of West and Central African cities', *EchoGéo*, No. 20.

Olvera, L. D., Guézéré, A., Plat, D. and Pochet, P. (2016) 'Earning a living, but at what price? Being a motorcycle taxi driver in a Sub-Sahara African city', *Journal of Transport Geography*, Vol. 55, pp. 165–174.

Pochet, P., Olvera, L. D., Plat, D. and Adolehoume, A. (2017) 'Private and public use of motorcycles in cities of Sub-Saharan African cities', in UITP (The International Association of Public Transport) (ed.) *Transport Trends 2017*, Bruxelles: UITP, pp. 103–105.

Roitman, J. (2005) *Fiscal Disobedience: An Anthropology of Economic Regulation in Central Africa*, Princeton: Princeton University Press.

Sakai, M. (2020) *Characteristics of Bike Taxis in African Rural Society: A Case Study of Dschang, West Cameroon, FFJ (Fondation France-Japon de l'EHESS) Discussion Paper #20-04*, Paris: FFJ (https://hal.archives-ouvertes.fr/hal-02904845) (accessed: 28 December 2020).

Uwizeyimana, L. (2009) 'Après le café, le maraîchage? Mutations des pratiques agricoles dans les Hautes Terres de l'Ouest Cameroun',

Cahiers d'Outre-Mer, Vol. 62, No. 247, pp. 331–344.
Warnier, J.-P. (1993) *L'ésprit d'entreprise au Cameroun*, Paris: Karthala.
Zafar, A. (2007) 'The growing relationship between China and Sub-Saharan Africa: Macroeconomic, trade, investment, and aid links', *The World Bank Research Observer*, Vol. 22, Issue 1, pp. 103–130.

Chapter 13

The Parallel Money Market and Money Changers' Resilience: Case of Masvingo and Harare, Zimbabwe

Manasa Sibanda, Simbarashe Gukurume and Mayu Hayakawa

1. Introduction: The Parallel Money Market in Zimbabwe

Almost four decades after independence, the majority of people in Zimbabwe remain poor. The socio-economic and political environment has been dynamically marked by the closure of industry and commerce, resulting in high unemployment levels, a hyperinflationary economy, reduced buying power among civil servants, inaccessible savings in banks, high taxes and lack of direct foreign investment. These factors have coalesced to exacerbate the challenges that people face with respect to livelihood. The combined effects have culminated in poor service delivery, lack of accountability in government and underdevelopment, condemning the country's citizens to poor access to resources and poverty.

Zimbabwe's ever-changing monetary policy has negatively impacted citizens' confidence in the banking sector, leading to the growth of a parallel money market for both basic commodities and currency. Furthermore, the informal sector's demand for foreign currency leads to proliferation of the parallel money market and allows the informal sector to thrive, with consequences for formal money supply. Although Zimbabwe's government has come under pressure to address inflation, unemployment and interest rate challenges while maintaining currency stability, the availability of cash to the general public from the banks has gradually diminished.

Research has examined local people's resilience to economic hardship (Gukurume 2019). However, the livelihood strategies for money changers have not been effectively and adequately analysed especially during and after the dollarisation of the economy. Similarly, few studies have focused on the cases in Harare and Masvingo.[1]

In conditions of high economic volatility, the parallel money market is essential to people's lives. We particularly focus on the impact of the country's socio-economic dynamics on money, along with the government's monetary policy, *de facto* suspension of the domestic currency after the hyperinflation of 2008, the introduction of a multi-currency system of 2009, and the subsequent enactment of the Statutory Instrument (SI) 142 and reintroduction of the new Zimbabwe dollar as the sole legal tender of 2019. We examine how people survived and developed resilient subjectivities in response to dynamic socio-economic circumstances, and show the influence and significance that the parallel money market holds for local livelihoods in Zimbabwe.

In the sections that follow, we examine the economic situation and subsequent rise of the parallel money market since the hyperinflationary period beginning in 2007. Following a detailed description of the country's policy environment, we will present a case study of money changers in Zimbabwe, and show how they profit from such economic circumstances. In conclusion, we discuss the case study in relation to three theoretical approaches that have informed the study: the actor-oriented approach, prospective theory and the sustainable livelihoods framework.

2. Background

2-1. The Parallel Money Markets in Zimbabwe and People's Resilience

From 2007 to 2009, Zimbabwe experienced astronomical hyperinflation. Following an interval of ten years, it has faced inflation resurgence. Recently, Trading Economics (2020) rated the country's inflation as the second highest globally after Venezuela, with 175.66 per cent.[2]

In October 2008, with hyperinflation raging, the Zimbabwean economy moved to partial dollarisation. The Reserve Bank of Zimbabwe (RBZ) selected companies and authorised them to trade their goods locally in foreign currencies, such as the United States dollar (USD) and South African Rand (ZAR). Dollarisation was officially expanded nationwide in January 2009, when a 'multi-currency system' was introduced.[3]

In 2014, the ZAR's value on the international market against the USD collapsed so acutely that local people, shops and transport operators could no longer accept it. Consequently, the ZAR disappeared from circulation. The scenario exacerbated shortages of small-denomination notes and coins, particularly for purposes of issuing change.

Two solutions were implemented to address this problem. First, cashless or electronic payments became operational. Such payments were made possible as shops installed the point of sale (POS) devices for debit cards while street vendors used mobile phones to accept mobile money transfers. Second, from the end of 2014, the 'bond currency' was introduced. This was a proxy currency released by the RBZ, whose exchange rate for the USD was officially fixed at 1:1.

Ironically, the adoption of electronic payments and the distribution of bond currency made the cash shortage chronic. Foreign currency became no longer available at banks but local currency whose daily withdrawal limit was set at low amounts, such as 300 dollars per month,[4] in order to manage the inflation that would ensue from the government's printing of the bond note.

A strange hierarchy between the currencies ensued. On the parallel market, the USD cash had a higher value than bond currency, while the official values remained equivalent.[5] In addition, on the parallel market, bond currency had a higher value than deposit or mobile money, while the official values were equivalent. The difference in value continued to grow as time went by.

People avoided depositing and spending their foreign currency through the official channels. They kept their money at home or used it on the parallel market where they would exchange it for local currency at a much higher rate than the banks. People were also obliged to develop innovative strategies to access their money from the banks, including developing social links to capitalise on as their money was locked down and consistently losing value (Gukurume 2015). The practice of arbitrage trading in foreign currency – called 'burning money' (*kupisa mari, kubhena mari*) – in response to inflated prices on the parallel money market allowed many to get by and support themselves in their everyday lives (ibid).

Thus, to address the issue of high inflation and its attendant livelihood challenges, many resorted to this illegal strategy. Consequently, the parallel money market expanded, the inflation of the bond and mobile money increased and the prices of basic commodities continued to rise.

Zimbabwe's government changed the 'politically' pegged exchange rate on 20 February 2019 (RBZ 2019a). The RBZ monetary policy statement declared that the bond and electronic currency be denominated as a new currency and the interbank exchange rate is allowed to operate autonomously to determine the official exchange rate. Subsequently on 24 June 2019, the RBZ abolished the multi-currency system (RBZ 2019b).[6] After the government eventually de-dollarised, the prices of basic commodities continued to increase considerably.

In September 2019, a new monetary policy was introduced that not only abolished the multi-currency system, but also criminalised any unofficial money changing (RBZ 2019c). In the following section, we turn to the policy environment in Zimbabwe.

2-2. Policy Environment in Zimbabwe

Zimbabwe's economic environment is complex and dynamic. It has been argued by Munangagwa (2009) and Bonga (2014) that the country's economic policy reforms have not resulted in improved socio-economic welfare for the populace. For them, policy changes have only resulted in economic decline that has inflicted widespread political discontent and disaffection.[7] They concluded that good economic policies are easily adopted, adequately financed and engage relevant stakeholders.

We consider economic policies to include decisions pertaining to government spending and taxation, the redistribution of income and the supply of money. We also consider that policy tools used by the government include interest rates, money supply, tax and tariffs, exchange rates and labour market regulations. We investigate the following policies as implemented by the government: the Basic Commodity Supply Side Intervention (BACOSSI) of 2008, the Zimbabwe Agenda for Sustainable Socio-Economic Transformation (ZIMASSET) of 2013 and the SI 142 of 2019.

2-2-1. Basic Commodity Supply Side Intervention (BACOSSI)

Recognising acceleration in food inflation, the RBZ financed quasi-fiscal expenditure from 2007 to 2008 that had not been budgeted for, according to critics (RBZ 2008).[8] Munangagwa (2009) asserted that high inflation in Zimbabwe was fuelled by a rapidly growing money supply due to excessive printing of money and expenditure in unplanned and unbudgeted programmes. Mackenzie and Stella (1996) argued that such expenditures by the RBZ may have had a huge impact on the financial operations of the central bank, other public financial institutions and the government. The BACOSSI initiative saw some companies receiving government subsidy while others did not. Companies that received such support were able to acquire basic commodities, which were imported and sold at highly subsidised prices considered affordable to poor citizens. This massive importation of basic commodities resulted in the central bank's high expenditure of foreign currency, which was already in short supply. Critics such as Munangagwa (2009) highlighted that the economic impact was such that the level of competitiveness among companies changed. For instance, while companies that received government subsidy relatively prospered, the rest and indeed the majority suffered. This situation was unsustainable. For instance, in

2007, Zimbabwe's government introduced price control without providing necessary subsidies to producers, as it could not continue to fund the BACOSSI initiative. This had consequences for producers who were unable to meet demand pressures, leading to shortages in basic commodities.[9]

To safeguard against further shortages at the household level, citizens hoarded the available goods and stocked at home, leading to severe shortages and elevated prices on the parallel market. The scarce commodities were sold using foreign currency in the informal sector. Consequently, citizens were compelled to acquire and use foreign currency to purchase goods before the country officially dollarised. Because of hyperinflation and price controls, many shops were no longer able to replace stock and shelves became empty. Those with access to foreign currency imported commodities from neighbouring countries like South Africa and Botswana for resale locally at exorbitant prices in the informal market. Thus, the demand for foreign currency in the informal sector drove the parallel money market and allowed the informal sector to thrive (Gukurume 2015).

Foreign currency was more readily available in the parallel market than in the banks as many people preferred to transact in the parallel market where the exchange rates were higher than the official rates offered at banks. It was also possible to exchange foreign currency for the local currency (but not vice versa) in the banks. Some parallel market actors could get foreign currency cheaply from the bank and sell it at a higher price in the parallel market. The Zimbabwe government also introduced the Agenda for Sustainable Socio-Economic Transformation (ZIMASSET) policy.

2-2-2. Agenda for Sustainable Socio-Economic Transformation (ZIMASSET)

ZIMASSET was implemented from October 2013 to December 2018. It is claimed that government officials consulted widely with a range of stakeholders from various ministries, the business community and the private sector. This was in response to a protracted economic recession in the country, characterised by high levels of unemployment and company closures. The Agenda was built around four strategic clusters: Food Security and Nutrition, Social Services and Poverty Eradication, Infrastructure and Utilities and Value Addition and Beneficiation. Projected as targets in the ZIMASSET blueprint, the economy was expected to grow by an average of 7.3 per cent, improve by 3.4 per cent in 2013, 6.1 per cent in 2014 and continue on an upward growth trajectory to 9.9 per cent by 2018. Seemingly hampered by the legitimacy challenges of the government, ZIMASSET did not entirely fulfil its objectives. Notwithstanding challenges experienced during the implementation period, the annual GDP growth rate slowed from 11.9 per cent in 2011 to under 1 per cent in 2015, 3.4 per cent in 2017 and 3.5 per cent in 2019 (Trading Economics 2020). It is alleged that the sanctions imposed on Zimbabwe by the USA through the enactment of the Zimbabwe Democracy and Economic Recovery Act (ZIDERA) in 2001 contributed to the 'poor achievements' (Hwengwere 2015).

Zimbabwe's current account balance of payment during the implementation of ZIMASSET was negative. Bonga (2014) attributed this to the government's failure to trade competitively. Several critics asserted that policy implementation was flawed owing to the limited collaboration between economic agents and various economic sectors, the existing judiciary, which was not politically independent, and the non-autonomous central bank charged with implementing monetary policy. Although the policy was aimed at developing infrastructure, increasing productivity for small to medium enterprises and maintaining the multiple currency regimes, only the last goal was relatively achieved. This had ripple effects on unemployment rate, inflation and the general welfare of local people. The informal sector thrived under these circumstances, including illegal money changing, which is the focus of this chapter.

In his assessment of ZIMASSET, Bonga (2014), recommended that governments should establish and strengthen the support of institutional and political frameworks 'for policymaking and work constantly toward improving it, so as to limit the scope for potentially damaging policy mistakes' (Bonga 2014: 3). The government's failure to reduce inflation and the parallel market money supply triggered the enactment of the SI 142 of 2019.

2-2-3. The Statutory Instrument 142 of 2019

On 24 July 2019, the Statutory Instrument 142 was enacted by the Minister of Finance and Economic Development under sections 44A and 64 of the RBZ Act. The instrument declares that the Zimbabwe dollar is the country's sole form of legal tender for all transactions. Aside from denouncing all other foreign currencies as legal tender, it criminalises retailers and manufacturers who price their goods or services in foreign currency and also criminalises individuals (including money changers) using foreign currency rather than the Zimbabwe dollar in any transaction carried out in the country. The instrument is enforced under several legal acts, including the Bank Use Promotion and Suppression of Money Laundering Act (Chapter 24:24), the Finance Act (No. 2) of 2009, the Financial Intelligence Unit (within the RBZ) and the Police Act (Chapter 11: 10). The Bank Use Promotion Act prohibits traders and other business people from hoarding or trading in cash and provides for the confiscation of cash illegally held. Therefore, the operations of money changers are criminalised as they exchange currencies informally in the parallel market.

Veritas (2019a) opined that the Minister of Finance and Economic Development was not empowered to make regulations amending or repealing Acts of Parliament, and it is arguable that by enacting SI 142, the Minister repealed the Finance Act's declaration of foreign currencies as legal tender. In a bid to circumvent this anomaly, the instrument was then passed in parliament. Veritas (2019b) notes that, 'SI 142 does not expressly state that foreign currencies cannot be used in transactions or to price goods. Instead it provides that the Zimbabwe dollar is the sole legal tender in Zimbabwe for all transactions'. In other words, SI 142 '… does not specifically forbid contracts that require payments to be made or calculated in a foreign currency … (ibid)'. In the meantime, *The Zimbabwe Standard* weekly newspaper of 24 November 2019, reported that in Matabeleland province, the Rand economy was thriving. It says that in the '… communities in the periphery of Zimbabwe's borders with South Africa and Botswana, foreign currency remains the sole medium of exchange in business transactions contrary to the government's efforts to reintroduce the mono-currency system of the Zimbabwe dollar'. It further elucidates how local people were unable to conduct any mobile banking due to inadequate local telecommunication infrastructure, which made it impossible to transact using mobile money transfers or to access local radio and television broadcasts. In spite of the Universal Services Fund (USF) drive by the Zimbabwe government to improve all citizens' access to telecommunications, particularly those living in peripheral areas, Matabeleland has witnessed only limited progress in achieving this. Rather than wait for the promised local service, they depend on neighbouring countries' mobile telephone networks as well as radio and television broadcasts. Similarly, for businesses to continue running in these areas, the parallel money market supplies foreign currency to facilitate access to goods from neighbouring countries that can then be sold locally. It also transpired that the local currency was in 'very short supply' compared to the ZAR and Botswana pula. Owing to this demand for foreign currency, local shops in Matabeleland South were not accepting purchases in local currency. The situation on the ground in this case amounts to a rejection of the country's own currency, which is contradictory to the recently promulgated SI 142 of 2019. Thus, the bulk of the money supply of foreign currency continues to grow in the informal sector.

3. Theoretical Framework

Three theories inform the present study: the actor-oriented approach, prospective theory and the sustainable livelihoods framework.

3-1. Actor-Oriented Approach

Norman Long's (2001) actor-oriented approach recognises the diversity of actors or stakeholders in the operationalisation of (illegal) parallel market discourse in Zimbabwe. These actors, comprising the general citizenry, money changers in their different categories, the elites (including politicians and business people), law enforcers and the government of Zimbabwe, have diverse interests. As they interact at various stages, they contribute to increase in money supply in the formal sector. The actor-oriented perspective treats actors as rational and active beings. In this study, money changers are conceived as active participants who process information and strategies in their everyday dealings with other actors, such as the general citizenry, elites and law enforcement agents. As this chapter will illustrate, this requires a more profound examination of the social and cultural discontinuities and ambiguities inherent in the battlefields of knowledge that have shaped relations between the actors and law enforcers and researchers (Bosman 2004). This image of the battlefields of knowledge was invoked by Long to illustrate the idea of contested arenas in which actors' understanding, interests and values are pitched against one another (Long 2001). In this study, the battlefield of knowledge refers to multiple meanings attached to money in its various forms in both the formal and parallel markets. We consider how the value of currency is negotiated in both the parallel and formal markets, what Long calls an interface. Thus, the study investigates how money changers exercise human agency and build resilience to transform their circumstances and livelihoods. We show how they engage with law enforcement agents to continue in their business in a context where their activities continue to be criminalised. In such cases, actors as individuals or groups may devise strategies to evade these rules to suit their interests.

3-2. Prospective Theory (Normative Theory)

Borrowing from psychology, prospective theory, developed by Kahneman and Tversky (1979), delineates how people make decisions in the face of certain and uncertain events. It is conjectured that people handle intricacy in decision making by purposively prioritising problems to levels that are manageable in a complex world, thereby reducing the cognitive demands. As such, prospective theory is less concerned with determining decision makers' ideal 'rationality' than it is attentive to identifying the conditions under which decision makers exhibit correct or erroneous reasoning. Simon (1957) acknowledges that prospective theory assumes that decisions are made within foreseeable capacity limits and that decision makers operate within 'bounded rationality'. Inherent in this approach is the possibility that irrationality may occur. Thus, decision making is guided by goals that may be adapted if they prove too difficult to attain (Hickson and Khemka 2014). The decision maker therefore searches for alternatives until a satisfactory alternative that meets the aspiration level ('satisficing') and is in accord with one's capacity limitations (Selten 2001) has been found. For the present study, considerations were given to several processes that actors in the parallel money market undertake with the aim of evaluating their perceptions regarding the extent to which selected livelihood options serve their interests in spite of not being the best options and their illegal nature.

3-3. Sustainable Livelihoods Framework

The sustainable livelihoods framework provides a basis from which to understand and analyse the livelihood strategies employed by money changers. Central to the framework are five different types of capital assets: natural, social, financial, physical and human (Scoones 1998) which people can tap into for them to make do and cope with existential challenges. Natural capital is characterised by natural resources stocks, which can be renewable and non-renewable. Physical capital incorporates things that can be commodified, such as secure infrastructures (e.g., houses), land and clean moderate energy. These are effectively formed by financial creation forms and can be used as collateral to access credit. Human capital alludes to skills, knowledge, ability to labour and good health (Carney (ed.) 1998). Financial capital is also referred to as monetary capital, which is basically generated through revenue acquired from various activities. In this study, financial capital is also taken to include the amount of profit generated from trading currency or 'burning money'. Social capital refers to the social resources, such as networks, social relations and associations, upon which people draw when pursuing different livelihoods requiring coordinated actors. For Bourdieu (1986), social capital explains how the relationship between power and control can be created and supported. The study will examine the different relationships established by money changers that sustain their existence and livelihoods in Masvingo and Harare as they pursue their illegal activities.

4. Methodology

The study applied both qualitative and quantitative methodologies. We collected primary data by triangulating approaches and methods such as focus group discussions, key informant interviews, participant observation, direct observation, a questionnaire survey (with both open and closed questions) and secondary sources. Data were collected from October 2018 to November 2019 by Sibanda and Gukurume. The study was conducted in Harare, the capital, and Masvingo city in Zimbabwe. Harare was purposively selected as it emerged that the parallel market rates were determined from there, while Masvingo was chosen for its proximity, as the two researchers resided in the city. Both researchers were also familiar with a number of money changers, which facilitated our entry and access to data.

The city of Masvingo also offered perspectives on dynamics in the parallel money market in a smaller city. Using the snowballing technique to identify money changers, a total of 80 questionnaires were self-administered (40 in each city) while six focus groups and 26 key informant interviews were conducted. The focus groups continuously increased in size from 12 to 18 as more money changers joined to share their experiences, as the subject under discussion was topical. The researchers joined the money changers on the streets to gain insight into what happens, who is involved, where it occurs and why it happens. Ethnographic material that captures the participants' voices with respect to their perceptions of the state, market and money in Zimbabwe is provided. Data were analysed using the SPSS package, which helped us to develop themes from the transcribed data. Content analysis was also performed, including secondary data consisting of hard and online sources, such as reports and published articles. Participants were advised of the study's objectives and their rights to volunteer and exit as they saw fit. Confidentiality was assured and maintained during the study. Pseudonyms are used throughout.

5. Results and Discussion

This section provides detailed results and discussion of the findings under three themes: state of the parallel money market, growth of the parallel market and legitimacy and survival.

5-1. The State of the Parallel Money Market

The parallel money market is where money is traded informally and is illegal in Zimbabwe. Its organisation is complex, involving individuals as well as more connected structures that include not only businesses and politicians but also principals in formal banks. During fieldwork, the local currency (bond and electronic money) was traded with USD, the ZAR, Botswana Pula and the British Pound. Money changers utilised the currency they had exchanged for various uses including injecting back into the informal market.

5-2. Categories of Money Changers and Their Money Supply

Key informants identified three categories (depending on their sources of money and how they are organised) of money changers and progression, who are sole traders, agents and the employee. Money changers who operated as employees formed the bulk of traders, constituting 82 per cent, followed by 13 per cent agents and 5 per cent sole traders.

5-2-1. The Sole Trader

Sole traders change local currency to secure foreign currency and spend it as they see fit. For example, they go to neighbouring countries to buy 'stuff' and sell locally, 'burn money' to generate more money, offload to the agents (described below) or retain it as savings while speculating an upward trend in the exchange rate with the local currency.

5-2-2. The Agent

A further category of money changers is that of agents, who independently change local currency to supply bulk buyers of foreign currency. These agents do not have a single consistent bulk buyer, but they change as and when they identify a lucrative bulk buyer in need of supply. Agents can have weekly targets (for example, 2,000 US dollars per agent) to meet in supplying the bulk buyers (wholesaling, retail, car parts and fuel importation) with foreign currency. Agents offer higher exchange rates than the sole traders, thus creating an immediate lucrative market. For example, on 11 November 2019, sole traders paid 20 Zimbabwe dollars (electronic) for 1 US dollar while agents paid 22 Zimbabwe dollars for the same. The amount for which sole traders sold their USD to agents accumulated to immediate profit per day, and the more they trade, the higher the chances the agents will meet their targets to supply the buyers. This high currency turnover in the parallel money market has consequences for the formal money market as more citizens use the parallel market owing to its efficiency in making local currency readily available while they lose confidence in the formal money market. This scenario continues unabated.

5-2-3. The Employee

The final category of money changers consists of those who are employed by elites. Participants identified elites as mostly comprising politically linked individuals (business people, bank employees, politicians) with access to bulk supplies of the local currency, which explains why local currency is readily available on the parallel market while extreme shortages afflict the banking sector. In several cases (11 per cent), the elites were linked to senior bank personnel. Employees assemble each morning at a given point or office and are given large sums of local currency to buy foreign currency on the street. They spend their day 'burning money' only to return at the end of the day to remit and reconcile. They are paid on commission: the more they sell, the more they earn. It was observed that these employees also act as sole traders who would also sell cash on the parallel market to earn extra money while simultaneously serving an employer. This strategy is referred to as *yemusana* (self-enrichment).

5-3. Sources of Local Currency for Money Changers

In the section that follows, we describe the money changers' sources of both local and foreign currency. These are local people who come directly to burn money, individuals going about their shopping and paying cash, elites, cross-border traders, till operators (point of sale) and remittances from the diaspora.

5-3-1. The Elites and Money Supply

As mentioned above, elites are the major source of local currency for the employee. One middle-aged man and employee in Harare described the situation as follows:

> Brother, I am an employee and at work right now. Money supply in the parallel market will never run dry unless it is stolen. My supply is readily available as and when I need it. Even now, if I contact my old man [employer] telling him that I am out of the local [bond] currency, it will be brought here in no time, coming from the RBZ. There is a lot of foreign currency with local people. My employer got the first batch of the new [bond] notes before the RBZ released it to the public (Harare, 9 November 2018).

It was also revealed during key informant interviews and group discussions that elites mostly determined the rates on the parallel money market. Because of the employees' juxtaposition,[10] the elites have a fairly large 'catchment area' from which they draw their money supply (particularly foreign currency). The above respondent added that, 'As harvesters of local and foreign currency, we keep injecting money into our system then we share the profits' (Harare, 9 November 2018). This keeps the flow of money in the parallel money market consistent, thereby sustaining it at local level.

5-3-2. Individuals and Shoppers

The sole traders and some agents have three major sources of local currency. Participants in a focus group discussion, including sole traders, agents and employees, reiterated that the main source is that of individuals who come directly to them to 'burn money' or those whom they approach and negotiate with while purchasing goods in retail shops as well as till operators in wholesalers and retail outlets. Individuals with cash trade directly with the sole traders after negotiating the exchange rate. Money changers pay electronically at the tills through mobile money or debit cards to willing shoppers intending to spend cash in the shops. Participants in the focus group discussion mentioned further that, depending on the money changer's negotiation skills, one can access more than 1,000 Zimbabwe dollars per day from willing customers. This cash will then be used to buy forcign currency in what is a typical 'money-burning' process. The results agree with those of a study conducted by Gukurume (2015), who indicated that money changers develop innovative ways of accessing money.

Unlike agents and employees, the results from the questionnaire survey indicated that all sole traders regarded individuals who come to 'burn money' as a reliable source of cash that is injected into the parallel money market, hence sustaining it. This suggests a threat to the formal money market as the money changers do not formally deposit their proceeds into the banks, and the retailers remit limited cash to the banking sector overall, affecting the availability of cash to customers withdrawing cash from the bank.

5-3-3. Remittances from the Diaspora

Remittances from the diaspora accessed via both formal (banks and registered *bureaux de change*) and informal channels (cross-border traders, cross-border bus drivers and friends coming from abroad) constantly inject foreign currency into the parallel money market. People from the diaspora can remit money through various platforms and Zimbabweans can access this money from banks and other financial institutions even without having a foreign currency account. One middle-aged female sole trader in Masvingo said:

> I do not have anyone influential supplying me with cash. So, I have to hunt for it. I am a hustler. I negotiate with potential customers intending to buy using cash in shops. When they accept, I swipe [debit card] or use EcoCash [mobile money] on their behalf. I have also established relations with those who receive remittances from the diaspora [via both formal and informal channels]. These are my special customers and they do not need to come to town; I actually travel to serve them in the comfort of their homes. However, potential customers in the shops are now a regular source of local currency for my business and those receiving remittances from abroad, a regular source of foreign currency (Masvingo, 29 November 2018).

The above sole trader points out the importance of providing customer care services to clients who regularly receive remittances from the diaspora. Such social capital assists the money changer in securing a regular supply of financial capital as foreign currency. This continues to sustain her money-changing business, and so it is her livelihood. On the one hand, such reciprocity of benefits can be explained by Mauss's (1925) gift exchange theory: while the money changer accesses foreign currency on a regular basis, the currency's supplier also accesses readily available local currency, which is difficult to obtain from the formal banking sector and at higher-than-interbank rates. On the other hand, the sole trader does not have an established social capital with influential people to supply cash, hence has to work extra hard to access it. This reflects Bourdieu's (1986) assertion that social capital is an asset for sustaining livelihoods. Indeed, our findings reveal that social capital and networks are a critical part of the money changing business. Access to significant networks from the politicians, bank officials and clients among other people mediated one's success in the money changing business. This resonates strongly with Gukurume (2019) who argued that informal ways of making do, '*kujingirisa*', are largely shaped by the density of one's social networks. Consequently, money changers with powerful networks tend to amass huge amounts of money through these illicit dealings in the streets as compared to sole traders who may not have such strong networks.

It also emerged during key informant interviews that informal transporters called *malaitshas*,[11] who ferry goods from neighbouring countries – particularly South Africa and Botswana (Nyamunda 2014) – to the doorstep were a regular and reliable source of foreign currency for sole traders. Demand for such services has not only created jobs for the transport operators but is also an informal source of foreign currency that propels the parallel money market in Zimbabwe. It can also be viewed as a regular injection of money into Zimbabwe's money market.

5-3-4. Retail Purchase Points and Willing Till Operators

In terms of competition with other money changers and connection challenges, the abovementioned sole trader further said that:

Because we are now so many of us chasing after the same customers, competition is becoming stiff. And cash is no longer readily available among people. *Zvapresa* [it is becoming tough]. Normally, I operate in wholesalers and hardware shops where large sums are traded. To beat the competition, I give willing till operators in the shops, my bank cards and PIN numbers to swipe and get cash for me. Obviously, *tinovapawo* cut [we give them a bribe] (Masvingo, 29 November 2018).

Here, the sole trader reveals that willing customers going about their business in retail shops are her main source of local currency and that the number of money changers seeking cash from such customers is increasing. This was also confirmed by results from the questionnaire survey, in which no respondent said that cash was readily available from the banks, suggesting that the availability of cash to the general public is diminishing. This could contribute to the shortage of cash deposits as many shoppers resort to electronic transactions.

The above sole trader also explained that till operators in retail shops are becoming a major access point for local currency. Till operators receive extra cash from the money changers while performing their day-to-day duties, all the time depriving their employer of the cash, which becomes channelled into the parallel market with consequences for the banking sector and the formal money supply market in general.

Another source of local currency for both sole traders and agents is the Mbare's Siyaso Musika area in Harare, where informal traders at the market exchange local currency in the form of notes and coins in the same way other commodities are sold at a market place. People can remit their deposits from mobile money to acquire local currency at a premium, depending on whether one needs notes (at 40 per cent) or coins (at 30 per cent). For instance, if somebody wants 10 Zimbabwe dollars in notes, they must remit 14 Zimbabwe dollars, while if they want the same in the form of coins, they must remit 13 Zimbabwe dollars. This suggests that local currency has been commodified when the same local currency is used to buy the same but in a different form (i.e., electronic money to notes or coins). The study established that coins were mostly bought for use as bus fare, usually by commuters in the city. This corroborates findings reported by Kopytoff (1986), who illustrated that the same currency but in a different form (electronic or hard currency) can be exchanged for itself, that is, from electronic into hard currency and at a different value. This also corroborates Davies and Davies's assertion that money is the supreme good (Davies and Davies 1996).

5-4. Growth of the Parallel Market and Security Risk of Money Changers

Almost all participants (97 per cent) agreed that the parallel market was growing. They reiterated that significantly more money changers are operating on the street than there were two years ago. For us, this rapid growth of street foreign currency trade is not only a symptom but also a consequence of the protracted socio-economic and political crisis, marked by hyperinflation and joblessness. This was reiterated by one middle-aged man who operated outside a popular food outlet in Masvingo said:

> In October last year [2018], it was the four of us operating from this part of the city. Now we are over 20 money changers here, comprising mostly young men. As you can see, there are now old women operating as money changers too. Their husbands lost their jobs and they are now resorting to this illegal business. You see those two boys at that corner by [name of shop]: they are graduates from the local university. There are no formal jobs. Industry has closed. So, they do not have any better option to survive but to change money. One of the pioneer money

changers here has even bought a 4X4 pickup truck from South Africa. We are surviving (Masvingo, 23 August 2019).

The results align with Long's actor-oriented approach, which holds that actors with different goals interact and make decisions (Long 2001). Money changers decide to engage in the illegal money trade as a livelihood option despite the risks involved (Kahneman and Tversky 1979), largely because they are unable to secure formal work. Meanwhile, elites access the needed foreign currency from the streets as it is not readily available from the formal banking sector. It was clear from the above that the parallel money market is not only growing but is also a lucrative livelihood option that generates financial capital, enabling the actors involved to acquire physical capital. Similarly, the participants suggested that the number of money changers was increasing, as observed at every strategic corner, including entrances to retail shops, where they openly advertise for cash. Such statements as, '*ma*Rands [ZAR] *ma*US [USD] cash *ne*EcoCash', to passers-by were not uncommon. This in part is due to the fact that it is fairly easy to enter into foreign currency trade business. Some participants told us that they joined as employees of the elites to earn an income, what they called '*zino*'. While the literal meaning of '*zino*' is a tooth, in the informal sector this relates to the mark-up that people charge when doing transactions. As such, many unemployed young people engage themselves in illegal money changing as a livelihood option. Indeed, Gukurume (2018) has argued that the informal sector has become a space through which many unemployed young people navigate livelihoods and reproduce themselves.

When asked about the police patrols and fear of possible arrest, participants acknowledged that they were aware of a new law that criminalises their activities and that they could face a maximum fine of 6,000 Zimbabwe dollars if caught. However, they were quick to tell the researchers that they find it easy to deal with the police: they take advantage of their relatively low salaries and offer bribes for their freedom. All money changers asserted that, although their operations were expanding, it was becoming increasingly risky and security was an issue. It was noted that the agents usually operate from cars. One middle-aged participant operating from Harare's Fourth Street described the situation as follows:

> We deal with large sums of money. So, it is a risk if you are not mobile. This city has eyes and thieves everywhere. Also, the police usually patrol this place and you must clear off before you are raided. Not to say that they are difficult to deal with, because you can give them a bribe, but we do not want that loss either (Harare, 6 November 2019).

Key informants stressed that being caught by police was one thing and being released conditionally (usually with a caution) was another. Accordingly, 50 per cent of the 'employees' reported that once apprehended by the police, they contact their bosses who will 'talk directly with relevant authorities' to have them released. This can be explained by normative theory in that decision makers operate within bounded rationality (Simon 1957). Another 35 per cent had established contacts within the police who negotiate or influence their release and have never paid a fine after being raided. Such relations or social capital must be maintained through regular donations of bribe money to the 'colleagues'. Interestingly, it is important to highlight that the risk of arrest, imprisonment and even confiscation of money by the police was not evenly spread across the street foreign currency landscape. We noted during interviews and observations that money changers with powerful political and business connections were less vulnerable to arrests and abuse from the police than those without.

Such relationships have repercussions for the formal money market, as transactions on the parallel market become increasingly socially legitimised by corrupt individual law enforcers. This practice has perpetuated the informal trade in currency. Similarly, the actor-oriented approach and normative theory are applicable in explaining the phenomena that sustain the illegal trade of money on the parallel market.

They also mentioned that the last two years have witnessed a dramatic increase in demand for their services as more people sell and purchase both foreign and local currency from the parallel market. Moreover, the interbank rate was always lower than that offered on the parallel market. Another factor that contributed to the expansion of the parallel money market was that some of those burning money were not paying relevant taxes. This was supported by results from group discussions and the questionnaire survey indicating that the parallel market charges neither the government-imposed two per cent tax under the SI 142 of 2019 nor swiping charges (charged by the banks for debit card use) on all transactions. They explained that these advantages of having readily available cash at a higher rate have continued to attract more customers to the parallel money market. Thus, the growing demand for services from the parallel money market has implications for formal money circulation.

5-5. Legitimacy and Survival

Money changers pointed out that the parallel money market derives its legitimacy from the socially and politically fragile law enforcement and economic environment prevailing in the country. During group discussions in Harare, money changers asked the following questions: Who is the criminal? Is it the money changer or those who come in search of their services, i.e., the elites (who come from high offices in government and political parties), the RBZ (who they accused of purchasing their foreign currency), the police who 'terrorise' them only to release them when they pay bribes or the local people and businesses who directly buy their currency?

5-5-1. Politics of Local Currency Supply by the Elites

One agent reported deriving his work's legitimacy from the fact that it is fully supported by elites who are influential and who have access to local currency from the formal sector – in particular, the RBZ – as and when he needs currency to supply the parallel market. This is consistent with Kahneman and Tversky's prospective theory, which would posit that the money changer has made a decision to be 'employed' (to undertake an illegal activity) by elites, as this provides both human and financial security in the face of apprehension by law enforcers. This guarantees a consistent flow of financial capital, which sustains money changers' livelihoods (Kahneman and Tversky 1979).

5-5-2. Fragile Law Enforcement and the Economic Environment

Key informants from the authorities blamed the prevailing economic environment that has triggered hyperinflation, placing the most basic commodities beyond the reach of civil servants, as causative. One authority said, 'People are tempted to accept bribes so that they can return home with a loaf of bread rather than apprehend someone who is also struggling to make ends meet.' This statement illustrates the extent to which the enforcement of relevant policies is fragile or compromised. However, the consequences do have a bearing on the formal money market and inflation in the country.

5-5-3. Mistrust in the Banking and Formal Sector

Mistrust in the banking and formal sector among the citizenry has also been a factor contributing to the social legitimacy of the burgeoning parallel money market. As mentioned by one female agent who linked the increase in demand for such services to people's lack of confidence in the banking system: 'In the past year [2018], people have not been accessing their cash from banks. Another culprit is the minister [Minister of Finance and Economic Development], who has stolen foreign currency from everyone who had a foreign currency account. Now, who can have faith in these banks? *Matsotsi aya.* These are crooks' (Harare, 1 November 2019). As such, the continued demand for money changers' services by various stakeholders for various reasons will strengthen the existence and social legitimacy of the parallel market, regardless of its illegality.

6. Conclusion

This chapter examined different actors involved in the growth of the parallel money market in Zimbabwe. It showed that policy implementation by respective authorities had a direct effect on the increased resilience of people in expanding activities of the parallel market. Money changers make decisions to continue operating in the illegal parallel market as they view it as a livelihood option, as rationalised by the sustainable livelihood framework and the social and political solicitude they derive from the elites in both the government and the banking sector. From a prospective theory perspective, they also derive employment and, more importantly, reduced risk of prosecution as elites provide the needed protection. Beyond these factors, the parallel money market in the study area is strengthened by the social capital created and maintained by the different actors, as elaborated by the actor-oriented approach. Indeed, the parallel money market will continue to grow as long as people have limited livelihood options from the formal sector. Unique to Zimbabwe is the local currency's commodification through the existence of the parallel money market and acute shortages from the banks. Local people have lost confidence in the banking sector owing to their inability to access their incomes; this is in addition to policies that not only make it difficult for them to access their money but also liquidate their savings into local currency that loses value on a daily basis.[12]

Endnotes

[1] Harare is the capital city and an industrial hub and commercial centre for Zimbabwe. In 2013, the city had a population of about 4.2 million

people, which was expected to reach 5 million by 2025 (*Daily News* 2013).

Masvingo is Zimbabwe's eighth-largest city with a population of 72,527. It is about 294 km from Harare in the southeastern part of the country, bordering Mozambique to the east and Matabeleland South to the south, the Midlands to the north and west and Manicaland to the northeast.

[2] *The Africa Confidential* online newspaper, reported that '… the Finance Minister … has written to the International Financial Institutions (IFIs) in Washington saying it takes responsibility for the recent policy missteps during late 2019, which have led to inflation currently running at an annual rate of over 500 per cent' (The Africa Confidential 30 April 2020).

[3] On 12 April 2009, the Zimbabwe dollar was effectively abandoned as an official currency.

[4] Consequently, long queues became commonplace in banks and at ATM points from early in the morning.

[5] The exchange rate of the local currency against the USD on the parallel market was 1:2 by the end of 2018. It changed to 1:5 in February 2019 and 1:10 in September 2019. Yet the official exchange rates were 1:2.5 in February 2019.

[6] The RTGS dollar (including bond currency) became the country's sole legal tender, referring to it as 'Zimbabwe dollar'.

[7] Zimbabwe's Finance and Economic Development Minister was quoted in *The Africa Confidential* as saying, 'The government and economy are near to collapse' (The Africa Confidential 30 April 2020).

[8] It was also reintroduced in 2019.

[9] In fact, the price control blitz by the government pushed basic commodities in the informal parallel market which was relatively beyond the purview of state control.

[10] Since employees have a wide range of clients they transact with.

[11] *Malayitsha* is the term for 'informal transport and courier businesses in Matabeleland, which operate across the Zimbabwe/South Africa border. The name *Malayitsha* is a SiNdebele term, which means the one who carries a heavy load' (Nyamunda 2014: 40).

[12] Zimbabwe's monetary policy has continued to evolve in 2020. In March, it saw the reintroduction of the use of foreign currency for domestic

transactions as legal tender, to mitigate the devastating impact of COVID-19 on the society and the economy (RBZ 2020a). In June, the fixed exchange rate was abandoned while the market-based-auction system was adopted (RBZ 2020b). Simultaneously, the RBZ also announced a suspension of the transactions through mobile money platform, which restricted the amounts of mobile money that could be transacted per day (RBZ 2020c). This affected transactions the money changers could avail per day as well as clients who would like to exchange large amounts.

Acknowledgements

This work was supported by JSPS KAKENHI Grant Number JP16H06318.

References

Bonga, W. G. (2014) 'Economic policy analysis in Zimbabwe: A review of Zimbabwe economic policies: Special reference to Zimbabwe agenda for sustainable socio-economic transformation (Zim Asset)', *SSRN Electronic Journal* (https://papers.ssrn.com/sol3/papers.cfm?abstract_id=2384863) (accessed: 28 December 2020).

Bosman, W. (2004) 'An analysis of the actor-oriented approach as tool in international development cooperation', Ph.D. Thesis, University of South Africa (http://uir.unisa.ac.za/bitstream/handle/10500/1777/thesis.pd) (accessed: 30 June 2020).

Bourdieu, P. (1986) 'The forms of capital', in J. G. Richardson (ed.) *Handbook of Theory and Research for Sociology of Education*, New York: Greenwood Press, pp. 241–258.

Carney, D. (ed.) (1998) *Sustainable Rural Livelihoods: What contribution can we make?*, London: Department for International Development.

Davies, R. and Davies, G. (1996) *A History of Money from Ancient Times to the Present Day*, Cardiff: University of Wales Press.

Daily News (2013) 'Population growth worries Harare', *Daily News*, 29 October 2013 (https://dailynews.co.zw/articles-2013-10-29-population-growth-worries-harare/) (accessed: 30 June 2020).

Gukurume, S. (2015) 'Livelihood resilience in a hyperinflationary environment: Experiences of people engaging in money-burning (*kubhena mari*) transactions in Harare, Zimbabwe', *Social Dynamics*, Vol. 41, No. 2, pp. 219–234.

——— (2018) 'Navigating precarious livelihoods: Youth in the SME sector in Zimbabwe', *IDS Bulletin*, Vol. 49, No. 5, pp. 89–104.

——— (2019) 'Navigating the crisis: University of Zimbabwe students' campus experiences during Zimbabwe's multi-layered crisis', *African Identities*, Vol. 17, No. 3-4, pp. 277–297.

Hickson, L. and Khemka, I. (2014) 'The psychology of decision making', *International Review of Research in Developmental Disabilities,* Vol. 47, pp. 185–229.

Hwengwere, M. (2015) 'A comparative study of Zimbabwe's economic performance under the Unilateral Declaration of Independence (UDI) and the Zimbabwe Democracy and Economic Recovery Act (ZIDERA)', unpublished dissertation for Bachelors Honours Degree, The Midlands State University (http://ir.msu.ac.zw:8080/xmlui/handle/11408/2049) (accessed: 28 December 2020).

Kahneman, D. and Tversky, A. (1979) 'Prospect theory: An analysis of decision under risk', *Econometrica*, Vol. 47, pp. 263–291.

Kopytoff, I. (1986) 'The cultural biography of things: Commoditization as process', in A. Appadurai (ed.) *The Social Life of Things*, Cambridge: Cambridge University Press, pp. 64–91.

Long, N. (2001) *Development Sociology: Actor Perspectives*, London/New York: Routledge.

Mackenzie, G. A. and Stella, P. (1996) *Quasi-Fiscal Operations of Public Financial Institutions, IMF Occasional Paper No. 142*, Washington: IMF (International Monetary Fund).

Mauss, M. (1925) *The Gift*, London: Routledge and Kegan Paul.

Munangagwa, L. C. (2009) 'The economic decline of Zimbabwe', *Gettysburg Economic Review*, Vol. 3, No. 9, pp. 110–129.

Nyamunda, T. (2014) 'Cross-border couriers as symbols of regional grievance?: The Malayitsha remittance system in Matabeleland, Zimbabwe', *African Diaspora*, Vol. 7, No. 1, pp. 38–62.

RBZ (Reserve Bank of Zimbabwe) (2008) *First Quarter Monetary Policy Statement: A Focus on Food, Foreign Exchange Generation, Producer Viability and Increased Supply of Basic Commodities* (http://archive.kubatana.net/docs/econ/rbz_monetary_policy_april_080430.pdf) (accessed: 30 September 2020).

———— (2019a) *Monetary Policy Statement* (https://www.rbz.co.zw/documents/mps/mpsfeb2019.pdf) (accessed: 30 September 2020).

———— (2019b) *Statutory Instrument 142 of 2019* (https://www.rbz.co.zw/documents/acts/SIs/S.-I.-142-of-2019-Reserve-Bank-of-Zim-Legal-Tender-Regulations-2019--1.pdf) (accessed: 30 September 2020).

———— (2019c) *2019 Mid Term Monetary Policy Statement* (https://www.rbz.co.zw/documents/mps/MPS-September-2019-.pdf) (accessed: 30 September 2020).

———— (2020a) *Interventions in Response to the Financial Vulnerabilities Caused by the COVID-19 Pandemic* [Press statement], 26 March 2020 (https://www.rbz.co.zw/documents/press/March/Press-Statement-COVID-Measures--website.pdf) (accessed: 30 September 2020).

———— (2020b) *On the Suspension of Monetary Transactions on Phone Based Mobile Money Platforms* [Press statement], 30 June 2020 (https://www.rbz.co.zw/documents/press/June/00104_STATEMENT-RESOLUTIONS-OF-THE-MONETARY-POLICY-

COMMITTEE-MEETING-HELD-ON-26-JUNE-2020.pdf) (accessed: 30 September 2020).

———— (2020c) *Resolutions of the Monetary Policy Committee Meeting Held on 26 June 2020* [Press statement], 27 June 2020 (https://www.rbz.co.zw/documents/press/June/SUSPENSION-OF-MOBILE-MONEY-TRANSACTIONS.pdf) (accessed: 30 September 2020).

Scoones, I. (1998) *Sustainable Rural Livelihoods: A Framework for Analysis, IDS Working Paper Vol. 72*, Falmer: IDS (Institute of Development Studies).

Selten, R. (2001) *Game Theory and Economic Behavior: Selected Essays*, Cheltenham: Edward Elgar Publishing.

Simon, H. A. (1957) *Models of Man, Social and Rational: Mathematical Essays on Rational Human Behavior in a Social Setting*, New York: John Wiley and Sons.

Trading Economics (2020) *Zimbabwe GDP1960–2019 Data* (https://tradingeconomics.com/zimbabwe/gdp) (accessed: 30 June 2020).

The Africa Confidential (2020) 'Zimbabwe government close to collapse as Ncube sends plea for cash', *The Africa Confidential*, 30 April 2020 (https://www.africa-confidential.com/article/id/12945/Zimbabwe_government_close_to_collapse_as_Ncube_sends_plea_for_cash) (accessed: 30 June 2020).

The Zimbabwe Standard (2019) 'Matabeleland switches to rand amid currency turmoil', *The Zimbabwe Standard*, 24 November 2019 (https://www.thestandard.co.zw/2019/11/24/matabeleland-switches-rand-amid-currency-turmoil/) (accessed: 30 June 2020).

Veritas (2019a) 'Bill Watch 15-2019 - The new monetary policy: Legal issues', *Veritas*, 21 March 2019 (http://veritaszim.net/node/3461) (accessed: 18 December 2020).

———— (2019b) 'Bill Watch 33/2019 - Monetary policy and the rule of law', *Veritas*, 4 July 2019 (http://veritaszim.net/node/3582) (accessed: 18 December 2020).

Index

D

E

F

G

U

V

W

Z